# WordPerfect 5.1
# Macro Handbook

# WordPerfect® 5.1 Macro Handbook

## Second Edition

Kay Yarborough Nelson

SAN FRANCISCO ■ PARIS ■ DÜSSELDORF ■ SOEST

Acquisitions Editor: Dianne King
Editor: Savitha Pichai
Technical Editor: Maryann Brown
Word Processors: Lisa Mitchell, Scott Campbell, Paul Erickson, Ann Dunn
Chapter Art: Charlotte Carter
Layout Artist: Lisa Jaffe
Screen Graphics: Cuong Le
Typesetter: Winnie Kelly
Proofreaders: Patsy Owens and Dina F. Quan
Cover Designer: Thomas Ingalls + Associates
Cover Photographer: Mark Johann
Screen reproductions produced by XenoFont.

XenoFont is a trademark of XenoSoft.

SYBEX is a registered trademark of SYBEX, Inc.

TRADEMARKS: SYBEX has attempted throughout this book to distinguish proprietary trademarks from descriptive terms by following the capitalization style used by the manufacturer.

SYBEX is not affiliated with any manufacturer.

Every effort has been made to supply complete and accurate information. However, SYBEX assumes no responsibility for its use, nor for any infringement of the intellectual property rights of third parties which would result from such use.

The text of this book is printed on recycled paper.

First edition copyright ©1989 by SYBEX Inc.

Copyright ©1990 SYBEX Inc., 2021 Challenger Drive, Alameda, CA 94501. World rights reserved. No part of this publication may be stored in a retrieval system, transmitted, or reproduced in any way, including but not limited to photocopy, photograph, magnetic or other record, without the prior agreement and written permission of the publisher.

Library of Congress Card Number: 90-71461
ISBN: 0-89588-687-1
Manufactured in the United States of America
10 9 8 7 6 5 4 3 2 1

For Newell Dudley Yarborough, Jr.

Now you can say you got your name(s, all of them)
in a book.
Personally, I will continue to call you
Buddy, so
this, Bud, is for you.

# Acknowledgments

Writing a book is always a team effort. Many people suggested tasks that they would like to have macros carry out for them. I would like to thank Martyn Perry of Network Equipment Technologies of Menlo Park, California, for his many valuable suggestions. In addition, special thanks to H. Lamar Henderson, AIA, of Palo Alto, California, for his recommendation for the bibliography macro.

# Contents at a Glance

Introduction   xv

## PART 1   A MACRO TUTORIAL

| | | |
|---|---|---|
| Chapter 1 | Learning to Use Macros | 3 |
| Chapter 2 | Editing Macros | 23 |
| Chapter 3 | More Complex Macro Techniques | 51 |
| Chapter 4 | Using Soft Macro Keyboards | 83 |
| Chapter 5 | Creating Menus with Macros | 115 |

## PART 2   WORDPERFECT MACROS

| | | |
|---|---|---|
| Chapter 6 | Text Entry and Editing Macros | 139 |
| Chapter 7 | Macros for Formatting Text | 203 |
| Chapter 8 | Graphics and Style Macros | 263 |
| Chapter 9 | Printing Macros | 323 |
| Chapter 10 | Specialized Macros | 363 |
| | | |
| Appendix A | Using Macro Command Language | 445 |
| Appendix B | WordPerfect's Reveal Codes | 493 |
| Appendix C | Converting Earlier Macros to WordPerfect 5.0 and 5.1 | 503 |
| Appendix D | WordPerfect Character Sets | 507 |
| Index | | 515 |

# Table of Contents

Introduction      xv

## PART 1    A MACRO TUTORIAL

### Chapter 1    Learning to Use Macros    3
- Recording a Macro    5
- Organizing Your Macros    10
- Assigning a Macro to the ⏎ Key    12
- Using Temporary Macros    13
- Other Simple Macros    15
- Starting WordPerfect with a Macro    19
- Summary    20

### Chapter 2    Editing Macros    23
- Editing Macros    24
- Macros That Search    26
- Using a Speed Value in Macros    36
- Documenting Macros    37
- Inserting a Pause as You Record a Macro    39
- Considerations in Designing Macros    40
- Combining Macro Commands    44
- Summary    47

### Chapter 3    More Complex Macro Techniques    51
- Special Search Techniques    52
- Sounding a Beep    59
- Chaining and Nesting Macros    62
- Using Any Number of Alt-Key Macros    77
- Executing Alt-Key Macros from Separate Subdirectories    79
- Summary    80

### Chapter 4    Using Soft Macro Keyboards    83
- Using Different Soft Keyboards    85

|  |  |  |
|---|---|---|
| | Creating a New Keyboard | 90 |
| | Creating Specialized Keyboards | 104 |
| | Summary | 112 |
| **Chapter 5** | **Creating Menus with Macros** | **115** |
| | Creating Menus with Macro Command Language | 117 |
| | Executing Macros from a Menu with Merge Commands | 130 |
| | A Few Final Words on Macro and Merge Command Language | 133 |
| | Summary | 134 |

## PART 2    WORDPERFECT MACROS

|  |  |  |
|---|---|---|
| **Chapter 6** | **Text Entry and Editing Macros** | **139** |
| | Splitting the Screen | 140 |
| | Scrolling Both Windows | 142 |
| | Displaying the Ruler Line | 143 |
| | Returning to a Full-Screen Window | 145 |
| | Viewing the Next Screens | 147 |
| | Creating a "Go To" Macro | 149 |
| | Moving to the Beginning of a Paragraph | 150 |
| | Starting the Speller | 151 |
| | Alphabetizing a List of Names | 152 |
| | Alphabetizing a List | 154 |
| | Capitalizing the First Letter of a Word | 156 |
| | Capitalizing the Next Few Words | 158 |
| | Lowercasing All but the First Letter | 159 |
| | Capitalizing a Word | 161 |
| | Capitalizing the First Word in a Paragraph | 162 |
| | Underlining (or Boldfacing) Several Words | 164 |
| | Italicizing a Number of Words | 166 |
| | Changing Underlining to Italics | 168 |
| | Changing Font Sizes Automatically | 171 |
| | Automatic Abbreviations | 173 |
| | Deleting to the Beginning of a Paragraph | 175 |
| | Deleting to the End of a Paragraph | 177 |
| | Deleting Words | 178 |
| | Deleting the Rest of Your Document | 180 |

| | | |
|---|---|---|
| Opening a New Blank Line | | 181 |
| Cutting and Pasting between Windows | | 183 |
| Inserting a Document Comment | | 185 |
| Transposing Words | | 186 |
| Transposing Two Characters | | 188 |
| Transposing Sentences | | 190 |
| Moving a Sentence (or Paragraph or Page) | | 191 |
| Marking Your Place | | 194 |
| Copying a Line | | 196 |
| Copying Text | | 197 |
| Creating Special Dashes | | 199 |
| Using Smart Quotes | | 200 |
| Summary | | 201 |

**Chapter 7  Macros for Formatting Text                 203**

| | |
|---|---|
| Clearing Tab Settings | 204 |
| Setting a Tab Stop at the Cursor's Position | 206 |
| Restoring Tab Settings | 207 |
| Inserting the Time | 209 |
| Inserting the Date and Time | 211 |
| Generating Mailing Labels (Version 5.0) | 213 |
| Creating Your Own Letterhead | 218 |
| Creating Hanging Indents | 220 |
| Setting a Quotation Style | 221 |
| Specifying a Paragraph Numbering Style | 222 |
| Numbering and Formatting Paragraphs | 225 |
| Automatic Memo Form | 227 |
| Writing Business Letters | 231 |
| Business Letter Header | 234 |
| Draft Format | 237 |
| Numbering Pages as Page *n* of *n* | 240 |
| Date and Page-Number Footer | 242 |
| Alternating Headers/Footers | 243 |
| Using Multiple Headers/Footers | 245 |
| Suppressing Headers and Footers | 247 |
| Switching to Single or Double Spacing | 249 |
| Setting Up a Column Format: Newspaper Columns | 251 |
| Setting Up a Column Format: Parallel Columns | 253 |
| Turning on Page Numbering | 254 |

| | | |
|---|---|---|
| Changing the Alignment Character | | 256 |
| Standardizing Spacing between Sentences | | 259 |
| Summary | | 261 |

### Chapter 8  Graphics and Style Macros — 263

| | |
|---|---|
| Converting WordPerfect Codes to Ventura Publisher | 265 |
| Creating a Masthead | 268 |
| Creating Presentation Graphics | 272 |
| Presentation Graphics: Creating a Bulleted Outline | 274 |
| Creating a Slide Show for Your Presentation Graphics | 282 |
| Creating an Organization Chart (Version 5.0) | 285 |
| Creating Boxes with Line Draw | 288 |
| Figure Border Macros: Double Borders | 290 |
| Figure Border Macros: Shaded Figures | 294 |
| Figure Border Macros: Borderless Shaded Figures | 296 |
| Figure Border Macros: Dashed Figure Borders | 297 |
| Figure Border Macros: Thick Borders for Figures | 299 |
| Figure Border Macros: Borders of Varying Sizes | 300 |
| Creating Sidebars and Displayed Quotations | 302 |
| Automatic Writing on the Screen | 304 |
| Changing Headings to Boldface | 306 |
| Changing Several Attributes in Headings | 309 |
| Changing Fonts with Macros | 311 |
| Styling Different Levels of Headings | 314 |
| Turning Styles On/Off | 317 |
| Summary | 320 |

### Chapter 9  Printing Macros — 323

| | |
|---|---|
| Canceling a Print Job | 325 |
| Stopping the Printer | 326 |
| Canceling All Print Jobs | 328 |
| Previewing the Document | 329 |
| Printing Two Copies of a Document | 331 |
| Sending a "Go" to the Printer | 333 |
| Changing Print Quality | 335 |
| Selecting a New Initial Font | 336 |
| Using Subscripts and Superscripts | 338 |

|   |   |   |
|---|---|---|
| | Printing Pages in Reverse | 340 |
| | Previewing Page Breaks | 342 |
| | Printing Envelopes or Mailing Labels | 343 |
| | Printing Selected Pages (Version 5.0) | 348 |
| | Switching to Italics | 352 |
| | Returning to Normal Type | 354 |
| | Draft Printing | 355 |
| | Printing Document Comments | 357 |
| | Summary | 360 |
| **Chapter 10** | **Specialized Macros** | **363** |
| | Changing the Outline Format | 364 |
| | Automatic Paragraph/Outline Numbering | 367 |
| | Using an Outline Style | 370 |
| | Numbering Items in a List | 376 |
| | Turning Line Numbering On and Off | 379 |
| | Changing Endnotes to Footnotes | 381 |
| | Changing Footnote Margins | 383 |
| | Resetting Margins | 386 |
| | Automatic Bibliography: Author-Date Method (Natural Sciences) | 388 |
| | Alphabetizing a Bibliography | 393 |
| | Automatically Numbering Equations | 396 |
| | Specifying a Chapter Number for Equation Numbering | 399 |
| | Changing the Font Used for Equations | 401 |
| | Creating an Area for Equations (Version 5.0) | 404 |
| | Creating Special Symbols with Macros | 408 |
| | Marking Text for Strikeout and Redline | 409 |
| | Marking a Word or Phrase for an Index | 411 |
| | Styling and Generating an Index | 413 |
| | Using Small Type for Footnotes | 415 |
| | Marking Items for a List | 417 |
| | Defining and Generating a List | 420 |
| | Sorting by Paragraph | 422 |
| | Creating Tables of Contents Automatically | 427 |
| | Setting Up a Table Format | 432 |
| | Creating an Invoice | 438 |
| | Summary | 444 |

| | | |
|---|---|---|
| **Appendix A** | **Using Macro Command Language** | **445** |
| | Using Variables | 446 |
| | Using Macro Control Characters in Displays | 447 |
| | The Macro Commands | 456 |
| **Appendix B** | **WordPerfect's Reveal Codes** | **493** |
| **Appendix C** | **Converting Earlier Macros to WordPerfect 5.0 and 5.1** | **503** |
| **Appendix D** | **WordPerfect Character Sets** | **507** |
| | Index | 515 |

# ❖ Introduction

Several years ago, I was writing with VisiWord as my IBM word processor of choice, simply because I had worked for the now-defunct company and there was a price incentive (i.e., it was free). One day a publisher (not SYBEX) called and asked if I could write six chapters of a database book in three weeks and named a figure I couldn't resist. Then they said it had to be written either in WordPerfect or Microsoft Word, neither of which I had or had ever seen before. I said, "Well, get me an evaluation copy of each one and I will meet your deadline."

So they sent me both Word and WordPerfect, along with their format requirements. I tried Word first, and it was a great program, but the problem was that I had to remember how to do something each time I did it. I had to actually learn the program, and I really didn't have time for that. I wanted to learn how to cut text and copy it, number pages and delete words, do a little basic formatting, and that was all. So I tried WordPerfect, hoping it would be easier. There were all those Alt, Shift, and Ctrl key combinations, and I didn't even have a manual, much less a function key template. But I discovered that if I could do something right *once*, I could record the process as a macro and never have to worry about why I was doing what I did—it just worked. I recorded a little Alt-X for Cut macro, an Alt-P for Paste, an Alt-F for Format, and so forth, and away I went, giving my concentration to what I was writing about rather than how I was doing it.

When I finished, I took the manuscript up to the publishers. "Which program did you use?" they said.

"WordPerfect," I said.

"You mean you learned it that fast?" they said.

"I used macros," I said, thinking of my little basic Alt-X, Alt-P, and Alt-F macros.

"Wow," they said, "you must be really good at word processing. How would you like to write a book on word processing?"

I smiled and nodded.

## WHO THIS BOOK IS FOR

It's been a while since then, and I have learned more about WordPerfect. But the point is that you don't really have to be expert at WordPerfect to start right out in this book. If you've mastered the basics, you can record macros. And once you've got macros for what you do most often, you can put off learning anything else until you really need to.

Macros can also help you with tasks that you don't have to do every day. For example, you probably don't have to create a table of contents every day, but you may have to once a month. Personally, I forget a procedure if I don't use it often, and I have to look everything up again the next time I do it. (At this point may I recommend to you the *Encyclopedia WordPerfect 5.1* also published by SYBEX, which covers everything my coauthor Greg Harvey and I could think of that you might want to do in WordPerfect.) But with a table of contents macro, all you have to remember is the macro's *name*. Once the macro starts, you're prompted to mark each heading, and the macro takes care of everything else for you: creating the contents page, generating it, and so forth. You can forget completely about which keys you have to press.

In addition to automating tedious, complicated procedures that are hard to remember, WordPerfect macros also automate repetitive, boring tasks. At first, I found myself constantly marking blocks of text, cutting them, switching to the Doc 2 window, pasting the cut text, moving to the end of it, inserting a hard return, and switching back to Doc 1 to look for another section of text to cut. Instead, I recorded a macro that would turn on blocking, pause to let me indicate which text I wanted to cut, and then would do all the cutting, pasting, moving, and switching automatically.

Macros are also faster than you are. You can write a macro that will change all of your boldfacing to italics, and it will zip through your document much faster than you can search for each boldface code, delete it, insert the code for italics, and search for the next boldface code, over and over again.

In addition, because you can pause a macro so that it will take input from the keyboard, you can write general-purpose macros that are useful in many specific situations. You can have an all-purpose header macro that will pause for you to enter the name of the document you are creating and then go on to date-stamp it and start a style of page numbering. You can create an automatic business letter that pauses for you to insert the recipient's address, then writes part of the letter, and then pauses again for you to choose which specific paragraph should be inserted at various points.

You can even use macros to set up tasks for others or even to write online tutorials for others. For example, you can create a data-entry form that can be used by others who don't have the slightest idea about how to use WordPerfect. All they need to know is how to start WordPerfect with the macro (by giving the startup command as **wp/m-*macroname***) that retrieves the form; prompts within the form direct the user about what to do next.

## USING THIS BOOK

*WordPerfect 5.1 Macro Handbook* consists of two parts. Part 1, Chapters 1–5, teaches you how to write macros; and Part 2, Chapters 6–10, contains step-by-step instructions for writing macros of all sorts.

Scattered throughout the margins are notes to guide you through the book.

 This symbol indicates a tip in the form of a special technique that a macro uses, a shortcut that may not be obvious, or a related macro that you might be interested in.

 This symbol indicates a note that may help you as you're using WordPerfect, or that further explains a point made in the text.

 This symbol indicates a warning about something that can go wrong.

You can write macros in two basic ways: first, by turning on the macro recorder and simply letting the program record your keystrokes; and second, by using WordPerfect's special Macro Command Language. Macro Command Language lets you write extremely complex macros that do all sorts of things, such as exception handling, conditional testing, branching, and so forth. In fact, it is a programming language in itself, and to get the most from it, you need a little background in programming. I'll show you several examples of how you can use Macro Command Language, but the emphasis in this book will be on the macros that you can record without it.

You don't have to understand much about macros to start recording and using them. So, if you like, you can start out by just following the steps to record some macros you want to use. (Or you can order them already recorded on disk; see the offer in the back of the book.) I'd recommend, though, that you at least review Chapter 1 before you start, especially if you haven't had any previous experience recording macros.

If you'd like to learn a bit about the various types of macros that WordPerfect supports, you can go through Chapters 1–5 in sequence. They start out with the simplest kinds of macros, those that insert text automatically, and build up gradually to complex menu systems that execute macros when you make a menu choice. Even if you decide to take this approach, you won't want to do everything all in one sitting. Instead, you'll probably want to read parts of the first five chapters, try out a few macros from the back of the book, explore a little more in the tutorial chapters, try out a few more macros, and so forth. You'll find that this approach lets you understand better what's going on in some of the more complex macros.

The step-by-step instructions have been kept short deliberately. They basically tell you what to do and give you an idea about why you're doing it, but they don't try to teach the complexities of some of WordPerfect's more specialized features. The idea behind this book is that you want to speed up your work, so you won't find any long discussions of the usefulness of merge printing or how to use Line Draw to create a form. You will find concise, numbered steps that, if followed accurately, will give you a working macro.

To help you check your work after you've recorded a macro, an illustration is provided for each one (unless it's so short and simple that you couldn't possibly get it wrong), showing the macro as it appears in the macro editor. You can compare the macro on your screen with the illustration to make sure that you've pressed all the right keys.

Even then, you may notice some discrepancies between your macro and the illustration in this book, because WordPerfect 5.1 lets you use either letters or numbers as menu choices. The macros in this book for the most part use the mnemonic alternatives (letters). If you're a diehard number person, go ahead and use numbers, but you are warned that many of the illustrations show the letter choices.

## *VERSION 5.1 AND VERSION 5.0 MACROS*

The screens shown in this book are for version 5.1, but there's very little difference between them and the version 5.0 screens. If you're using version 5.0, you will find that the 5.1 screens show more keystrokes and that the Action line that appears in version 5.0 screens is missing. If a macro has only a few different keystrokes for each version, only the version 5.1 keystrokes appear in the illustration, but the ones that differ are explained in the steps. If the macros have more than a few keystroke differences, screens are given for both versions.

The vast majority of macros in this book work with both versions of the program. However, a few of the macros will work only in one version and not in another (they're clearly labeled). This is because version 5.1 has added several new features—equations, tables, outline styles, and so forth—that are not available in version 5.0. Some macros in this book are for version 5.0 only, because they provide "workarounds" for features not easily available in that version, such as typing mathematical equations and printing mailing labels.

If you've recorded macros in version 5.0, you will probably find that most of them work fine in version 5.1. If the keystroke sequence is the same, the macro will need no further editing. However, WordPerfect 5.1 changed some key sequences, most notably on the Setup menu. If your 5.0 macro behaves erratically, check to see if the key sequence has changed; then edit it (as described in Chapter 2) to conform to the new sequence in version 5.1.

## *USING PULL-DOWN MENUS AND A MOUSE*

If you're using version 5.1, you know that you can use an alternate pull-down menu system with or without a mouse. When you record macros, choosing commands from the pull-down menu system is the same as pressing the command keys at the keyboard. You can use a combination of the two, or just the keyboard, or just the mouse. To display the pull-down menu, click the right mouse button; to remove the menu, click the right button again (or press F7 or the Spacebar). If you've set up your mouse as a left-handed mouse by using the Setup menu, remember that the right mouse button is the left mouse button and vice versa.

As you record macros, you can use the mouse just as you normally would, with one exception. Let's go over the basics quickly. When a pull-down menu is displayed, you can move the mouse pointer to an item and click the left mouse button to select it, or you can press and hold the left mouse button down and drag the pointer to an item, releasing the left mouse button to select it. When a regular menu is displayed, you can click on an item to select it or click with the right button to remove the menu from the screen.

You can also click on a prompt to select the highlighted command that the prompt is displaying, such as **Y**es (**N**o).

To use the mouse with the Search function, select Search, enter the pattern to search for, and press the right mouse button.

To cancel a command or restore a deletion with a two-button mouse, press either mouse button and hold it down. Click the other button and release both. On a three-button mouse, the middle button works like the F1 (Cancel) key.

The one exception? Don't use the mouse to position the cursor when you're defining a macro; use the arrow keys instead.

## *RECORDING THE MACROS*

You'll notice that most macros have a section entitled "Before You Begin." This is because macros operate accurately only if they're executed under the same conditions in which they were recorded. You may need to clear the screen, for example, or open a Doc 2 window before you begin to record a macro. You may also need to have some text on the screen for the macro to work on as you record it. The "Before You Begin" section will list any preliminary steps you'll need to take before you actually start to record.

If you're familiar with WordPerfect, you already know that it assigns names to the commands produced by the function keys in combination with other keys. Thus, Alt-F9 is Graphics, Shift-F1 is Setup, and so forth. You won't need to worry about memorizing those names; this book will give you both the key name and the corresponding keys to press. In the tutorial chapters, you'll sometimes see the alternate menu choices for the pull-down menu system. However, in the chapters that contain only the steps for recording macros, only the keyboard choices will be given; keep in mind that you can use the alternate menu system at any time, except to position the cursor. If you're using version 5.0, you'll find the key sequences for that version where they differ from version 5.1.

Who will ever have a complete understanding of WordPerfect? Not me. But these macros may help you see some things about the ways the program operates, and, at the very least, they'll help you get more from WordPerfect as you use it in your work.

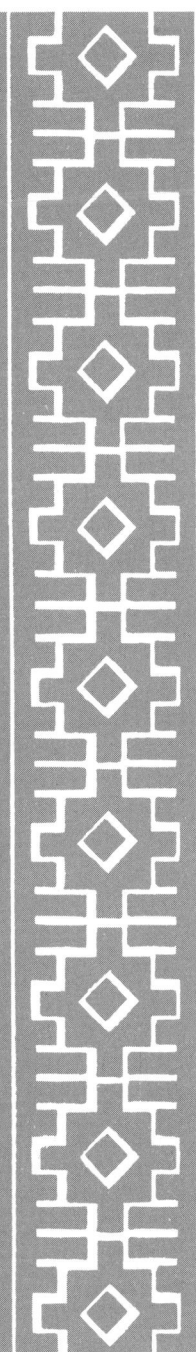

# *A Macro Tutorial*

PART

1

# *Learning to Use Macros*

CHAPTER

1

# CHAPTER 1

Get WordPerfect running and press Ctrl-F10. If you're using pull-down menus, choose Macro from the Tools menu; then select Define. You'll see the prompt

**Define Macro:**

Then type **name** and press ⏎ twice. You'll then see a flashing message, 'Macro Def.' Type your name; then press Ctrl-F10 again. With pull-down menus, select Macro from the Tools menu; then select Define again. You've just created your first *macro,* one that will type your name automatically.

To try it out, press Alt-F10, type **name**, and press ⏎. With pull-down menus, select Macro; then select Execute, type **name**, and press ⏎. Your name will automatically appear on the screen.

This is a simple example, but it illustrates how easy it is to record and use *macros,* which are simply recorded sequences of keystrokes that the program plays back for you. Anything you can do with the program can be recorded as a macro.

A macro can be ordinary text that you don't want to retype each time you use it, like your company's name and address or the standard clauses in a contract, or it can be a complex sequence of commands—for instance, one that sets up a document format, saves the document, and prints it. It's easy to think of ways to use macros for simple, boring tasks. However, you can also use them for complex sequences that you don't want to have to remember, such as marking text for a table of contents, formatting the table, and generating it.

You can do some incredibly sophisticated things with macros; what's surprising, though, is how easily you can create them. Whenever you turn the macro recorder on, WordPerfect simply records your keystrokes. All you have to do, then, is carry out a procedure once. If you make a mistake while you're recording the macro, just correct it, and WordPerfect will record the correction. When the macro is played back, it works so quickly that you normally can't see the mistake being corrected. As you'll see in Chapter 2, you can also edit macros after they've been created. But the macros we'll start out with in this chapter will be so simple that you won't have to worry about that yet.

## *RECORDING A MACRO*

Recording a macro, whether it's as simple as the one that types your name or as complex as one that creates a table of contents, consists of four basic steps:

1. Turn on the macro recorder by pressing Ctrl-F10. If you're using pull-down menus, choose Macro from the Tools menu; then select Define.

2. Assign a name to your macro and, if you like, enter a description of what it does.

3. Type the keystrokes that the macro is to carry out.

4. Turn off the macro recorder by pressing Ctrl-F10 again; or by selecting Macro from the Tools menu, then choosing Define again.

As we have seen, as soon as you press Ctrl-F10 (the Macro Definition key) to start recording a macro, you'll be prompted to define the macro. There are three ways to define a macro, and how you name a macro determines how you execute it:

- You can type a name that is from one to eight characters long, then press ←. WordPerfect automatically adds the extension .WPM (for WordPerfect macro) to each macro name you create. To execute a *named macro,* you press Alt-F10 (the Macro key), (or choose Macro from the Tools menu and then select Execute), enter the macro's name, and press ←.

- You can press and hold down the Alt key and type any letter from *A* to *z* (upper- and lowercase letters have the same effect). This creates a macro that will be executed each time you press Alt and the letter. For example, pressing Alt-A would execute the macro assigned to Alt-A; you don't have to press Alt-F10 first to execute it. Because Alt macros are faster to execute, this is the way to name the macros you use most frequently. But because they don't have descriptive names, it's harder to remember what they do.

- After turning on the macro recorder, you can simply press ⏎ to create a *macro*. For example, if you're typing a document that uses a complicated name or phrase over and over again, you might want to record it as a temporary macro the first time you type it so that you can just press Alt-F10 ⏎ to type it again without any mistakes.

After you've defined your macro by using one of these three methods, you can enter up to 39 characters to describe what it does. If you record a lot of macros—and I hope you plan to, with the help of this book—you'll want to get into the habit of always entering a short description for each one. Otherwise, it's easy to forget what a macro does. You'll see later how to look up and, if necessary, update these descriptions.

## *CREATING ANOTHER MACRO*

Let's try creating another simple macro. After all, just typing your name isn't something you need a macro to do for you.

However, you can record a macro that types a closing for a business letter. It types **Sincerely,** inserts blank lines for your signature, and types your name. This time, we'll take it slowly so that you can see what's going on:

1. Press Ctrl-F10, or select Macro from the Tools pull-down menu and then choose Define. You'll see the prompt 'Define Macro:' in the lower-left corner of the screen.

2. Type **close** as the macro's name and press ⏎.

3. You'll then see the prompt

    Description:

    in the lower-left corner. Type **business letter closing** as the description and press ⏎.

4. You'll then see the indicator

   **Macro Def**

   Whenever you see this message, as shown in Figure 1.1, it means that the macro recorder is on. Remember that any keys that you press will be recorded as part of the macro, including any mistakes you make. For example, if you type **x** and then press Backspace to delete it, the macro will also type an *x* and then delete it whenever you use the macro.

5. Type **Sincerely,** , press ← four times, and type your name. You can also press ← again and type your title under your name, if you're going to use this kind of closing.

6. Turn off the macro recorder by pressing Ctrl-F10 again. If you're using pull-down menus, select Macro, then Define.

```
_     First, you need to know what kind of printer is attached to
the other computer. You then install and select that printer just
as if it were attached to your own computer. Then you use the
Select Printer: Edit screen to specify the Other port. When you
select the Other port option (option 8), you will be prompted to
enter a device or file name. Enter the name that you are going to
use for the document file that you will take to the other
computer. The next time you use one of the regular print options
to print a file (as long as you have this printer selected), the
file will be created in ASCII format on disk under the file name
you just gave.




















Macro Def                                          Doc 2 Pg 1 Ln 1" Pos 1"
```

*Figure 1.1:* Whenever you see the 'Macro Def' indicator, whatever you do is being recorded as a macro.

▬ To see a listing of only the macros in the current directory, press F5, press End, backspace over the last *, and type **wpm** so that the end-of-prompt reads **\*.wpm**. Then press ←.

Turning off the macro recorder in step 6 automatically saved the macro, so you don't have to take the extra step of saving macros after you record them. If you press F5 to look at the List Files screen, you'll see your macro listed as CLOSE.WPM. You can't retrieve or execute a macro from the List Files screen, but you can use it to see the names of the macros you've created.

Notice that in the process of recording the macro you have executed its keystrokes on the screen. Naturally, then, if you had been working on another document, the macro would have become part of it. If you don't want this to happen, you can usually switch to an empty Doc 2 window to record the macro. However, as you'll see later, some macros require text to work on, and others require you to switch between the Doc 1 and Doc 2 windows, so recording in an empty window may not always work.

For now, press F7 (Exit) and type **N N** to clear the screen.

## *EXECUTING THE MACRO*

Now you can try executing your new **close** macro.

1. Press Alt-F10. If you prefer pull-down menus, choose Macro from the Tools menu, and then select Execute. You'll see this prompt:

   **Macro:**

2. Type **close** and press ↵. You can type CLOSE, close, or CloSE; it doesn't make any difference to WordPerfect. The message

   **\* Please wait \***

   is briefly shown, then **Sincerely,** and your name (and title, if you've typed one) appear on the screen.

From now on, whenever you're at the end of a letter, you can execute the **close** macro, and WordPerfect will automatically provide your personalized signature block. This simple macro (as you'll see in Chapter 3), can be linked to other macros that will, for example, take the recipient's name and address from the beginning of the letter, format the address as an envelope, and save the letter, so that you can automate the whole process.

Named macros, like the **close** macro you just created, are best used for tasks for which you need a reminder of what they do. Since their names indicate what tasks they carry out, it's easier to remember their purposes than those of Alt macros, whose names consist of just Alt plus a letter.

## RECORDING AN ALT MACRO

Alt macros are the fastest to execute because they run when you press Alt and the letter assigned to the macro. As I said earlier, they're best used for routine tasks that you carry out frequently. For example, when the lights begin to flicker, it's nice to have an Alt macro, like the one I'm going to call **Alt-S**, that quickly saves the document you're working on.

To record this macro, you'll need a document that you've previously saved. This is an example of how some macros operate only under specific conditions that you have to provide when you record them. In this case, to record a macro that saves a previously saved document, you have to have one actually on the screen. So either retrieve one from file or type something now and save it. Then follow these steps.

> You're not limited to only 26 Alt macros. As you'll see in Chapter 4, you can assign macros to other Alt and Ctrl key keyboard definitions, which gives you an almost unlimited range of possibilities.

1. Start the macro recorder. Remember, you can either press Ctrl-F10 or use the pull-down menus. This time, instead of typing a name, press the Alt key, hold it down, and type **S**. This names the macro **Alt-S**.

2. Type **saves document** as the description and press ↵. Although entering a description is optional, and you can bypass it by just pressing ↵ again, I've suggested descriptions for all the macros in this book.

3. Press F10 (Save), press ↵, and type **Y**. If you're using the pull-down menus, you can choose Save from the File menu. In WordPerfect 5.1, using the mouse to select from the pull-down menus records your keystrokes just as if you had typed them.

4. Turn off the macro recorder by pressing Ctrl-F10 again or by choosing Macro from the Tools menu and then selecting Define.

> As you learn to record other macros, use this Alt-S macro frequently. It's a good idea to save a document before you test a macro in it. That way, you can get the original back in case the macro does something unexpected to it.

Now you can save your document quickly just by pressing Alt-S. Try it.

You can record a similar Alt macro that not only saves your document but also lets you exit from WordPerfect. Let's name this one

**Alt-X** (for 'Exit'):

1. Press Ctrl-F10, then press Alt-X. (From now on, I'm assuming that you know you can use the pull-down menu system as an alternate way to choose commands in version 5.1.)

2. Type **saves and exits** as the description, and press ↵.

3. Press F7 (Exit), press ↵, wait for the next prompt, press ↵ again, and type **Y** in response to the next two prompts.

You won't need to press Ctrl-F10 again; WordPerfect will automatically turn off the macro recorder and save the macro when you exit.

When you record the macro, you'll exit to DOS. Start WordPerfect again so that you can record some more macros. From now on, you can save and continue by pressing Alt-S, or save and exit by pressing Alt-X.

You've now recorded four macros that have been stored in your current directory. Before we go any farther, let's pause and look at a better way to store macros.

## *ORGANIZING YOUR MACROS*

WordPerfect automatically records macros in the directory that you're in when you create them. If you move among directories frequently, you can wind up with macros in various directories and no record of which macro is in which. It can be frustrating to try executing a macro that you know you have recorded, only to get a message from WordPerfect that it can't be found.

A better way of organizing your macros is to set up a directory that contains all of them. You can use the Setup menu to tell WordPerfect which directory this is. Then, each time you record a macro, WordPerfect will store it in that directory. You'll be able to execute any of the macros from any of your other directories, no matter where you are.

First, use the List Files screen to create a subdirectory for macros under your regular WordPerfect directory:

1. Press F5 (List Files) twice.

2. Choose the Other Directory option (option 7) and then enter the path name for your new macros subdirectory. For

example, if you want to create a subdirectory for your macros under your WP51 directory, enter the path name as **C:\WP-51\MACROS**. You can use the End and Backspace keys to edit the line that WordPerfect is displaying.

3. Press ←; then respond **Y** to the prompt for creating the new directory.

4. You can now exit from the List Files screen and use the Setup key to indicate where your macros subdirectory is. Press F7, then press Shift-F1 (Setup). With pull-down menus, choose Setup from the File menu.

5. Select Location of Files (option 6 or L). (In version 5.0, this is called Location of Auxiliary files, and it is 7 or L.) Then select the Keyboard/Macro Files option (2 or K). (In version 5.0, this is option 3 or K.)

6. Type the path name you just used to create your macro directory, such as **C:\WP51\MACROS**; then press ← three times to return to your document.

From now on, all of your named and Alt macros will be automatically stored in this directory. If you want later to use a macro that is stored in another directory, just enter its full path name, such as C:\WP51\MATH\ALTY, after you press Alt-F10.

Figure 1.2 illustrates the contents of my macro directory.

If you've already been recording macros before you created this directory, you can move them to the new directory quite easily. Using the List Files screen (press F5), mark every macro (every file with the extension '.WPM') with an asterisk. Then select Move (option 3 or M). After confirming the move, type the path name of your new macro subdirectory and press ←. WordPerfect will move all of the marked files to your new MACROS subdirectory. You'll need to repeat the process in any directories where you've already recorded macros.

Using the Location of Files option to create a macro directory lets you create macros that can be executed from any directory. However, you may want to keep specialized macros, such as those that are for legal documents or mathematical typing, in separate directories. If you habitually do this, it's best *not* to use a central directory for your

> If you're marking several items to move, copy, print, or delete in List Files, use the PrtSc key instead of the asterisk at the top of the keyboard. On an enhanced keyboard, use the asterisk on the numeric keypad. Pressing Home-PrtSc (or Home-asterisk) will mark all the files in the directory.

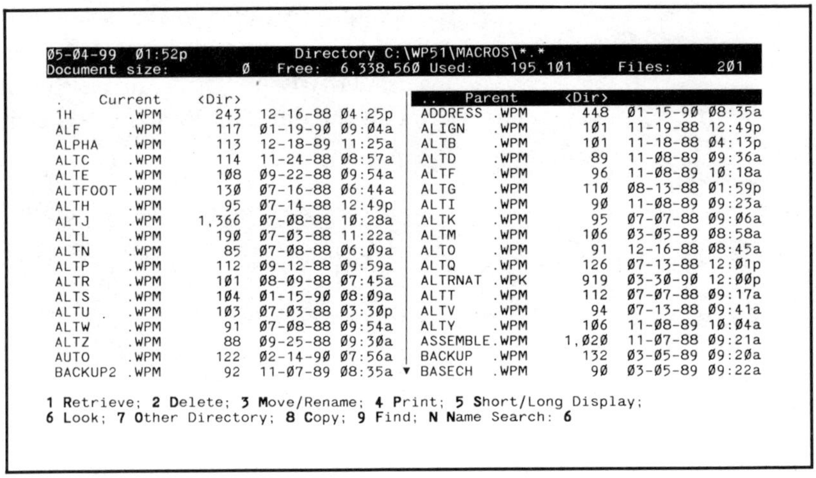

```
05-04-99  01:52p                 Directory C:\WP51\MACROS\*.*
Document size:        0     Free:  6,338,560 Used:     195,101    Files:     201

.       Current  <Dir>                   ..      Parent   <Dir>
1H         .WPM       243  12-16-88 04:25p    ADDRESS  .WPM       448  01-15-90 08:35a
ALF        .WPM       117  01-19-90 09:04a    ALIGN    .WPM       101  11-19-88 12:49p
ALPHA      .WPM       113  12-18-89 11:25a    ALTB     .WPM       101  11-18-88 04:13p
ALTC       .WPM       114  11-24-88 08:57a    ALTD     .WPM        89  11-08-89 09:36a
ALTE       .WPM       108  09-22-88 09:54a    ALTF     .WPM        96  11-08-89 10:18a
ALTFOOT    .WPM       130  07-16-88 06:44a    ALTG     .WPM       110  08-13-88 01:59p
ALTH       .WPM        95  07-14-88 12:49p    ALTI     .WPM        90  11-08-89 09:23a
ALTJ       .WPM     1,366  07-08-88 10:28a    ALTK     .WPM        95  07-07-88 09:06a
ALTL       .WPM       190  07-03-88 11:22a    ALTM     .WPM       106  03-05-89 08:58a
ALTN       .WPM        85  07-08-88 06:09a    ALTO     .WPM        91  12-16-88 08:45a
ALTP       .WPM       112  09-12-88 09:59a    ALTQ     .WPM       126  07-13-88 12:01p
ALTR       .WPM       101  08-09-88 07:45a    ALTRNAT  .WPK       919  03-30-90 12:00p
ALTS       .WPM       104  01-15-90 08:09a    ALTT     .WPM       112  07-07-88 09:17a
ALTU       .WPM       103  07-03-88 03:30p    ALTV     .WPM        94  07-13-88 09:41a
ALTW       .WPM        91  07-08-88 09:54a    ALTY     .WPM       106  11-08-89 10:04a
ALTZ       .WPM        88  09-25-88 09:30a    ASSEMBLE .WPM     1,020  11-07-88 09:21a
AUTO       .WPM       122  02-14-90 07:56a    BACKUP   .WPM       132  03-05-89 09:20a
BACKUP2    .WPM        92  11-07-89 08:35a ▼  BASECH   .WPM        90  03-05-89 09:22a

1 Retrieve; 2 Delete; 3 Move/Rename; 4 Print; 5 Short/Long Display;
6 Look; 7 Other Directory; 8 Copy; 9 Find; N Name Search: 6
```

*Figure 1.2:* The List Files screen for a macro directory shows that all the macros have the extension .WPM.

macros. Since WordPerfect will look in your current directory for a macro if you haven't specified a directory with the Setup menu, you can simply create macros in the directory where you plan to use them, and they will be stored and executed from there.

However, a word of warning: If you don't set up a central macro directory by using the Setup menu and you execute an Alt macro, such as **Alt-C**, WordPerfect will use the Alt macro that is in your current default directory. If you change to a different directory later (by pressing F5, typing =, and entering a path name) and try to execute a different **Alt-C** macro that you've stored there, the previous **Alt-C** macro will be executed instead! What happens is that WordPerfect keeps previously used macros in RAM and looks there first. To get around this limitation, either enter the full path name of the second Alt macro that you want to use, such as **C:\WP50\LET\ALTC**, or exit to DOS (Ctrl-F1 1) and then return to WordPerfect by typing **exit** to clear previously used macros from RAM.

## ASSIGNING A MACRO TO THE ← KEY

Let's imagine that you're typing a contract in which you have to repeat the phrase 'will exert all reasonable effort to meet the schedule as defined on or before October 28, 1991.' Because you're not going to be typing that phrase in another work session—the date's going to change—with WordPerfect you can assign it to a temporary macro just for this session.

1. Press Ctrl-F10; then press ⏎.
2. Type **will exert all reasonable effort to meet the schedule as defined on or before October 28, 1991.**
3. Press Ctrl-F10 again.

> You can also execute the macro you assigned to the ⏎ key by pressing the Spacebar or the right mouse button.

Now you can try it out. Clear the screen (F7 **N N**), press Alt-F10, and press ⏎. As you type your contract, you can repeat this phrase as often as you like by simply pressing Alt-F10 ⏎.

## USING TEMPORARY MACROS

Now we'll digress to take a look at some macros of a special kind: *temporary macros,* which don't require any storage at all.

Unlike named macros and Alt macros, temporary macros are erased from memory when you exit WordPerfect. They don't take up space on your disks or confuse you with macro definitions that you may never use again.

You can use temporary macros to type text that you need to repeat several times during a work session, such as a name and address in a letter or order form. In fact, that's all a temporary macro can do: insert text that you've previously typed. It can't carry out any of the program's other functions.

> Unfortunately, with temporary macros you can't use boldface and italics. To make appearance changes or to change the font, you have to record a regular Alt-key or named macro.

You can create ten temporary macros and assign them to the Alt key plus the number keys 0 through 9 by using the Ctrl-PgUp key, which is called the Macro Commands key.

There are two ways of doing this, and one gives you a little more flexibility than the other. The first way is to start the temporary macro and then type the text you want it to contain; the second way is to first type the text you want the temporary macro to type, then mark it as a block (that is, highlight it) and assign it to a macro. We'll begin with the first way.

1. Press Ctrl-PgUp. You'll see the prompt

   **Variable:**

2. To assign the macro to 1, type **1** (if you're using version 5.1, you'll also have to press ⏎). You'll then see the prompt

   **Value:**

3. Type the text that you want the macro to contain. You can type up to 79 characters. For practice, enter **SYBEX Computer Books** and press ⏎. When you press ⏎, macro definition will end, so you can only record text shorter than a paragraph in this way.

To test the macro you just recorded, press Alt and type **1**. The phrase 'SYBEX Computer Books' will appear on your screen.

Now you can try blocking text that you've already typed. There are two slight advantages to using this method instead of typing the text as you record the macro. First, you can type the text and correct any errors that may be in it without the macro recorder running. Second, if you use this method, you can record text that consists of several lines, such as addresses and standard openings and closings for business letters, as temporary macros. On the other hand, if you were typing the text as you were recording a temporary macro, pressing ⏎ would stop the macro recorder. With the blocking method, you can also type up to 128 characters, not just 79.

To try out this method, type the following address so that you can record it as a macro:

```
SYBEX Computer Books
2021 Challenger Drive
Alameda, CA 94501
```

Then mark it as a block with Alt-F4 and press Ctrl-PgUp. Type **2**⏎ to assign it as temporary macro 2. To test the macro, move the cursor to a blank line and press Alt-2. If there are any text enhancements such as underlining or boldface in the text you mark as a block for this kind of temporary macro, WordPerfect simply ignores them.

Temporary macros are often overlooked, but they can save you a great deal of time as you're doing routine typing.

## OTHER SIMPLE MACROS

Now let's take a look at some other simple permanent macros. You may want to add them to the library of macros you've already started to build. As you'll see shortly, WordPerfect lets you chain macros to each other so that one macro starts when another stops. Even the macros in this chapter, then, can be used as building blocks in other, more complex macros that you'll create later.

### DELETING TEXT WITH MACROS

The macros you've recorded up till now either typed text automatically for you or carried out a program function such as saving and exiting. However, macros can also do editing tasks such as deleting and moving text in your documents.

For example, suppose you're editing a document and realize that you'd like to delete everything from where the cursor is to the top of the page. Normally, you'd move the cursor to the top of the page, turn on block marking, and then highlight each line until you got back to where the cursor was originally. A macro can let you do this in three keystrokes.

To record a macro that deletes to the top of the page, you'll need a document on your screen, so retrieve one to use for recording these macros. Don't worry; you won't save it, so none of the changes you'll make will be permanent. You'll also need to put the cursor somewhere within a page. Then take the following steps:

If you're not sure whether you'll use a macro frequently, give it a name instead of an Alt-key assignment. It's easy to rename a macro later so that it is assigned to an Alt key, as you'll see in the next chapter.

1. Start the macro recorder by pressing Ctrl-F10 or choosing Macro from the Tools menu, then choosing Define. Enter **deltop** as the macro name, and press ←.
2. Type **delete to top of page** as the description and press ←.
3. Press Alt-F4 or choose Block from the Edit pull-down menu to turn on block marking.
4. Press Ctrl-Home and then press ↑.
5. Press Ctrl-Home twice to return the cursor to its original position. Then press Del and type **Y**.
6. Press Ctrl-F10 to stop recording the macro.

Try it out again: move the cursor to somewhere else on the page, press Alt-F10, and type **deltop**. The text to the top of the page is deleted immediately.

Because it's easy to mistakenly delete text with an Alt-key macro, you may prefer (as I have done in this example) to use names for macros that delete large amounts of text.

However, you can get deleted text back with the F1 key. You can try that here. Just press F1 (Cancel) and choose Restore (1 or R) or Previous Deletion (2 or P) to see the two previous deletions. If you want to move the text you just deleted, position the cursor at the location where you want it to appear and then restore it.

## *FORMATTING TEXT WITH MACROS*

Besides writing and deleting text with macros, you can also format it. Chapter 7 is full of formatting macros, but let's try one here to get an idea of some of the simpler formatting tasks WordPerfect can do for you. Up to now, the macros you've recorded have done only one or two things. With this one macro, however, you'll see how to get WordPerfect to apply several different kinds of font changes to the same block of text.

Suppose that you'd like to change a paragraph that you've already written to bold italic small type—a displayed quotation that you want to open a chapter with, for example. Normally, you'd have to highlight the paragraph, press F6 to apply the bold attribute, rehighlight the paragraph, press Ctrl-F8 S S to change the size to small, rehighlight the paragraph, and press Ctrl-F8 A I to change the appearance to italics. A macro can take care of all three changes for you at the same time.

To record this macro, you'll need to have a highlighted paragraph on the screen. Move the cursor to the beginning of the paragraph, press Alt-F4, and press ⏎ to highlight it.

> WordPerfect turns off block marking after you use a command on the block. To rehighlight the same block so that you can apply another command to it, press Alt-F4; then press Ctrl-Home (the Go To key) twice.

1. Start the macro recorder by pressing Ctrl-F10 or choosing Macro from the Tools menu, then choosing Define. Then press Alt-D (for Display).

2. Type **changes to small bold italics** as the description and press ⏎.

3. Press F6 (Bold).

4. Press Alt-F4; then press Ctrl-Home (Go To) twice. This rehighlights the last selection you highlighted.

5. Press Ctrl-F8 (Font) and type **S** for Size; then type **S** for Small.

6. Press Alt-F4; then press Ctrl-Home twice.

7. Press Ctrl-F8 and type **A** for Appearance; then type **I** for Italics.

8. Press Ctrl-F10 to stop recording the macro.

> If you need to refer to WordPerfect's format codes while writing any of the macros in this book, Appendix B lists all of them.

You won't see any changes on the screen except the boldfacing unless you've got a Hercules RAMFont card or a color monitor. However, if you press Alt-F3 (the Reveal Codes key), you'll see that the [SMALL][small], [ITALC][italc], and [BOLD][bold] codes surround your paragraph, as shown for the sample paragraph in Figure 1.3. To test the macro, highlight another paragraph—or another portion of text since it doesn't have to be a paragraph—then press Alt-D and check the Reveal Codes screen.

```
      The next time you use one of the regular print options to print a file
(as long as you have this printer selected), the file will be created in ASCII
format on disk under the file name you just gave.




Move cursor; press Enter to retrieve.              Doc 2 Pg 1 Ln 1" Pos 1"
[SMALL][ITALC][BOLD][Tab]The next time you use one of the regular print options
to print a file[SRt]
(as long as you have this printer selected), the file will be created in ASCII[S
Rt]
format on disk under the file name you just gave.[HRt]
[italc][bold][small]



Press Reveal Codes to restore screen
```

*Figure 1.3:* After you've used the **Alt-D** macro on a paragraph, you can check its codes by pressing Alt-F3 (the Reveal Codes key) or using the View Document feature (Shift-F7 V) at 100 percent.

## EDITING TEXT WITH MACROS

Macros can also be a great help in editing the words you write. You'll see a lot of macros in Chapter 6 that will transpose words and sentences and convert words and phrases to uppercase and lowercase. For now, let's look at a simple macro that will convert the character the cursor is on to uppercase. You've still got a sample document displayed, so press Alt-F3 to make the codes invisible; then put the cursor on any lowercase character. Note that this macro is an Alt macro, because you'll want to be able to use it quickly and often.

1. Start the macro recorder by pressing Ctrl-F10 or choosing Macro from the Tools menu, then choosing Define. Press Alt-U (for uppercase).

2. Type **capitalizes current character** as the description and press ↵ again.

3. Press Alt-F4 to turn on block marking.

4. Press →.

5. Press Shift-F3 and type **U** for uppercase.

6. Turn off the macro recorder by pressing Ctrl-F10 again or by choosing Macro from the Tools menu, then selecting Define.

Now you can test the macro on any other character in the document that's in lowercase. It won't have any effect on a character that's already in uppercase.

## REPEATING A MACRO

What if you want to capitalize more than one letter with the Alt-U macro? You can use WordPerfect's built-in Repeat function (the Esc key) to repeat a macro any number of times. All you have to do is:

1. Press Esc. You'll see the prompt

    Repeat Value = 8

2. Enter the number of times you want the macro to repeat. Don't press ↵.

3. Press Alt-F10, enter the macro's name, and press ←┘. If you're repeating an Alt macro, just press Alt and the letter of the macro.

For example, to capitalize three characters in a row, press Esc, enter 3, and press Alt-U.

This technique lets you do some very clever things, as you'll see throughout the book. For example, you can use it instead of the Search feature to locate all occurrences of something in a document, such as a specific word or phrase. How do you do this? By entering a repeat value larger than the number of instances that there can possibly be in the document, such as 100. WordPerfect will locate them all and then stop repeating the macro.

## *STARTING WORDPERFECT WITH A MACRO*

You can start WordPerfect with a macro that executes automatically when the program starts. For example, you can start WordPerfect with a macro that changes you to a different subdirectory or retrieves a certain document for you to work on. Or, if you always begin your day by writing letters, you can start WordPerfect with a macro that creates your letterhead, changes to a different font for business letters, and inserts the current date. Similarly, if you make a to-do list at the end of each day, you can have WordPerfect retrieve that list the next time it starts.

■ If you have a dot-matrix printer and you're using an early release of version 5.0, you can set print quality to Medium with a start-up macro. Otherwise you have to remember to change the print quality for each document you want to print in medium quality. You can't specify a print quality in early releases of version 5.0 with the Setup menu.

To start WordPerfect with a macro, you simply enter the start-up command as

   wp/m-*macroname*

You have to have recorded the macro first.

For example, to start WordPerfect and retrieve that to-do list (let's assume that you've saved it as **todo** in your working directory), just start the program by entering

   wp/m-todo

at the DOS prompt. To start WordPerfect with an Alt macro, such as **Alt-X**, enter it as

wp/m-altx

## SUMMARY

In this chapter, you've seen a few of the many things that macros can do for you. They can automate repetitive tasks or remember complex sequences of instructions for you. You can use them for editing as well as formatting text. In particular, you saw that:

- To record a macro, you can turn on the macro recorder by pressing Ctrl-F10. If you prefer to use version 5.1's pull-down menu system, you can choose the equivalent commands by selecting Macro from the Tools menu, then choosing Define. You can assign a name to your macro and, if you like, enter a description of what it does. You then type the keystrokes that the macro is to carry out and turn off the macro recorder by pressing Ctrl-F10 again, or by repeating the pull-down menu sequence and choosing Define again.

- To define a macro—that is, assign it a name—you can enter a name from one to eight characters, or you can press and hold down the Alt key and type a letter (A–z; uppercase and lowercase are the same). This creates a macro that will be executed each time you press Alt and that letter.

- To rename a macro once you have named it, you can use the Move/Rename option on the List Files screen (F5).

- To execute a macro after you have recorded it, press Alt-F10, enter the macro's name, and press ↵; or simply press the Alt-key combination you assigned to the macro without pressing Alt-F10 first. With pull-down menus, choose Macro from the Tools menu, then select Execute.

- To direct WordPerfect to store macros in a separate subdirectory, use the Setup menu (Shift-F1, or select Setup from the File menu).

- Temporary macros can be assigned to variables 0 through 9.
- You can block existing text and assign it to a variable to use as a temporary macro, or you can use the macro recorder to create a temporary text macro.
- To repeat a macro, press Esc, enter the number of times you want the macro to repeat, and then execute the macro.
- To start WordPerfect with a macro, enter the startup prompts as **wp/m-*macroname***.

Chapter 2 will expand on these skills as you learn to edit macros and construct more complex ones.

# *Editing Macros*

CHAPTER

2

# CHAPTER 2

Before you go any further with recording macros, you should acquire another skill: editing them. It's frustrating to have recorded a macro that doesn't work as you expect it to and then be forced to repeat each step all over again to get it right. WordPerfect comes with a built-in macro editor that you can use to correct steps in the macros you record.

This chapter will introduce you to the macro editor before you start creating slightly more complex macros than those you recorded in Chapter 1. That way, if you make mistakes in one of these longer macros, you'll know how to correct them in the final version without having to repeat the whole macro from scratch.

You'll also see in this chapter how to use macros with Word-Perfect's Search and Replace features, how to pause a macro so that you can input information from the keyboard, and how to chain a macro to itself so that it will repeat. In addition, you'll see how to copy a macro so that you can use it as the basis of another macro, and how to insert a delay factor in your macros so that you can actually watch them execute and debug them if something's going wrong. Then, before you begin to record some more complex macros in Chapter 3, we'll look at some general considerations that you should keep in mind when planning macros.

## EDITING MACROS

WordPerfect's built-in macro editor lets you delete steps from macros or add steps to them. When you want to change what a macro does, instead of repeating all the keystrokes necessary to create it again, you can delete only the keystrokes that are affected and replace them with others. For example, once you've recorded a macro that copies a sentence, it's a simple matter to edit it so that it moves the sentence instead, because only one keystroke changes.

> In version 5.1, you can just press Home before you press Ctrl-F10 to have the macro editor start as soon as you enter a name and description.

To edit a macro, press Ctrl-F10 (the Macro Definition key or Macro Def for short) and give the name of the existing macro as the macro to create. To edit the Alt-D macro you created in Chapter 1, enter **altd**. WordPerfect will ask if you want to replace it, edit it, or in version 5.1, edit its description. Select Edit (2 or E), and you'll see the macro editing screen, which is illustrated in Figure 2.1 with an edited version of the Alt-D macro you created in Chapter 1. If you are using version 5.0, your editing screen will appear slightly different. You will have two choices, 1 Description and 2 Action. Type 1 or D to change the macro's description; type 2 or A to edit the macro itself. In version 5.1 the cursor is immediately placed in the editing screen, so you do not have to type anything to begin.

Remember, this macro changes highlighted text to small bold italics. To see how to use the macro editor, we'll edit the macro so that it converts the highlighted text to small underlined italics instead.

1. Press Ctrl-F10 (Macro Def) or choose Macro from the Tools menu, then choose Define. Then press Alt-D. You'll see the prompt

   **ALTD.WPM Already Exists. 1 Replace; 2 Edit; 3 Description: 0**

2. Type **2** or **E** to edit the macro. If you choose Replace, you can input the macro again from scratch, including its description.

3. If you're using version 5.0, type **2** or **A** for Action when the macro editing screen appears. Typing **1** or **D** allows you to change the macro's description, or to enter a description if one isn't already there. Once you choose Action, you're in normal editing mode, so that pressing Backspace or Del deletes characters, End takes you to the end of the line, and so forth. In version 5.1, you are immediately placed in the editing screen so that you can begin editing.

4. To insert the underline instruction, press → to move past the {DISPLAY OFF} instruction, which WordPerfect automatically inserts at the beginning of macros. This instruction tells WordPerfect to execute the macro so that you don't see each step displayed on the screen.

5. Press Del to delete the {Bold} instruction.
6. Press F8 (Underline) to insert an {Underline} instruction in the macro. It should now resemble the one in Figure 2.1.
7. Press F7 (twice in version 5.0) to return to your document.

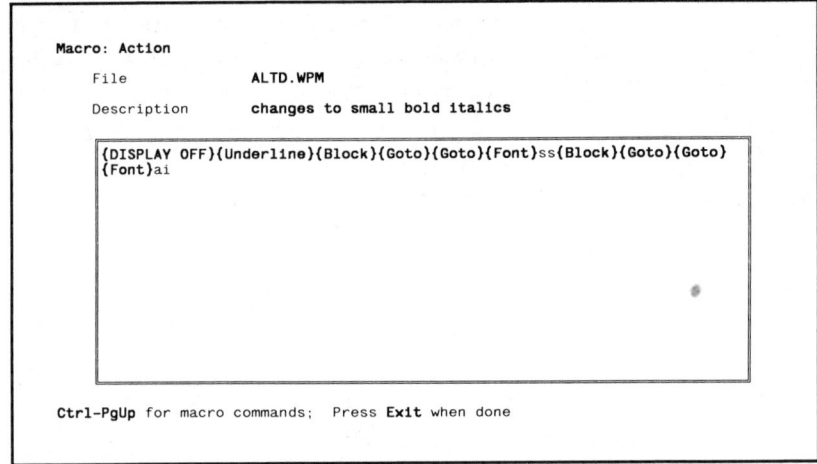

*Figure 2.1:* The macro editing screen allows you to edit macros once you have recorded them.

Now highlight a paragraph of text (by pressing Alt-F4 and then pressing ←) and then press Alt-D to see what happens. If you check the Reveal Codes window, you'll see that the [UND], [SMALL], and [ITALC] appearance codes surround the text after the Alt-D macro has been used on it. You can also use the View Document feature (Shift-F7 V) to see the results.

Now that you've had a quick introduction to the macro editor (we'll return to it later), you can try out some more complicated macros.

## MACROS THAT SEARCH

Combined with WordPerfect's Search features, macros become a powerful tool. Because you can have a macro locate something, such as a word or even a format code, by searching for it, search macros give you a way of moving around within a document quickly and accurately. When the macro locates what it's searching for, you can have the program change that item to something else—for example, change tabs to spaces, or underlining to boldface, or J.R. Elkins to Judith Rawls Elkins. You can also have the macro delete what it finds, or add something to what it finds. Or, as you'll see in Chapter 3, you can have the macro do one thing if it finds what it's looking for and do something completely different if it doesn't.

Let's start out by taking a simple example of a search macro that you can edit later to make more complex. Suppose that you've underlined various words in a document as you've introduced them, planning to create a glossary of new terms from them later. However, you're not sure that you've used underlining for that purpose only and no other. You need, then, to be able to *check* each instance of underlining and *take an action* on it (here, copy it) if it's a glossary term, or move on to the next underlined word if it's not.

First, you'll need to type the short document shown in Figure 2.2 so that the macro will have something meaningful to work on. After you've typed the document, save it as **glossary**. Then move to the top of it by pressing Home Home ↑. Then you can take the following steps to create a search macro.

```
     _    In traditional typesetting, the word kerning refers to
decreasing the spacing between specific pairs of letters, while
letterspacing refers to increasing the amount of space between
letters. WordPerfect uses letterspacing to mean either adjusting
or reducing the spacing between letters, but it uses kerning in
the traditional sense- -to decrease the space between letters.




C:\5\MB\GLOSEX                                 Doc 2 Pg 1 Ln 1" Pos 1"
```

*Figure 2.2:* To give the macro something to work on, create this short document and save it as **glossary**.

1. Turn on the macro recorder by pressing Ctrl-F10 or choosing Macro from the Tools menu, then choosing Define. Name the macro **Alt-G** (for glossary).

2. Enter **searches for underlined words** as the description and press ←┘.

3. Press F2 (Search); then press F8 (Underline) to generate the [UND] code.

4. Press F2 to start the search.

5. Turn off the macro recorder by pressing Ctrl-F10 or choosing Macro from the Tools menu, then choosing Define again.

WordPerfect stops at the beginning of the first word that has been underlined. If that were one of the words you were looking for, you could copy it at this point and then repeat the **Alt-G** macro to search for the next underlined word. However, there's a way to make the macro repeat itself each time it finds what it's looking for.

## *REPEATING A SEARCH*

☞ If you want to cancel the changes you've made as you're editing a macro, press F1 (Cancel). Enter **Y** to cancel them or press ←┘ to leave things as they appear on the screen.

To add the step that makes the macro repeat itself, you can edit it. Turn on the macro recorder and then press Alt-G. At the prompt, type **E** for Edit, and you'll see the Alt-G macro you just recorded on the screen (Figure 2.3). If you're using version 5.1, you can go to the macro editor by pressing Home before you press Ctrl-F10 and Alt-G. Note that the macro editor doesn't represent codes in the same way as the Reveal Codes screen. Formatting codes and other codes are shown in a macro within curly braces. Menu selections and text that you type are represented by their characters. Spaces are represented by centered dots.

This time, editing the macro will be a little different. To insert certain types of macro instructions, you have to be in Macro Define mode, which you can enter in either of two ways:

- You can press Ctrl-F10 (Macro Def) so that all the keys you press until you press Ctrl-F10 again will be entered as instructions in the macro. This method works best if you're entering several steps.

- You can press Ctrl-V so that only the next key you press is entered as an instruction in the macro. This method is best if you're entering only one or two steps.

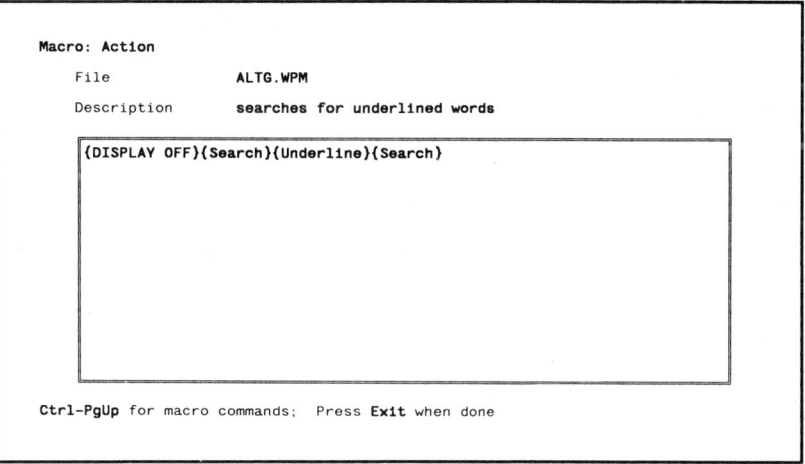

*Figure 2.3:* You can edit this **Alt-G** macro so that it will repeat itself until no more underlined words are located.

You'll see how this last method works as you edit your macro to repeat itself.

1. Press End to move to the end of the macro. If you're using version 5.0, you'll need to type **A** for Action first.

2. Press Alt-F10 to insert a {Macro} instruction code; then type **altg** (the name of the macro).

Now you need to insert an instruction for pressing the Enter key, but there's a problem: if you press ←, the macro editor simply moves to the next line. In fact, pressing Tab, Del, F1 (Cancel), F7 (Exit), or any of the cursor-movement keys, such as → or ←, works just as in WordPerfect, without any commands being added to your macro. Here's how to insert that {Enter} instruction:

3. Move to the place where you want the ← to occur in the macro—in this case, at the end.

4. Press Ctrl-V.

5. Press ←.

An {Enter} is then inserted in your macro so that the macro (when it executes) will call itself, type its own name, and press ←. You've just chained your macro to itself. It should now look like the one in Figure 2.4.

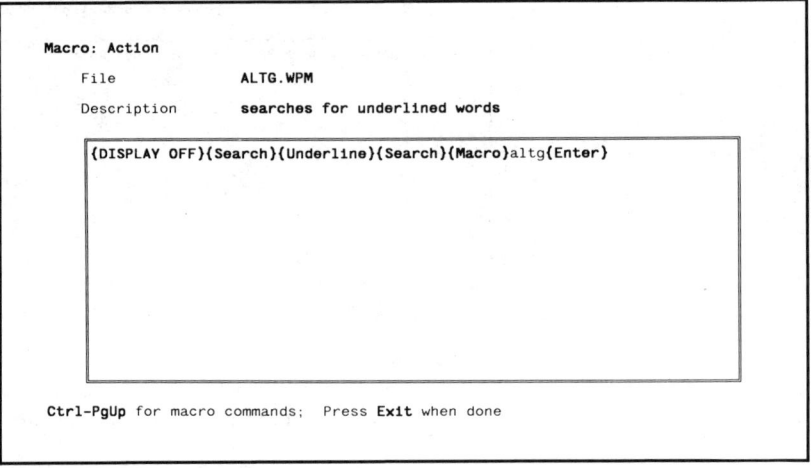

*Figure 2.4:* After you edit the macro to repeat itself, here's what you should see on your macro editing screen.

> WordPerfect automatically turns off a search macro when it can't locate any more occurrences of what it's searching for. This prevents the macro from going into an endless loop.

You can have a search macro repeat until it can't locate a pattern any longer. All you do is press Alt-F10 (the Macro key) at the end of the macro steps, enter the macro's name (the one you're recording), and press ⏎. If you know in advance that you want the macro to repeat over and over, you can add this step to the macro, and so avoid having to use the editor.

Another point to remember here is that in the WordPerfect macro editor, as we saw, simply pressing ⏎ moves the cursor to the next line and doesn't insert a hard return in your macro.

Now let's try out the edited **Alt-G** macro. Press F7 (twice in version 5.0) to exit from the macro editor. Then move to the top of the glossary document and press Alt-G. It seems like nothing happened. Look more closely. You'll see that the cursor is on the first character of the last underlined word. What happened was that the macro executed so quickly (remember that {DISPLAY OFF} instruction?) that you couldn't see what was happening on the screen. But you can fix that.

## PAUSING A MACRO

You can reedit the macro so that it will pause each time it locates an underlined word and wait for you to take an action on it. When a macro pauses, you can do anything except press ⏎. Pressing ⏎ starts the macro running again.

This technique makes your macro tremendously more useful, because you can enter information that it needs in order to work. For example, you can have a macro pause in a business letter so that you can type the recipient's name, or you can pause a macro so that you can choose a different font or enter new tab settings. You'll be using macro pauses in many of the macros in this book.

To insert a pause in your **Alt-G** macro so that you can take action on each occurrence of underlining, take the following steps:

> You don't have to use the macro editor to insert a pause in your macro; you can insert one as you're recording it. You'll see how before we get to the end of this chapter.

1. Turn on the macro recorder; then press Alt-G.

2. If you're using version 5.0, type **2 2** to edit the macro. You could type **E** for Edit and **A** for Action, but here's a case where typing a number is faster. Remember this trick, because you won't be reminded that you need to choose Action to enter the editor in version 5.0 from now on. If you have version 5.1, remember that the trick is to press Home before you press Ctrl-F10 to go to the macro editor.

3. Press → to move the cursor to just before the {Macro} command. Then press Ctrl-PgUp, which is called the Macro Commands key. A scrollable command menu appears in the upper-right corner of the screen. You can move through it with the ↑, ↓, PgUp, and PgDn keys. To insert any of the special commands listed there into your macros, highlight the command and press ⏎. (If you choose not to insert a command after it's highlighted, press F1 or Esc.) These commands are in WordPerfect's Macro Command Language, which you'll explore in Chapter 5. For now, all you need to know is how to insert a pause.

4. The menu has a built-in name search feature, so typing the first letter of the command you want to use will take you to

the command quickly. Type **pau** and press ⏎ to insert a {PAUSE}. (In version 5.0, you can just type **p**.)

Your macro should now look like the one in Figure 2.5.

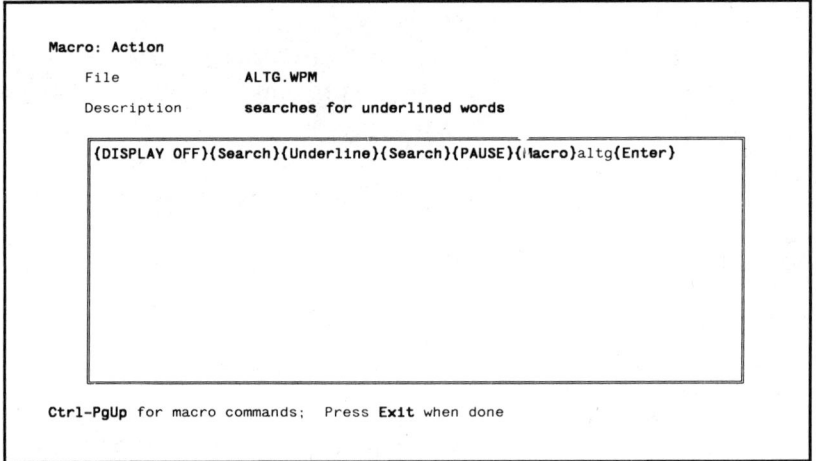

*Figure 2.5:* After you've inserted a pause with the macro editor, your macro should resemble this one.

When you pause a macro, none of your keystrokes are recorded until you press ⏎. With some macros, you'll need to enter something at this point for the macro to work on. For example, if you're pausing the macro in order to highlight text that the macro will move when it resumes, you'll need to highlight some text while the macro is paused. None of the text that you type or any cursor movements you make will be recorded while the macro is paused.

Now you can try out your newly edited macro. Return to your glossary document, go to the top of it, and press Alt-G. This time, the macro stops at the first underlined word, *kerning*. When you press ⏎, it moves to the next underlined word, and so on, until it can't locate any more underlined words in the document. However, you don't have to take an action every time the macro stops. When it stops at a word that you decide you don't want in your glossary, you can delete the underlining, so that the only words underlined are the words you want.

Now you can record a macro that automatically creates the word list for your glossary.

## *CREATING A GLOSSARY LIST*

Once you've used the **Alt-G** macro to clean up your document—that is, to make sure the only underlining left is under the words you want in your list—you've created a *unique identifier* for all those words. This is a special situation that lets you do several things with macros. You can search for this unique identifier and perform different kinds of operations. For example, you could change all the underlining to italics or boldface, or you could copy the words into the Doc 2 window and use them as the basis for creating a glossary. In fact, you can mark any kind of text with a unique identifier and use macros on it. You don't have to use underlining or boldface; you can use a symbol such as ## that isn't used anywhere else in your text. The macro can delete that symbol for you so that it won't be printed.

I often use a macro like this next one to copy marked text into the Doc 2 window and use that window as a workspace. For example, in this book's manuscript, all the level-1 headings begin with *A)*, which is a code for SYBEX's typesetting equipment. I can search for each *A)* and copy the line it's on to Doc 2 so that I have an automatic listing of all the level-1 headings, which are then used as a table of contents. (If you look at the "Cutting and Pasting between Windows" macro in Chapter 6, you'll see another example of this technique.)

To create a word list from the words you've underlined, you can record a macro that will search for each one, copy it, switch to the Doc 2 window, paste the copied word there, move to the next line, and go back to Doc 1 and search for the next underlined word. You'll use the **Alt-G** macro as the basis for this next macro, so you'll learn more about editing macros as well as copying and renaming them. In this way, you can use macros that you've already created as the basis for new macros, while keeping the old macro intact under its old name.

1. Press F5 (List Files), press End to move to the end of the line, delete the *.*, and enter the name of your macros subdirectory (if it isn't displayed). Then type **\*.wpm**. Press ⏎ to get a listing of your macros.

2. When the List Files screen appears, highlight ALTG.WPM.

3. Choose Copy (option 8 or C) and type **wrdlist.wpm** (don't forget the .wpm extension) as the name of the copy of the

macro; then press ←┘. You won't see the new macro listed on the List Files screen immediately, but the copy is there, and you can retrieve it to edit it. (Take care to remember what you called it, though.)

Now that you've got a copy of the **Alt-G** macro named **wrdlist**, you can edit it in Macro Define mode so that it will carry out the new steps.

1. Retrieve the **wrdlist** macro in the macro editor by turning on the macro recorder, entering **wrdlist**, pressing ←┘, and choosing to edit it.

2. Press End to move to the end of the line; press ← to move back to the {PAUSE}, then delete it. You don't want this macro to pause; you use the **Alt-G** macro for that as you check your document for underlined words.

3. Press Ctrl-F10 to go into Macro Define mode. You'll see the prompt

    **Press Macro Define to enable editing**

    When this prompt is present, each key you press is interpreted as a command. If you press Backspace, for example, a {Backspace} command appears in the macro editing screen, and nothing is deleted. You have to press Ctrl-F10 (Macro Def) again to get back to normal editing mode.

4. You want to add the keystrokes that copy the underlined word or phrase, switch to Doc 2, paste the copied word or phrase, move to the next line, and return to Doc 1 again, so take the following steps. (If you're unsure about what's happening, you can carry out the steps in your glossary document so that you can see them on the screen. Remember, if you need to correct a mistake, press Ctrl-F10 again to get back into editing mode.) With the cursor just after the second {Search}, press Alt-F4, which inserts a {Block} command into your macro.

5. Press F8 twice to generate the [UND][und] codes; then press ← to move over the last {Underline}, which generates the

[und] code. You need to search for the end of the underlining, which is the [und] code, so press Backspace to delete the first {Underline}, representing the [UND] code. Check Figure 2.6 if you lose your place here.

6. Press F2 to search for the [und] code represented by the remaining {Underline}. The underlined word or phrase will now be highlighted, so you can copy it.

7. Press Ctrl-F4 (Move) and type **B C** for Block Copy.

8. Press Shift-F3 (Switch); then press ⏎ to paste the copied text.

9. Press End to move to the end of the text; then press ⏎ again to move to the next line.

10. Press Shift-F3 to switch back to Doc 1.

11. Press Ctrl-F10 to return to normal editing mode.

12. Press → to move past the {Macro} command; then delete 'altg' and type **wrdlist** to have the macro repeat itself.

13. Press F7 (Exit) (twice in version 5.0) to stop editing the macro and to return to your document screen.

If you've followed along, your macro should look like the one in Figure 2.6. If you tried to correct any keystrokes as you recorded the

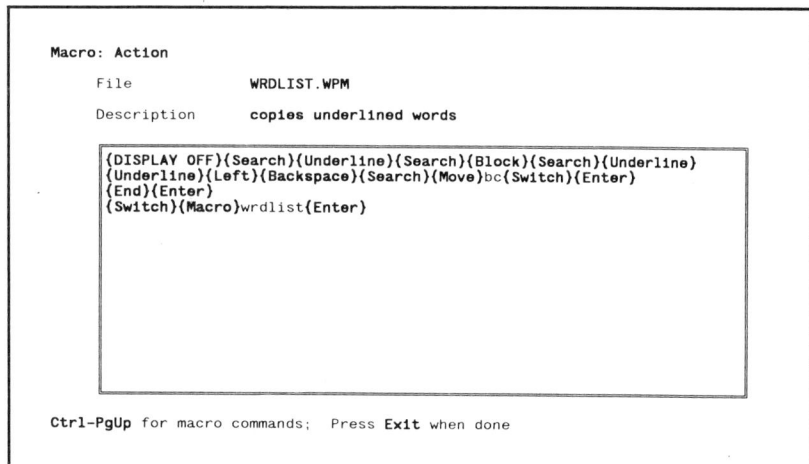

*Figure 2.6:* The **wrdlist** macro will automatically create a word list for you.

macro but didn't return to editing mode, they'll be followed by a {Backspace} code, as WordPerfect faithfully recorded every key you pressed, even the ones meant to correct your mistakes.

Now, return to the editing screen by pressing F7 (twice if you're using version 5.1), move to the top of the glossary document, and execute the **wrdlist** macro. When it finishes, switch to Doc 2 and see your new word list. WordPerfect will have copied each underlined word, and each one will be underlined on a separate line.

## USING A SPEED VALUE IN MACROS

Now that you've recorded a fairly complex macro, you may want to watch it as it executes. You can do so by inserting a *speed factor* in the macro, that is, a command that some or all of the macro's steps are to be executed at a certain rate.

To insert a speed factor in a macro, you have to use Macro Command Language, as you'll see in the following steps:

1. Retrieve your **wrdlist** macro into the macro editing screen.

2. Press Del to delete the {DISPLAY OFF} code.

3. Press Ctrl-PgUp (Macro Commands).

4. Type **S** and press ↓ to speed-search to the commands beginning with *S*. (In version 5.0, you'll need only to type **S**.) You should select the {Speed}100ths command. Press ↵ to insert the command in the macro.

5. Type **100 ~** to insert a speed factor of one second for each step of the macro. That way, you'll be able to see each step as it executes on the screen.

6. Press F7 (twice in version 5.0) to exit from the macro editor.

Now execute the **wrdlist** macro, and you'll see it slowly going through each step.

The speed factor you insert is in terms of hundredths of a second, so to have the macro delay half a second between steps, you would insert a delay of 50. For a two-second delay, insert 200, and so forth.

Another good reason for using a speed factor is to create macros that do automatic writing on the screen. If you create onscreen demonstrations, you may want to use this technique (there's a macro in Chapter 10 that demonstrates it).

## *DEBUGGING MACROS*

Using a speed value is also an excellent way of debugging a macro that isn't working as it should, because you can see each step that the macro takes as it executes on the screen. Once you spot where the problem is, you can edit the macro to correct it.

As you record macros, you may want to switch to an unused document window by pressing Shift-F3 (the Switch key), so that you can test and debug macros on sample text. As you've seen, it's not always possible to record a macro in a blank editing screen. For example, if you create a macro that moves a block of text, you must use some text that's previously been marked as a block. The sample text on which you use a macro won't be stored with the macro; only the macro keystrokes are recorded.

> See Appendix A for using Macro Command Language to specify the speed at which a macro runs, to make it wait a specified amount of time, or to execute it step by step.

## *DOCUMENTING MACROS*

When you use a macro, WordPerfect always assumes that the conditions under which you created it will exist in the document. For instance, if you execute a macro that copies a block of text without having first marked the block, either nothing or something unexpected will happen.

Also, some macros can get quite lengthy, and it's often good to be able to know exactly what operation is performed by a line that reads (for instance)

{Format}lt {Home}{Home}{Left}{Del to EOL}

(It clears all tab settings.)

To document the conditions under which a macro operates, you could add text to the macro description, but you're limited to only 39 characters. Instead, WordPerfect provides a Comment feature that lets you add descriptive comments in your macro. The comments do appear on the macro editing screen, but they aren't part of the macro and won't be printed when you execute it.

To add a comment to a macro as you're recording it, press Ctrl-PgUp and choose Comment (option 4 or C). You will see a 'Comment:' prompt, and you can type the text of your comment. WordPerfect inserts a semicolon (;) in the macro; anything after it is treated as a comment until it encounters a tilde (~). On the macro editing screen, you can see your comments, as Figure 2.7 illustrates.

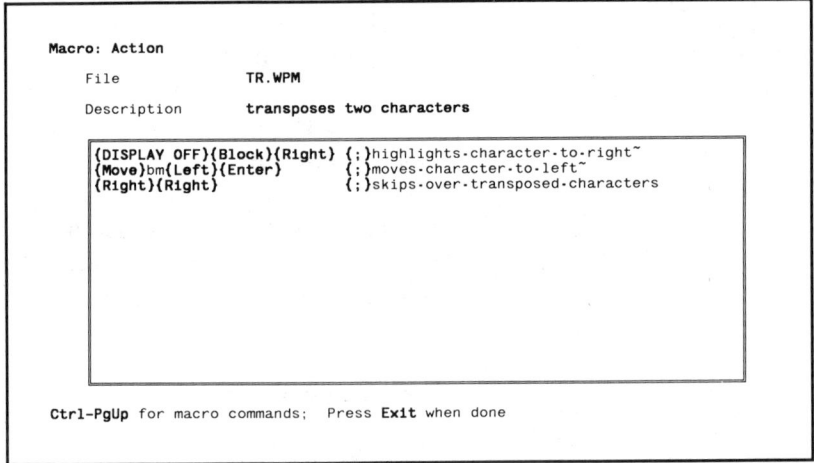

*Figure 2.7:* You can add comments to your macro so that you can see what each of its steps does.

● Just typing a semicolon in curly brackets won't insert a comment; you have to insert the {;} command by using the menu. However, you do have to type the tilde (~) that ends a comment.

If, while you're recording a macro, you're typing a comment and you reach the right edge of the screen, you won't be able to see the rest of the comment. However, you can insert longer comments by using the macro editor. To insert a comment with the macro editor, press Ctrl-PgUp (Macro Commands). A menu box appears, and {;}COMMENT~ is its first choice. This menu has WordPerfect's Name Search feature, so typing ; (a semicolon), and pressing ↵ inserts the {;} command. Anything you type after that will be considered a comment until you type ~.

If you become a serious macro writer, you'll want to set up a system for documenting your macros so that they're broken into logical sequences and are easy to understand. Since the macro editor has preset tabs, you can make it a practice to begin all your comments at one tab setting, as we saw in Figure 2.7. This makes it simpler for you or others to see at a glance what each sequence in a macro does. To break each line of the macro at a logical place, just press ⏎. Remember, pressing ⏎ in the macro editor doesn't insert a hard return in your document unless you've pressed Ctrl-F10 or Ctrl-V first.

As you get more deeply into macros, you'll find some tips in Chapter 4 that will help you. For example, you can use macros within the macro editor to move to the tab setting for your comment and then to insert the comment characters. Or you can use a macro to set up and format an {IF}{ELSE}{ENDIF} statement and position the cursor at the right place to start typing.

### CREATING A MACRO CATALOG

> If you want to rename a named macro as an Alt-key macro—for example, if you find that you're using it a lot—use the Move/Rename option on the List Files screen and type the new names as **alt*n*.wpm**, where **n** is the letter you want to assign it to.

If you find yourself editing macros often, you'll probably need to get hard copies of the macro editing screen. You'll find you can quickly refer to them to see the functions of each macro you've recorded as well as the exact keystrokes it contains. To get a printout of a macro editing screen, turn on your printer and press Shift-PrtSc (Print Screen on some keyboards). You can repeat this process for each macro you have created until you have a convenient catalog of your macro library.

### INSERTING A PAUSE AS YOU RECORD A MACRO

> WordPerfect 5.0 and 5.1 don't automatically sound a beep when a macro pauses, as earlier versions of WordPerfect did. To have a macro beep when it pauses, use the {BELL} command, which is described in Appendix A.

I said we wouldn't leave this chapter until I'd shown you how to insert a pause in a macro as you're recording it. You do that by using the technique we just discussed for adding comments, except that when you press Ctrl-PgUp, you choose Pause from the menu.

Once you've paused a macro, whatever you do remains unrecorded. You can type text, respond to a prompt, use a command, move to another place in the document—anything you like. Recording begins again only when you press ⏎. When you execute the macro, it will pause where you told it to and wait until you press ⏎ again.

A very useful macro, one that I use all the time, creates a footer for my document, but pauses to let me insert the chapter number before the page number. Here's how to create it:

1. Turn on the macro recorder, type **footer** as the macro's name (or name it **Alt-F**), and press ←.

2. Type **chapter and page number footer** as the description and press ←.

3. Press Shift-F8 (Format), type **P** for Page, **F** for Footers, **A** for Footer A, and **P** for Every Page.

4. When the footer editing screen appears, press Alt-F6 (Flush Right) so that the chapter and page number will be in the lower-right corner of every page.

5. Type **Chapter**, press the Spacebar, and insert a pause by pressing Ctrl-PgUp and typing **P**. Then resume the macro by pressing ←.

6. Type a hyphen (-), then press Ctrl-B. This tells WordPerfect to insert the number of the current page.

7. Press F7 twice to return to your document.

8. Turn off the macro recorder by pressing Ctrl-F10 or choosing Macro from the Tools menu, then choosing Define.

If you retrieve the macro to edit it, it should look like the one in Figure 2.8. Try it out. When the macro pauses, type a chapter number and press ←. Then use the View Document feature on the page (Shift-F7 V) to view the footer.

## *CONSIDERATIONS IN DESIGNING MACROS*

You've read and done a lot about building macros in this chapter, but there are a few other things you should consider as you begin to build a working library of macros. First, just how much of a process do you want to automate? As you've already seen, inserting pauses in macros lets you enter information from the keyboard, which

# EDITING MACROS 41

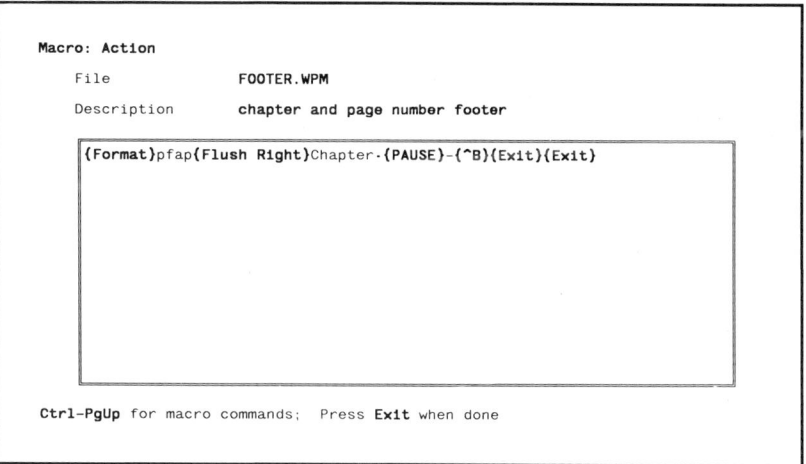

*Figure 2.8:* The **footer** macro pauses for you to type the chapter number.

makes the same macro useful under a variety of conditions. If you make a macro too specific to a particular document, it may not be of much use in another.

For example, if you frequently change from single to double spacing and back, instead of recording two macros—one for single spacing and one for double—you can use a single macro for both. First the macro enters the commands to change the line spacing (Shift-F8 L S) and then pauses for you to enter a value; then it resumes by pressing F7 twice to return you to the document. When you execute this macro, you can enter the number of line spaces and press ⏎ to enter the new value. This macro can be used whenever you need to change the line spacing, whether from single to double or in any other allowable way.

Also, be careful about following screen prompts as you're executing a macro. For example, when you define a header or footer, the prompt at the bottom of the screen reads

    Press **Exit** When Done

However, if you're executing a macro and it has paused for your input, you need to press ⏎, not F7. If you've already included the F7 (Exit) key as part of the macro definition, pressing F7 from the keyboard will still exit you from the screen, but the F7 in the macro may prevent it from working properly. Under some circumstances, for instance, it could exit you from your document.

Another thing to keep in mind is how the cursor moves in the program. If you're recording a macro, you can see the cursor move on the screen and correct its position. However, the next time you execute that macro, your correction will have been recorded also, and it may not be appropriate for the situation. Suppose, for example, that you want to highlight a five-letter word to the right of the cursor. You could press Alt-F4 and press → five times to highlight it, but from then on the macro would highlight only the five spaces to the right of the cursor. Instead, to select words, lines, sentences, or paragraphs, use WordPerfect's built-in cursor-control keys. For example, pressing Ctrl-← moves the cursor to the first character in the word to the left of the cursor, and it also jumps over any hidden formatting codes in the text. Pressing End takes you to the end of the current line, and Home-← takes you to the beginning of the line. In case you need a reminder of these cursor-control sequences while you're writing macros, Table 2.1 summarizes them for you. Likewise, Table 2.2 summarizes WordPerfect's quick-deletion methods.

*Table 2.1:* Moving the Cursor in WordPerfect

| To Move | Press |
|---|---|
| Character by character | ← or → |
| Word by word | Ctrl-← or Ctrl-→ |
| To the beginning of a line | Home ← |
| To the end of a line | Home → |
| To the end of the sentence | Ctrl-Home . |
| To the next occurrence of a character | Ctrl-Home <*character*> |
| To the top of the screen | Home ↑ or Gray − |
| To the bottom of the screen | Home ↓ or Gray + |
| To previous screens | Home ↑ or Gray − repeatedly |
| To following screen | Home ↓ or Gray + repeatedly |
| To the previous page | PgUp |

*Table 2.1:* Moving the Cursor in WordPerfect (continued)

| TO MOVE | PRESS |
| --- | --- |
| To the next page | PgDn |
| To the top of the page | Ctrl-Home ↑ |
| To the bottom of the next page | Ctrl-Home ↓ |
| To a specified page | Ctrl-Home <*page number*> ↵ |
| To the last cursor position before the cursor-movement command | Ctrl-Home Ctrl-Home |
| To the beginning of the last defined block | Ctrl-Home Alt-F4 |
| To the beginning of the document | Home Home ↑ |
| To the beginning of the document before any codes | Home Home Home ↑ |
| To the end of the document | Home Home ↓ |
| To the rightmost position on a line | Home Home → |
| To the leftmost position on a line | Home Home ← |

*Table 2.2:* Deleting Text in WordPerfect

| TO DELETE | PRESS |
| --- | --- |
| Character by character | Backspace (deletes to left of cursor) *or* Del (deletes character or space the cursor is on) |
| Word by word | Ctrl-Backspace |
| The word to the right of the cursor | Ctrl-→ or Ctrl-Backspace |

*Table 2.2:* Deleting Text in WordPerfect (continued)

| To Delete | Press |
|---|---|
| The word to the left of the cursor | Ctrl-← or Home-Backspace |
| Several words | Esc *n* (*n* = number of words to right of the cursor) Ctrl-Backspace |
| From the cursor right to the end of a word | Home-Del |
| To the end of a line | Ctrl-End |
| Several lines | Esc *n* (*n* = number of lines) Ctrl-End |
| To the end of a sentence (ending in a period) | Alt-F4 . Del Y |
| To to the end of a page | Ctrl-PgDn Y |
| A block | Alt-F4 <*highlight block*> Backspace or Del Y |
| A paragraph | Alt-F4 ← Del Y |

## COMBINING MACRO COMMANDS

You can combine the different commands that make the macro visible, that pause it or delay its execution, and that make it invisible. For example, you might want to record a macro that types the standard text of a business letter at a pace at which you can read it (with {DISPLAY ON}). At the places where you need to insert text, the macro can pause for your input. When you've finished typing the last text and you press ←, the macro can execute the F10 command to save the file as LTR (for letter) and pause again. At this pause, you can type an ending to the file name, such as 1028 (for October 28). You can then return the macro to invisible speed by inserting a {DISPLAY OFF} command and have it execute the keystrokes needed to print the letter (Shift- F7 1).

For example, to record a macro like this one, take the following steps. I'll keep it as short as possible (though it will still be quite long), so that you can see how to do it. Then later you can record one of your own for the kind of letter you'd normally write.

1. Turn on the macro recorder, type **letter** as the macro's name, and press ↵.

2. Type **writes and prints letter** as the description and press ↵.

3. To turn on the display so that you can see the macro as it writes, press Ctrl-PgUp (Macro Commands) and type **D**. If you haven't turned on the display previously, you'll see the prompt

    Display Execution? No (Yes)_

    Type **Y** to display the macro.

4. Insert the date by pressing Shift-F5 (Date/Outline); then type **T** for Text. You can insert the Date function instead if you want the date of the letter to change each time you retrieve or print it.

5. Press ↵ twice to insert a blank line.

6. Now you want the macro to pause so that you can type the recipient's name, street address, and city/state on three separate lines. Pressing ↵ at the end of each line will resume the macro, however, so you have to insert three separate pauses. Press Ctrl-PgUp, type **P**, and press ↵ twice—once to resume the macro and then again to move to the next line.

7. Press Ctrl-PgUp, type **P**, and press ↵ twice.

8. Press Ctrl-PgUp, type **P**, and press ↵ twice.

9. Now press ↵ again to insert a blank line. Then type **Dear** and press the Spacebar.

10. Insert another pause so that you can type the recipient's name. Press Ctrl-PgUp, type **P**, and press ↵. Then type : (colon).

11. Press ↵ twice to insert a blank line.

12. Then type the following text, inserting a pause by pressing Ctrl-PgUp, typing **P**, and pressing ↵ at each place indicated by {PAUSE}. The macro, when it executes, will pause

first for you to type your company name, then for you to type the recipient's company name, then to insert the discount that's being offered, and finally to insert the last date on which the offer is good.

> As you may be aware, we at {PAUSE} are preparing for our end-of-year inventory sale. We'd like to offer you at {PAUSE} a {PAUSE}% discount on any purchases you may make between now and {PAUSE}.

Be sure to use the spaces and punctuation that you need. You can look at Figures 2.9A and 2.9B to check your work.

13. When you've typed the last period, press ⏎ twice, type **Sincerely,** , press ⏎ three times to leave space for your signature, and type **Your Name**.

14. Now you can add the steps that save the letter and print it. These don't have to be displayed, so press Ctrl-PgUp, type **D**, and type **N** so that the display won't appear. Then press ⏎.

15. Press F10 (Save), enter **ltr**, and insert a pause again (Ctrl-PgUp **P**); then press ⏎ to save the file. The macro will pause here so that you can type up to five characters plus an

> This macro assumes that you haven't saved the letter previously. If you have, you'll be asked by the prompt whether you want to replace the existing version of the letter with the new one.

```
Macro: Action

    File              LETTER.WPM

    Description       creates business letter

    {DISPLAY ON}{Date/Outline}t{Enter}
    {Enter}
    {PAUSE}{Enter}
    {PAUSE}{Enter}
    {PAUSE}{Enter}
    {Enter}
    Dear {PAUSE}:{Enter}
    {Enter}
    As you may be aware, we at {PAUSE} are preparing for our end-of-year
    inventory sale. We'd like to offer you at {PAUSE}
     a {PAUSE}% discount on any purchases you may make between now and
    {PAUSE}.{Enter}
    {Enter}
    Sincerely,{Enter}
    {Enter}

Ctrl-PgUp for macro commands;   Press Exit when done
```

*Figure 2.9A:* The completed letter macro pauses for you to enter the information that changes from letter to letter.

```
Macro: Action
    File            LETTER.WPM
    Description     creates business letter

    {PAUSE}{Enter}
    {PAUSE}{Enter}
    {PAUSE}{Enter}
    {Enter}
    Dear {PAUSE}:{Enter}
    {Enter}
    As you may be aware, we at {PAUSE} are preparing for our end-of-year
    inventory sale. We'd like to offer you at {PAUSE}
     a {PAUSE}% discount on any purchases you may make between now and
    {PAUSE}.{Enter}
    {Enter}
    Sincerely,{Enter}
    {Enter}
    {Enter}
    Your Name{DISPLAY OFF}{Save}ltr{PAUSE}{Enter}{Print}1

Ctrl-PgUp for macro commands;   Press Exit when done
```

*Figure 2.9B:* Since the entire **ltr** macro is longer than one editing screen, this second figure shows its last few steps.

optional three-letter extension as the name of the letter. For example, you might name a letter written on December 21 as 1221, and you could add an extension identifying it as a form letter for the sale by typing .sal. In this example, you'd type **1221.sal** to save the letter as LTR1221.SAL. When you press ← to enter the file name as you use the macro, it will resume executing and carry out the last step, printing the letter.

16. Press Shift-F7 and type **1** to print the letter.
17. Press Ctrl-F10 to turn off the macro recorder.

Figure 2.10 shows a sample letter produced with this macro. I've underlined the places where the macro pauses to let you type.

## *SUMMARY*

In this chapter, you saw how to use the macro editor to insert new steps and commands in macros, how to clone macros so that you can edit them while keeping the original macro intact, and how to insert delays and pauses. In particular, you saw that:

- You can enter an existing macro's name at the Define Macro prompt and either replace it or edit it.

```
August 13, 1988

Harrison M. Starnes
3100 West Palace Court
Palo Alto, CA 94303

Dear Mr. Starnes:

As you may be aware, we at Consolidated Appliances are preparing
for our end-of-year inventory sale. We'd like to offer you at
Starnes Associates a 20% discount on any purchases you may make
between now and the first of October.

Sincerely,


Your Name




                                            Doc 2 Pg 1 Ln 1" Pos 1"
```

*Figure 2.10:* This sample letter was deliberately kept short, but it does give you an idea of how flexible document production can be with macros.

- In the macro editor, keystrokes are interpreted as commands after you press Ctrl-F10 or Ctrl-V (for the next keystroke only).

- Pressing Ctrl-PgUp while you're defining a macro lets you insert special macro commands if you're in the macro editor; if you're not in the editor, it lets you insert a pause, make the macro execute visibly, assign the macro to a variable, or insert a comment line in the macro.

- To have a macro repeat itself, you either press Alt-F10 (or, if you're using pull-down menus, choose Macro from the Tools menu, then choose Execute) and enter the macro's name at the end of the macro as you're recording it, or use the editor to create this last step in a macro you've already recorded.

- When you've paused a macro, your keystrokes aren't recorded until you press ⏎.

- Entering a delay factor into a macro lets you slow it down enough to see it execute on the screen.

- Renaming a macro with the Copy command in the List Files screen lets you work with a copy of the macro to alter it for another purpose.

With these skills, you can try out the more complex macros in Chapter 3, knowing that if anything goes wrong, you have ways to fix it.

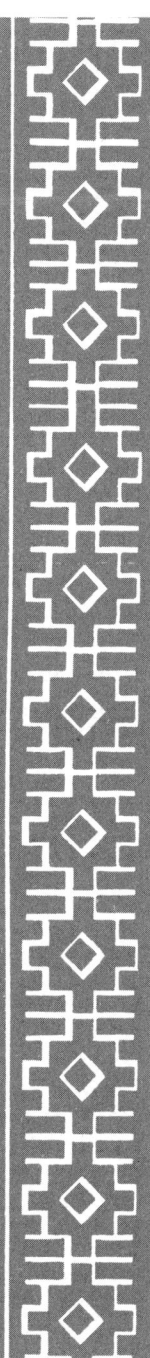

# *More Complex Macro Techniques*

CHAPTER

3

# CHAPTER 3

You've seen how to use the macro editor, and you've recorded some relatively sophisticated macros. Now you're ready for some of the more complex macro techniques, including a start on WordPerfect's special Macro Command Language.

This chapter, then, expands on the concepts of *chaining* and *nesting* macros, both of which are ways of having one macro call another after the macro has completed the tasks it was set up to do. Through chaining you'll get your original macro to execute another macro when it finishes; through nesting you'll have it branch to a macro that carries out a *subroutine* (a separate set of instructions), and then returns control to the master, or main, macro.

You'll also discover how you can use Macro Command Language to set up one macro to do one thing if a certain condition is met and do something else if it isn't. First, however, we'll look at some special (and not-so-special, but perhaps overlooked) techniques you can use to make your macros search.

## *SPECIAL SEARCH TECHNIQUES*

You can use the Search feature, which is an important part of many macros, to find not only specific text but also formatting codes or places where you've used a certain command—to change line spacing, for example. Searching for a particular code or use of a menu option allows you to instruct your macros to move to various locations in a document and carry out instructions there. Searching, and searching and replacing, are crucial operations in many macros.

### *SEARCHING FOR FORMAT CODES*

To have WordPerfect locate a particular format code, you use the appropriate Search function (Forward or Reverse) and then press the appropriate function key or key combination (including the number or letter of the menu option) instead of typing an alphanumeric search string. For instance, to perform a forward search to find the first occurrence of a hard page break (one that you entered), you press F2 (the Search key) and then press Ctrl-Return (the keys used to add a hard page break). In response, the program will display the format code as the search string:

   -> Srch: [HPg]

You then press F2 to perform the search. WordPerfect will position the cursor just after the first hard page break it finds. To delete this page break, press Backspace. To find the next occurrence of a hard page break, press F2 twice.

In version 5.1, to use the mouse with the Search function, select Forward or Backward Search, enter the pattern to search for, and press the right mouse button.

## *SEARCHING FOR PAIRED FORMAT CODES*

The Search function can also locate the second code (or lowercase version) in a pair of formatting codes such as [BOLD][bold] or [UND][und]. Searching for only the second code lets you record macros that perform a task just *after* a format code. For example, you might want to search for all instances of boldface, which is being used for headings, and add an extra line of space by pressing ←⎯.

When you perform a regular search for one of these paired codes, WordPerfect positions the cursor after the first uppercase code. For instance, to find the next use of underlining in a document, you press F2 and then F8 (Underline):

   -> Srch: [UND]

If you then perform the search and the next occurrence of underlining in the text is *Advanced Techniques in WordPerfect*, WordPerfect will position the cursor under the *A* in *Advanced*. If you press Alt-F3 (the Reveal Codes key), you will see that the cursor is really positioned right after the '[UND]' in '[UND]Advanced Techniques in Word-Perfect[und].' If you press Backspace, the underlining will be removed.

To search for the lowercase [und] code, you press F2 and then F8 twice. You will then see the following:

   -> Srch: [UND][und]

To search for just the second code [und], you need to modify the codes after the Search prompt. Press ← once and press Backspace. If you perform the search without deleting this first code, you will probably receive the message 'Not Found,' because it is likely that nowhere in your text will the codes [UND][und] occur together (that is, without any text between them).

Now, when you press F2 to perform the search mentioned above, your cursor will be positioned after the *t* in *WordPerfect*. If you open the Reveal Codes window, you will see that the cursor is really located *after* the '[und]' code in '[UND]Advanced Techniques in WordPerfect[und]'.

## *CHANGING PAIRED FORMAT CODES*

If you want to search for size or appearance codes, such as [SMALL][small], and change them throughout a document, you'll need to use a macro. Although you'd think that you could simply search for one code and replace it with another, the process isn't that simple. When you delete or change one of a pair of codes, WordPerfect deletes the *second* member of the pair also. So, if you replaced all the [SMALL] codes with [LARGE], you would turn on large type but never turn it off, and the rest of your document would be in the large type size. Instead, you can record a macro that searches for the first one of these codes, turns on blocking, searches for the second code in the pair, inserts the new size or appearance codes, and deletes the old ones.

This pattern, which is used in the following macro that changes all small type to large, can be used in any macro in which you want to change one of WordPerfect's paired sets of codes to another.

To record the macro, you'll need to have some text on the screen that's in small type, so clear the screen and type the following line:

**Converting small to large**

Then press Alt-F4 (or choose Block from the Edit pull-down menu), press Home-← to block the line, press Ctrl-F8, and type **S S** to insert the [SMALL][small] codes.

> All of WordPerfect's format codes are listed in Appendix B so that you can refer to them while recording macros.

1. Turn on the macro recorder and enter **large** as the name of the macro. Enter **changes small to large** as the description.

2. Press F2 to begin a forward search.

3. Press Ctrl-F8 (Font) and type **S S** to search for the [SMALL] code. Remember, if you prefer, you can choose from the Font pull-down menu, but typing seems to be faster.

4. Press F2 to execute the search.

5. When the macro locates the first code, turn on blocking (Alt-F4) and then search for the second [small] code to highlight the text. To do this, press F2, press Ctrl-F8 **S S** twice; then press ← to move over it. Press Backspace to delete the [SMALL] code.

6. Press F2 again to search for the [small] code.

7. The text is now highlighted, so press Ctrl-F8 (Font) and type **S** for Size; then type **L** for Large to insert [LARGE][large] codes around the highlighted text.

8. To delete the [SMALL][small] codes, press ←; then press Backspace and type **Y**.

9. To repeat the macro until no more [SMALL][small] codes are found in the document, press Alt-F10, type **large** (the name of the macro), and press ↵.

10. Turn off the macro recorder by pressing Ctrl-F10 or by choosing Macro from the Tools menu and then choosing Define.

Now, when you want to change small text to large text, you can use this macro to make the conversion quickly throughout a document. You can edit the macro to search for any combination of paired codes, so you can have it change double underlining to small caps, small type to italics, subscripts to superscripts, and so forth. If you want to check your work, the keystrokes for the final macro are shown in Figure 3.1. To view them, press Ctrl-F10, enter **large**, and type **2** to edit the macro.

## *SEARCHING FOR MENU OPTIONS*

You can also search to find format codes that require the use of menu options. For instance, to locate the place in the text where you first used WordPerfect's Newspaper Column format, you can use the Search function to find the [Col On] code required to activate your column definitions. After you press F2 (assuming that a forward search is required), you press Alt-F7 (the Columns/Table key, which defines the columns and turns them on and off). (In version 5.0 this key is called the Math/Columns key.) If you are using WordPerfect 5.1, type **C** for Columns, and you will see the following options:

**Column: 1 On; 2 Off; 3 Def: 0**

If you are using version 5.0, you will see

**Column: B Def C On D Off 0**

as soon as you press Alt-F7.

> When you access command menus to generate format codes that will be searched for, the menu options may not appear the same as in normal menus. All the options may be arranged horizontally, and some of them may be reworded or otherwise reorganized. In addition, some of the mnemonic shortcuts you are used to may not be in effect. You may have to enter an option number or letter different from the one you used to insert the format code originally.

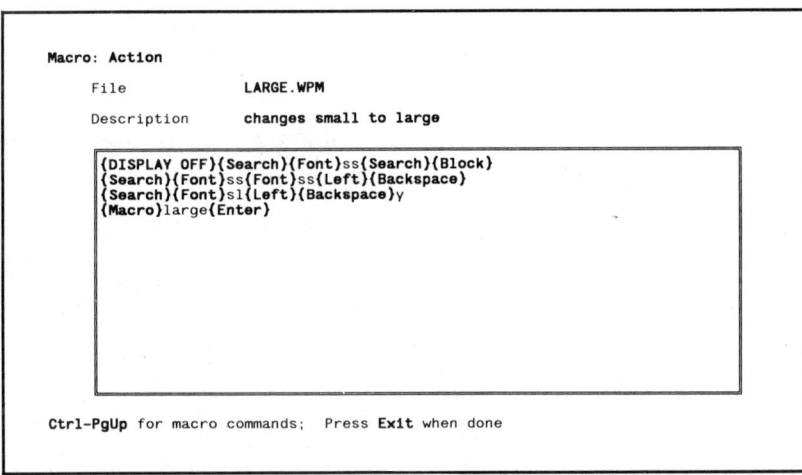

*Figure 3.1:* The pattern in this macro can be used in any macro that changes one paired format code to another.

*MORE COMPLEX MACRO TECHNIQUES* **57**

To search for the [Col On] code, you type **O** (in version 5.1) or **C** (in version 5.0), and you then see the following:

-> Srch: [Col On]

For example, after using several different column definitions within a document you may later decide that you want to use different styles of columns. You can record a macro that searches for each column definition in your document and displays the Text Column Definition screen, so that you can review the setting for each one. When you press ←, the macro will resume and search for the next definition. You will need a document containing a column definition in which to record this macro. To create one quickly, press Alt-F7, type **C** for Columns (version 5.1), type **D**, and press ←.

To record such a macro:

1. Turn on the macro recorder, type **colrev** as the macro's name, and press ←.

2. Type **review column settings** as the description and press ←.

3. Press F2 (Search); then press Alt-F7 (Columns/Table) and type first **C** for Columns, then **D**, then F2 again to search for the [Col Def] code. If you're using version 5.0, press Alt-F7 and type **B**.

4. Press Alt-F7 again and type **C** and then **D** to display the Text Columns Definition screen. In version 5.0, just type **D**.

5. Insert a pause by pressing Ctrl-PgUp and typing **P**.

6. Press ← three times to resume the macro and return to the editing screen.

7. WordPerfect will insert a new [Col Def] code that duplicates the old one, if you haven't changed anything; if you have changed settings, however, the new code will contain the changes. To delete the old code, just to keep your document clean, press ←, press Backspace, and then type **Y** to confirm the deletion.

8. Press → to move over the remaining [Col Def] code and continue the search.

9. Press Alt-F10, enter **colrev**, and press ← to have the macro repeat itself.

10. Turn off the macro recorder by pressing Ctrl-F10 or choosing Macro from the Tools menu and then choosing Define.

When you execute the macro, go to the top of your document by pressing Home Home Home ↑. Then press Alt-F10 (or choose Macro from the Tools menu and then choose Execute), enter **colrev**, and press ← to start the macro running. It will display each column definition screen in your document. Press ← to view the next column definition. While you are looking at each definition screen, you can make any changes that you like (without pressing ←, which will resume the macro—use F7 instead to enter your changes) or simply leave things as they are; WordPerfect will insert a new [Col Def] code at that point, but the macro will automatically delete the old one for you.

## *SEARCHING FOR SPECIAL CHARACTERS*

You can search directly for special characters that you have entered with WordPerfect's Compose feature (Ctrl-2 or Ctrl-V plus the appropriate character set and symbol numbers). To search for one of these characters, press Search (F2) and then repeat the sequence you originally used to generate the character. For example, to search for an uppercase umlauted *A* (Ä), press Ctrl-2, type **1,30**, and press ←. The Ä will appear as the search string. Next, press F2 to execute the search. Used in a macro, this technique lets you locate places where you've used any symbol from WordPerfect's character sets.

## *SEARCHING AND REPLACING*

As you already know if you have worked much with WordPerfect, you can also search for words or phrases and replace them with substitute words or phrases that you specify. This feature is like using a built-in macro. You can search for up to 59 characters and replace them with as many as 59 characters, including spaces. When you perform a search-and-replace operation, WordPerfect matches the capitalization of the first letter of the word or phrase it finds. For

> A macro that contains a search command will stop when an unsuccessful search ends, but a macro that replaces will not. You can therefore make many replacements with one macro.

example, if you ask it to search for *file list* and replace this phrase with *list files*, it will replace *File List* with *List files*, *file List* with *list files*, and so forth. This feature allows you to correctly replace words and phrases that are capitalized at the beginning of a sentence and lowercased within the text.

You can search for any WordPerfect code, but you can search and replace only some of them. Where you can't use the Replace function, just create a macro that uses the Search function to locate the appropriate code, performs any required deletion, and replaces the code with a new one.

## *SOUNDING A BEEP*

If you write macros that search, you can have them pause and sound a beep so that you can take an action each time the item you are searching for is located. Although this is a very simple use of Macro Command Language, it is also a handy one, since it warns you that your macro has paused and is waiting for your input.

The next macro speeds up the process of creating a table of contents by quickly locating each heading for you and beeping to alert you to enter the correct heading level. The macro searches for each heading in your document that you've previously marked with a unique identifier.

The only advance preparation you need to use a macro like the following is to decide which unique identifier you're going to use for the headings in your document. It must be an attribute or symbol that is used nowhere else in the document. In this example, we'll use the "at" sign (@). In your documents you could choose to use the [BOLD] code or a [LARGE] code instead. Just change that step in the macro to use whichever identifier you want; then, as you type your document, identify all your headings with that code. When you execute the macro, it will beep at each pause, letting you know that it's time to interact with the program.

To record the macro, you'll need a short document that contains at least a couple of marked headings. You can retrieve one that you've already created, or you can enter the text shown in Figure 3.2. You'll record the macro in two stages: first, by using the keyboard as a macro recorder, and then by using the editor to insert the {BELL} command.

```
@Using Soft Keyboards
     If you use macros frequently in your work, you may prefer to
map them to keys on your keyboard so that whenever you press that
key, the macro is executed instead of the character the key
normally generates.

@Assigning Macros to Keys
     This technique lets you execute named macros quickly from
another key combination, such as Ctrl-S, so that you aren't
limited to 26 quick macros on the Alt key. Because you can map
macros to Ctrl, Alt, and Shift combinations and the function keys
as well as to the lowercase keys, you can have more macros on one
keyboard definition than you'll ever be able to keep track of!

@Defining Separate Keyboards
     For example, if you do mathematical typing, you can set up a
MATH keyboard that executes macros that switch to superscript and
subscript, italicize highlighted text, create characters like
greater than or equals to, pi, and so forth.



C:\5\FIG3-2                                    Doc 2 Pg 1 Ln 1" Pos 1"
```

*Figure 3.2:* To record the **mark** macro, you'll need a short document with headings identified like these.

1. Turn on the macro recorder by pressing Ctrl-F10 or choosing Macro from the Tools menu and then choosing Define. Type **mark** as the macro's name, and press ←.

2. Type **marks headings for table of contents** as the description and press ←.

3. Press F2; then type @ to search for the @ symbols that mark the headings in the document. Then press F2 again to execute the search.

4. Press Backspace to delete the @ when it's been located.

5. Press Alt-F4 (Mark Block); then press ← to highlight to the next hard return. This ensures that if your headings are longer than one line, the lines following the first will be included, up to the next hard return.

6. Press Alt-F5 (Mark Text) and type **C** to mark the highlighted entry for the table of contents.

7. Press Ctrl-PgUp, type **P**, and press ← twice to insert a pause so that you can enter the correct level for the heading when the macro executes.

8. To chain the macro to itself so that it will repeat until all the headings have been located, press Alt-F10, type **mark**, and press ⏎.

9. Turn off the macro recorder by pressing Ctrl-F10 or choosing Macro from the Tools menu and choosing Define again.

To add a beep to this macro so that it will alert you each time it pauses, press Ctrl-F10 and retrieve the macro to the editing screen by typing **mark**, pressing ⏎, and typing 2. In version 5.0, you'll need to type 2 twice. Then move the cursor to just before the {PAUSE} command (Figure 3.3), press Ctrl-PgUp, type **B**, and press ⏎. Be sure to insert the {BELL} command before the pause, not after it, so that the macro beeps each time that it needs input from you.

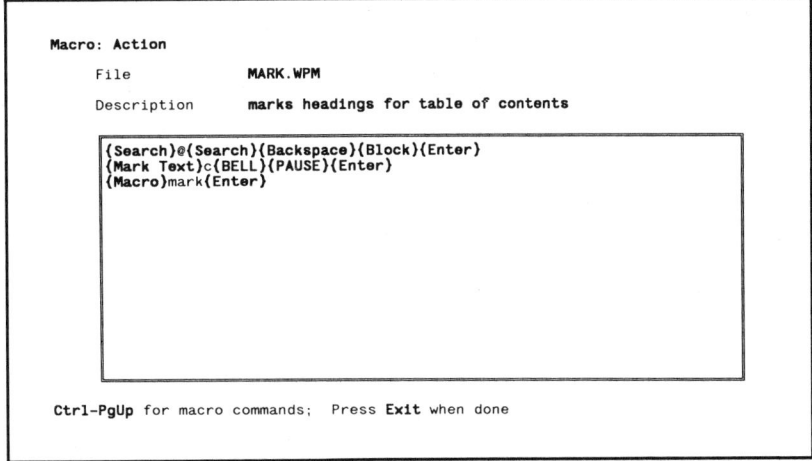

*Figure 3.3:* The **mark** macro lets you work interactively to indicate the level for each heading that WordPerfect locates and highlights on the screen.

When the macro executes, it will beep and pause for you to type the level of the heading that is highlighted on the screen. Pressing ⏎ resumes the macro so that it will search for the next heading marked with an @.

This macro that marks text for the headings in a table of contents can be used as a pattern for many other macros that pause and allow you to mark items in your document. For example, a similar macro can be used to mark items to be included in lists, such as a list of figure captions, or to search for specific phrases and mark them to be included in an index. You'll see other macros of this type in Chapter 10, Specialized Macros, which also has macros that define and generate tables of contents for you.

## CHAINING AND NESTING MACROS

You saw from the previous macro and in Chapter 2 that you can have a macro repeat until it can't locate any more occurrences of the pattern it's searching for. This, as we have seen, is called chaining, and it's a very powerful macro tool. You already know one way to chain a macro: by pressing Alt-F10 and entering the macro's name as you're recording or editing it. But there's another way as well.

### USING THE {CHAIN} COMMAND

You can use Macro Command Language to insert a {CHAIN}*file*~ command in a macro. Recall from Chapter 2 that to insert one of these special macro commands, you press Ctrl-PgUp (the Macro Commands key) while you're in the macro editor. To go quickly to the {CHAIN} command, you can just type **ch** after pressing Ctrl-PgUp; then press ↵ to insert the command in the macro.

You enter the macro's name in place of the *file*, so to chain a macro named **copy**, you'd enter **copy**~ . (Remember to type the tilde at the end.)

What happens when you use the {CHAIN} command? Instead of executing the chained macro at the point in the macro where the {CHAIN} command occurs, WordPerfect waits until all the steps in the original macro have been executed. Then it executes the chained macro. This is just like pressing Alt-F10 and entering the macro's name, which inserts a {Macro} command.

The {CHAIN} command lets you specify another macro to be executed after the current macro finishes, so in effect it transfers control from one macro to another. Practically speaking, this means that you can build a library of macros that carry out certain tasks for you, and just chain them to each other when you want to use them. For example, you could record a general macro that saves and prints a document and chain it to any other macro in which you want the last steps to be saving and printing. Or you could record a general-purpose macro that defines and generates a list, and use it in any macro that calls for that operation. By chaining macros, you save yourself the effort of typing the keystrokes for the second macro.

When WordPerfect completes a macro that includes a {CHAIN} command, it will search for the chained macro in your macros directory (or WordPerfect directory, if you haven't set up a separate directory for macros). You can specify a different directory by entering a path name before the macro name when you chain it. For example, to chain a macro named **cite** that you've stored in a subdirectory named REFS, you would enter the command

{CHAIN}\refs\cite

> If you've already recorded a macro and want to chain another macro to it, you must either use the macro editor or rerecord the macro.

You can also edit a macro to chain another macro to it. For example, suppose the **cite** macro that you've chained includes a {CHAIN} command that chains it to a macro named **generate**, which in turn generates the citation list. The **generate** macro could include a {CHAIN} command to a **print** macro, and so forth.

To see how this works, you can record a relatively simple macro that adds a new paragraph of so-called boilerplate text (standard clauses or instructions) to a document and then transfers control to the simple macro called **close** that you created in Chapter 1.

1. Turn on the macro recorder by pressing Ctrl-F10 or choosing Macro from the Tools menu and then choosing Define. Type **newpara** as the macro's name, and press ←.

2. Type **types standard paragraph** as the description and press ←.

3. Press Tab; then type **We'd like to remind you that your account is overdue. Enclosed is a postage-paid envelope for your convenience.** Then press ← twice to insert a blank line.

4. Press Ctrl-F10 to stop recording the macro.

5. To edit the macro and insert the {CHAIN} command, press Ctrl-F10 again, enter the macro's name (which is **newpara**) and press ←.

6. Type **2** to edit the macro. If you're using version 5.0, you'll need to type **2** again for Action.

7. Move the cursor to the end of the macro; then press Ctrl-PgUp, type **ch** to highlight the {CHAIN} command, and press ⏎.

8. Type **close** ~ to chain the **close** macro.

9. Press F7 (twice in version 5.0) to stop editing the macro.

The final macro should resemble the one in Figure 3.4. If you wanted to chain the **close** macro to a print macro, you would do so in the **close** macro, as Figure 3.5 shows. Then, when you executed the **newpara** macro, it would type the paragraph and go on to execute the **close** macro, which would then execute the **print** macro.

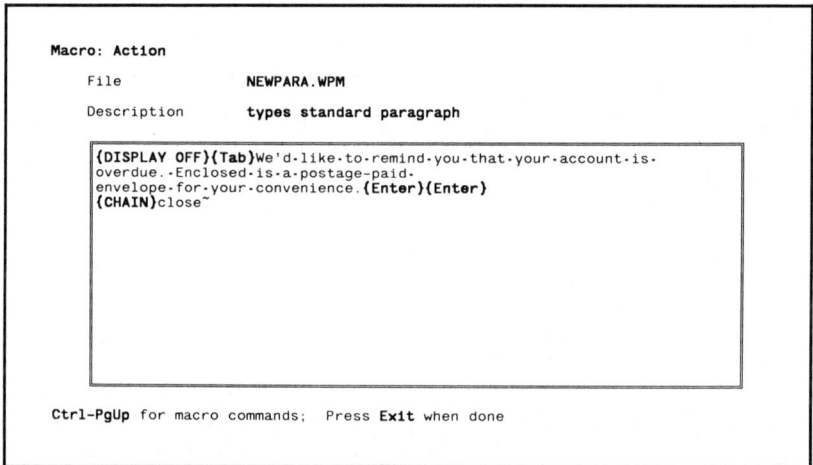

*Figure 3.4:* The **newpara** macro illustrates how you can chain one macro to another.

It's important to remember that you can put the {CHAIN} command anywhere within a macro, but the macro it calls won't be executed until the first macro finishes. To have a macro execute at its location in another macro, you should nest it instead (as you'll see in the next section).

## MORE COMPLEX MACRO TECHNIQUES  65

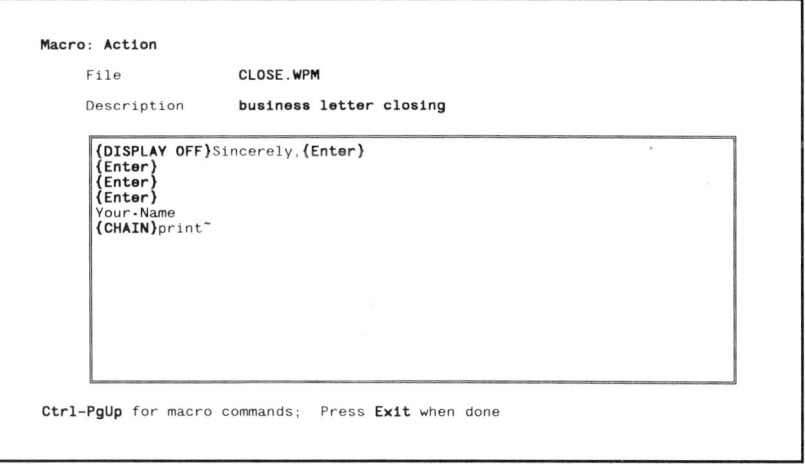

*Figure 3.5:* By chaining another macro at the end of the second macro, as here, you can continue the chain.

## *NESTING MACROS*

You can nest macros as well as chain them. When you use the {NEST} command, the nested macro is executed at the point where it occurs in the main macro (the macro that holds it), unlike a macro that's executed with the {CHAIN} command within a macro.

Alt macros, too, can be nested as you're recording other macros, but this technique is a little different from using the {NEST} command. When you press Alt and the letter of a previously recorded macro with the macro recorder running, the keystrokes of the Alt macro are executed immediately, and the command to execute the Alt macro is placed in the macro you're recording. For example, if you've recorded an **Alt-S** macro that saves and prints the document, your document will be saved and printed at that point. An {ALT S} command is also inserted in the macro.

In effect, a nested macro is like a subroutine. It says to Word-Perfect, "Go carry out these steps and then come back to this macro where you left off." Using nested macros gives you a lot of flexibility, because it lets you choose subroutines (other macros) freely from your macro library. With nested macros, you can record a main macro that moves to the top of the document, nest a macro that carries out a search-and-replace operation, move to the end of the document and create a blank page, nest another macro that defines and generates a list on that page, and so forth. In fact, the main macro doesn't have to do much besides move the cursor to various places in your document and carry out the nested macros.

As an example of how to nest macros, let's look at a set of nested ones that do a little final cleanup work on a document. As you know, format changes that you make in a document take precedence over the initial codes that you have established. If you change margins in a document, for example, that margin change takes effect at the cursor's position and continues in effect until another margin-change code is encountered. If you work on documents in separate work sessions or combine documents from various sources, you may find when you print your document that there are extra, unwanted format codes in it—several different headers, different page-numbering systems, and so forth. Instead of searching for each type of code that could possibly give you trouble, you can record a **cleanup** macro that does all the work for you.

You have to record nested macros before you can record a macro that calls them. First, then, we'll record a macro that searches for any extraneous margin changes and removes them, so that you can be sure your document's margins are consistent. You can add the **footer** macro you created in Chapter 2, which sets up a page-numbering system as a document footer. If you didn't record the **footer** macro, you can refer to Figure 3.6, which reproduces it.

To record the macro that searches for any extra [L/R Mar] codes and deletes them:

> You can nest several macros within one main macro. Just remember that the macro will execute them as it encounters them, not after it has finished, as it does with chained macros.

> You can use any of these macros separately in any of your documents. As you build a macro library, you can pick and choose macros to nest within each other, so you won't have to take the time to record them.

1. Turn on the macro recorder by pressing Ctrl-F10 or choosing Macro from the Tools menu and then choosing Define. Type **rmmar** as the macro's name, and press ⏎.

2. Type **remove extra margin change codes** as the description and press ⏎.

3. Press Home Home ↑ to go to the beginning of the document.

4. Press Alt-F2 (Replace) and press ⏎ to replace without confirming.

5. Press Shift-F8 (Format) and type **L M** to search for the [L/R Mar] code. Then press F2 to begin.

6. Press F2 again to replace each [L/R Mar] code with nothing.
7. Turn off the macro recorder by pressing Ctrl-F10 or choosing Macro from the Tools menu and choosing Define again.

The finished macro should resemble the one in Figure 3.7.

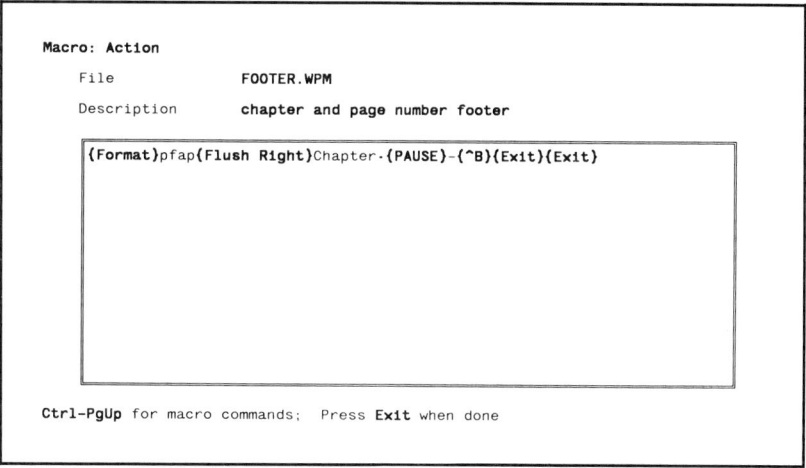

*Figure 3.6:* This macro inserts the current page number.

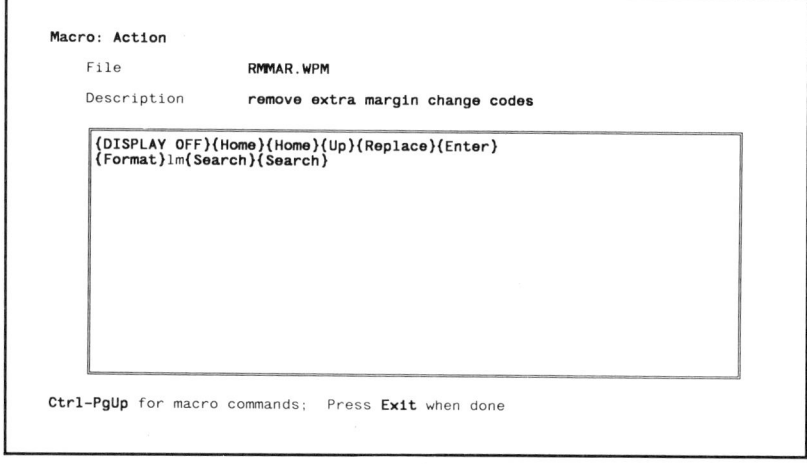

*Figure 3.7:* When you execute this macro, it strips out any extra margin-set codes in the document.

You've already recorded the macro that saves the document (see Chapter 1 under "Recording an Alt Macro" if you haven't), so now you can record the main macro that will contain all these macros you're going to nest.

1. Turn on the macro recorder by pressing Ctrl-F10 or choosing Macro from the Tools menu and then choosing Define. Type **cleanup** as the macro's name, and press ←.

2. Type **insert footer and fix margins** as the description and press ←.

3. Move to the beginning of the document by pressing Home Home ↑.

4. You'll nest the macros in the editor, so press Ctrl-F10 to stop recording the macro at this point.

5. Press Ctrl-F10 again, enter **cleanup**, press ←, and type **2** to edit the macro. If you're using version 5.0, you'll need to type **2** again for Action.

6. Press End to move to the end of the first line; then press ← to begin a new line so that your macro will be easier to read.

7. Press Ctrl-PgUp, type **N**, and press ← to insert the {NEST} command. Typing **N** activates the Name Search feature to take you to the {NEST} command.

8. Type **footer˜** to nest the footer macro; then press ← to move to the next line.

9. To nest the **rmmar** macro, press Ctrl-PgUp and then press ←, since {NEST} is already highlighted. Type **rmmar˜** as the name of the macro to nest.

10. Press F7 (twice in version 5.0) to return to your document.

The final **cleanup** macro should resemble the one in Figure 3.8. After you've recorded it, you can test it out by retrieving a short document in which you've changed the margins at some point.

If you haven't got a document in which you've changed margins, you can quickly change the margin settings in any document. Just retrieve a short document, move down a few lines, press Shift-F8, type **L M 3**, and press ← four times. This will change the left margin

## MORE COMPLEX MACRO TECHNIQUES   69

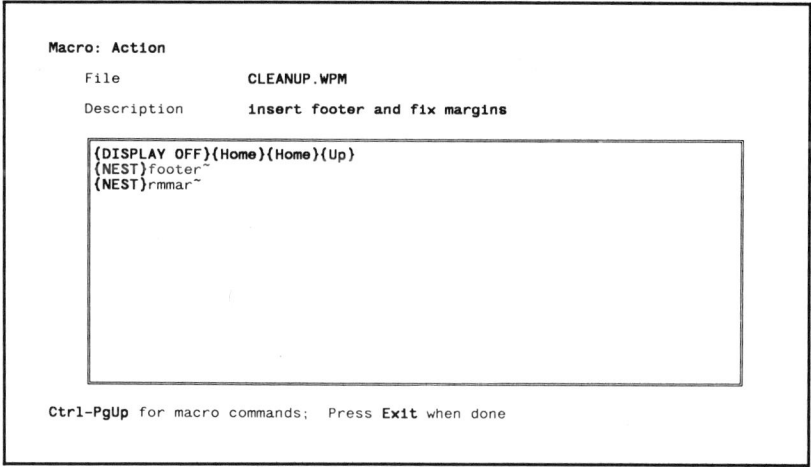

*Figure 3.8:* You can nest other macros within the subroutines represented by the nested macros, and so have the cleanup macro carry out additional cleanup tasks such as removing extra [Tab Set] codes.

to three inches. Then execute the **cleanup** macro. It will pause for you to type a chapter number and press ⏎, and then it will busily search for all the [L/R Mar] codes and remove them from the document.

As you can see from this example, once you've recorded macros, you can use them within other macros. As you build your macro library, you'll see why using that description line becomes more and more important, and why most of the macros in this book are named macros rather than Alt macros: You can remember what they do.

For example, suppose that you want to expand on your **cleanup** macro so that it will not only remove extraneous margin setting codes but will also strip out any footer codes other than the one the macro creates. To do this, you can nest a **rmftr** macro within the **cleanup** macro so that after it finishes, it will return to the top of the document and strip out any other [Footer A] codes that it finds.

1. First, you'll need to record the **rmftr** macro, so turn on the macro recorder, enter **rmftr** as the macro's name, and press ⏎.

2. Enter **remove extra Footer A codes** as the macro's description; then press ⏎.

3. Press Home Home ↑ to go to the top of the document so that the macro will search the entire document. Because you don't move over the format codes at the very beginning of the document, this ensures that all the codes you specify at the beginning will remain in place.

4. Press Alt-F2 (Replace); then press ⏎ to replace without confirming.

5. Press Shift-F8 (Format) and generate the codes for Footer A by typing **P F A**.

6. Press F2; then press F2 again at the 'Replace with:' prompt so that the Footer A codes will be removed (that is, replaced with nothing).

7. Turn off the macro recorder by pressing Ctrl-F10 or choosing Macro from the Tools menu and choosing Define again.

You've now created a macro (Figure 3.9) for stripping out your Footer A codes that you could use by itself or in other macros. (Note that it doesn't find multiple Footer A codes at the beginning of the document.) To use it in your **cleanup** macro, nest it by editing the **cleanup** macro so that the command

    {NEST}rmftr~

is its last line. Then test the macro out on a document that contains several margin and Footer A changes. You'll be prompted for the official footer at the top of the document, and then the macro will do its cleanup work for you.

As you probably have been gathering from this example, you could continue linking macros this way in order to search for and remove other types of codes, such as the ones for changing fonts or setting tabs, that you may have entered as you were working on a document. With such a set of macros, you could clean up the final version of a document, leaving only the codes at the beginning of it in effect.

You can use the pattern given in the **rmftr** and **rmmar** macros to set up any number of macros that will search for a particular code and strip it out. Then you can link the macros until you have a master

## MORE COMPLEX MACRO TECHNIQUES 71

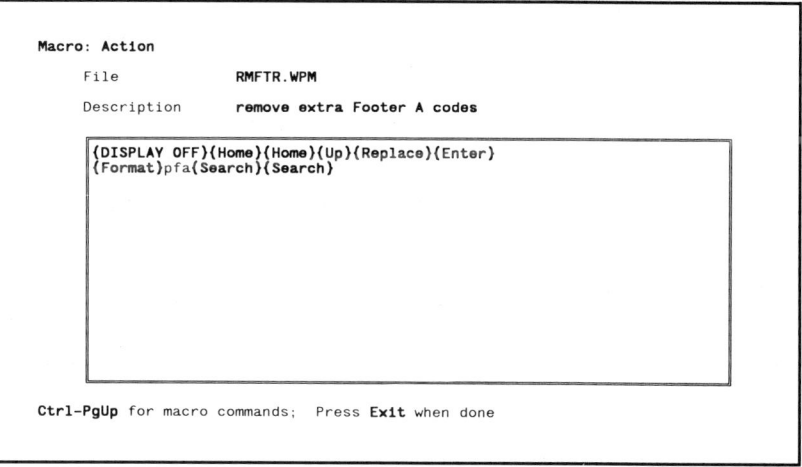

*Figure 3.9:* The **rmftr** macro will strip out any additional Footer A codes beyond the one at the beginning of the document.

**cleanup** macro that will ensure your document contains only one set of format codes, those at the beginning. To save yourself keystrokes, record macros only for the codes you normally use in your work. In addition to the [L/R Mar] and [Footer A] codes, for which you just recorded macros, here are a few other codes that you may want to strip out with macros and then use those macros in a **cleanup** macro.

> ⊙ Remember, you may *want* more than one of these codes in a document if you've deliberately changed a format somewhere in it.

| CODE | PURPOSE |
| --- | --- |
| [Col Def] | To remove extra column definitions |
| [Font] | To ensure that extra font changes are stripped out |
| [Header A], [Header B], [Footer A], [Footer B] | To remove extraneous headers and footers |
| [Ln Spacing] | To remove any changes from double to single spacing, or vice versa |
| [Paper Sz/Type] | To remove any changes in paper size or paper type |

| | |
|---|---|
| [Par Num Def] | To ensure that only one paragraph-numbering definition is used |
| [Pg Numbering] | To ensure that only one page-numbering system is used |
| [Suppress] | To make sure that no formats are suppressed on any pages |
| [T/B Mar] | To ensure consistent top and bottom margins |
| [W/O On] | To ensure that widow/orphan protection is turned either off or on (*widows* and *orphans* are printing terms for single lines at the top or bottom of a page, respectively) |

## CONDITIONAL MACROS

You can set up macros so that one macro will execute when the search pattern specified by another macro fails. Macros like these are called *conditional macros*. To create one in WordPerfect, you use Macro Command Language to tell the program what to do when the macro can no longer locate any occurrences of a search pattern.

None of the things we're going to do with these special commands in the rest of this chapter require you to have programming experience. Of course, it helps to have had such experience, but you won't need it to set up a conditional macro the way we're about to do.

To see how to use Macro Command Language for this purpose, you can record a short macro that searches for a period and then breaks each sentence onto a separate line. When it can't locate any more sentences, it moves to the top of the document and turns Outline mode on so that you can structure the sentences into an outline.

In this macro, you'll use three new commands from Macro Command Language:

- {ON NOT FOUND} tells the macro what to do when the search pattern is no longer located. It needs to be positioned as the first step in the macro.

> If you're used to writing conditional macros in earlier versions of WordPerfect, note that starting in WordPerfect 5 they no longer depend on searches. Instead, they use {IF} or {ON NOT FOUND} constructions instead.

- {LABEL} is the name of a subroutine. Think of it as the name of a macro-within-a-macro.
- {GO} tells the macro to go to a subroutine identified by a label.

The macro you're going to create will be recorded entirely in the editor, so just turn on the macro recorder, enter **breakup** as the macro's name, press ⏎, enter **breaks document into sentences** as the description, press ⏎ again, and immediately press Ctrl-F10 to stop recording the macro. Then retrieve the macro into the macro editor by choosing to define it again and selecting Edit.

In this macro you'll use two subroutines, one labeled **out**, which goes to the top of the document and turns on Outline mode, and one labeled **bust**, which breaks the document into its component sentences. You'll find the completed macro in Figure 3.10, if you want to refer to it as you go along. An extra line has been added between subroutines only for clarity; these extra lines are not necessary for the macro to function accurately.

First, you need to tell the macro what to do when it can no longer locate any instances of what it is to search for. You will do this with the

```
Macro: Action
    File            BREAKUP.WPM
    Description     breaks document into sentences

{DISPLAY ON}
{ON NOT FOUND}{GO}out~~

{LABEL}bust~
{Search}.{Search}{Enter}
{Enter}
{Del}
{GO}bust~

{LABEL}out~
{Home}{Home}{Up}{Date/Outline}o
```

Ctrl-PgUp for macro commands;   Press **Exit** when done

*Figure 3.10:* The **breakup** macro uses Macro Command Language to set up a conditional macro.

**out** subroutine that turns on Outline mode:

1. In the macro editor, move past the {DISPLAY ON} command, press ⏎ to start a new line if you want to (it just makes the macro more readable); press Ctrl-PgUp, and type **onf**. Press ⏎ to insert an {ON NOT FOUND} instruction in the macro.

2. Insert a {GO} instruction, which tells the macro to go to a subroutine, by pressing Ctrl-PgUp, typing **g**, and pressing ⏎.

3. Type **out** ~ ~ . This specifies the subroutine to branch to. Don't forget the two tildes; they are required by Macro Command Language.

4. Then insert a {LABEL} instruction: press Ctrl-PgUp, type **l**, and press ⏎.

5. Enter **bust** ~ as the name of the subroutine that breaks each sentence onto a separate line. The tilde indicates the end of the label—it's vital.

6. For the steps in this subroutine, press F2 (Search), type a period as the string to search for, and press F2 again.

7. Press ⏎ twice so that whenever the macro locates a period, it will put each sentence on a separate line with a blank line in between. You'll need to press Ctrl-V before each ⏎ to insert the instruction as {Enter}, as Figure 3.10 shows.

8. Press Ctrl-V; then press Del to insert the {Del} instruction and delete the extra space that will be at the beginning of the sentence—that is, if you're separating sentences with one space. (If you separate sentences with two spaces, guess what? You press Del twice.)

9. Enter another {GO} command that tells the macro to repeat the **bust** subroutine until it can no longer locate any periods. This is the same as chaining a macro to itself, which you're already familiar with. Type **bust** ~ immediately after the {GO} command.

10. Insert another {LABEL} command so that you can enter the steps for the **out** subroutine. This time, enter the label as **out˜**.

11. For the steps in **out**, press Ctrl-V Home Ctrl-V Home Ctrl-V ↑, press Shift-F5 (Date/Outline), and type **oo** to turn on Outline mode (only one **o** is necessary in version 5.0).

12. When your macro looks like the one in Figure 3.10 (remember, the blank lines are optional), press F7 (twice in version 5.0) to return to the editing screen.

Now you can try out the macro. If you've still got a document on the screen from the last example, just move to the top of it (Home Home ↑) and then take the following steps. Otherwise, retrieve a short document that contains several sentences. Then go to the beginning of the document and execute the **breakup** macro. Your short document will be broken into its component sentences (that end on a period), as the examples in Figure 3.11A (before) and Figure 3.11B (after) show. The Outline prompt in the lower-left corner of the screen in Figure 3.11B indicates that Outline mode is on. In that case, you can move to the beginning of any sentence, press ↵ and Tab to indent it to the appropriate level, and so generate an outline number, as Figure 3.12 shows.

```
If you use macros frequently in your work, you may prefer to map
them to keys on your keyboard so that whenever you press that
key, the macro is executed instead of the character the key
normally generates. This technique lets you execute named macros
quickly from another key combination, such as Ctrl-S, so that you
aren't limited to 26 quick macros on the Alt key. Because you can
map macros to Ctrl, Alt, and Shift combinations and the function
keys as well as to the lowercase keys, you can have more macros
on one keyboard definition than you'll ever be able to keep track
of. For example, if you do mathematical typing, you can set up a
MATH keyboard that executes macros that switch to superscript and
subscript, italicize highlighted text, create characters like
greater than or equals to, pi, and so forth.




C:\5\FIG3-11A                                    Doc 2 Pg 1 Ln 1" Pos 1"
```

*Figure 3.11A:* This is the sample paragraph before execution of the **breakup** macro.

```
    If you use macros frequently in your work, you may prefer to map
    them to keys on your keyboard so that whenever you press that
    key, the macro is executed instead of the character the key
    normally generates.

    This technique lets you execute named macros quickly from another
    key combination, such as Ctrl-S, so that you aren't limited to 26
    quick macros on the Alt key.

    Because you can map macros to Ctrl, Alt, and Shift combinations
    and the function keys as well as to the lowercase keys, you can
    have more macros on one keyboard definition than you'll ever be
    able to keep track of.

    For example, if you do mathematical typing, you can set up a MATH
    keyboard that executes macros that switch to superscript and
    subscript, italicize highlighted text, create characters like
    greater than or equals to, pi, and so forth.



Outline                                           Doc 2 Pg 1 Ln 1.16" Pos 1"
```

*Figure 3.11B:* This is the sample paragraph broken by the **breakup** macro. The macro searches for each period, inserts a blank line, and repeats until no more periods are found.

```
    I. If you use macros frequently in your work, you may prefer to
    map them to keys on your keyboard so that whenever you press that
    key, the macro is executed instead of the character the key
    normally generates.

        A. This technique lets you execute named macros quickly from
    another key combination, such as Ctrl-S, so that you aren't
    limited to 26 quick macros on the Alt key.

        B. Because you can map macros to Ctrl, Alt, and Shift
    combinations and the function keys as well as to the lowercase
    keys, you can have more macros on one keyboard definition than
    you'll ever be able to keep track of.

            1. For example, if you do mathematical typing, you can
    set up a MATH keyboard that executes macros that switch to
    superscript and subscript, italicize highlighted text, create
    characters like greater than or equals to, pi, and so forth.

Outline                                            Doc 2 Pg 1 Ln 4" Pos 2.3"
```

*Figure 3.12:* After using the **breakup** macro on your document, you can quickly structure it into an outline by pressing ⏎ and Tab at the beginning of each sentence.

## *USING ANY NUMBER OF ALT-KEY MACROS*

If you've run out of the combinations Alt-A through Alt-Z, you can set up a system that lets you use Alt plus a two-keystroke sequence such as Alt-AA, Alt-AB, Alt-A1, and so forth. You can execute these macros quickly by pressing Alt-A and then typing the letter or number. You're not confined to Alt-A for the master macro, either: You can assign your editing macros to Alt-E combinations, printing macros to Alt-P combinations, mail-merge macros to Alt-M, and so forth. If you use a lot of macros, taking the small amount of time it requires to set up a system like this can save you a lot of keystrokes, as it virtually eliminates the need to use named macros.

The basic method you use to do this is to set up a macro named Alt-A (or Alt-E, or Alt-M) that contains instructions to nest the macro whose letter you type next, so you can have a set of macros named AA, AB, A1, A2, and so forth, that will execute when you press Alt-A and then type the letter or number of the macro you want to use. (You can just think of them as Alt-AA and Alt-AB macros, but in reality they are an Alt-A macro plus a macro named AA or AB.)

You'll need to use a few commands from the macro editor to create the master Alt-key macro:

1. Press Home; then press Ctrl-F10; then press Alt-A. If you're using version 5.0, you'll need to record an empty Alt-A macro and then edit it, because pressing Home won't take you directly to the macro editor as it does in version 5.1.

2. At the description prompt, enter **master Alt-A macro** and press Enter.

3. In the macro editor, press Del to delete the existing {DISPLAY OFF} command, because you may use this macro with other macros in which you need to see prompts on the screen.

4. Press Ctrl-PgUp and type **g**; then press Enter to insert a {GO} command in the macro.

5. Type **mac**˜ and press Enter. This will tell WordPerfect to go to the instructions identified by the label *mac*. (The Enter just makes the macro easier to read, with one instruction per line.)
6. Press Ctrl-PgUp and type **l**; then press Enter to insert a {LABEL} command in the macro.
7. Type **mac**˜ and press Enter.
8. Press Ctrl-PgUp and type **char**; then press Enter to insert a {CHAR} command in the macro. Type **1**˜ ˜ and press Enter. This will store in variable 1 the next keystroke that is typed when the macro executes.
9. Press Ctrl-PgUp and type **n**; then press Enter to insert a {NEST} command in the macro. Type **a**, then press Ctrl-V and Alt-1 to insert the {VAR 1} command. End by typing a tilde (˜).
10. Press F7 (twice in version 5.0) to leave the macro editor.

Your macro should consist of the following lines:

```
{GO}mac~
{LABEL}mac~
{CHAR}1~ ~
{NEST}a{VAR 1}~
```

Now you can record a set of macros named AA, AB, A1, or whatever you want, as long as their two-character name begins with A and ends in a character or number. For example, to test your system, you can record an AA macro that types the word *doit* on the screen. Just press Ctrl-F10, type **aa**, press Enter twice to avoid entering a description, type **doit**, and press Ctrl-F10 again. Then press Alt-A and type **a**. (Note that you don't press Alt and hold it down while you type **aa**.) The word *doit*, created by the macro named A, appears on your screen.

You can go into List Files and rename existing macros to follow your new system by using the Move/Rename option. If you want to keep the macro under its old name as well as assign it to the new Alt-key system, copy it into another directory, rename it with a two-character name in the other directory, and then copy it back into your macros directory.

## EXECUTING ALT-KEY MACROS FROM SEPARATE SUBDIRECTORIES

If the above system doesn't appeal to you, here's another way to store large numbers of Alt-key macros that will exceed the 26-letter limit and to execute them quickly. With this system, you don't have to use Macro Command Language. You keep all the related printing macros (Alt-A through Alt-Z) in one subdirectory, all your merge macros in another subdirectory, all your formatting macros in another, and so forth. You then record a master macro named Alt-F, for example, that will allow you to type a for the Alt-A macro in that directory, b for the Alt-B macro, and so forth. The basic principle behind the way this method works is that after you press Alt-F10 (Macro) you can use a path name to any directory to execute a macro stored there.

For example, suppose you create a subdirectory named FORMAT and then record as many as 26 Alt macros for formatting and store them there. You then record a master macro named Alt-F (which resides in the macro directory you have specified in Location of Files). To record this macro, take the following steps:

1. Press Ctrl-F10; then press Alt-F. Enter **master format macro** as the description and press Enter.

2. Press Alt-F10 and enter the path to the FORMAT subdirectory plus the word **alt**—for example, **c:\wp51\format\alt**. (Remember, you can execute an Alt-key macro by either pressing Alt and the letter or by entering its name, such as **altb**.)

3. Press Ctrl-PgUp, type **p**, and press Enter twice.

4. Press Ctrl-F10 to turn off the macro recorder.

When you press Alt-F to execute the master macro, you will see the prompt 'Macro:c:\wp51\format\alt' and you can type a, b, c, and so forth, to execute the Alt macros stored in that directory.

You can set up other subdirectories such as PRINT for printing and use a master Alt-P macro to display a 'Macro: c:\wp51\print\alt' prompt.

## SUMMARY

In this chapter, you've reviewed some techniques you can use for searching and replacing within WordPerfect, as these operations are critical in many macros. Specifically, you may recall that

- You can search for text, format codes, and the use of menu options in a document.
- WordPerfect normally locates only the first code in a set of paired format codes, but you can have it search for the second code in a pair.
- To replace paired format codes, you have to use a macro that searches for the second code.
- You can search for special characters that you have created with WordPerfect's Compose feature.
- WordPerfect matches the capitalization of words in your text when it searches and replaces.

This chapter has also begun to introduce you to WordPerfect's Macro Command Language, which lets you write complex macros. In particular, you've seen how to chain macros together so that one macro starts when the other stops; and how to nest macros so that the nested macro will be executed at the point where it occurs. In particular, you've seen how to use the {BELL}, {CHAIN}, {NEST}, {ON NOT FOUND}, {LABEL}, and {GO} commands.

- You can use a {BELL} command to sound a beep when a macro pauses.
- You can use the {CHAIN} and {NEST} commands to chain and nest macros to each other in the macro editor.
- A macro automatically executes when you nest it.
- You can set up subroutines in the macro editor by using the {GO}, {ON NOT FOUND}, and {LABEL} commands to create conditional macros.

Next, in Chapter 4, we'll look at how you can assign the macros you write to special soft keyboards, so that pressing a key automatically executes a macro without your having to press Alt-F10 and enter a macro name. By creating soft keyboards, you can use different sets of macros for each type of specialized task that you do. You can set up a French or German keyboard, for example; or you can create a mathematical keyboard for typing equations and formulas if you're using version 5.0, which doesn't have an Equations feature as version 5.1 does. In addition, when you use soft keyboards you can assign macros to the Ctrl key as well as to the Alt key, which gives you access to many more single-key macros.

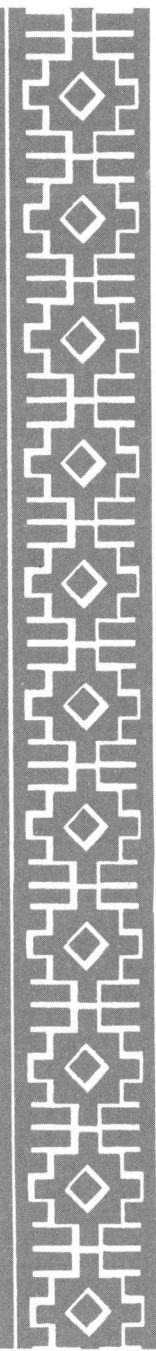

# *Using Soft Macro Keyboards*

CHAPTER

4

# CHAPTER 4

> A soft keyboard is really only a collection of macros. When you assign a new function to a key, in effect you're creating a macro for it. You'll find that the keyboard editor is virtually identical to the macro editor.

> You can even use a macro to switch to your different soft keyboards quickly! **Alt-F** can switch you to a FRENCH keyboard, **Alt-T** can take you to a text-merge keyboard, and so forth. You'll see such macros in this chapter.

If you use macros frequently in your work, you may prefer to map them to keys on your keyboard. Once a macro is mapped to a key, whenever you press that key, the macro is executed instead of the character the key normally generates. Mapping lets you execute named macros quickly from another key combination, such as Ctrl-S, so that you aren't limited to 26 easily executable macros on the Alt key. Because you can map macros to Ctrl, Alt, and Shift combinations and the function keys as well as to the lowercase keys, you can have more macros on one keyboard than you're ever likely to need.

Most people find that it's easiest to keep track of macros if they set up different *soft keyboards* for the different types of work they do and then assign the appropriate macros to each soft keyboard. These keyboards are called soft because the physical keyboard itself doesn't change; the software just redefines the function the key carries out when it's pressed. For example, if you do mathematical typing with version 5.0, you can set up a MATH keyboard that executes macros that switch to superscript and subscript, italicize highlighted text, create characters like $>$, $=$, $\pi$, and so forth. (Version 5.1 comes with a special EQUATION keyboard.) If you do foreign-language typing, you can assign macros to keys to generate an *e* acute, an *e* grave, an umlauted *u*, and so forth. (In fact, if you wish, you can even redefine the keyboard to use the AZERTY system used by French typists instead of our QWERTY.) If you do merge printing, you can set up a MERGE keyboard that executes macros you frequently use, such as sorting by zip code, deleting a record, and so forth. I have a BOOK keyboard that generates the special typesetting codes SYBEX uses.

Once you've defined one of these soft keyboards, you can switch to it instead of the normal keyboard definition and execute its special macros. For example, I have an **Alt-B** macro that creates a bullet in my BOOK keyboard, but the same **Alt-B** macro in my MATH keyboard inserts the Greek letter beta.

Using different soft keyboards in your work is an alternative way of using *menu systems,* which are discussed in Chapter 5. You'll need to be familiar with WordPerfect's Macro Command Language to set up menu systems. But you can map existing macros to keys on your keyboard easily, with no prior knowledge of any of the macro commands and no previous programming experience.

This chapter will give you the information you need to create, edit, and select soft keyboards. In addition, you'll get some ideas about how you can design keyboards to help you carry out specialized tasks. You'll see both how to save a key definition as a macro so that you can use it, no matter which keyboard you've selected, and how to map macros you've already defined onto keys. You may want to return to this chapter after you've created a number of macros for your own use; you will then be able to group them into specialized keyboards by following the instructions given here.

## *USING DIFFERENT SOFT KEYBOARDS*

When you use WordPerfect normally, specific commands are assigned to the function keys F1 through F10, used alone and in combination with the Shift, Alt, and Ctrl keys. In addition, the program assigns cursor-movement and deletion functions to the keys on the numeric keypad, or cursor pad if you're using that type of keyboard. However, with the soft keyboard feature, you can create many different kinds of keyboards. For example, you might want to have Ctrl-B instead of Alt-F4 turn on block marking, or to add new commands that make WordPerfect behave like another word processing program you may be more familiar with. WordStar, for example, uses many Ctrl sequences, and you can set up WordPerfect to work the same way. You might want to have Ctrl-Y delete a line of text, as it does in WordStar, instead of Home Home ← Ctrl-End, which is the key sequence required in WordPerfect.

You'll need the files KEYS.MRS and WP.MRS in your WordPerfect directory if you're going to use soft keyboards. Otherwise, you'll get an error message.

You can use the Keyboard Layout feature to create new keyboards from scratch, or you can edit the existing keyboard definitions that are supplied with WordPerfect. All the keyboards are automatically given the extension .WPK by the program.

## SELECTING A KEYBOARD

You may already be aware that WordPerfect 5.1 comes with five predefined keyboards—ALTRNAT, ENHANCED, MACROS, EQUATION, and SHORTCUT—that you can use unchanged or edit to add extra functions to them. (WordPerfect 5.0 comes with only the first three.)

The ENHANCED keyboard that comes with WordPerfect has definitions for many of the keys on the IBM Enhanced keyboard, which has 12 function keys and arrow keys between the numeric keypad and the regular keys. It reassigns the Home key (normally the 7 key on the numeric keypad) to the 5 key (the one in the center). It also provides several macros that move the cursor, copy text, and so forth:

| KEY | FUNCTION IN ENHANCED KEYBOARD |
| --- | --- |
| Alt-↑ | Move up one sentence (one paragraph in version 5.0) |
| Alt-↓ | Move down one sentence (one paragraph in version 5.0) |
| Alt-→ | Move right one column |
| Alt-← | Move left one column |
| Ctrl-Num 5 | Go to |
| Alt-F11 | Very large |
| Ctrl-F11 | Large |
| Shift-F11 | Italics |
| Alt-F12 | Copy block |
| Ctrl-F12 | Move block |
| Shift-F12 | Retrieve block |
| Home | Go to beginning of document, before any codes (Home Home Home ←) |

The ALTRNAT keyboard reassigns online help to F1, the cancel feature to the Esc key, and the Esc (repeat) feature to F3. If you regularly use other software programs that assign the cancel function to the Esc key and help to F1, you may want to select this keyboard layout.

The MACROS keyboard contains sample macros that are assigned to various Alt- and Ctrl-letter key combinations. Many of these macros make extensive use of WordPerfect's Macro Command Language, and they will be of interest to those of you who want to explore it in detail (as you can in Appendix A). Those of you who don't want to get that deeply into programmed macros will find macros in this book that carry out much the same functions without using Macro Command Language.

In version 5.0, there's not much documentation on these macros apart from their short descriptions; however, in version 5.1, comments have been added to the macros that explain what they do. (I had a hard time with the glossary macro, **Ctrl-G**, until I found out that one of the abbreviations was the developer's name). Here's what the macros do:

| *KEY* | *FUNCTION* |
|---|---|
| Alt-B | Restores the previous block. |
| Alt-C | Capitalizes the first letter of the word the cursor is on. |
| Alt-D | Deletes the current line. |
| Alt-E | Returns you to the main editing screen from any menu, from the Reveal Codes window, or from Help. If Block or Typeover is on, it is turned off. |
| Alt-F | Finds and deletes the <<<MARK>>> bookmark that is inserted when you use the Alt-M macro. |
| Alt-G | Sends a 'Go' to the printer. |
| Alt-I | Inserts a line just above the current line. |
| Alt-M | Inserts a <<<MARK>>> bookmark followed by a hard return. |
| Alt-N | Pauses and asks whether you want to edit a footnote or an endnote. |
| Alt-R | Replaces size, attributes, or text (differs in version 5.0). |

Alt-T     Transposes the two characters just before the cursor. (If the cursor is next to a format code, it will not be transposed.)

Alt-F9    Lists graphics files as you are defining a graphics box with Alt-F9 (version 5.0 only).

Ctrl-C    Displays a calculator on the screen.

Ctrl-D    Pauses and asks for your name; then allows you to choose a letter, memo, or itinerary form.

Ctrl-E    Prepares an envelope format from an address on a letter or memo and then prints the envelope.

Ctrl-F8   Gives a Temporary Font choice in addition to Normal on the Font key (Ctrl-F8). If you select Temporary Font, you'll see the Font menu, where you can select a new font. You can then enter text in the new font and simply press → to return to the original font, whose code is pushed along ahead of the cursor.

Ctrl-G    Expands the abbreviations *WP*, *WPC*, *ASAP*, *SY*, and *LC* to WordPerfect, WordPerfect Corporation, as soon as possible, Sincerely Yours, and Layne Cannon (the name of the Macro Command Language's developer), respectively.

Ctrl-P    Special mode for formula entry (version 5.1 only).

Ctrl-R    Recalculates formulas in a table (version 5.1 only).

Provided with version 5.1 are two additional keyboards, SHORTCUT and EQUATION. The SHORTCUT keyboard provides Alt- and Ctrl-key shortcuts for many of the program's often-used features. Alt-A, for example, lets you add an attribute, Ctrl-B lets you change the base font, Ctrl-T sets tabs, and so forth. One nice feature about this keyboard is its assignment of Alt-E, which lets you edit a code without going through the menu system. When the SHORTCUT keyboard is selected, you can just put the cursor on the code you want to change and press Alt-E; you'll then see the edit screen for that code.

The EQUATION keyboard is especially useful if you use version 5.1's equation editor; in fact, there's an option on the equation editor's menu that lets you select this keyboard without having to go through the Setup menu as described below. The EQUATION keyboard assigns special symbols, such as the integral, square root, infinity, and so forth, to Ctrl-key combinations and Greek lowercase letters, which are used as variables in mathematical typing, to Alt-key combinations.

> Press Ctrl-6 to return temporarily to the original keyboard definition after selecting a different one.

To select any of these keyboards, press Shift-F1 and select the Keyboard Layout option (5 or K). (It's option 6 in version 5.0.) If you're using pull-down menus, select Setup from the File menu; then choose Keyboard Layout. This brings up a screen that shows a list of all of the existing keyboards as well as the following menu options:

**1** Select; **2** Delete; **3** Rename; **4** Create; **5** Copy; **6** Original;
**7** Edit; **8** Map; **N** Name Search: 1

(In version 5.0, the Edit option is 5 or E, and there are no Copy and Map options.)

To select a keyboard, move the highlight bar to the name of the keyboard you want to use and then choose the Select option (1 or S).

For example, you can take a look at the online calculator macro that's been mapped to **Ctrl-C** on the MACROS keyboard. To see how it works, press Shift-F1 (Setup), type **K** for Keyboard, highlight the MACROS name, type **1** or **S**, and then press F7. Finally, press Ctrl-C. A special calculator box appears on your screen (Figure 4.1 shows the one for version 5.1), and you can use it to make calculations as you work with WordPerfect. (Press F7 to get this calculator box off your screen.)

> As you're using WordPerfect, you can check which keyboard is current by pressing Shift-F1 (Setup). The name of the keyboard that's currently being used is listed next to the Keyboard Layout option.

Once you've switched to a different keyboard, it remains in effect each time you start WordPerfect. Of course, you may switch to several different keyboards during each session, but the last one you switched to will be in effect the next time you start the program. To return to the original keyboard definition, press Shift-F1, type **K**, type **O** for Original, and press F7. You can also press Ctrl-6 to reset the keyboard for the current session only.

If you want to reset WordPerfect to the original keyboard definition each time you start it, use a startup macro that contains the keystrokes Ctrl-6, which resets WordPerfect to the original keyboard. If

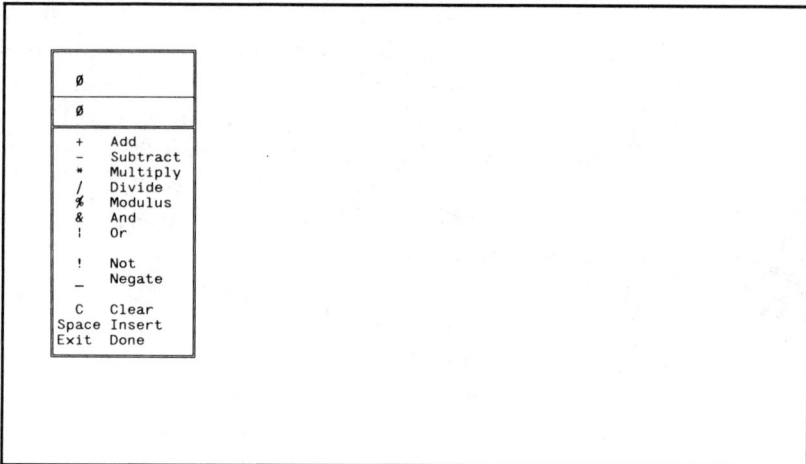

*Figure 4.1:* To experiment with a different keyboard definition, switch to the MACROS keyboard and press Ctrl-C to get this online calculator.

you name this macro **reset** or **Alt-R**, start WordPerfect with the command **wp m-/reset** or **wp m-/altr** at the DOS prompt, for example. Then the keyboard that's in effect on startup will be the original one, no matter which keyboard you used last.

## CREATING A NEW KEYBOARD

Although you can use any of the macros on the predefined MACROS keyboard simply by switching to it, you'll probably want to create new keyboards of your own. First, then, we'll look at how you create a keyboard from scratch, and then at how you can assign a few of the macros you've already recorded to such a keyboard.

### CREATING A KEYBOARD LAYOUT

To create a new keyboard layout, press Shift-F1 (Setup), type **K** for Keyboard Layout, and then select Create. If you're using pull-down menus, select Setup from the File menu, then Keyboard Layout.

When you select Create, you'll be prompted to enter a name for the keyboard file:

Keyboard Filename:

Keyboard layout files are saved on the same disk or in the same directory as your macros. To designate this drive or directory, you need to select the Location of Files option on the Setup menu, as you saw in Chapter 1. If you don't, these files will be saved on the drive or directory that contains your WordPerfect program files (C:\WP51 or \WP50 on a hard disk).

The file names that you enter here for your keyboard files must follow the DOS file-naming conventions (no more than eight characters long with no spaces). The program automatically appends the extension .WPK to the file names that you type, so don't enter extensions of your own. For this example, enter **NEW** and press ←.

The key sequences and the screens are slightly different in version 5.1 (Figure 4.2) and version 5.0 (Figure 4.3), so if you're using version 5.0, be patient; I'll summarize the way you redefine keys shortly.

After you assign a name to your keyboard file, choose Edit (7 or E). You'll see the Keyboard Edit screen and menu. The menu at the bottom of the screen contains the following options for defining the functions of the keys:

**Key: 1 Action; 2 Description; 3 Original; 4 Create; 5 Move;
Macro: 6 Save; 7 Retrieve: 1**

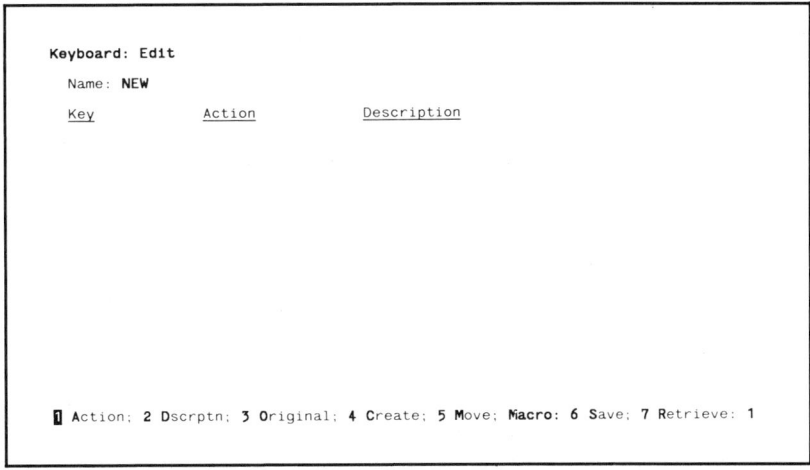

*Figure 4.2:* The Keyboard Edit screen appears when you create a new keyboard layout (version 5.1).

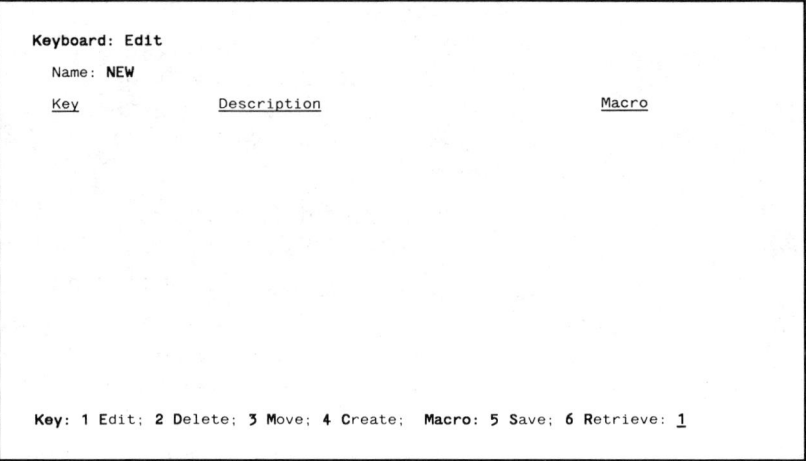

*Figure 4.3:* The Keyboard Edit screen appears when you create a new keyboard layout (version 5.0).

To begin defining the keys for your new NEW keyboard, select Create (4 or C). The menu options at the bottom of the screen are replaced by the prompt

**Key:**

In response to this prompt, press the key or key combination that you wish to define. For example, if you want Ctrl-S to move one character to the left, as it does in WordStar, press Ctrl-S. You then enter a description for the key combination (Ctrl-S in this example) and redefine its function in the editing area (Figure 4.4).

1. Enter **character left** as the description of the key's function, just as you enter a description for a macro. Then press ←.

2. Press Del to delete the {^S} that represents the normal function of Ctrl-S, press Ctrl-V so that the cursor key will be interpreted as a command, and press ←. Your screen should look like Figure 4.4.

3. Press F7 to return to the Keyboard Edit screen. You will see your Ctrl-S key listed as in Figure 4.5.

## USING SOFT MACRO KEYBOARDS 93

```
Key: Action
    Key          Ctrl-S
    Description  character left
    ┌─────────────────────────────────────────┐
    │ {Left}                                  │
    │                                         │
    │                                         │
    │                                         │
    │                                         │
    └─────────────────────────────────────────┘
    Ctrl-PgUp for macro commands;  Press Exit when done
```

*Figure 4.4:* The keyboard editor is virtually identical to the macro editor, because when you redefine a key, you're really creating a macro.

```
Keyboard: Edit
    Name: NEW
    Key          Action          Description
    Ctrl-S       {Left}          character left




    1 Action; 2 Dscrptn; 3 Original; 4 Create; 5 Move; Macro: 6 Save; 7 Retrieve: 1
```

*Figure 4.5:* After you have reassigned a key's meaning, its description appears on this screen.

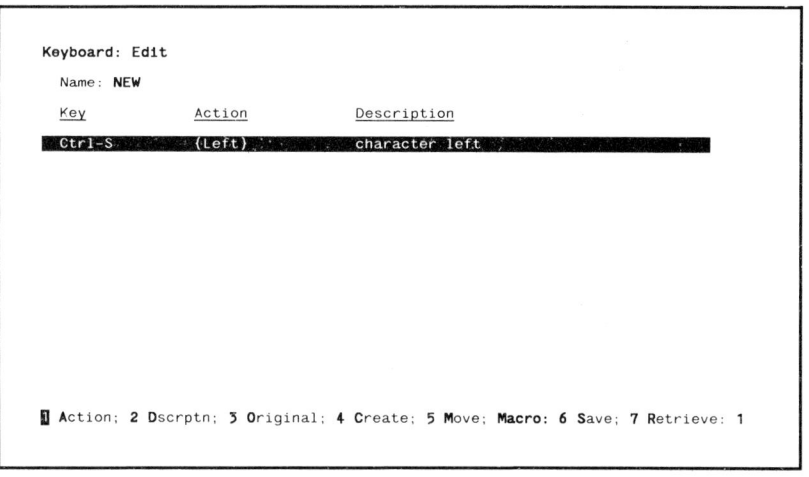 It's important to use a description for your new key assignment. If you don't enter one, you may forget what function you gave the key!

The way you do this in version 5.0 is just a little different. After you assign a name to your keyboard file, you'll go directly to the Keyboard Edit screen. Its menu is as follows:

**Key: 1 E**dit; **2 D**elete; **3 M**ove; **4 C**reate; **Macro: 5 S**ave
**6 R**etrieve: **1**

You choose Create, just as you do in version 5.1, and then press the key combination you want to use. This takes you to the keyboard editor (called the Key Edit screen), where you will need to type 1 or D for Description and 2 or A for Action, just as you do in the 5.0 macro editor. The rest of the sequence is the same.

When you reassign a key's meaning in the keyboard editor, WordPerfect shows you the current definition for the key or key combination you're creating (or editing). For instance, when you defined Ctrl-S, WordPerfect showed {^S} as the key's definition, since it has no other meaning in the program. If WordPerfect hasn't assigned a function to the particular key combination you're defining, you'll see just those keys represented in the Action editing area. For example, if you were creating a new definition for the key combination Alt-X, which has no function in WordPerfect, you would simply see {ALT X} in the editor. Press Del to delete any existing definition, just as you did in the example.

If you reassign a key that normally has a function, you won't be able to use that function unless you reassign it, too. For example, Ctrl-B normally inserts the current page number. If you want to have Ctrl-B do something else, reassign Ctrl-B's function to another key and then reassign Ctrl-B.

When you return to the Keyboard Edit screen, you'll see all the keys that you have redefined for that keyboard listed there. As you add new key definitions or delete them, this order will change.

What kinds of things can you use as key definitions? Basically, three different ones:

- You can assign a WordPerfect function, key, or key combination to a different key. Then, when you press that key, the function is carried out. For example, you might want to assign Block (Alt- F4) to Ctrl-B or assign Help (F3) to F1.

- You can assign special characters to keys in any of three different ways. First, you can assign characters from the IBM Extended Character set by pressing Alt and entering the ASCII decimal value for the character, using the numeric keypad. For example, holding down Alt and entering **133** creates an à character. Second, you can press Ctrl-2 (Compose) and enter **a** and ` , thus creating an *a* grave. Third, you can use the Compose feature and enter a number from WordPerfect's character sets. In this case, entering **1,33** creates an *a* grave, since it is character number 33 in character set 1. (When you use the Compose feature, your results will not be visible on the screen until you press ⏎.) To look up a character set and character number, see Appendix D.

- You can assign several different keystrokes to a key, in effect creating a macro that is executed when you press that key. Or you can assign macros that you've already created to keys.

You'll see later in this chapter how assigning special symbols to keys can be very helpful when you create foreign-language and mathematical keyboards.

Almost all the keys and key combinations on the keyboard can be redefined. However, WordPerfect won't allow you to assign new definitions to the Ctrl key when it's used with the numbers 0 to 9, the equals sign ( = ), semicolon (;), apostrophe ('), comma (,), period (.), or slash (/). You can, however, reassign the functions of these characters when they're combined with the Alt or Shift keys. The Alt-= combination will also work. You can even redefine the function keys F1 through F10, as well as their Shift, Alt, and Ctrl combinations. Remember, however, that the functions WordPerfect normally carries out through those keys won't be available to you if you redefine them.

Key definitions take precedence over any existing macros that have the same key combination. For example, if you've got a favorite Alt-S macro and you assign another definition to the Alt-S key combination on a soft keyboard, the new definition is used when that keyboard has been selected and you press Alt-S. To use your old Alt-S macro, you'll need to return to the original keyboard definition (Ctrl-6); or you can assign it to a different combination in the new keyboard.

## *MODIFYING KEYBOARD DEFINITIONS*

Once you've created a new keyboard, you can add new key definitions to it. Besides changing the function of a key definition, you can delete a key definition or even move an existing definition to a new key or key combination. In version 5.1, you can do this in two different ways, one of which is a little easier to visualize than the other. We'll first look at how you can create and edit keyboard definitions in both versions of the program, and then we'll look at version 5.1's Map option that lets you see all the key assignments for a particular keyboard (in "Mapping Key Assignments to Different Keyboards" below).

To edit a keyboard, press Shift-F1 or choose Setup from the File pull-down menu, type **K** for Keyboard Layout, highlight the name of the keyboard to be modified, and then type **E** for Edit. This will take you directly to the Keyboard Edit screen, which will show you all the keys you've already defined.

To locate the key description for the key or key combination you wish to modify, you can use the Name Search function by pressing F2 (the Search key). This can be useful if you have a long list of Alt- and Ctrl-key assignments. However, Name Search works somewhat differently here than it does in the List Files screen: instead of typing the first few matching characters, you press the key or key combination. For example, if you want to use Name Search to locate the key description of Ctrl-X, you press Ctrl and type **X** instead of typing **ctrl-x**.

To edit the function of a key definition, first highlight its description. You can change the key's description by typing **D** for Description or change its keystrokes or commands by typing **A** for Action. If you're using version 5.0, you'll need to choose Edit (1 or E) first. When you've finished modifying the key definition, press F7 (Exit) once in version 5.1 and twice in version 5.0 to save the changes and return to the Keyboard Edit screen. To return a key to its original definition, select Original (3 or O) when its description is highlighted. In version 5.0, this feature isn't available; instead, select the Delete option, which is 2 or D (you'll be asked to confirm the deletion).

> Make a backup copy of any keyboard definition files that you've worked long and hard to create, just as you would make a backup of any important file. Keyboard definition files are easily identified by the extension .WPK.

You can also move a key combination to another key; for example, you may decide that you'd like what's on Ctrl-S to be on Ctrl-F instead. To move an existing key definition to a new key or key combination, highlight the key description to be changed and then select Move (5 or M). (It's option 3 in version 5.0.) WordPerfect responds with the prompt:

 Key:

At this point, press the key or key combination that you now want to use. WordPerfect will immediately assign the description and keystrokes to this key combination. On the Keyboard Edit screen, you'll see the key description and macro number assigned to the key or key combination you just pressed. The former key(s) will no longer be listed on the menu, so this key or key combination can now be reassigned to some new function.

If you press F1 (Cancel) while you're modifying a key definition, you'll receive the prompt

 Cancel changes? No (Yes)

Type **Y** if you don't want the changes you've made to be saved. Typing **Y** also restores any key definitions that you've just deleted. You can also delete entire keyboard definitions. To do this, press Shift-F1 K, highlight the name of the keyboard you want to delete, and select Delete (2 or D) from the Keyboard Layout menu (you'll be asked to confirm the deletion).

## *CREATING A KEYBOARD FROM EXISTING MACROS*

Instead of creating key definitions from scratch, you can assign macros that you've already recorded to keys. This can be of great help if you've named a macro and find that you use it frequently. Instead of pressing Alt-F10 (Macro), entering a macro name, and then pressing ←, you can just reassign a macro to an Alt or Ctrl key on a soft keyboard.

As an example, we'll begin to create an alternate keyboard using some of the macros you've already recorded from this book, such as the **footer** macro that creates a footer and the **letter** macro that types a letter.

1. Press Shift-F1 (Setup) or choose Setup from the File menu; then choose Keyboard Layout.

2. Select Create. Enter **document** as the name of the new keyboard; then press ↵. In version 5.1, you'll then need to choose Edit (7 or E).

3. To assign the **footer** macro to Ctrl-F, type **R** for Retrieve. You'll see a prompt at the bottom of the screen

    Key:

    Press the key or keys you want to assign the macro to—in this case, Ctrl-F.

4. You'll then be prompted to enter a macro name, so enter **footer** and press ↵. WordPerfect will then assign the **footer** macro to Ctrl-F, and you'll see the macro's description appear on the screen, as in Figure 4.6. If your macro is stored in a directory other than \WP51, or in a directory that's not listed as the macro directory under Location of Files, enter the full path name.

> You'll probably never want a macro to be executed when you press a single letter key. You may, however, want to redefine some of the symbol keys that you use infrequently.

You can then press F7, select the DOCUMENT keyboard as the one you want to use, and try out the macro. Pressing Ctrl-F will execute the **footer** macro.

After you've recorded a few macros by following the steps given in Chapters 6 through 10 of this book, you'll be able to create key definitions for the ones you use frequently or for specialized tasks.

## *RECORDING A MACRO IN THE KEYBOARD MACRO EDITOR*

What if you want to assign a macro that you haven't recorded yet to a special key? In that case, you'd select Create (option 4) and then

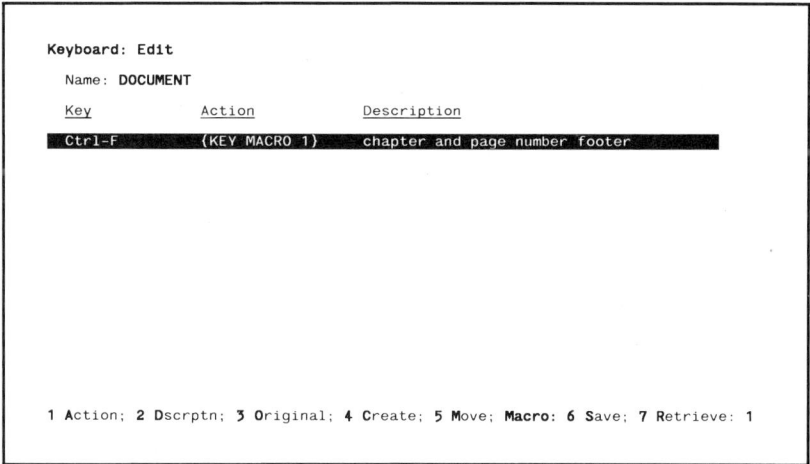

*Figure 4.6:* When you've assigned an existing macro to a key, its description appears on the Keyboard Edit screen.

type the key you want to assign the macro to. For example, type **C**, press Ctrl-K, and enter a description (in version 5.1) to create a Ctrl-K macro. You'll see the function of that key in WordPerfect, if there is one, in the action portion of the keyboard editing screen.

To record a different action, just delete that function and replace it with the other steps that you want the macro to perform, just as you did when you were using the macro editor in Chapter 2. Remember, pressing Ctrl-F10 puts you in Macro Command mode so that everything you do will be recorded as a step in the macro, while if you press Ctrl-V only the next key you press will have its literal meaning inserted in the macro.

Remember too that while you're recording a macro in the keyboard editor, the definitions for the current keyboard are active. For example, if you've assigned a macro to a key, pressing that key inserts that macro in the macro you're defining.

## *ASSIGNING A MACRO TO A KEY DEFINITION*

Finally, you can assign a key's new function to a macro in reverse: That is, if you've defined a key to carry out a certain sequence of actions, you can set up those actions to be a macro that you can use like any other macro. For example, say that you've recorded Ctrl-K in the keyboard macro editor so that it inserts a blank line of text when you use your special DOCUMENT keyboard. You decide that you'd also like to be able to use that macro when you use WordPerfect's original keyboard definition. To assign the function that Ctrl-K carries out to a normal macro— one that's named **open.wpm**, for example—so that you can execute it from your original keyboard, you'd take the following steps:

1. At the Keyboard Edit screen, highlight the key whose functions you want to make into a regular macro.

2. Type **S** for Save. You'll see the prompt

    **Define macro:**

    at the bottom of the screen. Enter the name that you want the function to have as a macro and press ↵. In this case, type **open** (or press Alt-O to assign it to Alt-O). WordPerfect will add the .WPM extension.

Although you won't see anything different on the screen, you've now created a macro that you can execute from any keyboard definition in the normal way: by pressing Alt-F10, entering the macro's name, and pressing ↵.

Once you've saved a key definition as a macro, however, you can edit it as you would any other macro that you create from the keyboard with Ctrl-F10 (Macro Def).

## COMBINING KEYS FROM OTHER KEYBOARDS

Once you've created several keyboards of your own, you can select key definitions from the various keyboards and combine them into one keyboard. The following procedure can save you a great deal of time, since you don't have to redefine each key definition each time you want to use it in a different keyboard.

1. Press Shift-F1 (Setup) and type **K** for Keyboard Layout.

2. Highlight the keyboard that contains the keys whose definitions you want to move, and press ↵ to select it. You may

---

*When you save a key definition as a macro, either give it a name or assign it to an Alt-key combination. You can't save it as a Ctrl- or Shift-key combination.*

*If you don't save an Alt-key combination as a macro and you press that key combination when the keyboard that uses that macro is not selected, you'll see the error message, 'ERROR: File not found—ALTn.WPM'.*

*This procedure copies key definitions to build new soft keyboards; it doesn't remove them from their original soft keyboards, which are left intact.*

also want to take a look (by choosing Edit) at the key definitions it contains, and make a note of the ones you want to copy and what their assignments are.

3. Type **K** to select Keyboard Layout again; then highlight the keyboard that is going to contain the new key definitions. Choose Edit to edit it. (If you haven't created that keyboard yet, type **C** or **4** to create it, and enter its name when you're prompted.)

4. Either choose Create to create a new key that will have the existing definition, or highlight a key that's already listed and choose Action or Description (in version 5.1) or Edit (in version 5.0) to edit it.

5. In version 5.0, when you see the keyboard editor, type **1** and enter a new description, or edit the old one if it needs editing. Then type **2** or **A** for Action.

6. Press Del to delete the original command for the key. Press Ctrl-V; then press the key from the other keyboard that has the macro you want to copy. For example, to copy a macro named **Alt-S** on the other keyboard, press Alt-S.

7. Press F7. You can continue to copy other key assignments and select other keyboards to copy the key assignments from by repeating steps 2 through 7.

## *MAPPING KEY ASSIGNMENTS TO DIFFERENT KEYBOARDS*

Version 5.1 contains a Map option that allows you to create macros and assign them to keys, change key assignments, and compose special characters that are assigned to keys. The advantage this feature has over version 5.0 is that it lets you view the key assignments of all the keys on the keyboard at a glance. When you choose Map (8 or M) from the Keyboard Layout menu, you will see a screen similar to the one in Figure 4.7, which is showing the keyboard map for the ENHANCED keyboard. The keyboard you see depends on which keyboard name was highlighted when you chose the Map option.

```
Keyboard: Map

  Name: ENHANCED

    Alt  Key     ABCDEFGHIJKLMNOPQRSTUVWXYZ1234567890-=\`[];',./
         Action  cccccccccccccccccccccccccccccccccccccc

    Ctrl Key     ABCDEFGHIJKLMNOPQRSTUVWXYZ[\]_           C = Command
         Action  ccccccccccccccccccccccccccc              M = Keyboard Macro

         Key     !"#$%&'()*+,-./0123456789:;<=>?@
         Action  !"#$%&'()*+,-./0123456789:;<=>?@

         Key     ABCDEFGHIJKLMNOPQRSTUVWXYZ[\]^_`
         Action  ABCDEFGHIJKLMNOPQRSTUVWXYZ[\]^_`

         Key     abcdefghijklmnopqrstuvwxyz{|}~
         Action  abcdefghijklmnopqrstuvwxyz{|}~

    Key          Action          Description
    Alt-A        (Cancel)

  1 Key; 2 Macro; 3 Description; 4 Original; 5 Compose; N Key Name Search: 1
```

*Figure 4.7:* The keyboard map for the ENHANCED keyboard

You can see all of the keys that can have different functions assigned to them. A bold **C** indicates that that key has been assigned a different function, but has not been assigned a macro. If a macro has been assigned to a key, a bold **M** is present. Notice that the function keys F1 through F10 are not represented. If you want to change their assignments, you need to use the method we discussed earlier, and edit the key assignment itself. If you're wondering why you might want to do this, here's a case in point. My brother resists using Word-Perfect and prefers Volkswriter. Although the rest of his company uses WordPerfect as WordPerfect, he had me create a Volkswriter keyboard for WordPerfect so that he could continue to use "Volkswriter" (actually WordPerfect) with the Volkswriter function keys instead of the WordPerfect function keys. By using macros, I have WordPerfect show a message on the screen when he switches to that keyboard: 'No longer in Kansas--switching to Volkswriter keyboard'; and 'Returning to Dodge City (WordPerfect)' when he switches back with Ctrl-6. It drives his secretary crazy because he uses her computer and forgets to switch back.

To change a key assignment, move the cursor to the key you want to assign a new meaning to. You can then choose Key to change one key's assignment to another, Macro to create a macro for the key, Description to write a description of the key's new action, Original to return the key assignment to its original meaning, and Compose to create a special character that will be assigned to the key. Typing **N** activates the Name Search feature so that you can move quickly to a key.

For example, suppose you wanted to reassign the Indent key to Alt-I. You would move the cursor to Alt-I, choose Key, and then press F4. As you move the cursor through the keys represented on the screen, you will see the 'Key', 'Action', and 'Description' items change at the bottom of the screen. If a macro has been assigned to the key, you will see its description listed there.

The Macro option lets you record a new macro for a key. After you type **M** for Macro, you'll be placed in the keyboard macro editor, where you can define the macro just as you would in the regular macro editor.

To assign a special symbol or character to a key, select Compose (5 or C) and then enter the character set number, a comma, the character number, and press ←, the method you saw earlier in this chapter for creating an à (a grave).

If you make a mistake while you're remapping keys, just choose Original (4 or O) to return the key to its original meaning; then start over again.

When you're using the Map feature, you have access to WordPerfect's Macro Command Language through the Macro option. This lets you create very sophisticated macros, as you'll see in the next chapter and in Appendix A. For now, one of the interesting things you can do with this feature is assign some of the ENHANCED keyboard functions to your keyboard even if you don't have an enhanced keyboard. For example, on the ENHANCED keyboard there are shortcuts for copying, moving, and appending blocks, and so forth. Here's how to get the Block Copy shortcut onto your keyboard:

1. Highlight the name of the keyboard you want to put the shortcuts on. Create a new one if you need to.

2. Choose Map (8 or M); then highlight the key that you want to assign the shortcut to. For example, let's assign Block Copy to Alt-C.

3. With the cursor on Alt-C, choose Macro (2 or M). When the macro editor appears, press Del to delete the key's original function. Then press Ctrl-PgUp.

4. Move the cursor to {Block Copy}; then press ⏎.
5. Press F7 to exit from the editor. Note that Alt-C now has the action "{Block Copy}".
6. Press F7 to exit from the Keyboard Map screen.
7. Then, to try out the new key assignment, select the keyboard you were just remapping and press F7 to return to the editing screen.
8. Highlight some text and press Alt-C. You'll see the 'Move cursor; press Enter to retrieve' prompt. When you press ⏎, the copy of the text will appear.

You can map the other ENHANCED keyboard shortcuts to keys on your keyboard in the same way.

## *CREATING SPECIALIZED KEYBOARDS*

One of the most popular uses of the soft keyboards feature is to let you create keyboards for foreign languages, mathematics, mail merge operations, and other specialized typing. In the next few sections, we'll take a look at several of the more specialized keyboards that you can create. From these examples you may get ideas for keyboards you want to set up for yourself by using the macros given in Part 2 of this book.

WordPerfect can reproduce all of the ASCII character set as well as the IBM Extended Character set. It also provides symbols and characters from its own extensive character sets (see Appendix D). Between all these sets, you'll find you have most of the special characters and symbols you need to type in many different languages. However, just because they are in the character sets, don't assume that your printer can print them. Before you go to the trouble of setting up any foreign-language or symbol keyboards, first retrieve the document named CHARACTR.DOC that came with WordPerfect and try printing the character set that contains the symbols or characters you want to use. If you have version 5.1, the program will create these characters graphically, so if you have a printer that can print graphics, you'll probably be able to print all of them, even the ones you can't see on the screen.

## *CREATING A FOREIGN-LANGUAGE KEYBOARD*

Figure 4.8 illustrates some of the special characters and symbols that you might want to map onto a German keyboard. They are created by using the Compose feature (Ctrl-2). For example, the macro that creates the uppercase umlauted *A* consists of the following keystrokes: Ctrl-2 1,30. Ctrl-2 turns on the Compose feature, and the *Ä* is in character set 1, character number 30.

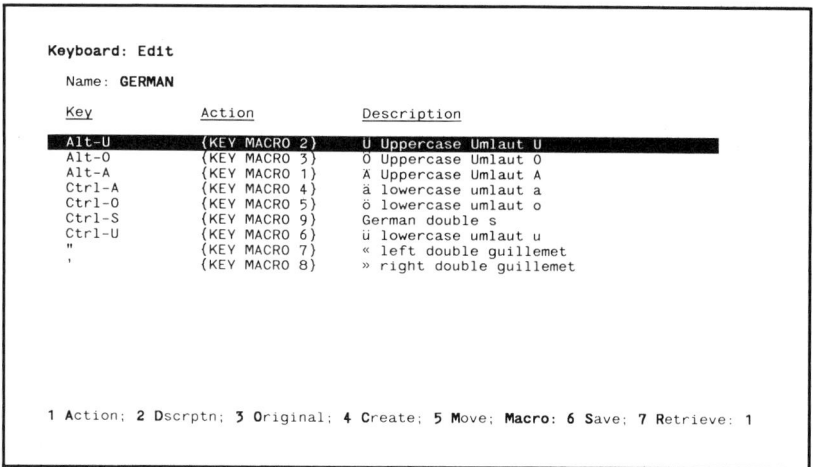

*Figure 4.8:* You can easily create a German keyboard like this one to simplify typing in German.

If you create keyboards like this one, you'll probably want to make a list of which key produces which character and keep it next to your keyboard. Here the Alt keys have been used as the uppercase characters (Alt-A for *A* umlaut, Alt-U for *U* umlaut, and so forth) and the Ctrl keys for the lowercase characters (Ctrl-A for *a* umlaut and Ctrl-U for *u* umlaut). However, you'll probably need more combinations than mnemonic association can provide, especially in languages with a large number of accented characters, such as French.

If you do much foreign-language typing, you should also be aware that WordPerfect is available in several different languages. Most of them come with separate dictionaries and thesauruses. To tell WordPerfect to switch to any of these languages, you insert a {Lang:} code in your document. You can include the steps for inserting this code in the macro that switches you to that keyboard. Of course, you must have a copy of the correct dictionary and/or thesaurus either in the directory you've specified (which you do with the Location of Files option on the Setup menu) or in your working directory. To obtain any of the foreign-language dictionaries, contact WordPerfect Corporation. The following languages are available:

| CODE | LANGUAGE |
|------|----------|
| AF | Afrikaans |
| BR | Brazilian Portuguese |
| CA | Catalan |
| CF | Canadian French |
| CZ | Czechoslovakian |
| DE | German |
| DK | Danish |
| ES | Spanish |
| FR | French |
| GR | Greek |
| IS | Icelandic |
| IT | Italian |
| NL | Dutch |
| NO | Norwegian |
| OZ | Australian English |
| PO | Portuguese |
| RU | Russian |
| SD | Swiss German |
| SU | Finnish |
| SV | Swedish |

UK   British English

US   American English

For example, to switch to your GERMAN keyboard and change the language code to DE, you can create the following macro:

1. Turn on the macro recorder; then press Alt-G.
2. Type **switch to German keyboard** as the description and press ↵.
3. Press Shift-F8 (Format) and type **O L DE**; then press ↵.
4. Press F7 to return to your document.
5. Press Shift-F1 (Setup) and type **K N G**; then press ↵ twice. If you have other keyboards beginning with G, you'll need to type enough letters to uniquely identify the keyboard after selecting Name Search (N).
6. Press F7 to return to your document.
7. Press Ctrl-F10 to turn off the macro recorder.

Now, when you press Alt-G, you're switched to your GERMAN keyboard and the language code is automatically changed to German as well.

## *CREATING A MATHEMATICAL KEYBOARD (VERSION 5.0)*

If you're using version 5.1, use the Equations feature instead. See the equation macros in Chapter 10.

WordPerfect's character sets 6 and 7 contain a wide variety of mathematical symbols that can be used for creating a math keyboard. In addition, character set 8 contains the complete Greek alphabet. If you will be creating formulas that use Greek letters, you can map them onto key combinations when setting up your keyboard.

Many equations and formulas can be entered without your using special symbols from these character sets. They require only the use of multiple levels of superscript and subscript characters and, perhaps, italics to denote the variables in the equation. You'll find macros that insert the {ITALC}{italc} codes as well as the codes for superscripting and subscripting in this book. (See the index for a list of all the macros.) Also, in Chapter 10, you'll find a macro that sets up a special equation area using WordPerfect's Line Draw feature and half-line spacing. On the keyboard shown in Figure 4.9 it has been assigned to Alt-E.

```
Keyboard: Edit

    Name: MATH

    Key           Action            Description

    Alt-E         (KEY MACRO 5)     creates equation area for line draw
    Alt-U         (KEY MACRO 10)    advance .25" up
    Alt-A         (KEY MACRO 6)     align on equal sign
    Alt-D         (KEY MACRO 11)    advance .25" down
    Ctrl-A        (KEY MACRO 4)     approximately equal to
    Ctrl-B        (KEY MACRO 9)     lowercase greek beta
    Ctrl-D        (KEY MACRO 3)     subscript
    Ctrl-E        (KEY MACRO 12)    equivalent symbol
    Ctrl-F        (KEY MACRO 17)    for all
    Ctrl-G        (KEY MACRO 13)    degree symbol
    Ctrl-H        (KEY MACRO 1)     there exists
    Ctrl-I        (KEY MACRO 14)    integral symbol
    Ctrl-O        (KEY MACRO 8)     lowercase greek theta
    Ctrl-Q        (KEY MACRO 7)     lowercase greek alpha
    Ctrl-S        (KEY MACRO 15)    summation symbol
    Ctrl-T        (KEY MACRO 16)    proportional symbol
    Ctrl-U        (KEY MACRO 2)     superscript

1 Action; 2 Dscrptn; 3 Original; 4 Create; 5 Move; Macro: 6 Save; 7 Retrieve: 1
```

*Figure 4.9:* You may want to set up a MATH keyboard similar to this one if you're using version 5.0.

Line Draw doesn't work well if you're using a proportional font, though. Although I haven't shown one in Figure 4.9, you could create an Advance Up macro that would allow you to control the placement of the vertical elements in a graphics box. Such a macro, perhaps named **Alt-U** (for Up), could contain the following keystrokes:

**Shift-F8 O A U Ctrl-PgUp P ↵ F7 F7**

What this means is that first it invokes the Format menu (Shift-F8), selects the Other option (O) and then the Advance (A) and Up (U) options, and then pauses to allow you to enter the distance that the characters are to be advanced and then press ↵. After the macro resumes, it presses the Exit (F7) key twice to return to the document editing screen. A similar Advance Down macro, Alt-D, could also be created.

Another useful macro for a MATH keyboard would change your units of measurement to WordPerfect 4.2 units (rows and columns). When you enter equations and formulas, you will need to rely on the Ln and Pos indicators to help you align the elements. Seeing these measurements in inches can be distracting if you are trying to count the number of characters and position a special symbol correctly. Such a macro would contain the following keystrokes, listed first for version 5.1 and then for 5.0:

Shift-F1 E U D U S U F7
Shift-F1 U D U S U F7

You could record a similar macro to change back to the default unit (inches) when you finished doing the mathematical typing. Or, as with the macro that automatically changes the language code to German, you could include these keystrokes in the macro that switched you to your MATH keyboard, so that WordPerfect 4.2 units would be used whenever you did mathematical typing.

One other useful macro that you might want to map onto a math keyboard is one that changes the alignment character to the equals sign so that all equations align on it. See the **align** macro in Chapter 7 for an example.

## *CREATING A SYMBOL KEYBOARD*

Even if you don't do any foreign-language or mathematical typing, you may want to set up a SYMBOL keyboard like the one illustrated in Figure 4.10. It creates most of the commonly used symbols, such as the paragraph symbol, the trademark, and the double dagger. All of these symbols are in WordPerfect's character sets (see Appendix D):

| SYMBOL | NAME | TO ENTER, PRESS CTRL-2 PLUS |
|---|---|---|
| • | Bullet | 4,3 |
| © | Copyright | 4,23 |
| † | Dagger | 4,39 |

| SYMBOL | NAME | TO ENTER, PRESS CTRL-2 PLUS |
|---|---|---|
| ¶ | Paragraph | 4,5 |
| ® | Registered trademark | 4,22 |
| § | Section | 4,6 |
| ™ | Trademark | 4,41 |
| ‡ | Double dagger | 4,40 |

```
Keyboard: Edit
  Name: SYMBOL

  Key           Action              Description
  Ctrl-B        (KEY MACRO 8)       solid round bullet
  Ctrl-C        (KEY MACRO 4)       copyright symbol
  Ctrl-D        (KEY MACRO 6)       single dagger
  Ctrl-P        (KEY MACRO 1)       ¶ symbol
  Ctrl-R        (KEY MACRO 2)       registered trademark
  Ctrl-S        (KEY MACRO 3)       § section mark
  Ctrl-T        (KEY MACRO 5)       trademark symbol
  Ctrl-Y        (KEY MACRO 7)       double dagger




  1 Action; 2 Dscrptn; 3 Original; 4 Create; 5 Move; Macro: 6 Save; 7 Retrieve: 1
```

*Figure 4.10:* A SYMBOL keyboard like this one lets you create special symbols without having to remember which character codes to use.

To quickly create a bullet with version 5.1, press Ctrl-2 (Compose); then type **. Type *o for an open bullet, *O for a large open bullet, and *. for a small bullet. For a case fraction, type /2 (for ½) or /4 (for ¼) after pressing Ctrl-2.

Character set 4 has many other useful everyday symbols, such as bullets (nice if you are creating organization charts or presentation graphics), ligatures such as ff and fl, case fractions such as ½ and ¼, and so forth.

## *CREATING A MERGE KEYBOARD*

If you do merge printing and sorting frequently, you may want, instead of a menu system, to create a customized keyboard in which certain keys automatically start merges that you have set up. In effect, this will let you automate most of your merge operations so that you can forget about exactly which keys to press.

You could also set up a system of this sort for others to perform merge operations in WordPerfect without having to learn the program's merge printing and sorting rules. You'll find several macros in Chapter 5 that are useful for starting merges, sorting, selecting records, adding records to merge files, and so forth. You could create a special keyboard with these functions:

- You could assign a macro named **merge1** to Ctrl-M. It would start a merge using the file that you specify.

- You could assign a macro named **merge2** to Ctrl-A. It would start a merge that would allow you to assemble a document.

- You could assign a macro named **report** to Ctrl-R. It would start a merge using a REPORT.PF file you created, which would allow you to fill out routine status reports.

- You could assign a macro named **form** to Ctrl-F. It would start a merge using a form that would prompt you for the information to be filled out.

- You could assign a macro named **sort** to Ctrl-S. It would sort your secondary file by zip code in preparation for mass mailings.

- You could assign a macro named **labels** to Ctrl-L. It would format the addresses on the screen as mailing labels.

- You could assign a macro named **envelope** to Ctrl-E. It would start a merge using ENVELOPE.PF as a primary file and take data from another secondary file.

- You could assign a macro named **print** to Ctrl-P. It would pause for you to select a printer and then print the merged documents on the screen.

- You could assign other sorting macros to other Ctrl keys. For example, one macro might sort alphabetically by company name, another by last name of contact, and so forth.

Using a system like this one, you (or someone else) would only have to remember these keys:

| | |
|---|---|
| Ctrl-A | Assemble letter |
| Ctrl-F | Fill out form |
| Ctrl-L | Labels for mailing |
| Ctrl-M | Merge customer records |
| Ctrl-P | Print merged documents |
| Ctrl-R | Report form |
| Ctrl-S | Sort by zip code |

You can record a macro that switches you to each of the keyboards you use frequently: **Alt-M** can take you to your MATH keyboard, **Alt-F** to your FRENCH keyboard, and so forth. The trick is to use the Name Search feature to select the keyboard; don't just highlight it and press ⏎ when you record the macro. For example, suppose you have a GERMAN keyboard that is the only keyboard beginning with G. You can record the following keystrokes as an **Alt-G** macro that switches you to that keyboard instantly: **Shift-F1 K N G ⏎ ⏎ F7**. If you have several keyboards beginning with the same letter, such as SPANISH and SYMBOL, you'll need to type more than one letter to identify its name after activating Name Search.

## *SUMMARY*

In this chapter you have seen how to map WordPerfect operations to keys on special soft keyboards, in effect creating macros that are carried out when the keys are pressed. In particular, you saw that:

- A soft keyboard (also called a keyboard definition or a keyboard layout) is really only a collection of macros.
- To select a different soft keyboard, you use the Setup menu; or you can record a macro for selecting each different keyboard you have created.

- To return to the original WordPerfect keyboard, you press Ctrl-6.
- To create a new soft keyboard, you use the Setup menu's Create option and give the keyboard a name. You can then define a new meaning for the keys. This new meaning is called a key definition.
- Once you have created a new keyboard definition, you can edit it to delete or change the functions of its keys.
- You can create a new keyboard from macros that you've already recorded, or you can record macros in the keyboard editor. You can also copy key definitions from one keyboard to another. With version 5.1, you can use the Map feature to see the entire keyboard's key assignments as you change them.

In addition, you've been shown several ways of creating specialized soft keyboards yourself, either by recording new macros or by assigning some of the macros provided later in this book to keys and key combinations.

Chapter 5 will take a look at how you can create menu systems that allow you to execute a macro when you make a selection from a menu.

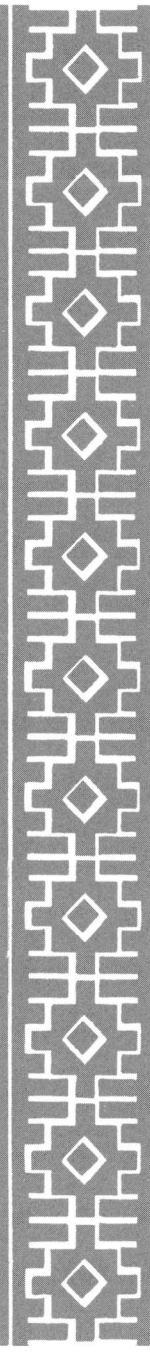

# Creating Menus with Macros

CHAPTER

5

# CHAPTER 5

As you become a more advanced WordPerfect user, you may find yourself called on to set up applications of WordPerfect for others to use. You may, for example, want to create an easy-to-use system for the specialized tasks that your office does, so that entry-level personnel can start using WordPerfect right away without knowing very much about it. By setting up menu systems of your own, you can automate and simplify complex tasks so that others can perform them easily.

You saw a few examples of this in Chapter 4, which demonstrated how to assign macros to keys so that a new user could, for example, simply press Ctrl-F to fill out a certain form, or press Ctrl-L to work with mailing labels. With a system like that, though, you have to give your users some indication of what the various keys do—perhaps by providing hard-copy instructions that they keep at their work stations.

However, you can use macros to create menu systems that prompt the user what to do next as well as present all the available choices on the screen. This chapter will show you how to create menus like this by using the program's built-in macro programming language to create menus just like the ones you use as you use WordPerfect.

By using these special commands, you can display messages on various parts of the screen, and you can also include in your macros error-handling routines that protect users from errors that might otherwise occur. In addition, you can allow the user more flexibility in making menu choices, just as WordPerfect does: You can create menus that permit number choices as well as mnemonic letter choices. For example, a menu choice called

**1 Create**

could be activated by the user typing **1**, **C**, or **c**.

To set up the menus discussed in this chapter, you'll need to record several macros and a certain amount of sample text so that your menu system will actually work and you can see how to set up menus on your own.

As you work through the examples in this chapter, you may want to refer to Appendix A, which presents the language with the syntax of its commands. As I said, it's not necessary that you be a programmer to use this language for setting up the menu systems in this chapter; you'll see step-by-step examples of how to create menus and prompts, and following them will allow you to create similar menus on your own.

## *CREATING MENUS WITH MACRO COMMAND LANGUAGE*

We'll create a menu that lets you assemble different types of documents from boilerplate text and back up your daily work. To work through this example, you will need to create several macros in the macro editor. If you want your system to be workable, you'll also need to create a short document containing some boilerplate text and save it as INQTEXT (see Figure 5.3 for some ideas). In addition, if you want to try out the **backup** macro presented here, you'll need a blank, formatted floppy disk on hand.

The Document Assembly menu system presents the menu shown in Figure 5.1 when you execute the **assemble** macro. You can type either an option number or an option letter, in either uppercase or lowercase, to view additional menus or execute macros. Option 1, L, or l presents the Letter Assembly menu shown in Figure 5.2. Options 2 and 3 present menus that are similar to the Letter Assembly menu, but list different types of reports and contracts. To keep your work to a minimum, we won't implement these two options, since they work exactly the same way as option 1; only the contents are different.

Option 4 executes a **backup** macro that automatically backs up your day's work to a floppy disk in drive B, so that you always have a floppy backup of your work. All you have to enter is today's date.

Option 5 exits you from the Document Assembly menu system and gives you a farewell message.

On the Letter Assembly menu, you have four choices. Choosing option 1 by typing **1**, **I**, or **i** displays a document named INQTXT that contains boilerplate text for customer inquiry letters, shown in

```
DOCUMENT ASSEMBLY MENU

1 Letter assembly

2 Contract assembly

3 Report assembly

4 Back up daily work

5 Exit from main menu

Enter option letter or number:
```

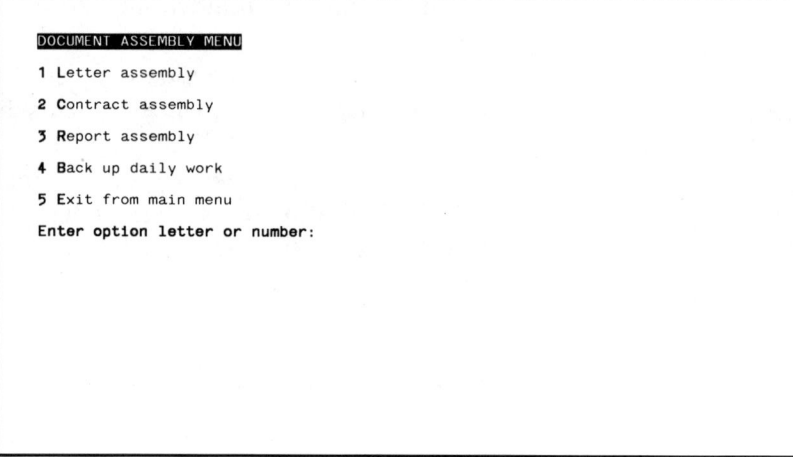

***Figure 5.1:*** You can create this Document Assembly menu system by using Macro Command Language.

```
LETTER ASSEMBLY MENU

1 Inquiry letters

2 Price quote letters

3 Overdue reminder letters

4 Go back to main menu

Enter option letter or number:
```

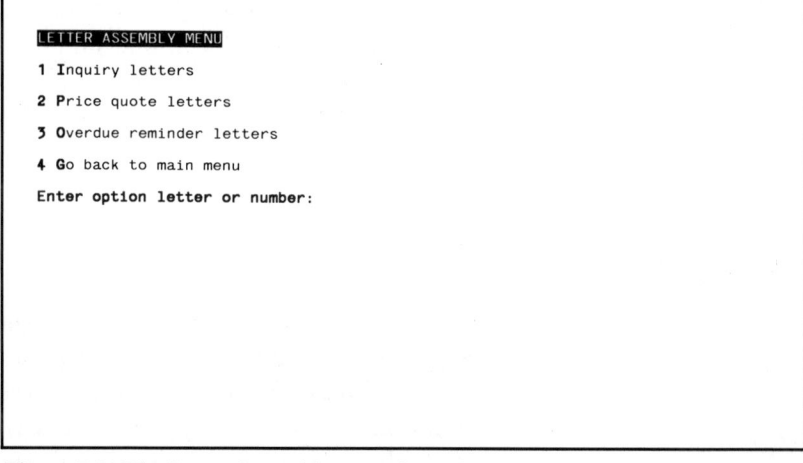

***Figure 5.2:*** The Letter Assembly menu is a submenu of the Document Assembly menu.

Figure 5.3. You can choose the paragraphs you want to use and delete the rest to quickly assemble a customer letter. Options 2 and 3 would present text for price quotations and different types of overdue-reminder letters if you were to implement them, but since

```
Your recent inquiry has been sent to the Accounting department.
Stephanie Cromek, the account representative, will be getting in
touch with you within ten days.

Your recent inquiry has been sent to the Sales department. Robert
Bridges, the account representative, will be getting in touch
with you within ten days.

Your recent inquiry has been sent to the Marketing department. R.
L. Stephenson, the account representative, will be getting in
touch with you within ten days.

Your recent inquiry is being processed and you will receive
further notification within ten days.

If you have further questions, please call me at (800) 555-1212.

If you have further questions, please call Debra Barnham at (800)
555-1200.



C:\5\INQTXT                                          Doc 2 Pg 1 Ln 1" Pos 1"
```

*Figure 5.3:* The INQTXT document contains all the boilerplate text for responding to customer inquiries.

they work exactly like option 1, we won't go through the steps you need to create them here.

Option 4 simply returns you to the main Document Assembly menu.

## CREATING THE DOCUMENT ASSEMBLY MENU

> If you need to review working with the macro editor, see Chapter 2.

To create the Document Assembly menu, turn on the macro recorder by pressing Ctrl-F10 or choosing Macro from the Tools menu and then choosing Define. Then enter **assemble**, press ←, and enter the description as **displays document assembly menu**. Then press Ctrl-F10 again to turn off the macro recorder. (With version 5.1, you can press Home before you press Ctrl-F10 and you'll be taken to the macro editor as soon as you enter the description and press ←.) You'll do the rest of the work in the macro editor, so retrieve the **assemble** macro by pressing Ctrl-F10 (Macro), typing **assemble**, pressing ←, and typing **E** for Edit. If you're using version 5.0, you'll then need to type **A** for Action.

Figures 5.4A, 5.4B, and 5.4C display the macro you're going to create. It's too large to fit in one macro editing screen, so some of the last lines in the screens have been repeated to help you keep your place. The instructions that follow will show you step by step how to create each line, but you may want to refer to these figures from time to time to see the completed macro.

```
Macro: Action

    File            ASSEMBLE.WPM
    Description     displays document assembly menu

    {DISPLAY OFF}
    {LABEL}assembly~
    {CHAR}1~(Del to EOP)
    {^R}DOCUMENT-ASSEMBLY-MENU{^S}
    {Enter}
    {Enter}
    {^]}1-L{^\}etter-assembly
    {Enter}
    {Enter}
    {^]}2-C{^\}ontract-assembly
    {Enter}
    {Enter}
    {^]}3-R{^\}eport-assembly
    {Enter}
    {Enter}

Ctrl-PgUp for macro commands;  Press Exit when done
```

*Figure 5.4A:* The **assemble** macro displays the Document Assembly menu.

```
Macro: Action

    File            ASSEMBLE.WPM
    Description     displays document assembly menu

    {^]}3-R{^\}eport-assembly
    {Enter}
    {Enter}
    {^]}4-B{^\}ack-up-daily-work
    {Enter}
    {Enter}
    {^]}5-E{^\}xit-from-main-menu
    {Enter}
    {Enter}
    {^]}Enter-option-letter-or-number:{^\}-~
    {CASE}{VAR 1}~1~letters~l~letters~L~letters~
    2~contracts~c~contracts~C~contracts~
    3~reports~r~reports~R~reports~
    4~backup~b~backup~B~backup~
    5~exit~e~exit~E~exit~~

Ctrl-PgUp for macro commands;  Press Exit when done
```

*Figure 5.4B:* The {CASE} command is used to branch to each subroutine.

1. Press → and ↵ to move to the line after the {DISPLAY OFF} command; then press Ctrl-PgUp, type **L**, press ↵, and enter **assembly**~. (Don't forget the tildes in this macro, or it won't work.) Press ↵ to move to the next line.

2. Press Ctrl-PgUp, type **char**, and press ↵ to enter the {CHAR} command. Then type **1**~. This tells WordPerfect

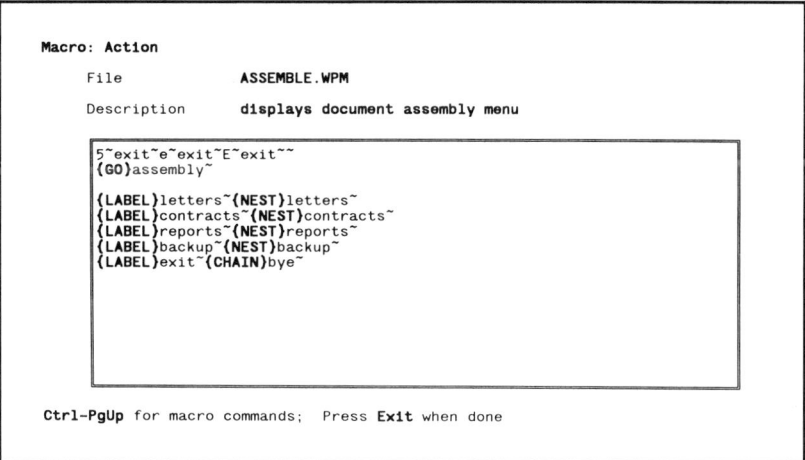

*Figure 5.4C:* The {LABEL} command identifies each of the subroutines.

that the user will type a one-character response to the information beginning with the menu title and ending with the onscreen prompt 'Enter option letter or number' shown in Figure 5.4B.

3. Then press Ctrl-L. Pressing Ctrl-L inserts the {Del to EOP} command in the macro, which tells WordPerfect to clear the screen and position the cursor in the upper-left corner.

4. Move to the next line and press Ctrl-R. Pressing Ctrl-R turns on reverse video in the resulting menu so that the menu title will be highlighted. Pressing Ctrl-S turns off reverse video, so type the title ( **DOCUMENT ASSEMBLY MENU** ) and then press Ctrl-S.

5. On the next line, press Ctrl-V and then press ⏎ to insert an {Enter} command. Do the same thing on the next line so that you have two

    {Enter}
    {Enter}

    commands to separate the menu title from the options in the final display.

6. The next few lines of the menu will display the user's choices. To display in boldface the numbers and letters that the user

can type to make a choice from the menu, you use the {^]} and {^\} commands, which respectively turn bold on and off. Press Ctrl-]; then type **1 L**; then press Ctrl-\ and type **etter assembly** to create the

**1 Letter assembly**

option.

7. Repeat steps 5 and 6 for the rest of the menu choices. Enter the following:

    {Enter}
    {Enter}
    {^]}2 C{^\}ontract assembly
    {Enter}
    {Enter}
    {^]}3 R{^\}eport assembly
    {Enter}
    {Enter}
    {^]}4 B{^\}ack up daily work
    {Enter}
    {Enter}
    {^]}5 E{^\}xit from main menu
    {Enter}
    {Enter}
    {^]}Enter option letter or number:{^\} ~

    Note the spacing of the last line: there is a space and a tilde at the end to allow the user to input one character.

8. Now you will use the {CASE} command to direct Word-Perfect to the appropriate subroutine that will be executed when the user types an option or letter number that goes into variable 1. Press Ctrl-PgUp, type **cas**, and press ⏎ to insert the {CASE} command. Press Ctrl-V and then press Alt-1 to insert the {VAR 1} command. Then enter the following text just as it is shown, with tildes surrounding the various letters and numbers that the user can type.

    ~1~ letters~ letters~L~ letters~
    2~ contracts~ c~ contracts~ C~ contracts~
    3~ reports~ r~ reports~ R~ reports~

4 ~ backup ~ ~ backup ~ B backup ~
5 ~ exit ~ e ~ exit ~ E ~ exit ~ ~

These instructions tell WordPerfect to execute the *letters* subroutine when 1, L, or l is typed; the *contracts* subroutine when 2, C, or c is typed, and so forth.

9. To enter the {GO} command on the next line, press Ctrl-PgUp, type **G**, and press ←. Then enter **assembly** ~ . This command, together with the {LABEL} command on the second line of the macro, tells WordPerfect to redisplay the menu if the user presses anything other than the letter and number choices that you just defined in the preceding lines.

Now you can set up the {LABEL} commands that direct WordPerfect to the instructions that are to be executed when the user makes a choice. The *letters* subroutine executes a macro named **letters** that presents the Letter Assembly menu you saw in Figure 5.2; you'll create that macro soon. Likewise, the *contracts* and *reports* subroutines would execute macros named **contracts** and **reports**, respectively. (You don't have to name them the same thing; you could have a subroutine named *contracts* that would execute a macro named **hello**, for example. The same names are being used here to help identify what is going on, as it's complicated enough without having to keep track of more names.)

10. Press ← twice to insert a blank line. Then press Ctrl-PgUp, type **L**, and press ← to insert the {LABEL} command. Type **letters** ~ ; then insert the {NEST} command and type **letters** ~ as the name of the macro to nest. Continue in this way to type the next four lines:

{LABEL}contracts ~ {NEST}contracts ~
{LABEL}reports ~ {NEST}reports ~
{LABEL}backup ~ {NEST}backup ~
{LABEL}exit ~ {CHAIN}bye ~

The last command tells WordPerfect what to do when the user wants to exit from the menu. Here the {CHAIN} command immediately executes a macro named **bye**, which displays a goodbye message and clears the screen. You'll record it later.

Your macro should now resemble the one shown in Figures 5.4 A–C. Check it over before you go on. Check the tildes, especially; they're easy to leave out.

When you're satisfied that you've typed all the steps correctly, press F7 twice to leave the macro editor.

## CREATING THE LETTER ASSEMBLY MENU

Creating the Letter Assembly menu is relatively easy, since you can just copy the **assemble** macro by using the List Files screen and name the copy **letters.wpm**. You can then retrieve the **letters** macro into the editor and edit it to become the macro shown in Figures 5.5A–B.

> You won't see any macros that you copy within the same directory listed on the List Files screen until you display the List Files screen again with F5 ⏎ (pressing F5 twice doesn't update the List Files screen).

```
Macro: Action
    File            LETTERS.WPM
    Description     displays letter assembly menu

    {DISPLAY OFF}
    {LABEL}letters~
    {CHAR}1~{Del to EOP}
    {^R}LETTER-ASSEMBLY-MENU{^S}
    {Enter}
    {Enter}
    {^]}1-I{^\}nquiry-letters
    {Enter}
    {Enter}
    {^]}2-P{^\}rice-quote-letters
    {Enter}
    {Enter}
    {^]}3-O{^\}verdue-reminder-letters
    {Enter}
    {Enter}

Ctrl-PgUp for macro commands;   Press Exit when done
```

*Figure 5.5A:* The **letters** macro creates the Letter Assembly menu.

Instead of calling another submenu, the Letter Assembly menu retrieves various documents containing boilerplate text. The subroutine named *inquiry* executes a macro named **inquiry** (shown in Figure 5.9) that retrieves a document named INQTXT. Likewise, the *prices* and *dun* subroutines would execute macros that retrieve other boilerplate documents. The *assemble* subroutine calls back the Document Assembly menu you created with the **assemble** macro, so it returns you to the main menu.

```
Macro: Action
    File              LETTERS.WPM
    Description       displays letter assembly menu

    {Enter}
    {^]}4-G{^\}o-back-to-main-menu
    {Enter}
    {Enter}
    {^])Enter-option-letter-or-number:{^\}-~
    {CASE}{VAR 1}~1~inquiry~i~inquiry~I~inquiry~
    2~prices~p~prices~P~prices~
    3~dun~o~dun~O~dun~
    4~assemble~g~assemble~G~assemble~~
    {GO}letters~

    {LABEL}inquiry~{NEST}inquiry~
    {LABEL}prices~{NEST}prices~
    {LABEL}dun~{NEST}dun~
    {LABEL}assemble~{CHAIN}assemble~

Ctrl-PgUp for macro commands;  Press Exit when done
```

*Figure 5.5B:* The middle portion of the **letters** macro

When you've finished editing the **letters** macro (remember to edit the description line also), you can go on to record the various macros that these menu systems use. Without these macros, you'll be able to display the menus, but they won't do much.

## *RECORDING THE MACROS FOR THE MENUS*

You'll need to record three macros. They are illustrated in Figures 5.6 through 5.9:

- **backup**, used in the Document Assembly menu, backs up your day's work to a disk in drive B. The keystrokes in version 5.0 and 5.1 are slightly different; Figure 5.6 shows them for version 5.0 and Figure 5.7 shows them for version 5.1, which has been named **backup1**.

- **bye**, used in the Document Assembly menu, presents an exit message when you exit (Figure 5.8).

- **inquiry**, used in the Letter Assembly menu, retrieves boilerplate letter text (Figure 5.9).

```
Macro: Edit

        File              BACKUP.WPM
    1 - Description       backs up day's work to drive b:
    2 - Action

    ┌─────────────────────────────────────────────────┐
    │ {DISPLAY ON}{List Files}{Enter}                 │
    │ wcd{Enter}                                      │
    │ {PAUSE}{Enter}                                  │
    │ {Enter}                                         │
    │ {Enter}                                         │
    │ cyb:{Enter}                                     │
    │                                                 │
    └─────────────────────────────────────────────────┘

Selection: 2
```

*Figure 5.6:* The **backup** macro backs up your day's work (version 5.0).

```
Macro: Action

        File              BACKUP1.WPM
        Description       backs up day's work to b: (5.1)

    ┌─────────────────────────────────────────────────┐
    │ {DISPLAY ON}{List}{Enter}                       │
    │ fcd{PAUSE}{Enter}                               │
    │ {Enter}                                         │
    │ p{Home}*cyb:{Enter}                             │
    │                                                 │
    └─────────────────────────────────────────────────┘

Ctrl-PgUp for macro commands;   Press Exit when done
```

*Figure 5.7:* This **backup1** macro shows the keystrokes version 5.1 requires.

In addition, to make the **inquiry** macro work, you'll need a document named INQTXT. You can either create the document shown back in Figure 5.3 or you can save any short document as INQTXT, just to give the macro a document to retrieve.

Note that all three of these macros begin with the {DISPLAY ON} command so that WordPerfect will display them on the screen.

```
Macro: Action
    File            BYE.WPM
    Description     gives exit message

    {DISPLAY ON}{PROMPT}{Del to EOP}
       Exiting·from·Document·Assembly·menu...~
    {WAIT}20~
    {Exit}ny




Ctrl-PgUp for macro commands;  Press Exit when done
```

*Figure 5.8:* The **bye** macro presents you with a message on exiting.

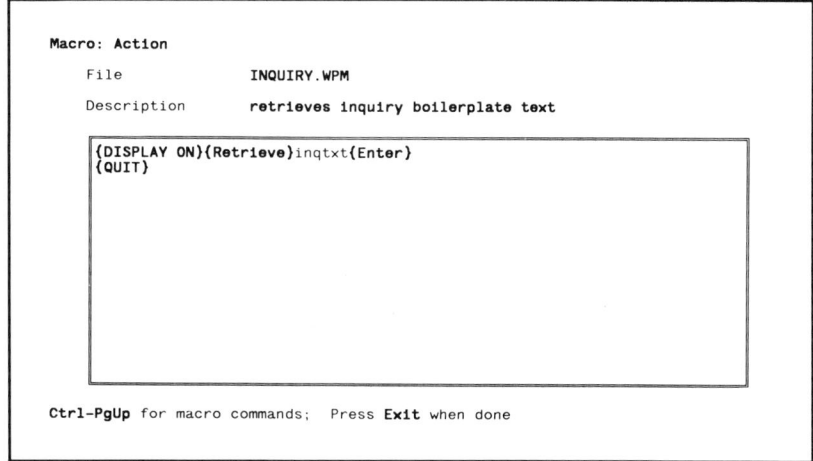

*Figure 5.9:* The **inquiry** macro retrieves boilerplate text for cutting and pasting into a letter.

To record the **backup** macro, take the following steps:

1. Press Ctrl-F10, type **backup** as the macro's name, and press ←⎯.

2. Type **backs up day's work to drive b:** as the description and press ←⎯.

3. To turn the display on, press Ctrl-PgUp and type **D Y**.
4. Press F5 (List Files); then press ⏎.
5. Type **f** for Find (in version 5.1) or **w** for Word Search (in version 5.0); then type **c d** and press ⏎. This tells WordPerfect to use Find (or Word Search) to set up Conditions, and to use the Date as the search condition.
6. Pause the macro so that you can enter the date when the macro executes. Press Ctrl-PgUp, type **P**, enter the date, and press ⏎.
7. Press ⏎ twice more to indicate that you want only one day's files and to begin the search. In version 5.1, type **P** next to perform the search.
8. WordPerfect will locate all the files you have created that day. In version 5.0, it will mark them with an asterisk and display the contents of the directory on the screen. Type **c y b:** and press ⏎ to copy all the marked files to drive B. In version 5.1, the program will display just the selected files on the screen. Press Home-* (or Home-1 if you are using an enhanced keyboard) to mark all of the files with an asterisk; then type **c y b** to copy all of the files to the floppy disk in drive B.
9. Press Ctrl-F10 to stop recording the macro.

When you use the macro, WordPerfect will pause for you to enter today's date in the format 11/19/91. When you press ⏎, the macro will resume and locate all the files in your current directory that have been saved on today's date. It will then copy them to a floppy disk you have inserted in drive B. If you use a blank floppy, all the files will be copied automatically with no prompts. If there are files on the floppy that have the same names as the files the macro is copying, you will be prompted as to whether you want to overwrite the existing files.

To record the **bye** macro, take the following steps:

1. Press Ctrl-F10, type **bye** as the macro's name, and press ⏎.
2. Type **gives exit message** as the description and press ⏎.

3. Press Ctrl-F10 to stop recording the macro.
4. Retrieve the **bye** macro into the macro editor.
5. Delete the {DISPLAY OFF} command and insert a {DISPLAY ON} command instead. Then insert a {PROMPT} command and press Ctrl-L to position the cursor at the upper-left corner of the screen.
6. On the next line, press Tab; then type **Exiting from Document Assembly menu...~**.
7. Enter a {WAIT}20~ instruction so that WordPerfect will display the message for two seconds.
8. On the next line, press Ctrl-V; then press F7 to enter an {Exit} command. Type **n y** to respond to the exit prompts and clear the screen.
9. Exit from the macro editor by pressing F7 twice.

When this macro executes (when you choose option 5 on the Document Assembly menu), you will see the farewell message and then the screen will clear, leaving you in WordPerfect.

The **inquiry** macro, illustrated in Figure 5.9, simply retrieves the document named INQTXT and quits the menu system so that you can work with the text file to create your form letter. You can record the steps that retrieve the document by using the macro recorder, but you will then need to retrieve the **inquiry** macro into the macro editor to add the {DISPLAY ON} and {QUIT} commands.

## *USING THE MACRO MENU SYSTEM*

To exit from your new menu system, press F1 (Cancel).

Your document assembly system is now ready for a test run. Execute the **assemble** macro by pressing Alt-F10, typing **assemble**, and pressing ⏎. You can then use the menus just as you would any other menu in WordPerfect, either with number choices or with mnemonic letter choices. (Remember that you haven't enabled options 3 and 4 on the Document Assembly menu or options 2 and 3 on the Letter Assembly menu; choosing those options will get you a message that the files can't be found.) Choosing any option not listed on these menus simply redisplays the menus.

If your menu system doesn't work right, check your **assemble** and **letters** macros carefully against the macros in the figures in this chapter. Chances are that a misplaced or missing tilde is causing the trouble.

### *CHANGING THE DISPLAY OF MENUS ON THE SCREEN*

By using control characters, you can control how onscreen messages that use the {PROMPT} and {CHAR} commands, as well as other macro commands, are displayed on the screen. You saw in the previous examples how to use boldface, but you may also want to use reverse video or underlining, position messages in different places on the screen, or turn on and off text attributes such as large type or italics. Refer to Appendix A for details about how to use these special control characters to change the appearance of your menus.

### *EXECUTING MACROS FROM A MENU WITH MERGE COMMANDS*

You can also set up a menu system using merge prompts that will let you execute any macro that you have recorded. To do this, you first use the {PROMPT},{KEYBOARD}, and {CHAIN MACRO} merge codes (or ^O, ^C, and ^G in version 5.0) to present the menu on the screen as a prompt. (If you're using version 5.1, to access these commands you press Shift-F9 and choose More.) Then you pause the program (with the {KEYBOARD} or ^C code) so that you can enter a macro name. A sample menu of this type is shown in Figure 5.10. Figure 5.11 shows how the codes would appear in version 5.0. These menus contain macros from Chapter 7.

The program stops at the {KEYBOARD} code, so anything you type will be considered to be a macro name when you press ↵, because of the {CHAIN MACRO} or ^G codes (in version 5.0). Thus, the program will treat your input as a macro name. If you want to execute a macro that you haven't listed on this menu, just type its name and press ↵. In fact, because you can name macros with one-character names, you can even number your macros (or rename macros you've already recorded) and execute them by

```
{PROMPT}
                        MACRO MENU

    Macro Name          Function

    hang                create hanging indent
    labels              generate mailing labels
    letter              generate letterhead
    memo                create memo form
    para                number and format paragraph
    pstyle              change paragraph numbering style
    quote               format a displayed quote
    tab                 set tab at cursor position
    time                insert current time
    restore             restore tabs to previous settings

                    <<Press Shift-F9 to exit>>


        ~{CHAIN MACRO}{KEYBOARD}~
    C:\WP51\MACRO2.PF                              Doc 2 Pg 1 Ln 1" Pos 1"
```

*Figure 5.10:* You can execute any macro on this menu (or any macro that you have recorded) by typing the macro's name and pressing ⏎ (version 5.1).

```
    ^O
                        MACRO MENU

    Macro Name          Function

    hang                creates hanging indent
    labels              generates mailing labels
    letter              generates letterhead
    memo                creates memo form
    para                numbers and formats paragraph
    pstyle              changes paragraph numbering style
    quote               formats a displayed quote
    tab                 sets tab at cursor position
    time                inserts current time
    restore             restores tabs to previous settings

    <<Press Shift-F9 to exit>>


        ^O^G^C^G
                                                   Doc 2 Pg 1 Ln 1" Pos 1"
```

*Figure 5.11:* You can execute any macro on this menu (or any macro that you have recorded) by typing the macro's name and pressing ⏎ (version 5.0).

number from such a menu, as Figure 5.12 shows with the version 5.1 codes.

You will first need to create the menu itself and save it as a primary file named MACRO2.PF. When you create this menu, don't use the

```
{PROMPT}
                    MACRO MENU


            1 - create hanging indent
            2 - generate mailing labels
            3 - generate letterhead
            4 - create memo form
            5 - number and format paragraph
            6 - change paragraph numbering style
            7 - format a displayed quote
            8 - set tab at cursor position
            9 - insert current time
           10 - restore tabs to previous settings


            <<Press Shift-F9 to exit>>



     ~(CHAIN MACRO)(KEYBOARD)~
C:\WP51\MACRO2.PF                          Doc 2 Pg 1 Ln 1" Pos 1"
```

*Figure 5.12:* If you name your macros as numbers, you can execute them by typing the appropriate number at this menu.

Center, Tab, Indent, or Margin Set commands; just use the Spacebar to position your text. Also, if you're using version 5.0, be sure to use the Shift-F9 key to insert the ^O, ^C, and ^G codes; typing a caret and a letter won't work. If you're using version 5.1, be aware that typing curly brackets around a command won't work, either.

List on your menu all the macros you want to execute and a short description of each, so that you'll know which does what. You'll also want to add a reminder, such as the one in Figure 5.10, to press Shift-F9 to exit from the macro menu without making any choices.

Then, after you've created and saved the primary file, like the menu example used earlier in this chapter, you will want to record a macro that displays this menu:

1. Turn on the macro recorder and press Alt-M to name the macro menu macro **Alt-M**.

2. Type **displays macro menu** as the description and press ←⎯.

3. Press Ctrl-F9 (Merge/Sort) and type **M** for Merge.

4. Enter **macro2.pf** as the name of the primary file to use and press ←⎯ to bypass using a secondary file.

WordPerfect automatically turns off the macro recorder when the merge starts, so there's no need to press Ctrl-F10.

When you use the **Alt-M** macro, WordPerfect displays your macro menu, as shown in Figure 5.13. It is displayed in boldface since it is basically one large prompt. When you enter a macro name and press ⏎, that macro is executed.

```
                    MACRO MENU

              1 - create hanging indent
              2 - generate mailing labels
              3 - generate letterhead
              4 - create memo form
              5 - number and format paragraph
              6 - change paragraph numbering style
              7 - format a displayed quote
              8 - set tab at cursor position
              9 - insert current time
             10 - restore tabs to previous settings

                <<Press Shift-F9 to exit>>


Macro:
```

*Figure 5.13:* The macro menu in action: enter a macro name and press ⏎ to execute it.

> You can also set up a series of macro menus that display the names and functions of all the macros you've recorded. The menu you retrieve with an Alt-A macro can display all your macro names beginning with *A*, Alt-B can display all the macros beginning with *B*, and so forth.

You are limited to one screen of choices at a time, but you can record a macro named **seemore** that will display another menu of macros and add as the last option on the menu the choice

    **SEEMORE**   See another macro menu

This menu can also display a macro choice—SOMEMORE, perhaps—that takes you to yet another macro menu, and so forth.

## *A FEW FINAL WORDS ON MACRO AND MERGE COMMAND LANGUAGE*

By using version 5.1's Merge Command Language along with the program's Macro Command Language, you can create entire document management systems. Such sophisticated systems are beyond the scope of this book, but you have seen how you use the basic commands in both of these languages to produce some pretty spectacular results. We don't have room to cover all of the commands here, but there are lots of them. For example, you could use an {IF BLANK}field~ command to check to see if a field were blank (if a customer's name had been omitted, for instance) and then replace the salutation in that letter with a generic salutation, such as "Dear Cardholder:".

## SUMMARY

This chapter has presented ways you can create menus in WordPerfect by using Macro Command Language. In particular, you have seen that:

- You can use Macro Command Language to create systems like the ones the program uses.
- The {CHAR} command interprets a one-character response made by the user and stores it in a variable.
- The {CASE} and {GO} commands tell WordPerfect to execute specific sets of commands identified by the {LABEL} command.
- Subroutines can be used to nest and chain macros.
- Other special commands allow you to position the cursor, use reverse video, and use boldface in your menus.
- The {PROMPT} command (or the ^O merge code, in version 5.0) can be used to display a message for the user of your menu system.
- The {KEYBOARD} command (or the ^C merge code, in version 5.0) pauses the program.
- The {CHAIN MACRO} command (or the ^G merge codes, in version 5.0) allow you to call a macro from a menu.

- The {WAIT} command inserts a pause, measured in tenths of seconds.
- The {QUIT} command terminates a macro.

The rest of the chapters in this book present various types of macros you can use in your everyday work. By using the techniques in this chapter, you can set up a menu system that will execute any of these macros after you have recorded them. If you prefer not to record the macros yourself, you can order a disk with the macros on it. See the back of this book for details.

For additional information about WordPerfect's Macro Command Language, see Appendix A.

# *WordPerfect Macros*

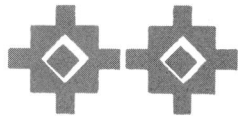

PART

2

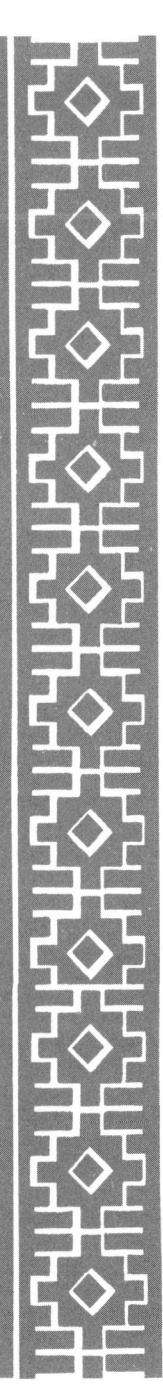

# *Text Entry and Editing Macros*

CHAPTER

6

# CHAPTER 6

In this chapter, you'll find macros that streamline the process of editing text as well as that of entering it. You've already seen how macros can save your document quickly and do some other routine chores. In this chapter you'll see macros that do much more: They let you delete to the beginning of a line or paragraph, for instance, or insert a place marker so that you can return later for further editing. There are macros here that will cut and paste material into a workspace, display the ruler line, and even alphabetize a phone list by last name.

Many of the macros in this chapter are quick and easy to record and deal with common, everyday tasks, so it's a good place to begin your macro library. The macros you choose to record will of course be the ones that carry out tasks you do most often. If you do a lot of editing, for example, you'll probably want to record several of the deletion macros as well as those that transpose characters, words, or sentences. If you work with lists, the macros in this chapter that sort lists can save you a great deal of time. Most people, no matter what kind of work they do, can make use of the "Go To" and "Starting the Speller" macros that are given in this chapter. And if you prepare material for publication, you'll find macros that create em dashes and typesetter's quotation marks.

## *SPLITTING THE SCREEN*

This macro, named **win2**, splits the screen into two equal windows. Use it whenever you need to compare two versions of the same document or when you need to use a Doc 2 window as a workspace for cutting and pasting text.

### *BEFORE YOU BEGIN*

Before you begin to record the macro:

- The cursor should be in a Doc 1 window.

## RECORDING THE MACRO

To record the macro, take the following steps:

1. Turn on the macro recorder by pressing Ctrl-F10 or choosing Macro from the Tools menu and then choosing Define. Enter **win2** as the name of the macro.

2. Enter **splits the screen** as the macro description; then press ↵.

3. Press Ctrl-F3 (Screen) and type **1** for Window.

4. Enter **11** for the number of lines to be in the window; then press Enter.

5. Press Shift-F3 (Switch) to switch the cursor to the Doc 2 window.

6. Press Ctrl-F10 to stop recording the macro.

7. Press Shift-F3 to move back to the Doc 1 macro, so that the program stops recording in both windows.

The final macro should resemble the one in Figure 6.1.

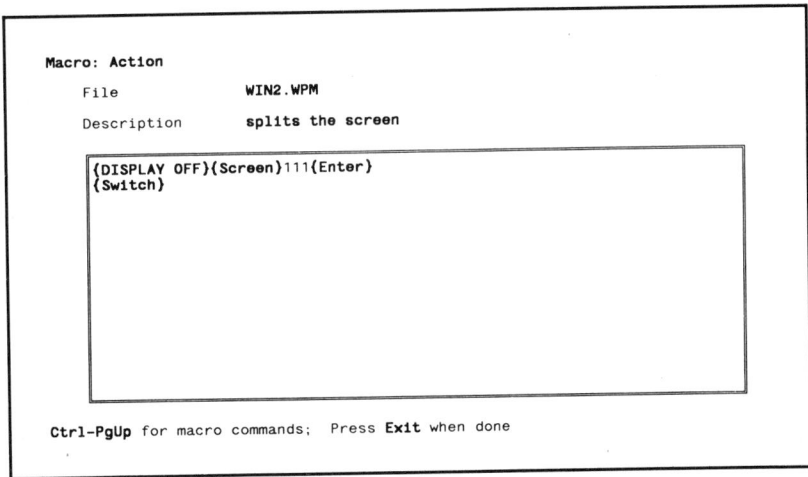

*Figure 6.1:* This **win2** macro splits the screen into two equal views.

## USING THE MACRO

When you use the macro, your screen will split into two equal-sized windows. You can retrieve another document into the lower window or use it as a cut-and-paste space. For example, you might want to review your document to make notes on terms to be indexed. You can highlight them, copy them into a second window, and later use that list as the basis of a concordance file. If you're making extensive revisions to a document, you can use the second window as a scratch area in which to make notes or hold cut sections of text until you decide what to do with them.

## SCROLLING BOTH WINDOWS

This macro, named **Alt-R**, scrolls the documents in both windows simultaneously. You can use it for comparing different versions of the same document or in any other situation in which you want to view the contents of two windows simultaneously. It's assigned to an Alt key so that you can execute it quickly and repeatedly.

### BEFORE YOU BEGIN

Before you begin to record the macro:

- You must either have executed the **win2** macro that opens two windows and splits the screen, or else you must have split the screen previously. The cursor should be at the bottom of either screen.

> If you start to record a macro and get as far as entering its name before you change your mind and decide not to record it, press F1 (Cancel) to stop. If you press ↵, WordPerfect will enter the macro's name, and you will have created a macro without a description and without any keystrokes.

### RECORDING THE MACRO

To record the macro, take the following steps:

1. Turn on the macro recorder by pressing Ctrl-F10 or choosing Macro from the Tools menu and then choosing Define. Press **Alt-R** as the name of the macro.

2. Enter **scrolls documents simultaneously** as the macro description; then press ↵.

3. Press the Screen Down key (the plus key on the numeric keypad). Remember to press Num Lock to use the numeric keypad.
4. Press Shift-F3 (Switch).
5. Press Screen Down.
6. Press Shift-F3.
7. Press Ctrl-F10 again to stop recording the macro.

The final macro should resemble the one in Figure 6.2.

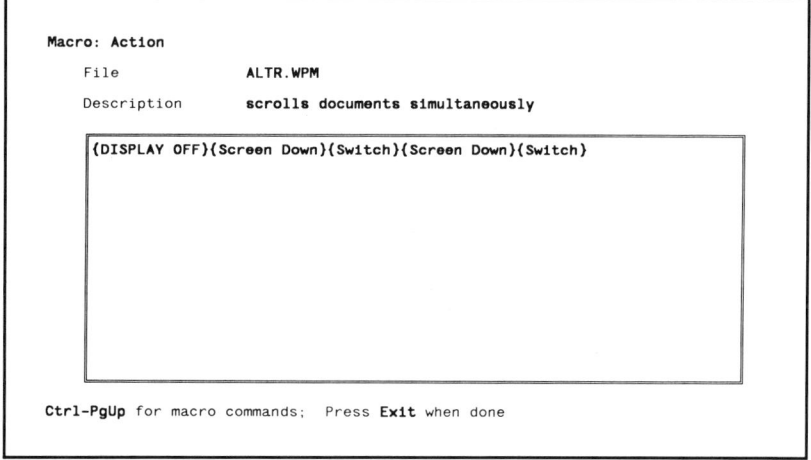

*Figure 6.2:* This **Alt-R** macro will allow you to scroll through two documents simultaneously.

### USING THE MACRO

When you use the macro, you will scroll downward through the information in both documents, half a screen at a time. You can record a similar macro using the minus key on the numeric keypad to scroll upward.

## DISPLAYING THE RULER LINE

This macro, named **display**, displays the ruler line at the bottom of a full-screen window. (You may want to name it **rule** or **Alt-R** instead.) If you are setting up complex tables with tabs, you will find that it is easier to work with the tabbed columns if you can see the ruler line, which shows the tab settings.

## *RECORDING THE MACRO*

To record the macro, take the following steps:

1. Turn on the macro recorder by pressing Ctrl-F10 or choosing Macro from the Tools menu and then choosing Define. Enter **display** as the name of the macro.

2. Enter **displays ruler line** as the macro description; then press ↵.

3. Press Ctrl-F3 (Screen) and type **1** for Window.

4. Type **22** in version 5.1 or **23** in version 5.0 as the number of lines to be displayed in the window. (In version 5.1, if you have the menu bar displayed, it takes up one line.)

5. Press ↵.

6. Press Ctrl-F10 to stop recording the macro.

The final macro should resemble the one in Figure 6.3. Figure 6.4 shows how, after you use this macro, the ruler line appears as you work.

```
Macro: Action
    File           DISPLAY.WPM
    Description    displays ruler line

    {DISPLAY OFF}{Screen}122{Enter}




Ctrl-PgUp for macro commands;  Press Exit when done
```

*Figure 6.3:* This **display** macro displays the ruler line at the bottom of the screen.

*TEXT ENTRY AND EDITING MACROS* **145**

```
      The Document Management/Summary options on the Setup menu allow
you to set defaults to use with your document summaries. You can have
WordPerfect automatically prompt you to create a summary the first time you
save each document by setting the Create Summary on Save/Exit option (1 or
C) to Yes. The characters RE: are the default Subject Search Text, but you can
change them to another subject heading, such as SUBJECT:, by using the
Subject Search Text option (2 or S). You can also specify with the Long
Document Names option (3 or L) whether you want to use a long document
name (up to 30 characters, including spaces) when you save each document. If
you set this option to Yes, WordPerfect will prompt you to enter  the long
document name, the document type (see below), and the DOS file name for the
document each time you save it. The Default Document Type option (4 or D)
C:\WP51\A-G                                       Doc 2 Pg 15 Ln 7.21" Pos 1"
```

*Figure 6.4:* After you execute the **display** macro, the ruler line remains visible as you work.

### USING THE MACRO

When you use this macro, a ruler line appears at the bottom of your screen. To get rid of it, use the **win1** macro described next.

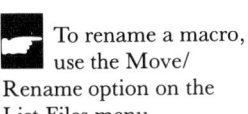 To rename a macro, use the Move/Rename option on the List Files menu.

If you need to see the ruler line frequently, you might consider renaming this macro as an Alt macro.

## RETURNING TO A FULL-SCREEN WINDOW

This macro, named **win1**, returns you to a full-screen window if you've split the screen to display a Doc 2 window or a ruler line at the bottom of it.

### BEFORE YOU BEGIN

Before you begin to record the macro:

- You should have split the screen into two windows, either by using the **display** macro or the **win2** macro, or by pressing Ctrl-F3, choosing Window, and selecting the number of lines you want in the window.

### RECORDING THE MACRO

To record the macro, take the following steps:

1. Turn on the macro recorder by pressing Ctrl-F10 or choosing Macro from the Tools menu and then choosing Define. Enter **win1** as the name of the macro.

2. Enter **returns screen to one window** as the macro description; then press ↵.

3. Press Ctrl-F3 (Screen) and type **1** to choose Window.

4. Type **24** as the number of lines in this window; then press ↵.

5. Press Ctrl-F10 again to stop recording the macro.

The final macro should resemble the one in Figure 6.5.

```
Macro: Action
    File              WIN1.WPM
    Description       returns screen to one window

  ┌─────────────────────────────────────────────────────┐
  │ {DISPLAY OFF}{Screen}124{Enter}                     │
  │                                                     │
  │                                                     │
  │                                                     │
  │                                                     │
  └─────────────────────────────────────────────────────┘

Ctrl-PgUp for macro commands;   Press Exit when done
```

*Figure 6.5:* The **win1** macro returns you to one full-screen window.

### USING THE MACRO

When you use the macro, your screen will return to a full-screen display. If you have a document in the Doc 2 window, it will still be there; you can switch to that window by pressing Shift-F3 (Switch).

## VIEWING THE NEXT SCREENS

These two macros for editing, named **next** and **prev**, let you view the screen of text below or above the cursor without moving the cursor from the line it's on. Without them, you have to use the Screen Up or Screen Down keys and then reposition the cursor to continue editing where you left off.

### BEFORE YOU BEGIN

Before you begin to record the macro:

- You should have a document that is longer than one page on the screen.

### RECORDING THE MACRO

To record the first macro, which views the next screen, take the following steps:

1. Turn on the macro recorder by pressing Ctrl-F10 or choosing Macro from the Tools menu and then choosing Define. Enter **next** as the name of the macro.

2. Enter **view next screen** as the macro description; then press ⏎.

3. Press Ctrl-Return to create a hard page break. Then press + (Screen Down).

4. Press Ctrl-Home (Go To); then press ↑ to go to the top of the page.

5. Press Backspace to delete the hard page break.

6. Press Ctrl-F10 again to stop recording the macro.

Then, to record the next macro, the one that displays the preceding screen, take the following steps:

1. Turn on the macro recorder by pressing Ctrl-F10 or choosing Macro from the Tools menu and then choosing Define. Enter **prev** as the name of the macro.

2. Enter **view preceding screen** as the macro description; then press ↵.

3. Press Ctrl-Return to create a hard page break. Then press ←.

4. Press Ctrl-Home (Go To); then press ↓ to go to the bottom of the page.

5. Press Home Home → to move the cursor onto the hard page break; then press Del to delete it.

6. Press Home; then press ↑ three times to adjust the bottom line.

7. Press Home; then press ↓ twice to move the cursor to the bottom line.

8. Press Ctrl-F10 again to stop recording the macro.

The final macros should resemble those in Figures 6.6 and 6.7.

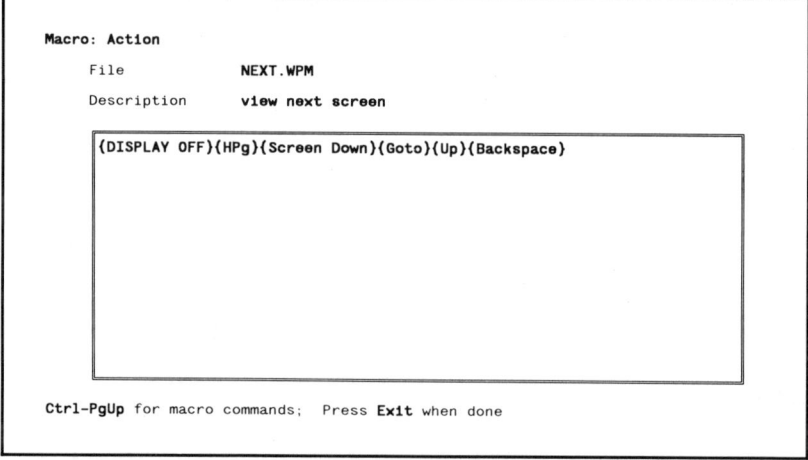

*Figure 6.6:* This macro shows the next 22 or 23 lines without moving the cursor.

## USING THE MACRO

When you use the **next** macro, the line containing the cursor will move to the top of the screen, which allows you to view the following

TEXT ENTRY AND EDITING MACROS    149

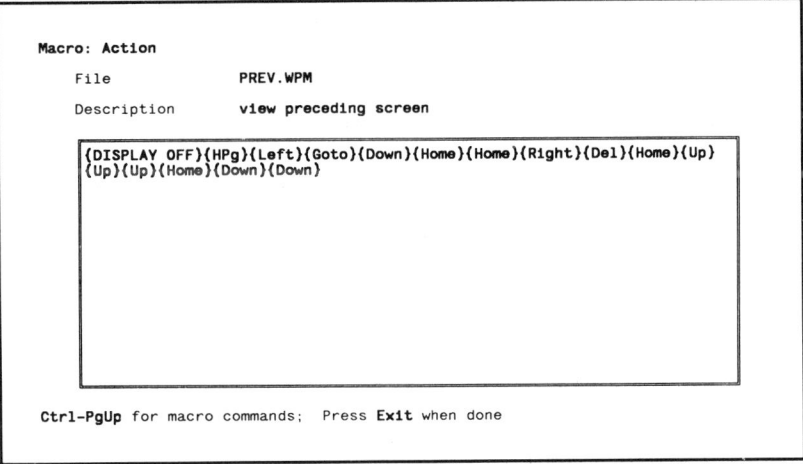

*Figure 6.7:* This macro shows the preceding 22 or 23 lines.

22 or 23 lines. If you use the **prev** macro, the line containing the cursor moves to the bottom of the screen, showing up to 23 of the previous 23 lines. In either case, the cursor remains in position so that you can continue editing where you were. (The exception to this is if there are less than 23 lines above the cursor.)

If, when you use the **next** macro, the cursor is already on the first line on the screen, nothing will happen, because you're already viewing the next 23 lines of text.

If you find that you use these macros frequently, rename them as **Alt-N** and **Alt-P** so that you can execute them quickly.

## CREATING A "GO TO" MACRO

This macro, named **Alt-G**, lets you specify which page you want to go to next. It's a very simple macro, but it's easier to remember than Ctrl-Home, which does the same thing.

Using Go To (or this **Alt-G** macro) and entering the number of the page you're on takes you to the beginning of the page, before any format codes that may have been entered. You'll see in Chapter 7 how this can come in handy; if you're creating a header, for instance, its code needs to come first on the page.

### RECORDING THE MACRO

To record the macro, take the following steps:

1. Turn on the macro recorder by pressing Ctrl-F10 or choosing Macro from the Tools menu and then choosing Define. Then press **Alt-G.**

2. Enter **go to specific page** as the macro description; then press ↵.

3. Press Ctrl-Home.

4. Press Ctrl-F10 again to stop recording the macro.

### USING THE MACRO

When you use the macro, you will be prompted in the lower-left corner of the screen for the page number you want to go to. If you enter a character instead of a page number, WordPerfect will go to the next occurrence of that character.

## MOVING TO THE BEGINNING OF A PARAGRAPH

This macro, named **gopp** (for go to beginning of paragraph), moves the cursor to the beginning of the current paragraph. Yes, it's an ugly name. Name yours whatever helps you remember it.

### BEFORE YOU BEGIN

Before you begin to record the macro:

- You should have a paragraph that begins with a tab indent on your screen.

### RECORDING THE MACRO

To record the macro, take the following steps:

1. Turn on the macro recorder by pressing Ctrl-F10 or choosing Macro from the Tools menu and then choosing Define. Enter **gopp** as the name of the macro.

2. Enter **goes to beginning of current paragraph** as the macro description; then press ⏎.
3. Press Shift-F2 to search backward.
4. Press Tab; then press F2 to begin the search.
5. Press Ctrl-F10 again to stop recording the macro.

The final macro should resemble the one in Figure 6.8.

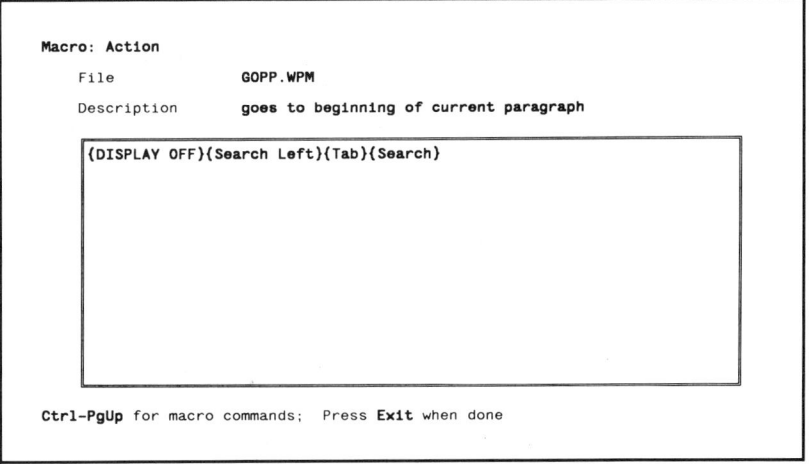

*Figure 6.8:* The **gopp** macro takes you to the beginning of the paragraph you're working on if you've indented it with the Tab key.

## USING THE MACRO

When you use the **gopp** macro, WordPerfect will return to the [Tab] code just above the cursor. This macro won't operate properly if you haven't begun each paragraph by pressing the Tab key. In that case, have the macro search for hard returns.

You can record a similar macro that takes you to the end of a paragraph (searches for the next hard return). Simply have the macro search forward for a [HRt] code in steps 3 and 4 above.

## STARTING THE SPELLER

This macro, named **Alt-S**, saves your document, starts Word-Perfect's Speller, and begins to check the entire document with it.

## BEFORE YOU BEGIN

Before you begin to record the macro:

- You should have a document on the screen that you've previously saved.

## RECORDING THE MACRO

To record the macro, take the following steps:

1. Turn on the macro recorder by pressing Ctrl-F10 or choosing Macro from the Tools menu and then choosing Define. Enter **Alt-S** as the name of the macro.

2. Enter **saves document and starts Speller** as the macro description; then press ⏎.

3. Press F10; then press ⏎ to save the document in its current state. Type **Y** in response to the prompt.

4. Press Ctrl-F2 (Spell); then type **3** for Document. WordPerfect will start the Speller. Press F1 to exit; then press any key in response to the prompt.

5. Press Ctrl-F10 to stop recording the macro.

## USING THE MACRO

When you use the macro, WordPerfect saves your document and presents the Speller menu. After you've checked the spelling in your document, remember to save it again.

## ALPHABETIZING A LIST OF NAMES

All too often you get lists of names and phone numbers with first names first and last names last. If you want to create a directory of names, though, you usually want them alphabetized by last name so that you can find Brian and Alice Aldiss at the same time and know where to look for Roger Zelzany. This macro, named **alf** (for alphabetic), sorts on the second word in a list so that it sorts by last name.

## BEFORE YOU BEGIN

Before you begin to record the macro:

- The items to be sorted must be in rows and columns, like names and phone numbers in the following unalphabetized phone list. Each item should be separated by at least one blank space, as in the following:

    ```
    Brian Aldiss      2770
    Roger Zelzany     4500
    Alice Aldiss      7623
    Susan Spencer     5612
    ```

    Press Alt-F4 or choose Block from the Edit menu and highlight the items in the list.

## RECORDING THE MACRO

To record the macro, take the following steps:

1. Turn on the macro recorder by pressing Ctrl-F10 or choosing Macro from the Tools menu and then choosing Define. Enter **alf** as the name of the macro.
2. Enter **Alphabetic sort on second word in list** as the macro description; then press ⏎.
3. Press Ctrl-F9 (Merge/Sort).
4. When the Sort by Line screen appears, type **3** or **K** for Keys.
5. Press → twice; then type **2** so that the list will be sorted on the second word first.
6. Press → twice so that WordPerfect will then sort on the first word; then press F7 (Exit).
7. Type **1** to start sorting.
8. Press Ctrl-F10 again to stop recording the macro.

The final macro should resemble the one in Figure 6.9.

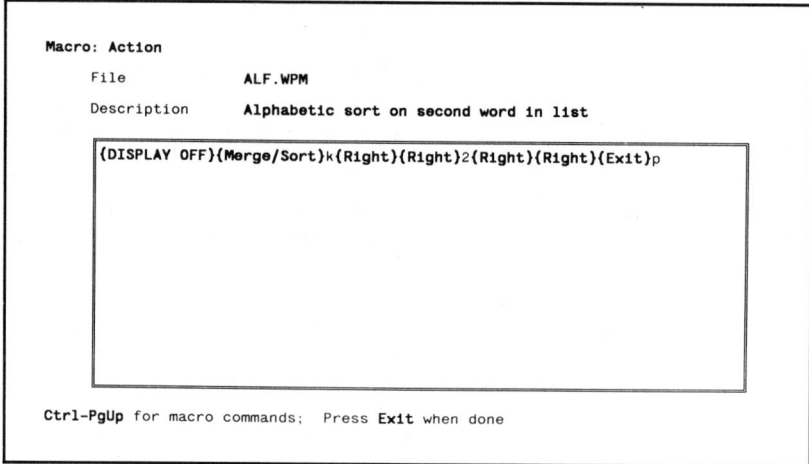

*Figure 6.9:* This **alf** macro sorts first on the second word and then on the first word in a list.

### *USING THE MACRO*

This macro instructs WordPerfect to sort a highlighted list (marked with Alt-F4) alphabetically (A–Z) on the second word in the line and then on the first word in the line. To use the macro, mark the list of names, press Alt-F10, type **alf**, and press ⏎. (If the names have initials, either remove the space between the first name and the initial or delete the initials.) When the macro finishes, the names will still be in the format first name/last name, but they will have been alphabetized by last name and then by first name within last name, so that Alice Aldiss will come before Brian Aldiss and Susan Spencer will come before Roger Zelzany.

## *ALPHABETIZING A LIST*

This macro, named **Alt-A**, alphabetizes by first word only. The list to be alphabetized may have more than one word in each item, like a bibliography, as long as each item is separated by a hard return. It will also sort numerically if the first character in each item is a numeral. In the sorted list, items beginning with numerals will come before items beginning with letters.

## *BEFORE YOU BEGIN*

Before you begin to record the macro:

- You should have a list of words on the screen, and each discrete item to be sorted should be separated by a hard return.
- If you are sorting only part of a document, mark it as a block first.

## *RECORDING THE MACRO*

To record the macro, take the following steps:

1. Turn on the macro recorder by pressing Ctrl-F10 or choosing Macro from the Tools menu and then choosing Define. Enter **Alt-A** as the name of the macro.
2. Enter **sorts list alphabetically** as the macro description; then press ←.
3. Press Ctrl-F9 (Merge/Sort) and type **T L 1** to choose a line sort. (If you have used a different type of sort previously, this clears the previous sort type.)
4. Press Ctrl-F10 again to stop recording the macro.

The final macro should resemble the one in Figure 6.10.

## *USING THE MACRO*

When you use the **Alt-A** macro, WordPerfect will sort the list you have highlighted alphabetically by the first word in each list. If you haven't marked a block, it will sort all the items separated by hard returns on the screen. If the first item in the list is a numeral such as a zip code, an item number, a client record number, or a department number, don't worry; the macro sorts alphanumerically, so it will sort the numerals too (they'll end up first in the list). If your list is in the format last name/first name, you'll get a list alphabetized by last name. If it's in the format first name/last name, use the **alf** macro on it instead.

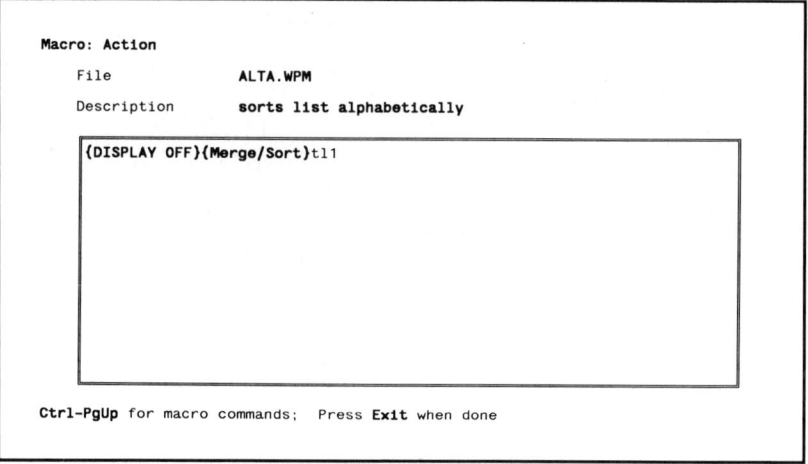

*Figure 6.10:* This **Alt-A** macro sorts a list of words alphanumerically on the first word.

## CAPITALIZING THE FIRST LETTER OF A WORD

This macro, named **cap**, capitalizes the first letter of the word your cursor is on. It can save you a lot of time as you work because you don't have to move the cursor to the beginning of the word, delete the first letter, and retype it.

This macro is on the alternate MACROS keyboard that comes with WordPerfect. The instructions for recording it are given here so that you can see how the macro works. (Refer to Chapter 4 for a discussion of using the alternate soft keyboards supplied with WordPerfect.)

### BEFORE YOU BEGIN

Before you begin to record the macro:

- Your cursor should be within a word on the screen—anywhere except on the first letter.

## RECORDING THE MACRO

To record the macro, take the following steps:

1. Turn on the macro recorder by pressing Ctrl-F10 or choosing Macro from the Tools menu and then choosing Define. Enter **cap** as the name of the macro.

2. Enter **capitalizes the first letter of a word** as the macro description; then press ←⎯.

3. Press Ctrl-← to move to the beginning of the word.

4. Press → to move one character to the right.

5. Press Alt-F4 to turn on blocking; then press ← twice to select the first letter of the word.

6. Press Shift-F3 (Switch) and type **1** or **U** to uppercase the letter.

7. Press Ctrl-→ to move to the next word.

8. Press Ctrl-F10 again to stop recording the macro.

The final macro should resemble the one in Figure 6.11.

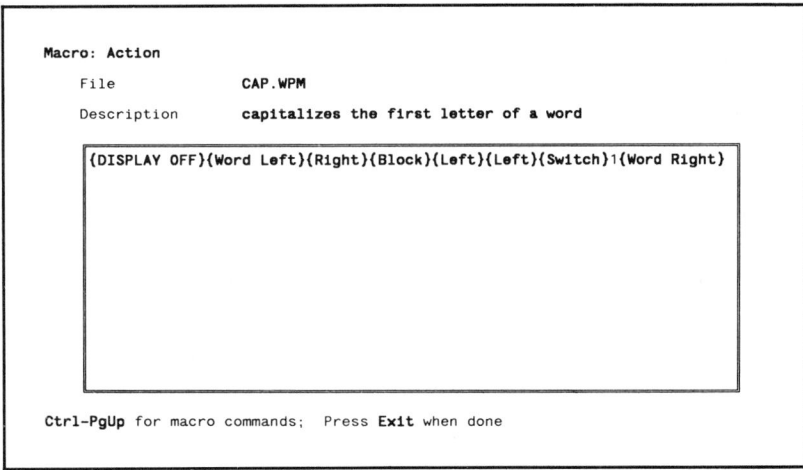

*Figure 6.11:* This **cap** macro automatically capitalizes the first letter of the word your cursor is on.

### USING THE MACRO

When you use the **cap** macro, the first letter of the current word is capitalized. If you find that you use it often, rename it **Alt-C**.

## CAPITALIZING THE NEXT FEW WORDS

The **cap** macro works fine if you want to capitalize the word the cursor is in. But what if you notice that a whole string of words needs to be capitalized? Neither the **Alt-C** macro on the MACROS keyboard nor the **cap** macro will help you in this situation. This next macro, named **capn** (for "capitalize any number"), will capitalize as many words as you tell it to.

### BEFORE YOU BEGIN

Before you begin to record the macro:

- You should have several lowercased words in front of the cursor (to its right).

### RECORDING THE MACRO

To record the macro, take the following steps:

1. Turn on the macro recorder by pressing Ctrl-F10 or choosing Macro from the Tools menu and then choosing Define. Enter **capn** as the name of the macro.

2. Enter **capitalizes n words** as the macro description; then press ←.

3. Press Ctrl-→; then press Alt-F4.

4. Press →.

5. Press Shift-F3 (Switch) and type **1** or **U** to uppercase the letter.

6. Press Ctrl-F10 to stop recording the macro.

The final macro should resemble the one in Figure 6.12.

```
Macro: Action
    File                CAPN.WPM
    Description         capitalizes n words

    {DISPLAY OFF}{Word Right}{Block}{Right}{Switch}1




Ctrl-PgUp for macro commands;  Press Exit when done
```

*Figure 6.12:* By using the Esc key with this macro, you can tell WordPerfect to capitalize any number of words.

> You can record a macro to lowercase any number of words that have been capitalized by substituting **2** or **L** for the 1 or U in the **capn** macro.

## USING THE MACRO

When you use the macro, press Esc and enter the number of words you want to capitalize. For example, if you want to capitalize the next five words, press Esc, type **5**, and execute the macro.

## LOWERCASING ALL BUT THE FIRST LETTER

Another situation where an editing macro can save you time and patience is one in which you have uppercased headings in a document and decide that they would really look better in capitals and lowercase. This macro, named **lower**, converts the whole line that the cursor is on to lowercase. You can then use the **capn** macro on individual words to change them to caps and lowercase.

## BEFORE YOU BEGIN

Before you begin to record the macro:

- You should have several words in uppercase on the screen. Position the cursor anywhere in the line.

## RECORDING THE MACRO

To record the macro, take the following steps:

1. Turn on the macro recorder by pressing Ctrl-F10 or choosing Macro from the Tools menu and then choosing Define. Enter **lower** as the name of the macro.

2. Enter **lowercases a line** as the macro description; then press ⏎.

3. Press Home-← to move to the beginning of the line.

4. Press Alt-F4 (Block); then press End.

5. Press Shift-F3 (Switch) and choose Lowercase (2 or L).

6. Press Home-← to move back to the beginning of the line.

7. Press Ctrl-F10 to stop recording the macro.

The final macro should resemble the one in Figure 6.13.

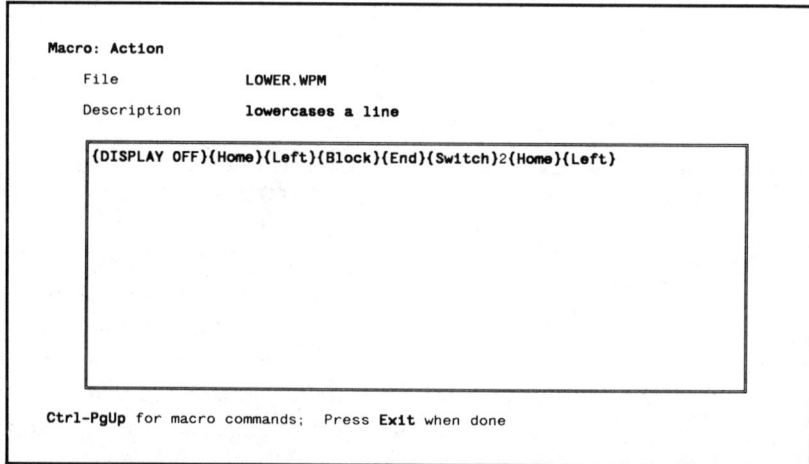

*Figure 6.13:* You can easily convert uppercase headings to lowercase by using this macro.

## USING THE MACRO

When you use the **lower** macro, all the words in the line that the cursor is on will be lowercased. For example, if you have a heading such as

**MADISON'S CABINET STRUCTURE**

executing the **lower** macro will change it to

**madison's cabinet structure**

If you want to capitalize the first letter in each word, use the **capn** macro on that line. In the example given, press ← (to move the cursor off the first letter in the line), press Esc, type **3** (as there are three words to capitalize), and then execute the **capn** macro.

To capitalize words one at a time, move the cursor to each one and use the **cap** macro.

# CAPITALIZING A WORD

This macro, named **Alt-K**, changes the word that the cursor is on to all caps. You'll find it a handy editorial tool as you work, because you won't have to block the word and then convert it to uppercase.

## BEFORE YOU BEGIN

Before you begin to record the macro:

- You should have some text on the screen, and the cursor should be within a word that you want to change to all capital letters.

## RECORDING THE MACRO

To record the macro, take the following steps:

> You can easily record a similar macro that lowercases a capitalized word. Just substitute **2** or **L** for the 1 or U in the macro.

1. Turn on the macro recorder by pressing Ctrl-F10 or choosing Macro from the Tools menu and then choosing Define. Press **Alt-K** to define the macro.

2. Enter **capitalizes current word** as the macro description; then press ↵.
3. Press Ctrl-← to move to the beginning of the word.
4. Press Alt-F4 and press Ctrl-→ to select the word.
5. Press Shift-F3 (Switch); then type **1** or **U** to capitalize the word.
6. Press Ctrl-F10 again to stop recording the macro.

The final macro should resemble the one in Figure 6.14.

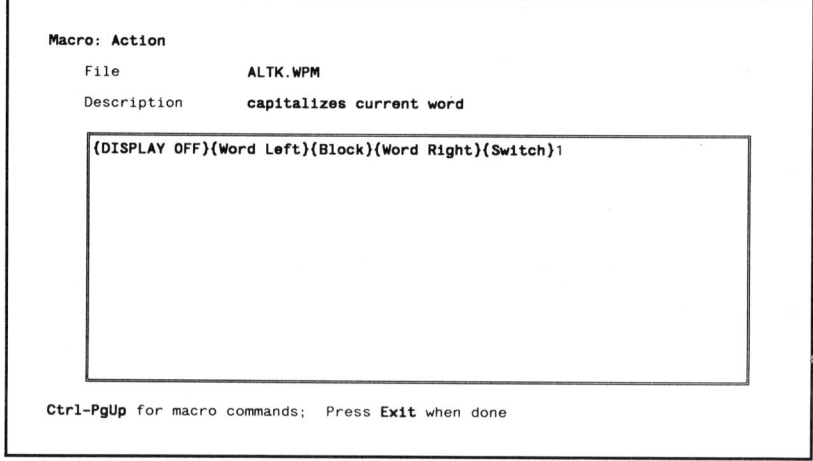

*Figure 6.14:* This macro puts the current word in all caps.

### USING THE MACRO

When you use the macro, the word that the cursor is in will be capitalized. If the cursor is between words, the word to the left of the cursor will be capitalized.

## CAPITALIZING THE FIRST WORD IN A PARAGRAPH

Sometimes in editing you discover that, because you have deleted text, the word that begins the paragraph is now all in lowercase.

Instead of moving to the beginning of the paragraph, deleting the lowercase letter, pressing the Shift key, and typing a capital letter, this macro automatically capitalizes the first word in the paragraph for you.

## *BEFORE YOU BEGIN*

Before you begin to record the macro:

- You should have a paragraph beginning with a tab on the screen.

## *RECORDING THE MACRO*

To record the macro, take the following steps:

1. Turn on the macro recorder by pressing Ctrl-F10 or choosing Macro from the Tools menu and then choosing Define. Press **Alt-T** to define the macro. You may want to choose a letter that helps you remember what it does.

2. Enter **capitalizes first word in paragraph** as the macro description; then press ↵.

3. Press Shift-F2 (Reverse Search); then press Tab.

4. Press F2 to start the search.

5. Press Alt-F4 to turn on blocking; then press → to highlight the first letter.

6. Press Shift-F3 (Switch) and type **1** or **U** for Uppercase.

7. Press Ctrl-F10 to stop recording the macro.

The final macro should resemble Figure 6.15.

## *USING THE MACRO*

When you execute the macro, WordPerfect searches backward to the last [Tab] (which it assumes to be the beginning of a paragraph) and converts the character that it finds there to uppercase. So, if you

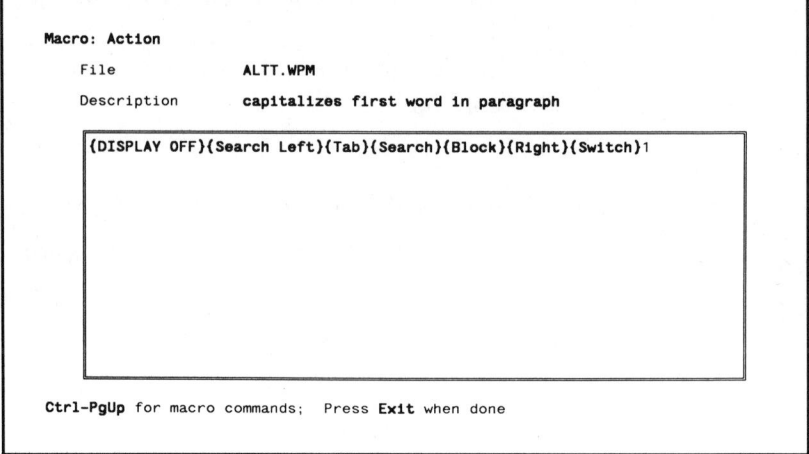

*Figure 6.15:* This macro automatically changes the first letter in a paragraph to uppercase.

aren't indenting paragraphs with the Tab key, this macro won't work. Have it search backward for the last [HRt] instead.

## UNDERLINING (OR BOLDFACING) SEVERAL WORDS

This macro, named **Alt-N**, will underline the number of consecutive words in a row that you specify. It's useful in editing because you don't have to block the words and then press F8 to underline them. You can modify it so that it will boldface several words instead.

### BEFORE YOU BEGIN

Before you begin to record the macro:

- You should have a few words on the screen, and the cursor should be on the first character of the first word.

## RECORDING THE MACRO

To record the macro, take the following steps:

1. Turn on the macro recorder by pressing Ctrl-F10 or choosing Macro from the Tools menu and then choosing Define. Press **Alt-N** to define the macro.

2. Enter **underlines n words** as the macro description; then press ←┘.

3. Press Alt-F4 to turn on block marking; then press Ctrl-→ to highlight the word the cursor is on.

4. Press F8 (Underline).

5. Press Ctrl-F10 again to stop recording the macro.

The final macro should resemble the one in Figure 6.16.

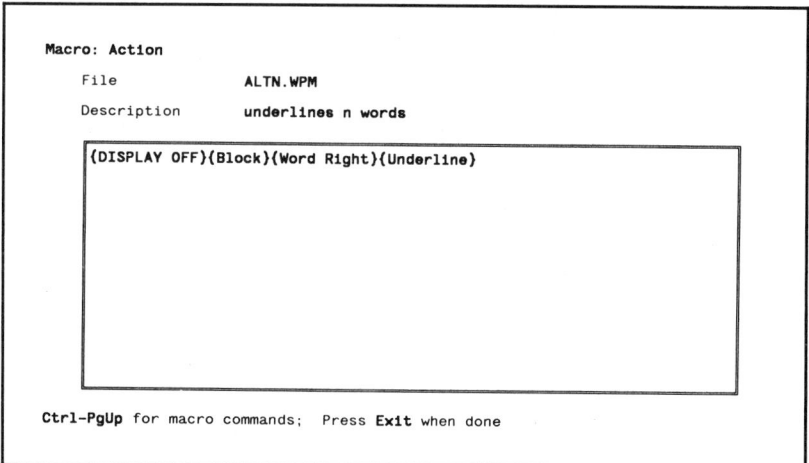

*Figure 6.16:* The **Alt-N** macro underlines as many words as you specify.

This macro produces words that are continuously underlined. If you want each word to be underlined individually, change the default underlining style by using the Other submenu of the Format menu. The key sequence is Shift-F8 **O U N**.

### USING THE MACRO

When you use the **Alt-N** macro, press Esc, enter the number of words to underline, and then press Alt-N.

### OTHER USES

You can edit this macro so that it boldfaces instead of underlines: just substitute Bold (F6) for Underline (F8). Of course, you can record this edited version separately by starting out with step 1 and making the change in step 4.

You can also record a macro to italicize any number of words, as we shall see next.

## ITALICIZING A NUMBER OF WORDS

This macro, named **Alt-I**, italicizes the number of consecutive words you specify. You will find it useful if you often type documents that contain many book titles, which are usually set in italics, or italicized foreign phrases. You can type out your whole article without worrying about the italics and then return to it to insert them.

Using this macro has another advantage over switching to italics as you type: because it acts on blocked text, you don't have to worry about changing back to your normal font at the end of each italicized word or phrase. WordPerfect automatically inserts the [italc] code at the end of each italicized word and returns you to the normal font.

### BEFORE YOU BEGIN

Before you begin to record the macro:

- You should have several words on the screen, and the cursor should be where the italics should begin.

## *RECORDING THE MACRO*

To record the macro, take the following steps:

1. Turn on the macro recorder by pressing Ctrl-F10 or choosing Macro from the Tools menu and then choosing Define. Press **Alt-I** to define the macro.

2. Enter **switches to italics** as the macro description; then press ↵.

3. Press Alt-F4 to turn on block marking; then press Ctrl-→ to highlight the word.

4. Press Ctrl-F8 (Font) and type **A** for Appearance.

5. Type **I** for Italic.

6. Press Ctrl-F10 again to stop recording the macro.

When you view the macro, your screen should resemble the one in Figure 6.17.

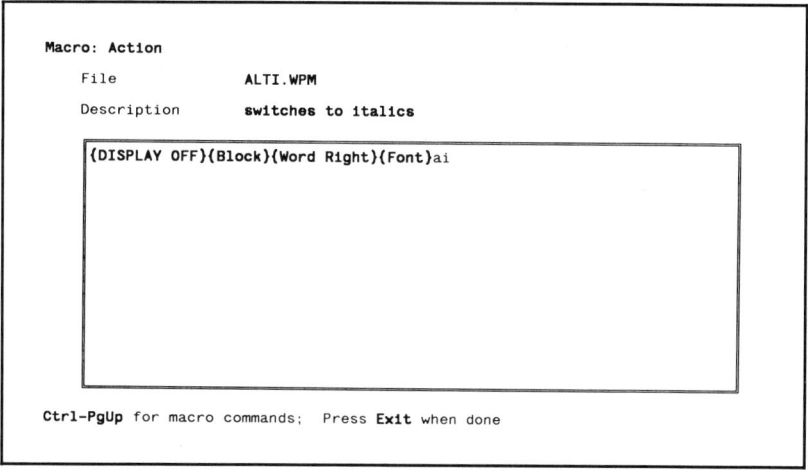

*Figure 6.17:* The **Alt-I** macro italicizes any number of consecutive words you specify.

### USING THE MACRO

When you use the macro, press Esc, enter the number of words you want to italicize, and then press Alt-I. WordPerfect will return you to the normal font at the end of the italicized words without your having to do anything else.

### OTHER USES

Using this macro as a model, you can record macros that change to any of the other type styles that your printer can handle, such as double underlining, outline, shadow, small caps, strikeout, or redlining.

As strikeout and redlining usually operate on entire lines, you'll find a macro (named **strike**) that will strike out *n* lines in Chapter 10, which contains a variety of such specialized macros.

## CHANGING UNDERLINING TO ITALICS

It's much faster to underline as you type instead of italicizing. Underlining takes one keystroke at the beginning and one at the end; italicizing requires four keystrokes in each case. This macro, named **italics**, will search through your document and change everything that you have underlined to italics automatically. For example, if you've referred to *The Joy of Cooking* several times and marked it for underlining, **italics** will locate that book title for you and mark it for italics. Likewise, if you've underlined foreign-language words or phrases such as *nolo contendere* or *res ipsa loquitur*, it will mark those for italics also.

> You may have been printing on a printer that does not support italics and have been using underlining as a substitute. When you buy a new printer that can handle italics, you'll probably want to change the underlining in some of your existing documents to italics. This macro will quickly convert the text for you.

### BEFORE YOU BEGIN

Before you begin to record the macro:

- You should have several words on the screen, they should be underlined, and the cursor should be where you want the underlining to begin.

- You will probably want to open the Reveal Codes window, if you are interested in what is going on.

## *RECORDING THE MACRO*

To record the macro, take the following steps:

1. Turn on the macro recorder by pressing Ctrl-F10 or choosing Macro from the Tools menu and then choosing Define. Enter **italics** as the name of the macro.
2. Enter **changes underlines to italics** as the description.
3. Press F2 to begin a forward search.
4. Press F8 to generate the [UND] code.
5. Press F2 to execute the search.
6. When the macro locates the first code, turn on blocking (Alt-F4), and then press F2 to search for the second [und] code to highlight the underlined text. To generate the [und] code, press F8 twice.
7. Delete the [UND] code by pressing ← and Backspace.
8. Press F2 again to search for the [und] code.
9. Press Ctrl-F8 (Font) and choose option 2 (Appearance). Then choose option 4 (Italics) to insert [ITALC] [italc] codes around the highlighted text.
10. To delete the underlining codes so that the text won't be both underlined and italicized, press ← twice; then press Del and enter **y** in response to the prompt.
11. End the macro definition by pressing Ctrl-F10.

The final macro should resemble the one in Figure 6.18.

## *USING THE MACRO*

When you use the macro, go to the beginning of your document by pressing Home Home ↑. Then press Esc and enter a number that you know is larger than the number of occurrences of underlining in your document—say, 100. You can then execute the **italics**

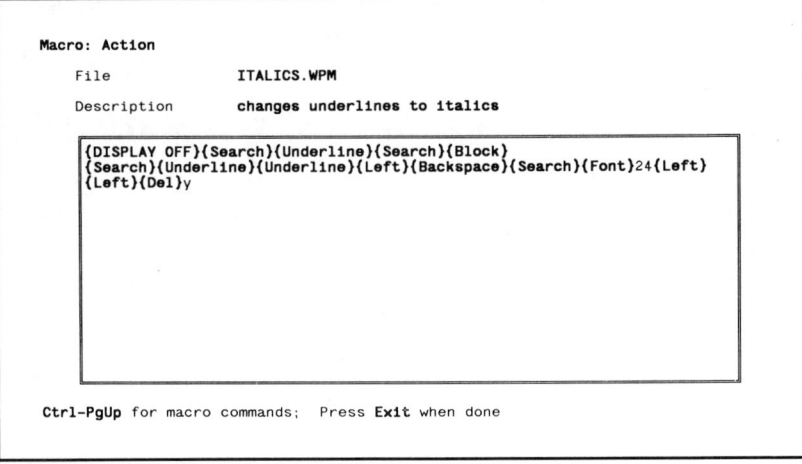

*Figure 6.18:* This **italics** macro will convert all underlining in the document to italics.

> This macro shows you how you can edit a macro you've already recorded to chain it to itself. By using this procedure, you can have a search macro repeat itself until it no longer locates what it's searching for.

macro, and it will repeat until all instances of underlining have been located and changed to italics.

There is another way that you can have the macro repeat until no more occurrences of what it is searching for are found: you can chain it to itself. To do this, you'll need to edit the macro as follows:

1. Retrieve the macro by pressing Ctrl-F10 and entering **italics** as the macro name.
2. Type **2** or **E** to edit the macro.
3. When the macro editing screen appears, type **2** or **A** for Action, if you're using version 5.0.
4. Move the cursor to the end of the macro codes (press Home Home ↓); then press Ctrl-PgUp, type **ch**, and press ↵. WordPerfect will insert a {CHAIN} code into your macro.
5. Type **italics** ~ (the name of the macro plus a tilde) to chain the macro to itself.
6. Press F7 twice to exit and return to your document.

Now, WordPerfect will search automatically for underlined characters and convert them to italics until it can no longer find any

# TEXT ENTRY AND EDITING MACROS    *171*

underlining in your document. Try it in a document that contains several occurrences of underlining.

## OTHER USES

Like many of the macros in this book, the **italics** macro can easily be adapted to perform other functions. You can write similar macros to search for almost any appearance or size code and change it to something else. For example, you might want to search for underlining and change it to double underlining, or search for Large codes and change them to Small (as you will do in the next macro).

# CHANGING FONT SIZES AUTOMATICALLY

This macro, named **small**, is given as an example of how you can quickly and automatically convert one font change code to another consistently throughout a document. If you have printed your document and then decided that your Large heads would look better in Small type, this macro will convert all the codes for you.

## BEFORE YOU BEGIN

Before you begin to record the macro:

- You should have a document on the screen with several occurrences of Large type codes in it. The cursor should be somewhere above the first occurrence of a Large code.

## RECORDING THE MACRO

> This macro shows you how to chain a macro to itself as you are recording it.

To record the macro, take the following steps:

1. Turn on the macro recorder by pressing Ctrl-F10 or choosing Macro from the Tools menu and then choosing Define. Enter **small** as the name of the macro.

2. Enter **converts Large text to Small** as the macro description; then press ⏎.

3. Press F2 to begin a forward search.
4. Press Ctrl-F8 and type **S L** to generate the [LARGE] code.
5. Press F2 to execute the search.
6. When the macro locates the first code, turn on blocking (Alt-F4) and then search for the second [large] code to highlight the large text. Press F2; then, to generate the [large] code, press Ctrl-F8 and type **S L**. Press Ctrl-F8 again; then type **S L** again.
7. Move over the [LARGE] code and delete it by pressing ← and Backspace.
8. Press F2 again to search for the [large] code.
9. The text is still highlighted, so press Ctrl-F8 (Font) and type **S S** to insert [SMALL] [small] codes around the highlighted text.
10. To delete the Large codes, press ← twice; then press Del and enter **y** in response to the prompt.
11. Chain the macro to itself by pressing Alt-F10 and entering **small** as the name of the macro. Then press ↵.
12. Press Ctrl-F10 again to stop recording the macro.

The final macro should resemble the one in Figure 6.19.

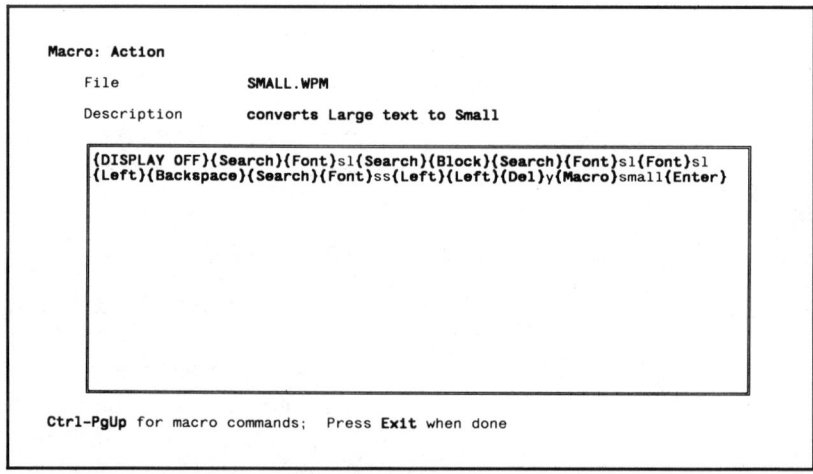

*Figure 6.19:* The **small** macro is an example of how you can automatically convert one size of type to another.

## USING THE MACRO

When you use the macro, it will search through the document and change each instance of Small type to Large, stopping only when there are no more occurrences of the [LARGE][large] codes.

## OTHER USES

You can record similar macros to convert Fine to Small, Small to Fine, Large to Vry Large, and so forth. Remember that the actual size of type that you will get in the printed document depends on the size of your base or your initial font. If you're using 12-point type as your initial font, Small gives you 10-point type and Fine gives you 8-point type. However, if your initial font is 14-point type, Small probably gives you 12-point and Fine probably gives you 10-point. This is one reason that it's nice to have a macro to change font sizes for you: If you don't like what you get when you test-print a document, you can quickly change to another size.

# AUTOMATIC ABBREVIATIONS

You saw in Chapter 1 that you can mark a block of text and assign it to an Alt-number key to use as a temporary macro that automatically inserts the text in a document. Temporary macros, however, are erased whenever you exit WordPerfect. This can be a nuisance when you have to type a long document containing complex names, words, and phrases that will not be complete until you have worked on it for several sessions. This macro, named **Alt-B**, lets you assign an abbreviation to the @ key (or any other key you choose, as long as it's not a character that you are using in the document) and later replace each @ with a complex name, address, or standard clause in a contract (up to 59 characters).

## BEFORE YOU BEGIN

Before you begin to record the macro:

- You should have a few @ characters on the screen, and the cursor should be before the first @.

## RECORDING THE MACRO

To record the macro, take the following steps:

1. Turn on the macro recorder by pressing Ctrl-F10 or choosing Macro from the Tools menu and then choosing Define. Press **Alt-B** as the definition of the macro.

2. Enter **replaces @ for abbreviations** as the macro description; then press ⏎.

3. Press Alt-F2 (Replace) and press ⏎ to replace without confirming.

4. Type @ as the character to replace and press F2.

5. Pause the macro so that you can enter the text you abbreviated as @. Press Ctrl-PgUp, type **p**, and press ⏎. When the macro executes, it will pause at this point so that you can enter the full text of your abbreviation. (The 'Replace with:' prompt can be ignored.)

6. Press F2 to begin the search and replace operation.

7. Press Ctrl-F10 again to stop recording the macro.

The final macro should resemble the one in Figure 6.20.

## USING THE MACRO

You can test the macro by pressing Alt-B and entering the word **test** to replace each @ in your document. When you actually use the macro, WordPerfect will pause and allow you to enter the full text that is to replace each @.

## OTHER USES

You can record other similar macros that use seldom-used characters, such as #, ^, &, and *, to replace other phrases in a document. Because you determine what the replacement text should be at

## TEXT ENTRY AND EDITING MACROS

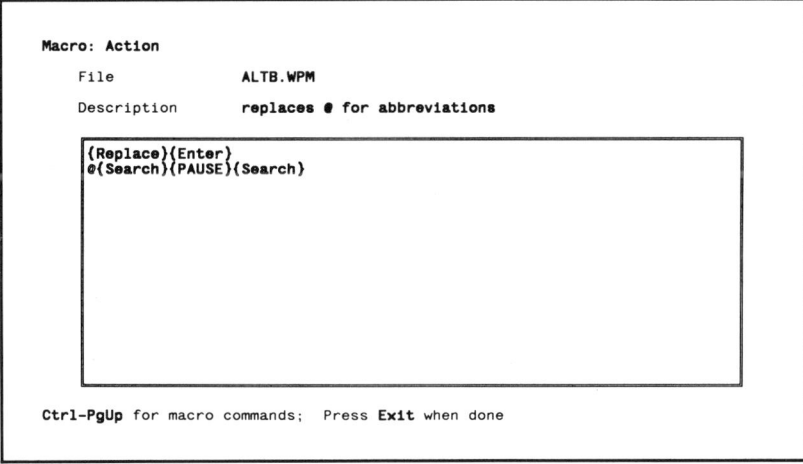

*Figure 6.20:* You can use a macro like this one to replace abbreviations in your text.

replacement time, you can record one of these macros and use it in many documents to replace the symbol with whatever you may need to specify. You can even have the macro prompt you for what you want to replace (see Appendix A for a discussion of using prompts in macros).

## *DELETING TO THE BEGINNING OF A PARAGRAPH*

■ An Alt-D macro on your MACROS keyboard deletes the line that the cursor is on.

This macro, named **bpp**, deletes text from the cursor's position backward to the beginning of a paragraph that has been indented with the Tab key.

### *BEFORE YOU BEGIN*

Before you begin to record the macro:

- You should have a paragraph of text, beginning with a tab, on the screen.
- The cursor should be somewhere within that paragraph.

## RECORDING THE MACRO

To record the macro, take the following steps:

1. Turn on the macro recorder by pressing Ctrl-F10 or choosing Macro from the Tools menu and then choosing Define. Enter **bpp** as the name of the macro.

2. Enter **deletes to beginning of the paragraph** as the macro description; then press ⏎.

3. Press Alt-F4 to turn on block marking.

4. Press Shift-F2 (Reverse Search).

5. Press Tab; then press F2 to start the search.

6. Press Backspace and type **y**.

7. Press Ctrl-F10 again to stop recording the macro.

The final macro should resemble the one in Figure 6.21.

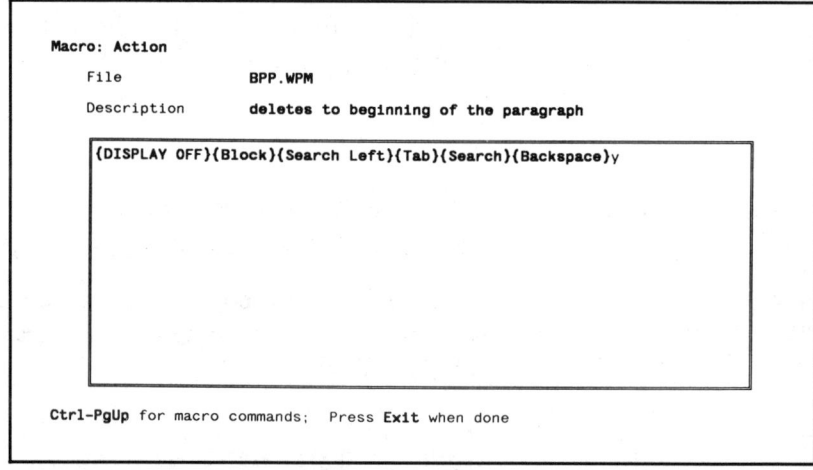

*Figure 6.21:* Macros like this one can delete to the beginning of a paragraph.

You can have WordPerfect search for special format codes by pressing Ctrl-V and then another Ctrl-key sequence, as follows. Press Ctrl-V at the 'Search' prompt; then press Ctrl-J to search for a [HRt] code, Ctrl-M for a [SRt], Ctrl-L for a [HPg], and Ctrl-K for a [SPg].

## USING THE MACRO

When you use the macro, the text from the cursor's position backward to the beginning of the paragraph will be deleted. Use F1 to restore the text if you change your mind about deleting it.

## *OTHER USES*

If you usually indicate a paragraph with an extra line of space instead of indenting paragraphs with the Tab key, edit the macro to search backward for a hard return code instead of a tab.

# *DELETING TO THE END OF A PARAGRAPH*

This macro, named **epp**, deletes to the end of the paragraph you are currently in.

## *BEFORE YOU BEGIN*

Before you begin to record the macro:

- You should have a paragraph of text on the screen (ending in a hard return), and the cursor should be located within it.

## *RECORDING THE MACRO*

To record the macro, take the following steps:

1. Turn on the macro recorder by pressing Ctrl-F10 or choosing Macro from the Tools menu and then choosing Define. Enter **epp** as the name of the macro.

2. Enter **deletes to the end of a paragraph** as the macro description; then press ↵.

3. Press Alt-F4 to turn on block marking.

4. Press F2 (Search).

5. Press ↵; then press F2 to start the search.

6. Press Backspace and type **y**.

7. Press Ctrl-F10 again to stop recording the macro.

The final macro should resemble the one in Figure 6.22.

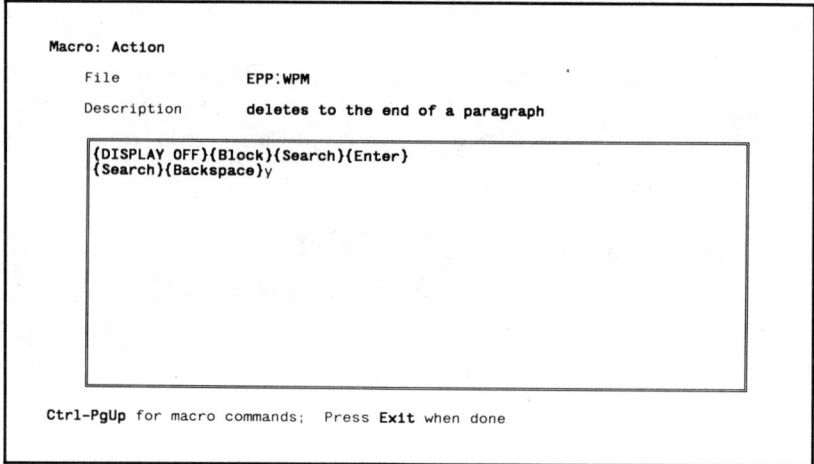

*Figure 6.22:* Similar to the **bpp** macro, the **epp** macro deletes text to the end of a paragraph.

## USING THE MACRO

When you use the macro, text that is between the cursor and the next hard return will be deleted.

## DELETING WORDS

Although pressing Ctrl-Backspace deletes the word the cursor is on, it can be hard to remember. In addition, those keys are not very close together. You can record an Alt macro like the following to delete by word instead of pressing Ctrl-Backspace. It may not save any keystrokes, but you may save yourself some frustration.

### BEFORE YOU BEGIN

Before you begin to record the macro:

- You should have a few words on the screen.
- The cursor should be somewhere within the words.

## RECORDING THE MACRO

To record the macro, take the following steps:

1. Turn on the macro recorder by pressing Ctrl-F10 or choosing Macro from the Tools menu and then choosing Define. Press **Alt-W** to define the macro.
2. Enter **deletes current word** as the macro description; then press ←┘.
3. Press Ctrl-← to move to the beginning of the word.
4. Press Alt-F4 to turn on block marking.
5. Press Ctrl-→ to highlight the word.
6. Press Del and type **y**.
7. Press Ctrl-F10 again to stop recording the macro.

The final macro should resemble the one in Figure 6.23.

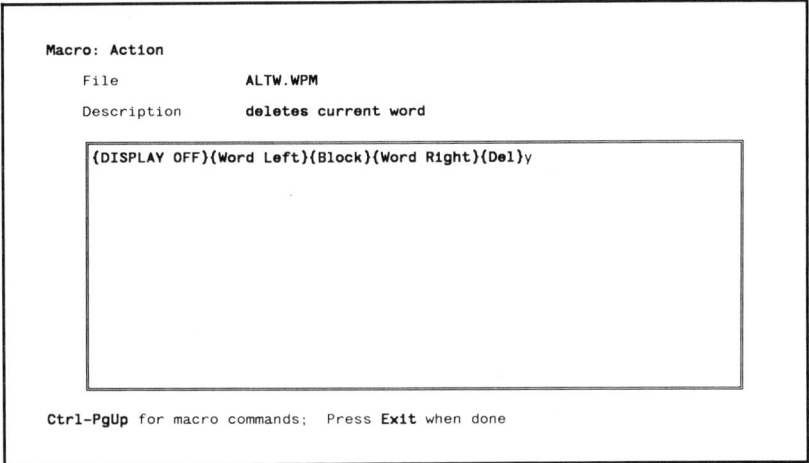

*Figure 6.23:* The **Alt-W** macro deletes the current word.

## USING THE MACRO

When you use the macro, WordPerfect will delete the word that the cursor is in. If it's between words or on the very first character of the word, it will delete the word to the left. To delete several words, press Esc, type the number of words (counted *backward* from the cursor's position) that you want to delete, and then press Alt-W.

## DELETING THE REST OF YOUR DOCUMENT

This macro, named **enddel**, will actually delete from the cursor's position to the end of the document; you don't have to mark large sections as blocks and delete them individually. So use it with care—and remember that you can get deleted text back by pressing F1 (Cancel) right away.

### BEFORE YOU BEGIN

Before you begin to record the macro:

- You should have a document on the screen. Although you'll delete a large portion of it, if you've saved it first you can always get it back.

### RECORDING THE MACRO

> Don't assign macros that delete large amounts of text to Alt keys; it's too easy to press Alt when you intend to press Shift. Give them names instead.

To record the macro, take the following steps:

1. Turn on the macro recorder by pressing Ctrl-F10 or choosing Macro from the Tools menu and then choosing Define. Enter **enddel** as the name of the macro.

2. Enter **deletes to the end of the document** as the macro description; then press ↵.

3. Press Alt-F4 to turn on blocking; then press Home Home ↓.

4. Press Backspace; then type **y**.

5. Press Ctrl-F10 again to stop recording the macro.

The final macro should resemble the one in Figure 6.24.

```
Macro: Action
    File             ENDDEL.WPM
    Description      deletes to the end of the document

    {DISPLAY OFF}{Block}{Home}{Home}{Down}{Backspace}y




    Ctrl-PgUp for macro commands;   Press Exit when done
```

*Figure 6.24:* This macro will delete text from the cursor's position to the end of the document.

## *USING THE MACRO*

When you use the macro, all the text from the cursor to the last character in the document will disappear. If there's a large amount of text, such as 30 or 40 pages, to be deleted, this will take several seconds.

To restore text that you've inadvertently deleted, press F1 (Cancel). If you've previously saved the document, you can just clear the screen and retrieve the saved version instead.

## *OPENING A NEW BLANK LINE*

This macro, named **Alt-O**, opens a blank line and returns the cursor to the end of the previous line. Normally, when you press ↵ to insert a blank line, the cursor moves to the beginning of the next line. However, you may want to keep on adding blank lines below the text you are typing.

WordStar has a command for this, but WordPerfect doesn't. If you're used to WordStar, you will appreciate this macro.

## RECORDING THE MACRO

To record the macro, take the following steps:

1. Turn on the macro recorder by pressing Ctrl-F10 or choosing Macro from the Tools menu and then choosing Define. Press **Alt-O** to define the macro.

2. Enter **opens a new blank line** as the macro description; then press ↵.

3. Press ↵; then press ↑ End.

4. Press Ctrl-F10 again to stop recording the macro.

The final macro should resemble the one in Figure 6.25.

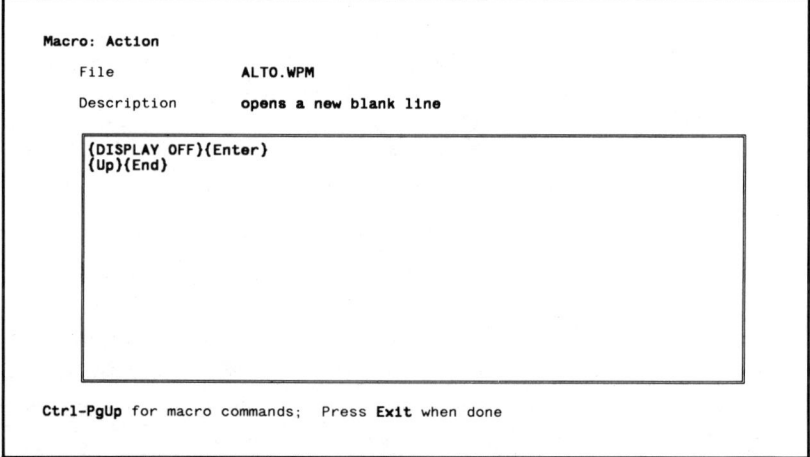

*Figure 6.25:* This **Alt-O** macro opens a new line and keeps the cursor in place.

## USING THE MACRO

When you use the macro, WordPerfect will insert a new blank line under the line you are typing, but the cursor, instead of moving to the beginning of the new line, will remain in place on the old one.

If you are used to using WordStar, you may want to rename this macro **Alt-N**.

# CUTTING AND PASTING BETWEEN WINDOWS

This macro, named **Alt-Q**, allows you to cut and paste between documents in your Doc 1 and Doc 2 windows with a minimum of keystrokes. If you need to cut blocks of text and store them in a second window, you can use this macro. It pauses to let you mark the text; then it pastes it into the Doc 2 window, moves to the end of the pasted block, inserts a hard return, and switches back to Doc 1, where you can browse for more text to cut.

## BEFORE YOU BEGIN

Before you begin to record the macro:

- You should have some text on the screen, and the cursor should be at the beginning of the text that is to be cut.

- The Doc 2 window should be empty, but it doesn't have to be open.

## RECORDING THE MACRO

To record the macro, take the following steps:

1. Turn on the macro recorder by pressing Ctrl-F10 or choosing Macro from the Tools menu and then choosing Define. Press **Alt-Q** to define the macro.

2. Enter **Cuts text to Doc 2 and returns to Doc 1** as the macro description; then press ↵.

3. Press Alt-F4 (Block) and insert a pause by pressing Ctrl-PgUp P ↵. When you use the macro, it will pause here so that you can mark the text you want to cut.

4. Press Ctrl-F4 and type **B** for Block. Type **C** for Copy, if you want this to be a copying macro, or type **M** for Move if you want it to cut text.

5. Press Shift-F3 (Switch) to go to the Doc 2 window.

6. Press ⏎ to paste the cut or copied text.
7. Press Home Home ↓ to move to the end of the newly pasted text in the Doc 2 window.
8. Press ⏎ to insert a blank line.
9. Press Shift-F3 (Switch) to go back to the Doc 1 window.
10. Press Ctrl-F10 to stop recording the macro.

The final macro should resemble the one in Figure 6.26.

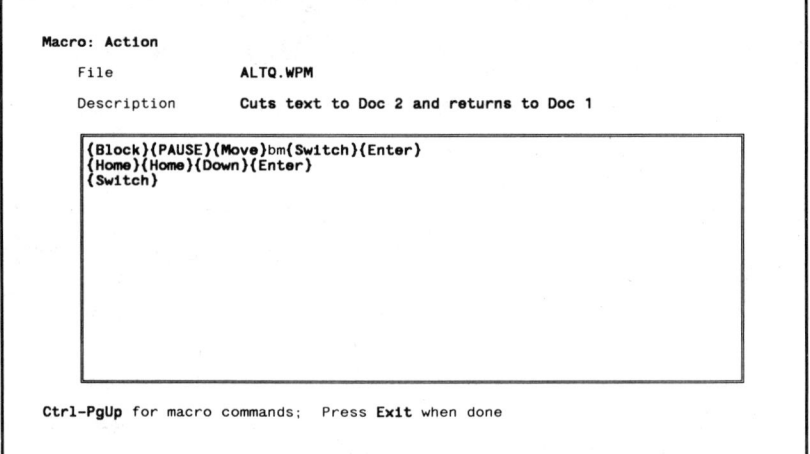

*Figure 6.26:* This handy macro cuts (or copies) text from Doc 1 to Doc 2.

## USING THE MACRO

When you use the macro, you can cut or copy blocks of text quickly into Doc 2 and then return to where you were in Doc 1.

## OTHER USES

You'll find these same keystrokes useful in any macro that creates a list in the Doc 2 window. For example, I have several macros that have been modified to search for all lines beginning with the word Figure, in boldface, and copy them to Doc 2. In this way I create an instant figure list so that I don't have to bother compiling one.

If you are rearranging text to edit, this macro is also useful for cutting out all the paragraphs that you want to relocate and holding them temporarily in the Doc 2 window. For the quickest way to duplicate the macro so that you can edit it to cut (if you recorded it to copy) or copy (if you recorded it to cut), use List Files to copy **Alt-Q** to another name in the same macro directory. (See Chapter 2 if you need help on this.) You can then edit it under a new name to change it to cut or copy, as described in step 4 above.

## INSERTING A DOCUMENT COMMENT

This macro, named **Alt-D,** inserts a document comment at the cursor's position. If you frequently use comments in your documents, you'll find that this macro saves you many keystrokes.

### RECORDING THE MACRO

To record the macro, take the following steps:

1. Turn on the macro recorder by pressing Ctrl-F10 or choosing Macro from the Tools menu and then choosing Define. Press **Alt-D** to define the macro.

2. Enter **inserts document comment** as the macro description; then press ↵.

3. Press Ctrl-F5 (Text In/Out) and type **C** for Comment.

4. Type **C** for Create.

5. Press Ctrl-F10 again to stop recording the macro. Press F7 to exit.

The final macro should resemble the one in Figure 6.27.

### USING THE MACRO

When you use the macro, WordPerfect will pause for you to type the text of the comment and press F7 (Exit). Don't worry if the comment appears to cut a sentence in two; the sentence will be printed

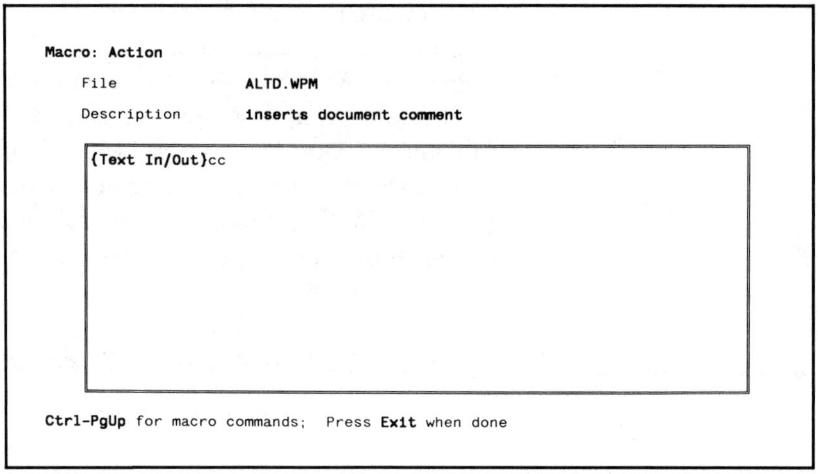

```
Macro: Action
    File           ALTD.WPM
    Description    inserts document comment

    {Text In/Out}cc




Ctrl-PgUp for macro commands;  Press Exit when done
```

*Figure 6.27:* The **Alt-D** macro inserts a document comment at the cursor's position.

correctly when you print the document. Document comments in WordPerfect are never printed in documents.

## TRANSPOSING WORDS

This macro, named **Alt-Y**, transposes the word that the cursor is on with the word to its left. It's useful when you're editing text and see that *to move* should really be *move to*, for example. A surprisingly large number of keystrokes is required for such a simple operation.

### BEFORE YOU BEGIN

Before you begin to record the macro:

- You should have a few words on the screen.
- The cursor should be somewhere inside a word that you want to switch places with the word on its left, not on the first character of the word.

## *RECORDING THE MACRO*

To record the macro, take the following steps:

1. Turn on the macro recorder by pressing Ctrl-F10 or choosing Macro from the Tools menu and then choosing Define. Press **Alt-Y** to define the macro.

2. Enter **transposes word to left** as the macro description; then press ⏎.

3. Press Ctrl-← to move to the beginning of the word the cursor is on; then press Alt-F4 to turn on blocking.

4. Press Ctrl-→ to highlight the whole word.

5. Press Ctrl-F4 (Move) and type **B M**.

6. Press Ctrl-← to move to the word to the left; then press ⏎.

7. Press Ctrl-→ twice to move to the right of the two words you have just moved, so that you will be able to continue typing or editing.

8. Press Ctrl-F10 again to stop recording the macro.

The final macro should resemble the one in Figure 6.28.

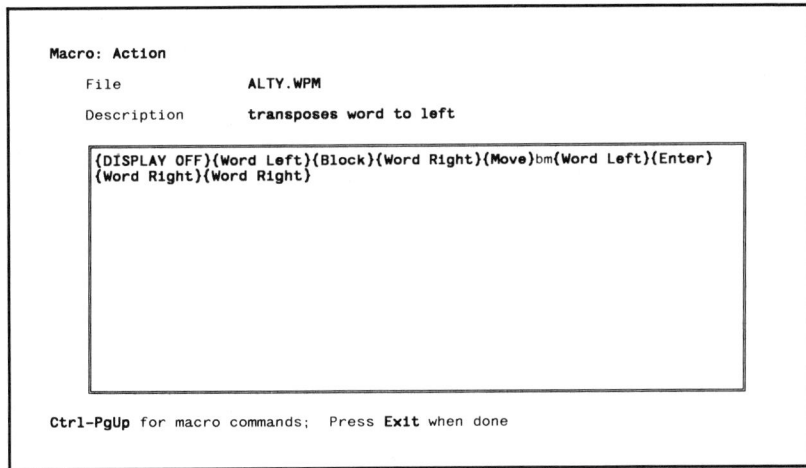

*Figure 6.28:* This **Alt-Y** macro transposes the current word with the word to its left.

## USING THE MACRO

When you use the macro, WordPerfect will switch the word the cursor is on with the word to its left. If the word you are moving is at the end of a sentence, WordPerfect will move the punctuation with it, and you'll have to delete the punctuation. The space following the word moves with it, so if there is no space following the word, you will need to edit any run-together words.

## OTHER USES

If you prefer to switch in the opposite direction—by transposing the word to the cursor's right—you can edit this macro or record another in which you press Word Right (Ctrl-→) in step 3 above instead of Word Left (Ctrl-←). The rest of the keystrokes are the same.

# TRANSPOSING TWO CHARACTERS

This macro, named **tr**, transposes two characters. You will probably want to record it as an Alt macro if you plan to use it often. A slightly different version of it, named Alt-T, can be found on the soft MACROS keyboard supplied with WordPerfect; to use it, press Shift-F1 (Setup), type **K**, and select the MACROS keyboard. However, if you want to see the steps that are involved (at a slightly less sophisticated level) in creating such a macro, here they are.

## BEFORE YOU BEGIN

Before you begin to record the macro:

- You should have several characters on the screen, and the cursor should be on one of them.

## RECORDING THE MACRO

To record the macro, take the following steps:

1. Turn on the macro recorder by pressing Ctrl-F10 or choosing Macro from the Tools menu and then choosing Define. Enter **tr** as the name of the macro.

2. Enter **transposes two characters** as the macro description; then press ↵.

3. Press Alt-F4 (Block); then press → to highlight the character the cursor is on.

4. Press Ctrl-F4 (Move) and type **B M** to move the block.

5. Press ← to move one character to the left.

6. Press ↵.

7. Press → twice to move over the transposed characters.

8. Press Ctrl-F10 again to stop recording the macro.

The final macro should resemble the one in Figure 6.29.

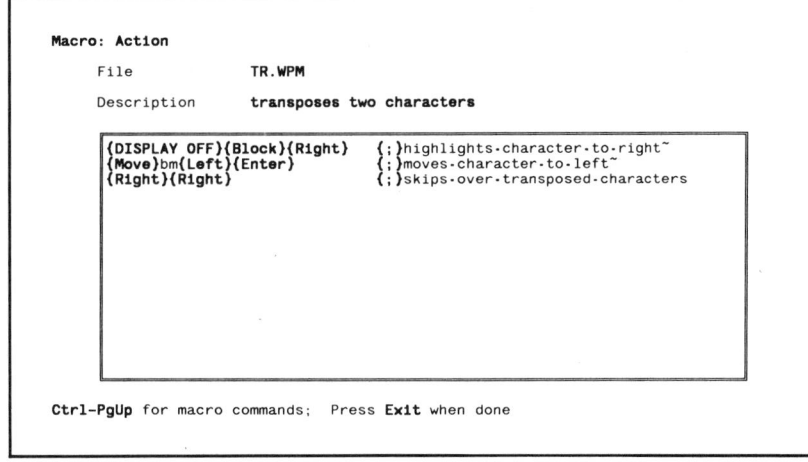

*Figure 6.29:* A slightly different version of this **tr** macro is supplied on your MACROS keyboard.

> You can't edit macros that are on the MACROS keyboard (or other soft keyboards) by pressing Ctrl-F10 (Macro) and choosing the Edit option. Instead, press Shift-F1 (Setup) and choose to edit the keyboard the macro is on. Then highlight the macro and choose to edit it. You'll be placed in the normal macro editing screen.

## USING THE MACRO

When you use the **tr** macro, WordPerfect transposes the character that the cursor is on with the character to its left. A typo like *hte* becomes *the*, for example, if you've placed the cursor on the *t* when you execute the macro. The cursor then moves to the next character.

The Alt-T macro supplied by WordPerfect uses an IF-THEN-ELSE construction to check whether you're in the editing screen and protect against deleting an invisible character. The simpler version that you've just recorded will transpose an invisible character, such as a [Tab] or other format code, if it's one of the two characters you're transposing.

## TRANSPOSING SENTENCES

This macro, named **trsent**, transposes the current sentence with the sentence just preceding it.

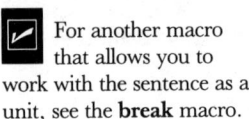 For another macro that allows you to work with the sentence as a unit, see the **break** macro.

### BEFORE YOU BEGIN

Before you begin to record the macro:

- You should have several sentences on the screen, and the cursor should be in any of them except the last.

### RECORDING THE MACRO

To record the macro, take the following steps:

1. Turn on the macro recorder by pressing Ctrl-F10 or choosing Macro from the Tools menu and then choosing Define. Enter **trsent** as the name of the macro.

2. Enter **transposes sentences** as the macro description; then press ←.

3. With the cursor located within a sentence, press Ctrl-F4 (Move) and type **S M**.

4. Press F2 (Search) and type a period.

5. Press F2 to start the search. WordPerfect will locate the end of the next sentence to the right, as long as it ends in a period.

6. Type a space (or two spaces); then press Enter.

7. Press Ctrl-F10 again to stop recording the macro.

The final macro should resemble the one in Figure 6.30.

```
┌─────────────────────────────────────────────────────────────┐
│  Macro: Action                                              │
│      File              TRSENT.WPM                           │
│      Description       transposes sentences                 │
│  ┌───────────────────────────────────────────────────────┐  │
│  │ {DISPLAY OFF}{Move}sm{Search}.{Search}.{Enter}        │  │
│  │                                                       │  │
│  │                                                       │  │
│  │                                                       │  │
│  │                                                       │  │
│  │                                                       │  │
│  └───────────────────────────────────────────────────────┘  │
│  Ctrl-PgUp for macro commands;   Press Exit when done       │
└─────────────────────────────────────────────────────────────┘
```

*Figure 6.30:* This **trsent** macro will transpose entire sentences.

### USING THE MACRO

When you use the macro, WordPerfect will highlight the sentence the cursor is in and cut it. It will then search for the next occurrence of a period and paste the cut sentence there. You decide when you record the macro whether you want one space or two between sentences. Two spaces is traditional for typing, but if you're using proportional fonts (typefaces in which each character occupies a different amount of space), or preparing material for a typeset look, you may want to use only one space between sentences.

### OTHER USES

You can easily edit this macro so that it will transpose a paragraph or even a page by selecting one of the other options on the Move menu in step 3 above.

## MOVING A SENTENCE (OR PARAGRAPH OR PAGE)

This macro, named **sm**, highlights and cuts a sentence so that you can move it to any other position in the document. (You'll probably want to assign it to an Alt key, such as Alt-M, but there's been an Alt-M macro in the book already.) WordPerfect considers a sentence to be the block of text from the first capitalized letter up to from one to three spaces after a period, question mark, or exclamation point.

Instead of recording the macro to move a sentence, you can record it so that it will move a paragraph or a page, or you can record one macro for each purpose. In WordPerfect, a paragraph is a block that extends from one hard return up to and including the next hard return. When it selects a paragraph, it also selects the final hard return. A page is a block of text from one hard page break [HPg] or soft page break [SPg] to the next. The final page break code is also included when WordPerfect selects a page.

## *BEFORE YOU BEGIN*

Before you begin to record the macro:

- You should have a document on the screen. If you're recording the macro to move a paragraph or page, the screen should contain a paragraph or page of text.

## *RECORDING THE MACRO*

To record the macro, take the following steps:

1. Turn on the macro recorder by pressing Ctrl-F10 or choosing Macro from the Tools menu and then choosing Define. Type **sm** to define the macro.

2. Enter **moves sentence** as the macro description; then press ↵.

3. Press Ctrl-F4 (Move) and type **S M** to move the sentence. (Type **P M** to move a paragraph or **A M** to move a page.)

4. Press Ctrl-F10 again to stop recording the macro.

The final macro should resemble the one in Figure 6.31.

```
Macro: Action
        File            SM.WPM
        Description     moves sentence
    ┌─────────────────────────────────────────────────┐
    │ {DISPLAY OFF}{Move}sm                           │
    │                                                 │
    │                                                 │
    │                                                 │
    │                                                 │
    │                                                 │
    └─────────────────────────────────────────────────┘
Ctrl-PgUp for macro commands;  Press Exit when done
```

*Figure 6.31:* This simple **sm** macro can move a sentence, paragraph, or page for you.

## USING THE MACRO

When you use the macro, WordPerfect highlights and cuts the current sentence. Move the cursor to where you want the sentence to appear; then press ⏎.

When you cut a sentence (or paragraph or page) by using the Move key (Ctrl-F4), the text goes into a buffer that is different from the one used when you delete text. This means that you can cut and paste a block of text by deleting it with the Del or Backspace keys or pressing Ctrl-End and then restoring it with the Cancel key. When you're at the location where you want the sentence, press F1, type **R**, and press ⏎.

If you're moving large sections of text—entire pages, for instance—you may find it handy to be able to move two sections at once. You do this by deleting one page and moving another with this macro. That way you can get them both back in two separate locations without having to move one page and then go back and move the second one.

> You can retrieve the last text you moved (with Ctrl-F4) by pressing Shift-F10 (Retrieve) and pressing ⏎.

> Version 5.1 has a shortcut for Block Move (Ctrl-Del) and Block Copy (Ctrl-Ins) if you have an enhanced keyboard. If you don't, Chapter 4 tells you how you can map these shortcuts to your keyboard.

## OTHER USES

As I said earlier, you can modify this macro to move a paragraph or page or record separate macros that move paragraphs or pages. Just select those options from the Move menu in step 3 above.

You can also use the macro to cut text. Once it's in the Move buffer (when you see the 'Move cursor; press Enter to retrieve' prompt), just press F1 (Cancel). You can't use the Undelete feature (F1) to restore text you delete in this way, but you can get it back by pressing Shift-F10 (Retrieve) and then pressing ⏎.

## MARKING YOUR PLACE

This macro, named **mark1**, marks your place so that you can return to it later. If you work with long documents, you'll appreciate a macro like this because it lets you move around quickly without losing your place. (You'll probably want to record it as an Alt-macro. Use Alt-M, for Mark, if you haven't already used that combination.)

There is a fine macro named **Alt-M** on the MACROS keyboard that inserts a <<<MARK>>> code into your document and an even finer **Alt-F** macro that finds it (take a look at **Alt-F**; you'll see what I mean). But if you don't want to use the MACROS keyboard, here is a common, garden-variety macro that does the same thing, with a little variation.

You'll actually need to record two macros: one that marks your place, and one that searches to find your place markers.

> You can even put a marker in the middle of a word—like th@@@is—and WordPerfect will locate it. The Search feature won't search for an exact match unless you tell it to by using spaces or punctuation.

### BEFORE YOU BEGIN

Before you begin to record the macro:

- You should have a document on the screen.

### RECORDING THE MACRO

To record the macro that inserts the place marker:

1. Turn on the macro recorder by pressing Ctrl-F10 or choosing Macro from the Tools menu and then choosing Define. Enter **mark1** as the name of the macro.

*TEXT ENTRY AND EDITING MACROS* **195**

2. Enter **marks place** as the macro description; then press ↵.

3. Since it's unlikely that you will ever type a word that has @@@ in it, you can use that as your marker. Type @@@.

4. Press Ctrl-F10 again to stop recording the macro.

Then, to record the forward search macro:

1. Turn on the macro recorder by pressing Ctrl-F10 or choosing Macro from the Tools menu and then choosing Define. Enter **Alt-F** to define the macro.

2. Enter **searches for marker** as the macro description; then press ↵.

3. Press Home-F2 (Extended Search) and type @@@. (With an extended search, WordPerfect will search headers, footers, notes, and graphics captions, as well as text.)

4. Press F2 again to begin the search.

5. Press Ctrl-F10 again to stop recording the macro.

The final macro should resemble the one in Figure 6.32.

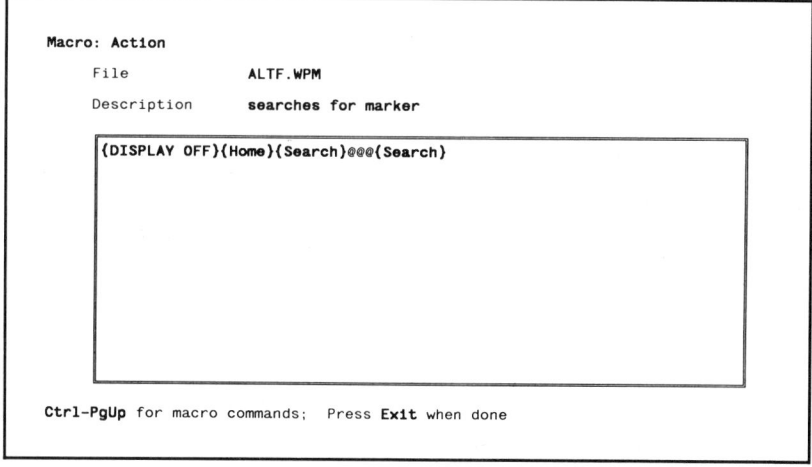

*Figure 6.32:* This **Alt-F** macro locates the marker you've inserted with the **mark1** macro.

### USING THE MACRO

Use the **mark1** macro to mark the place in your document to which you want to return for rewriting. If you mark more than one place, you can immediately type **2** after you execute the **mark1** macro the second time, **3** after the third time, and so forth, so that you can keep track of your markers. (They'll look like @@@1, @@@2, @@@3, and so forth.)

To search for a marker, press Home Home Home ↑ before you execute Alt-F, to go to the beginning of the document before any codes. WordPerfect will go to the beginning of the document and begin the search. Repeat the **Alt-F** macro until you locate the marker you're searching for.

## COPYING A LINE

This macro, named **copyl**, copies the line that the cursor is on. You can then move to where you want the copy to appear and press ↵ to retrieve it.

### BEFORE YOU BEGIN

Before you begin to record the macro:

- You should have some lines of text on the screen.

### RECORDING THE MACRO

To record the macro, take the following steps:

1. Turn on the macro recorder by pressing Ctrl-F10 or choosing Macro from the Tools menu and then choosing Define. Enter **copyl** as the name of the macro.

2. Enter **copies current line** as the macro description; then press ↵.

3. Press Home three times; then press ←. This moves the cursor to the beginning of the line, before any codes, such as a [Tab] or an [Indent], that may be there.

4. Press Alt-F4 (Block); then press End to highlight the entire line.

5. Press Ctrl-F4 (Move) and type **B C** to copy the block.

6. Press Ctrl-F10 to stop recording the macro.

The final macro should resemble the one in Figure 6.33.

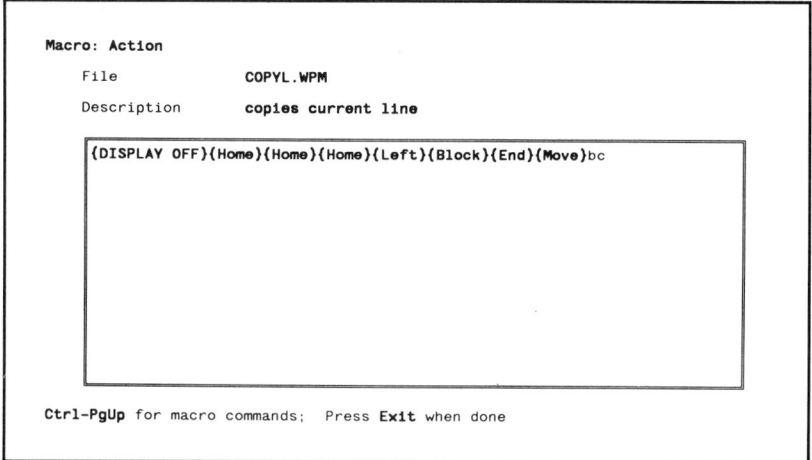

*Figure 6.33:* This **copyl** macro copies the current line.

### *USING THE MACRO*

When you use the macro, WordPerfect copies the line that the cursor is on. It will also copy any formatting codes that precede the line, so you can use it to copy the first line of a paragraph or a centered line, and the copied line will retain the formatting.

## *COPYING TEXT*

This macro, named **cc**, copies whatever text you highlight when the macro pauses.

### *BEFORE YOU BEGIN*

Before you begin to record the macro:

- You should have some text on the screen.

## RECORDING THE MACRO

To record the macro, take the following steps:

1. Turn on the macro recorder by pressing Ctrl-F10 or choosing Macro from the Tools menu and then choosing Define. Enter **cc** to define the macro.
2. Enter **copies selected text** as the macro description; then press ↵.
3. Press Alt-F4 (Block); then insert a pause by pressing Ctrl-PgUp and typing **P**. So that the macro will have something to work on, highlight a couple of lines of text and then press ↵.
4. Press Ctrl-F4 (Move) and type **B C** to copy the block.
5. Press Ctrl-F10 again to stop recording the macro.

The final macro should resemble the one in Figure 6.34.

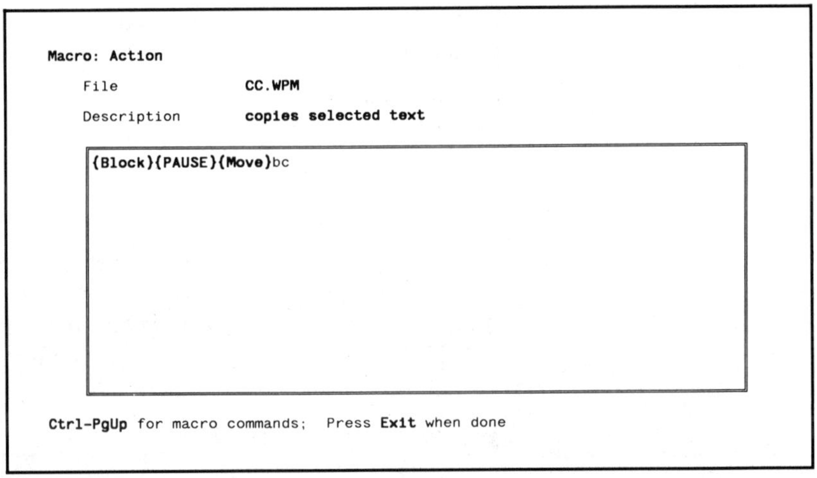

```
Macro: Action
    File           CC.WPM
    Description    copies selected text

    {Block}{PAUSE}{Move}bc




Ctrl-PgUp for macro commands;  Press Exit when done
```

*Figure 6.34:* This **cc** macro copies whatever text you have selected.

## USING THE MACRO

When you use the macro, it will pause for you to highlight text. To do so, you can use any of WordPerfect's cursor-movement techniques. For example, you can drag across text with the mouse, or press End once to highlight to the end of a line, ⏎ once to highlight the paragraph, or ⏎ several times to highlight succeeding paragraphs. Pressing Home Home ↓ will highlight to the end of the document; pressing Home Home ↑ will highlight to its beginning.

After you've highlighted the text you want to copy, press ⏎. Then move the cursor to where you want the copied text to appear and press ⏎ again.

## OTHER USES

You can edit the macro to cut instead of copy by changing the **C** in step 4 above to **M**.

## CREATING SPECIAL DASHES

This macro, called **em**, creates an em dash, so named because it usually occupies about as much space as the width of the letter *m* in a font. You may know it as a long dash or nonbreaking dash; in any case, it looks like this: —.

There's also an en dash. It's used mostly to link inclusive numbers in a series, as in the dates 1949–50 or page numbers 248–61. Neither of these dashes is the hyphen (-), but in word processing you often see them replaced by the hyphen, especially if the printer can't print them. They're available in WordPerfect, however, if you use them from character set 4.

> Test-print a page that contains dashes produced by these macros to see whether your printer can print them. Some dot-matrix printers can't, but most laser printers can.

> WordPerfect 5.1 will print any character in any of the character sets if your printer can print graphics, even if the character is not in the font you're using.

### RECORDING THE MACRO

To record the **em** macro, take the following steps:

1. Turn on the macro recorder by pressing Ctrl-F10 or choosing Macro from the Tools menu and then choosing Define. Enter **em** as the name of the macro.

2. Enter **creates em dash** as the macro description; then press ⏎.

3. Press Ctrl-2.

4. Type **4,33**.

5. Press Ctrl-F10 again to stop recording the macro.

For a macro that creates an en dash, substitute **4,34** in step 4 above.

### USING THE MACRO

When you use the macro, WordPerfect creates an em (or en) dash at the position of the cursor, so you can easily type these special dashes as you work.

## USING SMART QUOTES

This macro, named **oq** (for open quote), creates double opening quotation marks ("). Quotes of this type are also often called typesetter's quotes, or "smart" quotes. If you look closely, you'll see that the opening quotes in this book are slightly different from the closing quotes. Your printer probably prints quotation marks that look exactly alike; most printers do unless you tell them explicitly which quote characters to use. If you are using WordPerfect to prepare material for publication, you will want to use typesetter's quotes.

### RECORDING THE MACRO

To record the macro, take the following steps:

1. Turn on the macro recorder by pressing Ctrl-F10 or choosing Macro from the Tools menu and then choosing Define. Enter **oq** as the name of the macro.

2. Enter **creates open quote** as the macro description; then press ↵.

3. Press Ctrl-2.

4. Type **4,30**.

5. Press Ctrl-F10 again to stop recording the macro.

To record the **cq** macro that creates the closing quotes, substitute **4,31** in step 4 above.

## *USING THE MACRO*

When you use the **oq** macro, WordPerfect inserts an open quote ("). When you reach the end of the quoted material, use the **cq** macro. You'll get smart quotes like the ones in this book instead of the straight up-and-down ones that your printer normally produces.

# *SUMMARY*

In this chapter, you've seen macros that manipulate windows, move the cursor through your document, sort different kinds of lists, capitalize and lowercase words, and delete, copy, or move text. You've also seen macros that will allow you to perform some specialized tasks like inserting document comments or creating special characters. What all of these macros have in common is that they're used either as you type new text or edit existing text.

Chapter 7 will allow you to expand your macro library by providing formatting macros. You'll find macros that create headers and footers, convert text to columns, and set up standard document formats such as memos and business letters. Like the macros in this chapter, you probably won't find all of them worth recording; just choose the ones that are most useful for the kinds of work you do. If you want to use the macros but don't want to record them, you can send for a disk of all the macros in this book, prerecorded for you. See the back of the book for details.

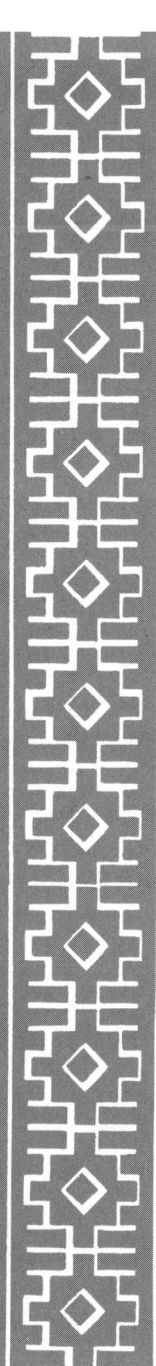

# *Macros for Formatting Text*

CHAPTER

7

# CHAPTER 7

The macros in this chapter all have one thing in common: They speed up the tedious process of formatting text. Once you get accustomed to using macros, you'll probably find that it's faster just to type out your text and then go back and use macros to carry out the formatting for you. Here you'll find macros ranging from simple ones that set a tab at your cursor's position to macros that automatically format and fill out forms for you, pausing for you to insert the information needed on each line.

Some of the macros in this chapter use Macro Command Language. Even without having any programming background, you'll find that some of the macro language commands are very easy to use and will produce quite sophisticated results in your macros. In various macros in this chapter, you'll see how to use the {PROMPT} command to produce onscreen prompts, which can be useful in macros that you create both for yourself and for others to use. The **memo** macro, which sets up an automated memo system for you, is an example of using prompts.

Another relatively easy-to-use macro command is {TEXT}, which you will see in the **lttr** macro. It also creates onscreen prompts, but in a slightly different way from the {PROMPT} command.

While the macros you'll create in this chapter are self-explanatory, you may want more details about how to use Macro Command Language. If so, see Appendix A.

## *CLEARING TAB SETTINGS*

This macro, named **clear**, clears all tab settings at the current cursor position. It is useful when you need to reset tabs—when defining math columns, for example, or when setting up a table of data.

## RECORDING THE MACRO

1. Turn on the macro recorder by pressing Ctrl-F10 or choosing Macro from the Tools menu and then choosing Define. Enter **clear** as the name of the macro. Enter **Clears all tabs** as the macro description; then press ⏎.
2. Press Shift-F8 and type **L**; then type **T**.
3. Press Home Home ← to move to the beginning of the line.
4. Press Ctrl-End to delete the tabs.
5. Press Ctrl-F10 to stop recording the macro.

The final macro should resemble the one in Figure 7.1.

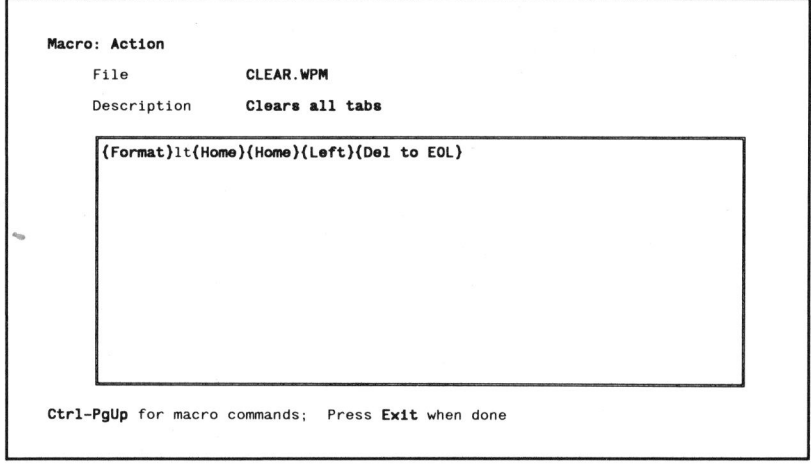

*Figure 7.1:* This macro deletes all tab stops so that you can set new ones.

## USING THE MACRO

When you use the macro you've just recorded, all the tab stops at the current cursor position will be deleted. Pressing Home Home ← positions the cursor at the left edge of the paper, not the left margin, so that all tab stops are deleted, not just the ones normally visible on the screen. You can then set new tabs.

## OTHER USES

You may want to include **clear** in a macro for establishing a math column definition, as the first math column begins at the first tab setting WordPerfect locates. You may also want to include it in a macro that establishes your own standard table format.

## SETTING A TAB STOP AT THE CURSOR'S POSITION

This macro, named **tab**, sets a tab at the location of the cursor. If you are used to setting tabs on a typewriter by first moving to the spot where you want the tab, you will find **tab** handy. It also lets you see exactly where the tab will appear, which is useful if you are setting up columns of figures.

In version 5.1, the tabs you set with these macros will be relative tabs—that is, they remain in place relative to the left margin so that even when you change the left margin, a tab set as +1 remains one inch from the left margin. In version 5.0, tabs are set at an absolute distance from the left margin. An absolute tab will remain in the same position even when you change margin settings; the tab ruler shows it as a distance from the left edge of the page. To change the type of tab from relative to absolute in version 5.1, select Type from the tab ruler menu; then choose Absolute.

### BEFORE YOU BEGIN

Before you begin to record this macro:

- The cursor should be located at the position where you want to set the tab.

### RECORDING THE MACRO

1. Turn on the macro recorder by pressing Ctrl-F10 or choosing Macro from the Tools menu and then choosing Define. Enter **tab** as the name of the macro.

2. Enter **sets tab at cursor position** as the macro description; then press ←.
3. Press Shift-F8 (Format) and type **L T L**. The last *L* sets a left-justified tab.
4. Press F7 twice to exit.
5. Press Ctrl-F10 to stop recording the macro.

When you have finished, your screen should resemble Figure 7.2.

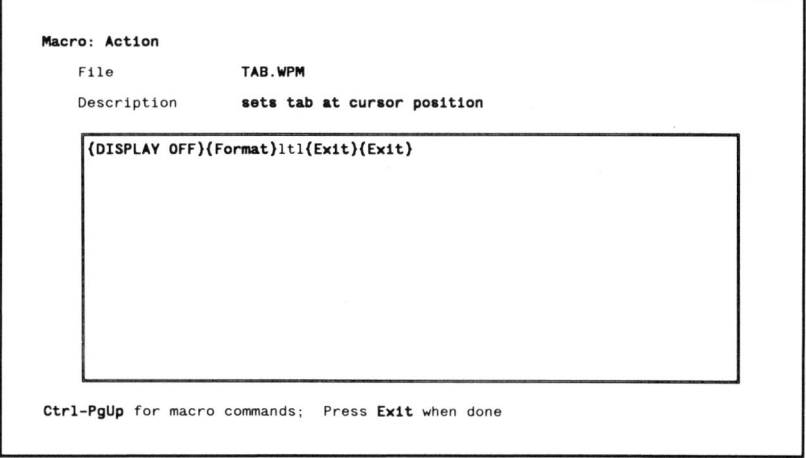

*Figure 7.2:* This macro lets you set tabs as if you were using a typewriter.

## RESTORING TAB SETTINGS

If you've reset tabs for math columns, this macro is especially handy for restoring the tabs for main text.

This macro, named **oldtab**, restores the tab settings to the ones you used previously. If you have set up tabs in a document and then switched temporarily to different ones—say, for a table—this macro will return you to the ones you switched from.

### BEFORE YOU BEGIN

Before you begin to record this macro:

- You must have a document on your screen with two different tab settings in it (two [Tab Set] codes).

- The cursor must be positioned after the last [Tab Set] code.

## *RECORDING THE MACRO*

As this sequence is slightly complex, you may want to record it with the Reveal Codes window open so that you can see exactly what is going on.

1. Turn on the macro recorder by pressing Ctrl-F10 or choosing Macro from the Tools menu and then choosing Define. Enter **oldtab** as the name of the macro.

2. Enter **reset tabs to previous settings** as the macro description; then press ←⎯.

3. Type ## as a place marker; then press Shift-F2 (Reverse Search).

4. To generate the [Tab Set] code to search for, press Shift-F8 (Format) and type **1 7**. Press F2 to begin the search.

5. WordPerfect locates the [Tab Set] code that was used when you changed tab settings. The code before this one is the one you want to copy, so press Shift-F2 and F2 again to search in reverse for the previous [Tab Set] code.

6. When the program locates the code, press Alt-F4 to turn on blocking. Press ← twice to move over the [Tab Set] and [Block] codes.

7. You can now copy the highlighted [Tab Set] Code. Press Ctrl-F4 (Move) and type **1 2** to copy the block.

8. Press F2 (Search) and type ## to search for your place marker. Then press F2 again to execute the search.

9. When WordPerfect locates the ##, press Backspace twice to delete it. Then press ←⎯ to insert the copied [Tab Set] code.

10. As a finishing touch, press → to move the cursor over the code you just copied so that you will be able to start typing text in the original format immediately.

11. Turn off the macro recorder by pressing Ctrl-F10 or choosing Macro from the Tools menu and then choosing Define.

When you have finished, your screen should resemble Figure 7.3.

### USING THE MACRO

When you use the macro you've just recorded, WordPerfect marks the current cursor position. It locates the last [Tab Set] code and then finds the one before that. It then copies that [Tab Set] code, searches for your marker, and pastes it there.

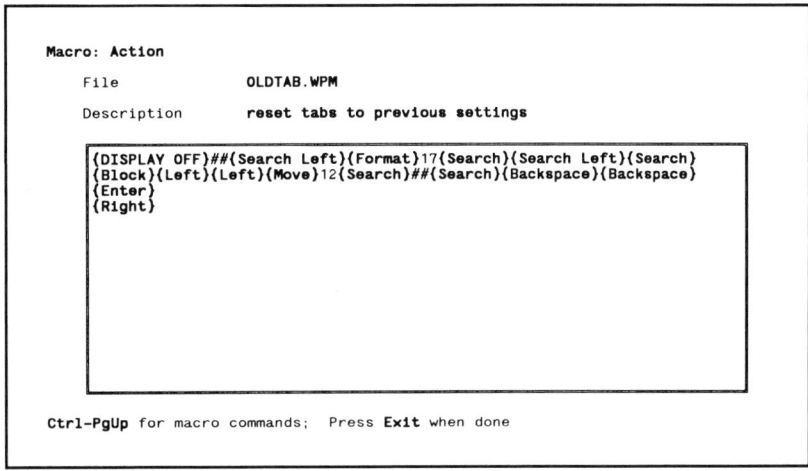

*Figure 7.3:* This macro searches backward for the [Tab Set] code you used before you reset tabs for a table, so you can use it to return to regular text.

## INSERTING THE TIME

This macro, named **time**, inserts the current time into the document you are working on. It is useful because WordPerfect does not normally insert the time when it inserts the date unless you change the date format.

### RECORDING THE MACRO

1. Turn on the macro recorder by pressing Ctrl-F10 or choosing Macro from the Tools menu and then choosing Define. Enter **time** as the name of the macro.

2. Enter **Inserts current time** as the macro description; then press ←.

3. Press Shift-F5 (Date/Outline). Type **F** to change the format to insert the time.

4. Type **8:9 0** and press F7 (Exit). This formats the time in 12-hour format with *am* or *pm* added at the end.

5. Type **T** to insert the time as Text.

6. Press Shift-F5 and type **F 3 1,4** to reset the date to its normal format (as in "February 16, 1991") so that the next time you want to insert the date in this document, WordPerfect will insert the date and not the time.

7. Press F7 twice to return to your document without inserting the date.

8. Press Ctrl-F10 to stop recording the macro.

When you have finished, your screen should resemble Figure 7.4.

### USING THE MACRO

When you use the macro you've just recorded, the current time in the format "10:05 am" will be entered in your text. It is entered as text so that it effectively time-stamps the document. If you entered it as a function (by typing **F** instead of **I** in step 5), the time would change each time you retrieved or printed the document.

### OTHER USES

The macro can be included in header or footer macros to time-stamp documents. You can also use it as a quick way to check the time as you work. Execute the macro; then press Backspace to erase the time.

# MACROS FOR FORMATTING TEXT 211

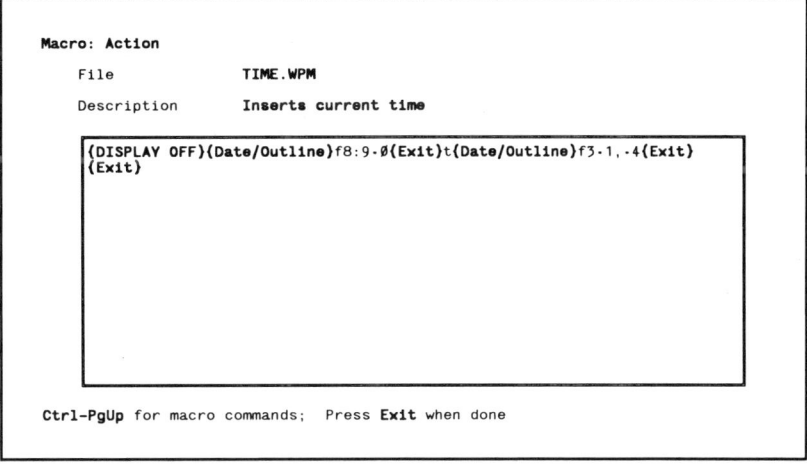

*Figure 7.4:* This macro, named **time**, time-stamps your document.

## INSERTING THE DATE AND TIME

This macro, named **DT**, inserts both the date and time. Instead of using the 12-hour format, it uses the 24-hour format and inserts the day of the week so that dates appear as in "Mon, 26 Dec 88, 23:45." If you are working on scientific documents or government contracts, you may prefer this format to the conventional date format that WordPerfect normally uses.

### RECORDING THE MACRO

1. Turn on the macro recorder by pressing Ctrl-F10 or choosing Macro from the Tools menu and then choosing Define. Enter **DT** as the name of the macro.

2. Enter **Inserts 24-hour time and date** as the macro description; then press ⏎.

3. Press Shift-F5 (Date/Outline) and type **F** to change the format.

4. Type %**6,** %**1** %**3 5, 7:9**. This format results in dates and times such as "Tue, 06 Dec 88, 23:45." The % tells Word-Perfect to use a three-letter abbreviation for the day of the week and to enter leading zeros in numerals under 10.

5. Press F7; then type **T** to insert the date and time as text.

6. To return to the default format, press Shift-F5, type **F**, and enter **3 1, 4**. Then press F7 twice to return to your document.

7. Press Ctrl-F10 to stop recording the macro.

When you have finished, your screen should resemble Figure 7.5.

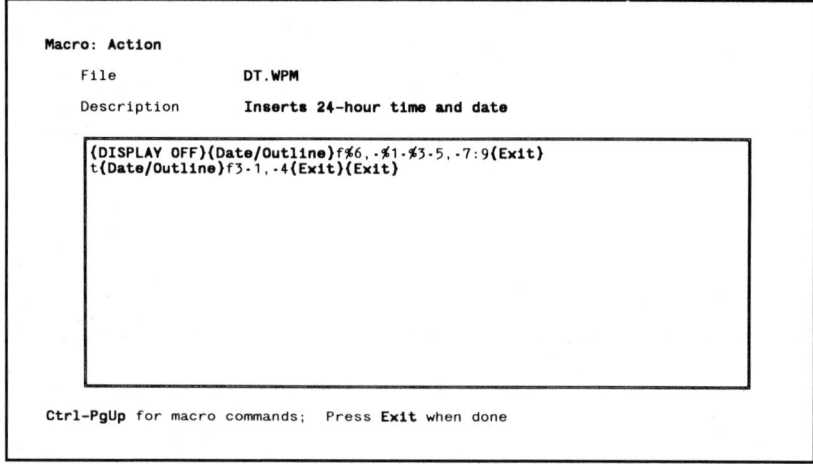

*Figure 7.5:* This **dt** macro inserts the time in 24-hour format and the date in military-style format.

## USING THE MACRO

When you use the macro you've just recorded, the date and time will be inserted in the format just described. Dates you insert without using the macro will be in the WordPerfect default format as in "January 12, 1991."

## OTHER USES

You may want to include this macro in a header or footer macro so that it will date- and time-stamp the document you're working on. If you want the date to be updated each time you retrieve or print the document, use the Date Function code instead of the Date Text code in step 5 of the macro.

---

If you have the WordPerfect Library, you will find that its Calendar feature provides you with calendars of years from A.D. 1600 to 20,000 (no, that's not a typo). If you write historical or science fiction novels, you can use this feature to check the accuracy of your dates—whether July 14, 19,999 will be on a Thursday, for example.

## GENERATING MAILING LABELS (VERSION 5.0)

This version 5.0 macro, named **labels**, merges a primary file that you have formatted for mailing labels with the names and addresses in any secondary file that you specify. It pauses for you to enter the name of the secondary file.

### BEFORE YOU BEGIN

If you're using version 5.1, use the LABELS macro supplied with the program instead of this one.

Before you begin to record the macro:

- You should have created a primary merge file named **labels.pf**; it should contain the appropriate field codes for your secondary merge file, and be formatted for the type of labels you are printing on (see the notes at the end of this macro). You may need to modify this merge file for the types of labels you prefer to use.

- You should clear the screen, because WordPerfect will merge the names and addresses to the screen.

### RECORDING THE MACRO

To record the macro, take the following steps:

1. Turn on the macro recorder by pressing Ctrl-F10 or choosing Macro from the Tools menu and then choosing Define. Enter **labels** as the name of the macro.

2. Enter **generates mailing labels** as the macro description; then press ↵.

3. Press Ctrl-F9 (Merge/Sort) and type **1** or **M** for Merge.

4. Type **labels.pf** as the name of the primary file and press ↵.

5. Press Ctrl-PgUp and type **P** to pause the macro so that you can enter the name of the secondary file containing the names and addresses you want to use. Then press ↵.

Note that you do not have to stop recording this macro because WordPerfect will stop recording it when the merge starts. The final macro should resemble the one in Figure 7.6.

```
Macro: Action
    File          LABELS.WPM
    Description   generates mailing labels

{Merge/Sort}mlabels.pf{Enter}{PAUSE}{Enter}




Ctrl-PgUp for macro commands;  Press Exit when done
```

*Figure 7.6:* The **labels** macro can be used to create mailing labels.

## USING THE MACRO

When you use the macro, WordPerfect will pause for the name of the secondary file you want to use. It will then carry out the merge so that you have one mailing label for each name and address in the secondary file.

To print the labels, chain the macro that you use for printing (see Chapter 8) to the end of this macro, or execute the print macro when this macro stops. Be sure that your printer is loaded with the mailing labels. If your printer allows you to position the paper in relation to the printhead, line the labels up so that the printhead is at the very top of the first label before you give the print command.

## CREATING A PRIMARY FILE FOR MAILING LABELS

The actual primary file you create for your mailing labels will depend on two factors:

- The order of the fields in your secondary files that contain the names and addresses.
- The physical dimensions of the mailing labels you are using.

In this example, we will assume that your secondary file is structured as follows:

F1: name

F2: address

F3: city, state zip

We will also assume that you are using tractor-fed mailing labels that measure 4 inches wide by 1½ inches top to bottom.

First, you will need to open a new document and create the merge field codes by pressing Shift-F9, typing **F**, and entering each field number as follows:

```
^F1^
^F2^
^F3^ ^F4^
```

WordPerfect will add the carets (^) around each code. Each of these lines should end with a hard return.

Next, you need to move to the top of the document and format it for the physical dimensions of the labels, in this case, 4 inches by 1½ inches. WordPerfect doesn't have a predefined paper size for mailing labels, because their dimensions vary according to the type of labels you are using. Because the "page size" of a typical label is quite small, you will need to change the top and bottom margin settings before the program will permit you to change the paper size for the overall label dimensions. You will also need to adjust the right and left margins for the correct label size, and you may need to choose a smaller font size so that the longest line in your addresses will fit on the labels you are using.

1. Set the top margin to ⅜ inch (or rather .37″, since WordPerfect uses decimals and the ″ symbol) and the bottom margin to ¼ inch (.25″). If you are not using inches as your default units of measurement, you can still enter the figures in inches. Just add ″ after the figure—as .25″, for example—and WordPerfect will automatically convert the inches into the units you are using.

2. Then select the Paper Size/Type option. Because there is no predefined size for a 4-inch by 1½-inch paper size, select the Other option (O). WordPerfect will display the prompt

   **Width: 8.5"**

   at the bottom of the screen. After you type **4** (which replaces the 8.5" default) and press ⏎, the prompt

   **Length: 11"**

   will appear. Type **1.5** and press ⏎.

3. From the Paper Type menu, select option 4 (Labels) and press ⏎.

4. Next, change the left and right margins for the labels. Set a left margin of .75" and a right margin of .25" by using the Margin option (option 7) of the Line menu. Then press F7 (Exit) to return to your document.

You can now perform the merge. Clear the screen, press Ctrl-F9 (Merge/Sort), and type **M** for merge. Enter the names of the primary and secondary files to use.

As you scroll through the resulting merged document (or press Ctrl-F3 twice to rewrite the screen), you will see that soft page breaks precede each of the hard page breaks inserted between each address during the merge operation. These soft page breaks are a result of the greatly reduced page length (from 11 inches to 1½ inches). Even with the smaller top and bottom margin settings, this new page length is just sufficient to have each address printed on a single page (that is, a label).

However, before printing the labels, you must delete the hard page breaks. The simplest and fastest way to do this is by using WordPerfect's Search-and-Replace feature. Press Alt-F2 (Replace); then simply press ⏎ to delete the hard page breaks without confirmation. Press Ctrl-Enter to insert the [HPg] code as the search string; then press F2 (Search). When you are prompted for a replacement, press F2 to replace each [HPg] code with nothing.

Before you send the newly formatted document containing the addresses to the printer, it's a good idea to use the View Document feature to check the layout of the addresses on the mailing label. If everything appears as you want it, save the file as LABELS.PF. You can then use it as your primary file in the **labels** macro.

## *PRINTING MULTICOLUMN LABELS*

To print addresses on sheets of labels that have multiple columns (usually, two or three columns across a sheet), you use WordPerfect's Parallel Column feature. The number of labels across the page determines the number of columns to specify when you define the parallel columns.

For example, one common label sheet contains labels in three columns, and each label measures 2⅝ inches wide by 1 inch top to bottom. The edge of the first row of labels starts ½ inch down from the top of the sheet, and the bottom edge of the last row ends ½ inch from the bottom of the sheet. For this type of label sheet, set both the top and bottom margins to .62" (⅝ inch). The left edge of the first column of labels and the right edge of the last column of labels are each ³⁄₁₆ inch from the left and right edges of the page respectively, so set both the left and right margins at .25".

For labels this small, you will also probably need to use a smaller font, either by using the Font key (Ctrl-F8) to set the size to Small or by selecting a new font in a smaller size if you have a laser printer. (Times, or Times Roman, is the most space-saving font that is widely available.) After you have inserted the font change and modified the margin settings, define three parallel columns. For the distance between columns, use a setting of .25". WordPerfect automatically calculates the correct margin settings for the three columns. When you turn the columns on, WordPerfect reformats the addresses for your mailing labels. You can use the View Document feature to preview the new format before you print the labels.

WordPerfect has been known to take out the [HPg] codes that separate each address and format the remaining addresses in a single column when it reaches the second row of addresses. If you have this type of formatting problem, locate the cursor on the first character of each address that needs to be reformatted and press Ctrl-Enter to insert a hard page break. The address will then be reformatted in the proper column.

## CREATING YOUR OWN LETTERHEAD

This macro, named **letterhd**, uses WordPerfect's abilities to create and format a custom letterhead. It centers the letterhead on the line where the cursor is when you execute the macro.

### RECORDING THE MACRO

To record the macro, take the following steps:

1. Turn on the macro recorder by pressing Ctrl-F10 or choosing Macro from the Tools menu and then choosing Define. Enter **letterhd** as the name of the macro.

2. Enter **generates letterhead** as the macro description; then press ↵.

3. To create a centered letterhead, press Shift-F6. Then press F6 (Bold).

4. Type the first line of your letterhead. In this example, we've used the line **Central Systems West**.

5. Press ↵, press Shift-F6 (Center) again, and type the second line of the letterhead: **2400 West 48th Street**, or your own address.

6. Press ↵, press Shift-F6 (Center), and type the last line, **Palo Alto, CA 94303**, or your own city, state, and zip code. Then press F6 again to turn off boldfacing.

7. Press ↵ three times to insert two blank lines into your document.

8. Press Ctrl-F10 again to stop recording the macro.

The final macro should resemble the one in Figure 7.7.

### USING THE MACRO

When you use the macro, WordPerfect inserts your letterhead on the line where the cursor is. If you only want to use it on the first page of

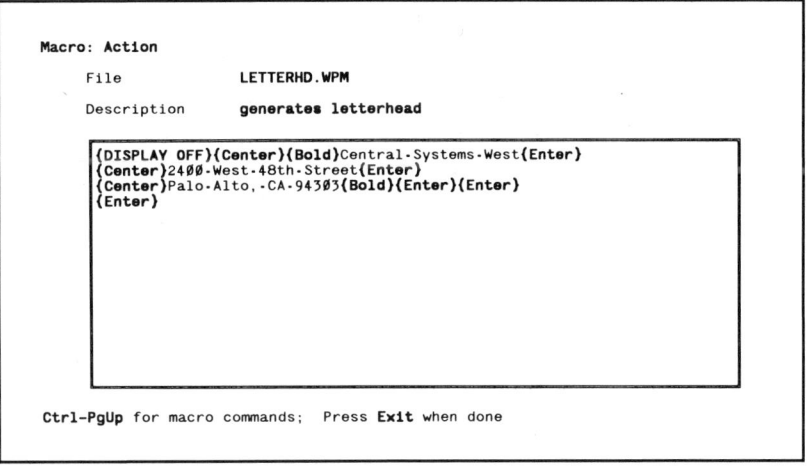

*Figure 7.7:* This macro creates a letterhead of your own design in the font you specify.

business letters, you could add two or three blank lines to its beginning so that the letterhead would appear slightly lower on the printed page.

## *OTHER USES*

You can also add the date function as the last step of the macro so that WordPerfect will insert the current date at the beginning of each business letter.

Depending on your printer's capabilities, you might also want to change fonts at the beginning of the macro and change back to your text font at the end. If you have a laser printer, you can probably choose a typeface for your letterhead that is larger and different from the one you normally use for text. If your printer supports line drawing, you may also want to use WordPerfect's Line Draw feature to create a border around your letterhead, or you may want to put the letterhead in a graphics box as described in Chapter 8.

To create a different effect from boldface for the letterhead, you could switch to italics. To do this, edit the macro to change the last part of step 3 above to:

Press Ctrl-F8 (Font), type **A** (for appearance), and type **I** (for italics).

Then change step 6 so that instead of turning off boldface by pressing F6 again, you enter the keystrokes Ctrl-F8 **3** to return to your normal text font.

## CREATING HANGING INDENTS

This macro, named **hang**, formats your text so that the next paragraph you type is formatted as a hanging indent until you press ⏎. In a hanging indent, the first line of text is "outdented" and the rest are indented at a common tab setting.

> This is an example of a hanging indent. This type of indent is often used in itemized lists and bibliographic entries.

### BEFORE YOU BEGIN

Before you begin to record the macro:

- The document in which you record the macro should have a tab at the left margin.

### RECORDING THE MACRO

To record the macro, take the following steps:

1. Turn on the macro recorder by pressing Ctrl-F10 or choosing Macro from the Tools menu and then choosing Define. Enter **hang** as the name of the macro.
2. Enter **creates hanging indent** as the macro description; then press ⏎.
3. Press F4 (Indent); then press Shift-Tab (Left Margin Release).
4. Press Ctrl-F10 again to stop recording the macro.

The final macro should resemble the one in Figure 7.8.

### USING THE MACRO

When you use the macro, all the text you type after the first line will be indented one tab stop. You will return to normal paragraph formatting as soon as you press ⏎.

```
Macro: Action
    File              HANG.WPM
    Description       creates hanging indent
┌─────────────────────────────────────────────────────┐
│ {DISPLAY OFF}{Indent}{Left Mar Rel}                 │
│                                                     │
│                                                     │
│                                                     │
│                                                     │
│                                                     │
└─────────────────────────────────────────────────────┘
Ctrl-PgUp for macro commands;  Press Exit when done
```

*Figure 7.8:* You can create hanging indents automatically by using this macro.

## *OTHER USES*

If you want text to be indented by a larger amount, reset the tab stops. To indent text equally from both margins with this macro, you can edit it. Change {Indent} to {L/R Indent} by deleting the {Indent} code and pressing Shift-F4 instead.

# *SETTING A QUOTATION STYLE*

You can use macros instead of the Styles feature to instruct WordPerfect to use a certain format. This macro, named **quote**, sets up a format in which all the text you type until you press ⏎ is indented from both margins and set in a Small font size. This is a common practice for material that is displayed as long quotes in text, as in the following paragraph:

> Fourscore and seven years ago, our forefathers brought forth upon this continent a new nation, conceived in liberty and dedicated to the proposition that all men are created equal.

### RECORDING THE MACRO

To record the macro, take the following steps:

1. Turn on the macro recorder by pressing Ctrl-F10 or choosing Macro from the Tools menu and then choosing Define. Enter **quote** as the name of the macro.

2. Enter **formats a displayed quote** as the macro description; then press ⏎.

3. To instruct WordPerfect to use the Small type size, press Ctrl-F8 (Font); then choose Size (option 1). Choose Small (option 4). The actual size that will be used depends on the size of the initial or base font you are using. If you are using 12-point type, Small will probably produce 10-point type.

4. Press Shift-F4 (L/R Indent).

5. Insert a pause by pressing Ctrl-PgUp and typing **P**.

6. Press ⏎ three times to end the quote and insert a blank line.

7. Press Ctrl-F8 and choose Normal (option 3) to return to normal text size after typing the quote.

8. Press Ctrl-F10 to stop recording the macro.

Your screen should resemble the one in Figure 7.9.

### USING THE MACRO

When you use the macro, the text you type next will be indented from the right and left margins and set in a smaller type size than the size you are using in the document. You will return to normal paragraph formatting and type size as soon as you press ⏎.

## SPECIFYING A PARAGRAPH NUMBERING STYLE

This macro, named **pstyle**, lets you select a custom style for paragraph numbering. Normally WordPerfect will use the Outline style (I., A., 1., and so forth) for all your automatic numbering, whether

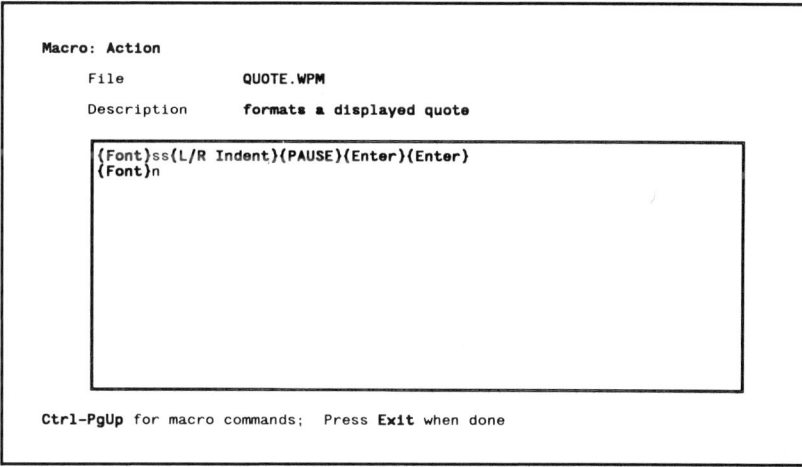

*Figure 7.9:* Macros like this one can be used in place of WordPerfect's Styles feature.

you are outlining or numbering paragraphs. Once you have defined the style you want to use, WordPerfect will follow it each time you create a numbered paragraph by pressing Ctrl-F5 (Date/Outline) and choosing Para Num (option 5). The next macro will number the paragraphs for you after you have selected the style by using this macro.

## RECORDING THE MACRO

To record the macro, take the following steps:

1. Turn on the macro recorder by pressing Ctrl-F10 or choosing Macro from the Tools menu and then choosing Define. Enter **pstyle** as the name of the macro.

2. Enter **change paragraph numbering style** as the macro description; then press ←.

3. Press Shift-F5 (Date/Outline) and choose Define (option 6).

4. You will see the paragraph number definition screen. Press Ctrl-PgUp and type **P** to insert a pause; then press ←. When you execute the macro, you can choose the style you want to use.

By using **para**, the next macro in this book, you can choose a fixed style if you don't want your paragraph numbering style to change each time you press Tab. Make a note of which level produces the exact style you want to use. For example, in Bullet style, level 1 gives solid bullets and level 2 gives open bullets.

5. Press F7 twice to exit from the paragraph number definition screen and return to your document.
6. Press Ctrl-F10 again to stop recording the macro.
7. Press Backspace to delete the [Para Num Def] code you just inserted.

The final macro should resemble the one in Figure 7.10.

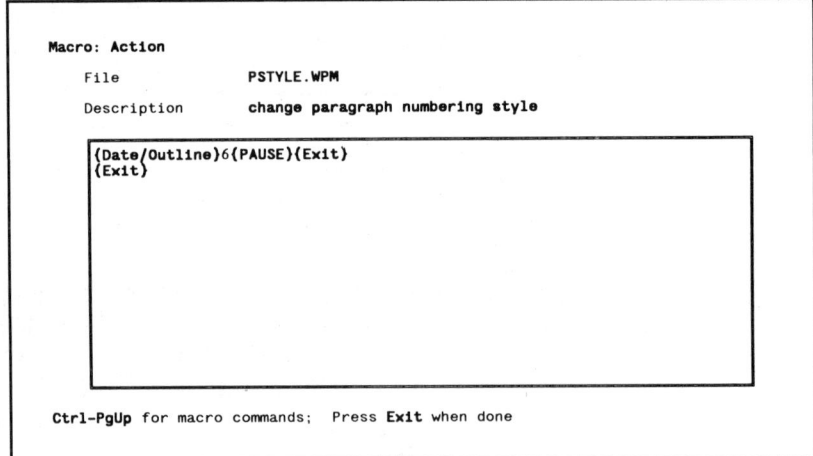

*Figure 7.10:* This macro, named **pstyle**, lets you customize the paragraph numbering style you want to use.

## USING THE MACRO

When you use the macro, WordPerfect will pause for you to choose the style you want to use. Enter its number (**2** for Paragraph, **4** for Legal, or **5** for Bullets) and press ←┘. From that point on in your document (until you define a new style), WordPerfect will follow the style you have chosen each time you insert an automatic paragraph number (Shift-F5 **5**). You do not have to begin automatic paragraph numbering right away; you can use this macro to establish a style at the beginning of a document and then actually number paragraphs much later in the document.

### *OTHER USES*

To number paragraphs or bulleted items consistently throughout a document, no matter which tab stop your cursor is on, use the next macro, called **para**, after you have chosen a style.

## NUMBERING AND FORMATTING PARAGRAPHS

WordPerfect is preset to use the Outline style (I., A., 1., and so forth), but if you are numbering paragraphs, you may want to use a different style of numbering. WordPerfect also generates automatic paragraph numbers in the style that corresponds to your cursor's position when you number the paragraph, so that you get a level-1 style number (such as I.) if your cursor is on the left margin, a level-2 style number (A.) if it's on the first tab stop, and so forth. However, you may also want to use the same style of numbering no matter where your cursor is. You may also want the text of your paragraphs to align instead of wrapping back to the left margin on the second line.

This macro, named **para**, automatically numbers paragraphs and indents them so that they align like this:

> (1) WordPerfect will not automatically number paragraphs in a certain style and align text unless you instruct it to.

If you use it after you have executed the **pstyle** macro, it produces numbered paragraphs in the style you have indicated by that macro. If you haven't changed the numbering style, it uses WordPerfect's default Outline style.

This macro uses fixed paragraph numbering so that you can produce the same level of numbering no matter where your cursor is when you execute the macro. In this example, we will use level 5, which produces (1), (2), (3) if you are using the program's default setting.

## RECORDING THE MACRO

To record the macro, take the following steps:

1. Turn on the macro recorder by pressing Ctrl-F10 or choosing Macro from the Tools menu and then choosing Define. Enter **para** as the name of the macro.
2. Enter **numbers and formats paragraphs** as the macro description; then press ⏎.
3. Press Shift-F5 (Date/Outline) and type **p** for Para Num.
4. Type **5** for level 5 and press ⏎.
5. Press F4 (Indent).
6. Press Ctrl-F10 again to stop recording the macro.

The final macro should resemble the one in Figure 7.11.

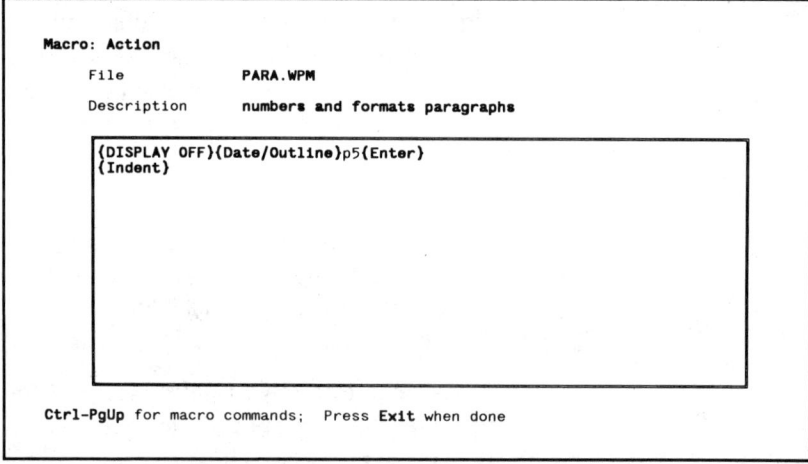

*Figure 7.11:* This macro lets you number paragraphs in a fixed style.

## USING THE MACRO

When you use the macro, the program will automatically number the next text you type and will consider the text to be one item until you press ⏎. If you later delete any item or add new numbered items by using the macro again, WordPerfect will automatically renumber the other numbered items that you created with this macro. You can use it in any situation in which you want to maintain accurately numbered lists, such as for test questions or steps in a procedure.

To change to a different paragraph numbering style instead of the default Outline style, execute the **pstyle** macro before you use this macro. WordPerfect will follow whatever style is currently in effect and will use the style of the level you indicated in step 4 of this macro, which is level 5.

### OTHER USES

You may want to use a style other than level 5. For example, to use fixed numbering in the Paragraph style so that you get numbers like i), ii), iii), type **7** for level 7 in step 4 above, or edit the macro.

If you number paragraphs often or create bulleted lists that you want to have formatted in this way, rename the macro **Alt-P** or **Alt-B** so that it will be quicker to execute.

## AUTOMATIC MEMO FORM

This macro, named **memo**, creates a memo form that automatically pauses for you to fill it out. You can adapt it for any style of memo format that your company uses.

### RECORDING THE MACRO

To record the macro, take the following steps:

1. Turn on the macro recorder by pressing Ctrl-F10 or choosing Macro from the Tools menu and then choosing Define. Enter **memo** as the name of the macro.

2. Enter **create memo form** as the macro description; then press ↵.

3. To set the alignment character so that your headings will align on the colon as shown in Figure 7.12, press Shift-F8, type **O** (for Other) and **3** (or **D**) for Decimal character.

4. Type a colon (:).
5. Press ⏎; then press F7 (Exit).
6. Press Tab; then press Ctrl-F6 to turn on tab alignment. Whatever you type will not be aligned correctly until you type a colon.
7. Type **TO:**.
8. Press the Spacebar to insert a space; then insert a pause in the macro (Ctrl-PgUp **P**).
9. Press ⏎ twice to resume the macro and move to the next line.
10. Repeat steps 6–9, entering text for a 'FROM,' 'SUBJECT,' and 'DATE' line, as shown in Figure 7.12. To enter the date, press Shift-F5 (Date/Outline), type **1**, and press ⏎ twice.
11. To create a dashed line, press Esc, enter **65**, and type a hyphen. Then press ⏎.
12. Press Ctrl-F10 again to stop recording the macro.

Your macro should resemble the one in Figure 7.12, up to the last two lines. You will add the final {PROMPT} and {CHAIN} commands in the next set of instructions.

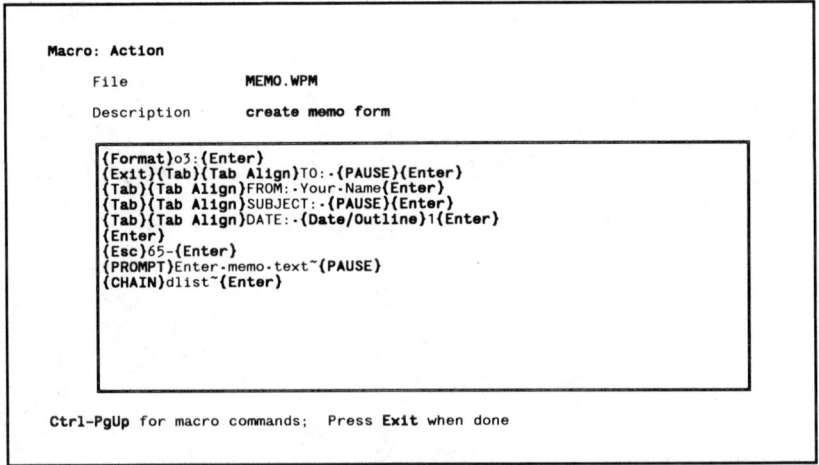

*Figure 7.12:* This macro produces the memo format shown in Figure 7.13, where steps have been added to create a distribution list at the bottom.

## USING THE MACRO

When you use the macro, WordPerfect will pause after the 'TO' line for you to enter the recipient's name. After you enter the name and press ⏎, it will insert your name and pause for you to enter the subject of the memo. After you enter the subject and press ⏎, it will insert today's date as text and then draw a full-screen dashed line to separate the headings from the body of the memo.

## OTHER USES

> The **memo** macro will produce text in any existing document that you've got on the screen. Clear the screen before you use it, if that's not what you want.

You can chain this macro to a couple of other useful macros and have it prompt you for the memo text. For example, suppose you have a standard distribution list of six people to whom you normally send a copy of each memo you write. You can edit this macro so that it will pause for you to type the memo paragraph; when you press ⏎, it will retrieve your distribution list. It will then save the memo and print the same number of copies as there are people on your distribution list, plus one for yourself.

First, you'll need to create the distribution list macro named **dlist**. This macro consists of a list of the six names to whom you send memos, each separated by a hard return, and the instructions to save the memo and pause for you to enter its name. A sample **dlist** memo is shown in Figure 7.13; of course, you'll want to type the names of your own recipients. Figure 7.14 shows the **dlist** macro itself. Note that it calls a print macro named **P7** that prints seven copies, and you will need to record this macro also (the keystrokes are Shift-F7 **N 7** ⏎ 1).

Finally, you can edit the **memo** macro to prompt you for the memo text, chain the **dlist** macro, and nest the **P7** print macro.

1. Turn on the macro recorder by pressing Ctrl-F10 or choosing Macro from the Tools menu and then choosing Define. In version 5.1, you can press Home before you press Ctrl-F10 as a shortcut for editing macros. Enter the macro's name (**memo**); then press ⏎ to edit the description, and then go to the macro editor. In version 5.0, this shortcut isn't available, so press Ctrl-F10, enter **memo**, and type **2 2** to edit it.

2. Press Home Home ↓ to move to the end of the **memo** macro.

```
            TO: Elaine Beebe Nelson
          FROM: Your Name
       SUBJECT: Current Inventory
          DATE: August 15, 1991
-----------------------------------------------------------------
On-hand quantities of 5-1/4" floppy disks have reached the
reorder mark. Please issue the appropriate purchase order.

L. Olsen
R. Maccabee
B. Swift
V. Hughes
S. Seton
W. Canaris


                                              Doc 1 Pg 1 Ln 0.2" Pos 0.5"
```

*Figure 7.13:* This sample memo was prepared with the **dlist** macro; the macro also saves and prints the document.

```
Macro: Action

    File             DLIST.WPM

    Description      inserts distribution list and saves

    L.·Olsen{Enter}
    R.·Maccabee{Enter}
    B.·Swift{Enter}
    V.·Hughes{Enter}
    S.·Seton{Enter}
    W.·Canaris{Save}{PAUSE}{Enter}
    {Macro}p7~




Ctrl-PgUp for macro commands;   Press Exit when done
```

*Figure 7.14:* When the **dlist** macro is chained to the **memo** macro and the **P7** macro is nested inside it, you have an automated memo system.

3. Press Ctrl-PgUp, type **PR**, and press ⏎ to insert a {PROMPT} command. Type **Enter memo text ~**.

4. Press Ctrl-PgUp, type **pau** (just **P** will be sufficient in version 5.0), and press ⏎ to insert a pause so that you can type the text of the memo when the macro executes.

5. Press ← again; then press Ctrl-PgUp, type **CH**, and press ← to insert {CHAIN} into your macro. Type **dlist~** as the name of the macro to execute.

6. Press F7 (twice in version 5.0) to stop editing the macro.

The final **memo** macro should resemble the one in Figure 7.12.

Now you have a fully automated memo system that prompts you for your memos, saves them, and creates the correct number of hard copies. You can adapt this system for any type of report you issue regularly.

## *WRITING BUSINESS LETTERS*

This macro, named **lttr**, sets up a business letter format for you with a particular font, centers the letter on the page, inserts the current date, and inserts your return address. You can use it with any of the boilerplate text macros to automate the task of letter writing.

### *BEFORE YOU BEGIN*

Before you begin to record the macro:

- You should open a new document window.

### *RECORDING THE MACRO*

To record the macro, take the following steps:

1. Turn on the macro recorder by pressing Ctrl-F10 or choosing Macro from the Tools menu and then choosing Define. Enter **lttr** as the name of the macro.

2. Enter **formats business letter** as the macro description; then press ←.

3. The instruction for centering the letter on the page must come first, so press Shift-F8 (Format) and type **P C Y** (omit the Y in version 5.0). Then press F7 ←.

4. Pause the macro so that you can type the recipient's name. Press Ctrl-PgUp, type **P**, and press ⏎ twice.

5. Pause the macro so that you can type the recipient's street address. Press Ctrl-PgUp, type **P**, and press ⏎ twice.

6. Pause the macro so that you can type the recipient's city, state, and zip code. Press Ctrl-PgUp, type **P**, and press ⏎ twice.

7. Press Alt-F6 (Flush Right). Type your street address (or your company's) and press ⏎.

8. Press Alt-F6 (Flush Right). Type your city, state, and zip code, and press ⏎.

9. Press Alt-F6 (Flush Right). Insert the Date function so that each time you write a business letter, it will have the current date. Press Shift-F5 (Date/Outline) and type **C** for Code; then press ⏎.

10. Press ⏎ twice more to insert extra lines between the address block and the salutation. Then type **Dear** and press the Spacebar.

11. Press Ctrl-F10 again to stop recording the macro.

A sample letterhead being formatted with this macro is shown in Figure 7.15, and the final macro should resemble the one in Figure 7.16.

## *USING THE MACRO*

When you use the macro, WordPerfect will format the letter for you. It will pause for you to type three lines—one for the recipient's name, one for the street address, and one for the city, state, and zip. As soon as you press ⏎ the third time (for the last line), your address and the date will appear. Your cursor will be positioned to type the salutation.

If you are using double spacing as a default setting, you will want to insert the code for single spacing in this macro so that your business letters will be single-spaced. If you do, be sure to put it after the Center Page (top to bottom) command (step 3 above), as WordPerfect needs to read the Center Page command first to position the letter properly on the page.

```
               R.M. Harshaw
               Wiles Iron Works
               San Francisco, CA 94109
                                                              7201 Paradise Court
                                                              Palo Alto, CA 94304
                                                              August 15, 1991



               Dear
```

*Figure 7.15:* The **lttr** macro will produce a letterhead like this one, with your own address, and in the font you select.

```
Macro: Action
     File               LTTR.WPM
     Description        formats business letter

     {Format}pcy{Exit}
     {Enter}
     {PAUSE}{Enter}
     {PAUSE}{Enter}
     {PAUSE}{Enter}
     {Flush Right}7201·Paradise·Court{Enter}
     {Flush Right}Palo·Alto,·CA·94304{Enter}
     {Flush Right}{Date/Outline}c{Enter}
     {Enter}
     {Enter}
     Dear·


Ctrl-PgUp for macro commands;   Press Exit when done
```

*Figure 7.16:* When you record this macro, use your own address and select the font you want to use.

## OTHER USES

Once you've executed this macro, you can use a boilerplate text macro to write the standard text of your letter for you. You can also link it to macros that format and print the envelope or mailing label automatically. (See the **labels** macro in this chapter and the **busenv** macro in Chapter 9.)

If you're comfortable with using the macro editor, you can edit this macro so that it prompts you for the recipient's name, street address, and city, state, and zip code. To do this, you'll need to retrieve the macro into the editor and edit it as shown in Figure 7.17, because prompts have to be inserted by using the editor. You will assign the text of each prompt to a variable and then give the instruction for entering the variable into the document when the user presses ⏎. To do this for the first prompt:

1. Delete the three {PAUSE}{Enter} lines, as shown in Figure 7.17.

2. Press Ctrl-PgUp and type **T** for Text. Press ⏎ to insert the {TEXT} command into the macro.

3. To assign the first text (which the user will enter as a result of the prompt) to variable 0, type **0˜**. Be sure to include the tilde.

4. Then type the message of the first prompt: **Enter recipient's name:** ˜. Remember the tilde.

5. To insert the {VAR 0}{Enter} instructions that tell WordPerfect to enter the text stored in variable 0, press Ctrl-V, press Alt-0, press Ctrl-V again, and press ⏎.

You have now inserted the first prompt. To create the second and third prompts, repeat steps 1–5, assigning the text of the prompts—

```
Macro: Action
    File              LTTR.WPM
    Description       formats business letter

    {Format}pcy{Exit}
    {Enter}
    {TEXT}0~Enter recipient's name: ~{VAR 0}{Enter}
    {TEXT}1~Enter street address: ~{VAR 1}{Enter}
    {TEXT}2~Enter city, state ZIP: ~{VAR 2}{Enter}
    {Flush Right}7201 Paradise Court{Enter}
    {Flush Right}Palo Alto, CA 94304{Enter}
    {Flush Right}{Date/Outline}c{Enter}
    {Enter}
    {Enter}
    Dear
```

Ctrl-PgUp for macro commands;    Press Exit when done

*Figure 7.17:* You can edit the **lttr** macro to prompt you as you use it.

"Enter street address: ˜ " and "Enter city, state ZIP: ˜ "—to variables 1 and 2. When you have finished, press F7 (twice in version 5.0) to return to your document. Then clear the screen (F7 **N N**) and try out the macro. As it executes, you will be prompted at the bottom of the screen for each item of information. Enter the text and press ⏎ to resume the macro after each prompt.

## *BUSINESS LETTER HEADER*

If you write business letters, you know that it's often not possible to plan in advance whether a letter's going to fit on one page or whether it will require more than one. If you do spill over onto several pages, it's easy to forget to number them or insert a header that dates the letter. This macro remembers for you. You can use it at the beginning of any business letter, and as long as you don't go onto a second page you'll get no page numbering and no header. If you do write a second or even third page, they'll be numbered and date-stamped automatically.

This macro, named **bltr**, creates a header with the date text and the page number. It then immediately suppresses these formats for the current page.

### *RECORDING THE MACRO*

To record the macro, take the following steps:

1. Turn on the macro recorder by pressing Ctrl-F10 or choosing Macro from the Tools menu and then choosing Define. Enter **bltr** as the name of the macro.

2. Enter **creates header for multiple-page letter** as the macro description; then press ⏎.

3. Press Home Home ↑ to move to the beginning of the document. This makes sure that the header code comes near the top of the document and also lets you use the macro at any time while you're writing a letter.

4. Press Shift-F8 (Format); then type **P H A P** to create a Header A on every page.

5. When the header editing screen appears, press Shift-F5 (Date/Outline) and type **T** for Date Text. (If you use the date function, your letter will be updated each time you retrieve it or print it, which is probably not what you want.)

6. Press Alt-F6 (Flush Right); then type **Page**, press the Spacebar, and press Ctrl-B. This creates a page numbering style like "Page 2" in the upper-right corner of the page.

7. Press F7; then type **U A** to suppress this format for the current page.

8. Press F7 to return to your document.

9. Press Ctrl-F10 again to stop recording the macro.

The final macro should resemble the one in Figure 7.18.

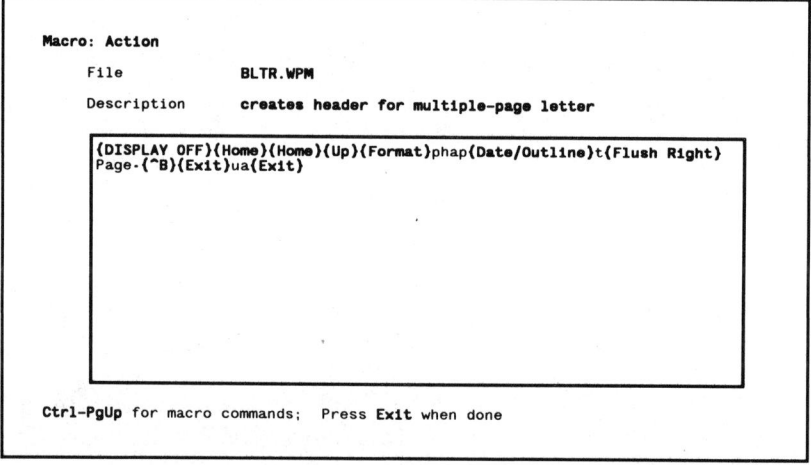

*Figure 7.18:* The **bltr** macro creates a header on all but the first page of a letter.

## USING THE MACRO

When you use the macro, WordPerfect creates a header like the following on all pages but the first of your letter:

August 28, 1991    Page 2

## OTHER USES

You may want to edit the macro so that it will pause for you to create a custom header, perhaps including the recipient's name or your initials. To do this, just insert a pause after step 3 above.

## DRAFT FORMAT

If you often prepare draft manuscript before you prepare final versions of reports or chapters, you can use this macro or one very similar to it. The macro, named **ms**, creates a manuscript format that uses double spacing, a ragged right margin, and a 2-inch left margin, which leaves plenty of room for comments. It also inserts a footer that says "Draft version - Not for Final Release" and numbers the pages for you.

### BEFORE YOU BEGIN

Before you begin to record the macro:

- Open a new document window.

### RECORDING THE MACRO

To record the macro, take the following steps:

1. Turn on the macro recorder by pressing Ctrl-F10 or choosing Macro from the Tools menu and then choosing Define. Enter **ms** as the name of the macro.

2. Enter **ms format** as the macro description; then press ⏎.

3. Press Shift-F8 (Format) and type **L J L** to set Left Justification. (In version 5.0, type **N** for No Justification.)

4. Type **S 2** and press ⏎ to change to double spacing.

5. Type **M 2"** and press ⏎ three times to set a 2-inch left margin and return to the Format menu.

6. Type **P F A P** to insert a footer on each page.

> When you execute a macro that creates a header, be careful where your cursor is. Word-Perfect needs to read header instructions at the beginning of a page; otherwise, the header will show up on the next page. It doesn't matter where footer instructions go, as long as they are on the page where you want the footer.

7. Type **Draft - Not for Final Release**.

8. Press Alt-F6 (Flush Right), type **Page**, press the Spacebar, and press Ctrl-B. This will number the pages in the format Page 1, Page 2, and so forth, in the lower-right corner of the printed page. (If you would rather number pages as "Page *n* of *n*," see the **pg#** macro shown in Figure 7.21.)

9. For an elegant touch, switch to small type for the footer. Move to the beginning of the line (press Home-←) and press Alt-F4 to turn on blocking. Press End to block the entire footer. Then Press Ctrl-F8 (Font) and type **S S** to select the Small size.

10. Press F7 twice to return to your document.

11. Press Ctrl-F10 to stop recording the macro.

The final macro should resemble the one in Figure 7.19; Figure 7.20 illustrates a sample page prepared by using it.

## USING THE MACRO

When you use the macro, WordPerfect automatically formats your document to be like the one shown in Figure 7.20. You can change the wording of the footer easily by editing the macro.

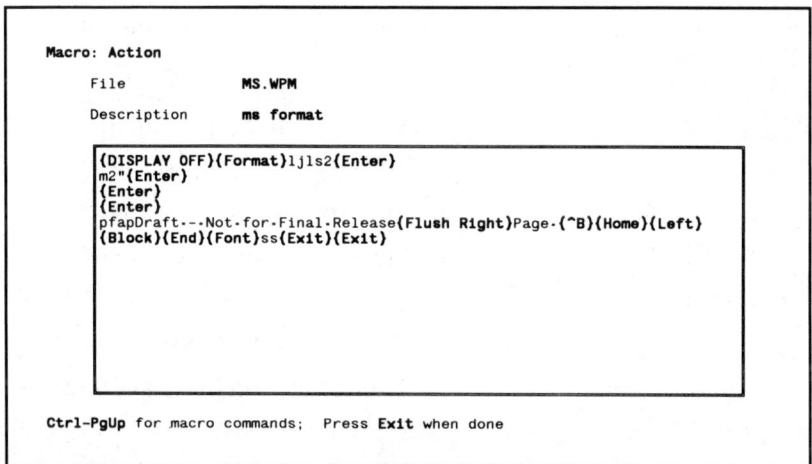

*Figure 7.19:* This **ms** macro sets up a draft report form for you.

```
WELCOME

Welcome to MagnaCorp. We hope this employee handbook
will help to guide you through your first few days
here. In addition, it contains valuable information
about employee services and benefits available to
you. Ask your manager or call the personnel office
if you have any questions for which you cannot find
the answers in this handbook.

ITEMS OF INTEREST

Work Day

The official work day at MagnaCorp is 8:30 a.m. to
5:00 p.m. Flexible hours can be arranged with your
manager.

Parking

As parking is limited, please apply to the personnel
office for a parking slot assignment. They are
issued on a first-come, first-served basis.



Draft - Not for Final Release                                Page 1
```

*Figure 7.20:* A sample page created with the **ms** macro; here, the footer is in small type.

To reset WordPerfect's format settings to their original default values for one session with the program, start WordPerfect with the command **wp/x**.

You can start WordPerfect with a format macro like this one so that the macro will be executed as soon as WordPerfect opens a new document window. To start WordPerfect with a macro, give the startup command as **wp/m-*macroname*.**

You can customize a format macro like this one even further by adding instructions for turning on page numbering, specifying Widow/Orphan protection, and so forth.

## NUMBERING PAGES AS PAGE N OF N

This macro, named **pg#**, numbers pages in the style "Page 1 of 50" if there are 50 pages in your document. You can use it within other formatting macros to set this style of page numbering for you. It uses WordPerfect's Cross Reference feature (called Automatic Reference in version 5.0) to number the pages.

### BEFORE YOU BEGIN

Before you begin to record the macro:

- You should have a document on the screen.

### RECORDING THE MACRO

To record the macro, take the following steps:

1. Turn on the macro recorder by pressing Ctrl-F10 or choosing Macro from the Tools menu and then choosing Define. Enter **pg#** as the name of the macro.

2. Enter **page n of n** as the macro description; then press ⏎.

3. Press Shift-F8 (Format) and type **P F A P** to create a footer on each page.

4. Press Shift-F6 (Center) to center the page-number line. (Press Alt-F6 if you'd rather have it flush right.)

5. Type **Page**, press the Spacebar, press Ctrl-B, press the Spacebar, type **of**, and press the Spacebar.

6. Now you can create the automatic reference. In a header or footer, you have to mark the reference (the actual reference) and target (what is being referred to) separately. Press Alt-F5 (Mark Text) and type **R R P**. Type **endp** as the target name.

7. Press F7 three times to return to your document.
8. Now you can mark the target. Press Home Home ↓ to go to the end of the document.
9. Press Alt-F5 (Mark Text), and type **R T** and press ⏎ to mark the target.
10. To generate the correct page number for the target, press Alt-F5 (Mark Text) and type **G G Y**.
11. Press Ctrl-F10 to stop recording the macro.

The final macro should resemble the one in Figure 7.21.

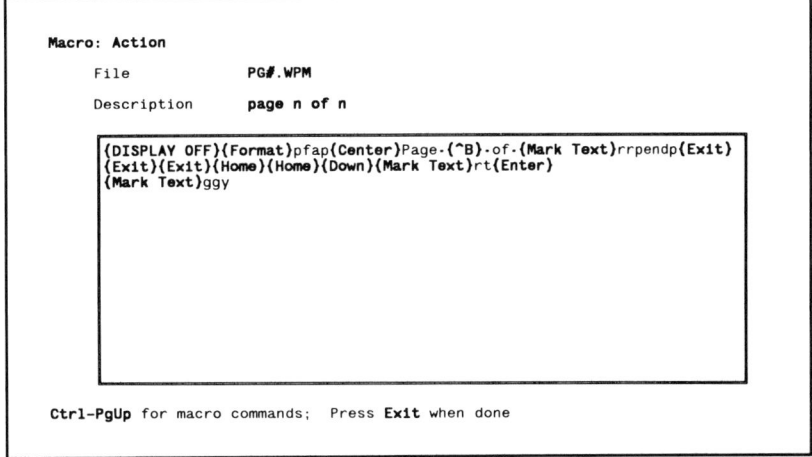

*Figure 7.21:* This page-numbering macro uses automatic referencing to determine the last page number in your document.

## *USING THE MACRO*

When you use the macro, WordPerfect will read the last page number in your document and generate the correct number to use in the footer. If you add pages to the document, you will need to generate the document again so that the page number will be accurate. If you've changed the page count and you try to print the document, WordPerfect will prompt you that the document may need to be generated. If you want the page numbers to be accurate, press ⏎ and then execute the **pg#** macro again. It will automatically generate the right page numbers, and you can then print the document.

## DATE AND PAGE-NUMBER FOOTER

This macro, named **foot**, inserts the date and page number as a footer on each page of your document.

### RECORDING THE MACRO

To record the macro, take the following steps:

1. Turn on the macro recorder by pressing Ctrl-F10 or choosing Macro from the Tools menu and then choosing Define. Enter **foot** as the name of the macro.

2. Enter **inserts date and page number** as the macro description; then press ↵.

3. Press Shift-F8 (Format) and type **P F A P** for a footer on each page.

4. When the header/footer editing screen appears, press Shift-F5 (Date/Outline) and type **C** to insert the date code. (If you want the date to remain the same each time you retrieve and print the document, type **T** for Date Text instead.)

5. Press Shift-F6 (Center) and insert a pause by pressing Ctrl-PgUp, typing **P**, and pressing ↵. When you execute the macro, it will pause here so that you can enter the title of the document, such as April Report or Chapter 14.

6. Press Alt-F6 (Flush Right) and insert the code that will generate a page number on each page by pressing Ctrl-B.

7. Press F7 (Exit) twice.

8. Press Ctrl-F10 again to stop recording the macro.

The final macro should resemble the one in Figure 7.22. It creates a footer with the date flush left and the page number flush right. The name you gave the document is centered:

February 16, 1991           Final Report           100

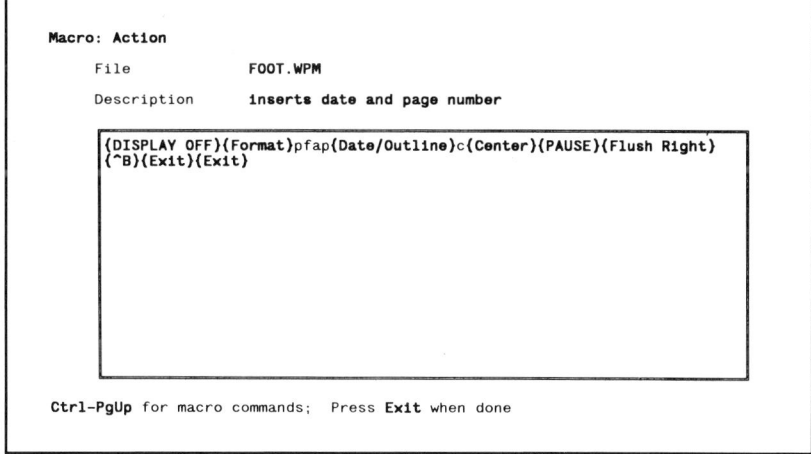

*Figure 7.22:* This **foot** macro pauses to let you insert the title of the document in the center position.

### USING THE MACRO

When you use the macro, it will pause for you to type a document name and press ←┘. If you don't want to have the document's title appear at the bottom of the page, just press ←┘ when the macro pauses.

### OTHER USES

You can record this macro as a header by typing **H** for Header instead of F for Footer in step 3 above.

If you want the footer (or header) to be in Small type, add one step to the macro: before the date code, press Ctrl-F8 (Font), and type **S S** to select Small. You might want to use italics or boldface in the same way.

## *ALTERNATING HEADERS/FOOTERS*

WordPerfect will let you have a variety of headers and footers in your document. You can define a Header A, a Header B, a Footer A, and a Footer B, and you can choose whether they're to appear on every page, only on odd pages, or only on even pages. If you work with classified documents, for example, you may want to have header or footer text that remains the same on every page but also header or footer text that changes on each page to indicate the classification of the material there. This macro, named **altfoot**, inserts a report number (you can substitute whatever text you want) in the lower-left corner of the page and pauses to let you type the text, such as CONFIDENTIAL, that appears in the lower-right corner. To use the macro, execute it at the beginning of the document and then execute it each time the classification changes, or each time you want the variable text to change. As it is a footer, it doesn't matter where you are on the page when you execute it. However, if this were a header, you would have to be careful to position the cursor at the very beginning of the page where you wanted it to change, because WordPerfect has to read the header code first to get the header on that page.

### *RECORDING THE MACRO*

To record the macro, take the following steps:

1. Turn on the macro recorder by pressing Ctrl-F10 or choosing Macro from the Tools menu and then choosing Define. Enter **altfoot** as the name of the macro.

2. Enter **alternating footer text** as the macro description; then press ←.

3. Press Shift-F8 (Format) and type **P F A P**.

4. Type **Report No. 9000** as the text that will never vary.

5. Press Alt-F6 (Flush Right) and insert a pause by pressing Ctrl-PgUp, typing **P**, and pressing ←.

6. Press F7 twice.

7. Press Ctrl-F10 again to stop recording the macro.

The final macro should resemble the one in Figure 7.23.

### *USING THE MACRO*

When you use the macro, WordPerfect will pause for you to change the text that appears flush right. Execute the macro on each page where you want the text to change.

# MACROS FOR FORMATTING TEXT    245

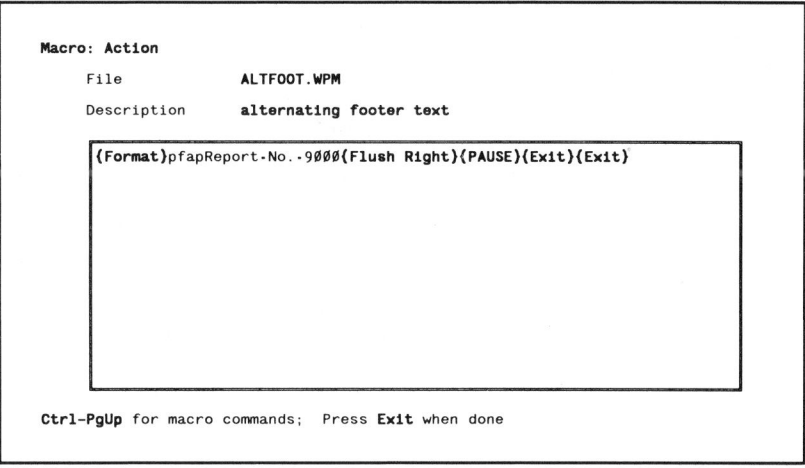

*Figure 7.23:* The **altfoot** macro lets you insert variable text on a page-by-page basis.

## USING MULTIPLE HEADERS/FOOTERS

This macro, named **hdrs**, uses a Header A on odd pages and a Header B on even pages. It pauses to let you enter whatever text you like.

### RECORDING THE MACRO

To record the macro, take the following steps:

1. Turn on the macro recorder by pressing Ctrl-F10 or choosing Macro from the Tools menu and then choosing Define. Enter **hdrs** as the name of the macro.

2. Enter **create header A (odd) & header B (even)** as the macro description; then press ←.

3. Press Home Home Home ← to move to the very beginning of the document, before any other codes.

4. Press Shift-F8 (Format) and type **P H A O** to create a Header A on all odd (right-hand) pages.

> If you change the margins in your document, header and footer margins won't be updated unless the margin-change code occurs before the header or footer code.

5. Press Alt-F6 (Flush Right) so that the text of the header will be flush against the right (outside) margin.

6. Pause the macro by pressing Ctrl-PgUp, typing **P**, and pressing ⏎ twice.

7. Press F7 (Exit).

8. To create Header B, type **H B V**. As it will be on even (left-hand) pages, you can leave the text flush left.

9. Pause the macro by pressing Ctrl-PgUp, typing **P**, and pressing ⏎.

10. Press F7 (Exit) twice.

11. Press Ctrl-F10 to stop recording the macro.

The final macro should resemble the one in Figure 7.24.

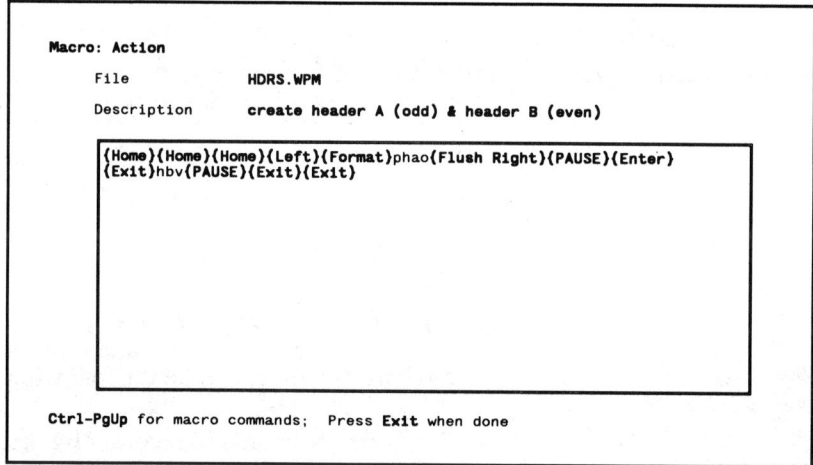

*Figure 7.24:* The **hdrs** macro creates a Header A on odd pages and a Header B on even pages.

## USING THE MACRO

When you use the macro, WordPerfect will pause for you to enter the text of Header A, the header that will appear on all the odd (right-hand) pages in your document. After you type the text and press ⏎, it will pause to let you enter the text for Header B, the one for all the even (left-hand) pages. The instructions for moving to the very beginning of the document are part of the macro, so you can be sure that you will get the headers on each page of your text.

If you are using a title page or a contents page, though, you may not want headers on them. Use the **suppress** macro given later in this chapter (Figure 7.26) to suppress headers and footers on those pages.

To record this macro so that it will create footers instead of headers, type **F** instead of **H** in steps 4 and 8.

See the **lttr** macro for instructions on how to assign variables.

To insert a prompt for the user, retrieve the macro into the editor and edit it as illustrated in Figure 7.25, assigning the prompt 'Enter text for odd pages:' to variable 0 and 'Enter text for even pages:' to variable 1. Note that there is a space after each colon for better readability on the screen.

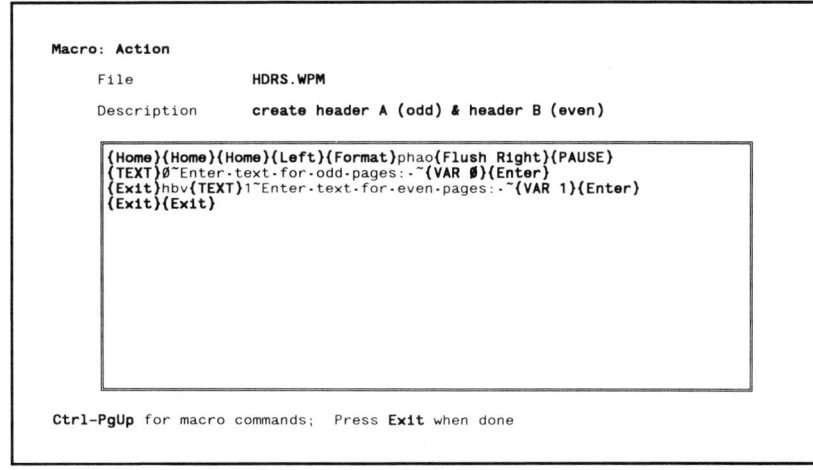

*Figure 7.25:* You can add prompts to the **hdrs** macro so that it will tell the user which text to type.

## *SUPPRESSING HEADERS AND FOOTERS*

This macro, named **suppress**, suppresses headers, footers, and page numbers on the page where you execute it. In order to suppress these page-formatting items on other pages, move the cursor to each page and execute the macro.

## RECORDING THE MACRO

To record the macro, take the following steps:

1. Turn on the macro recorder by pressing Ctrl-F10 or choosing Macro from the Tools menu and then choosing Define. Enter **suppress** as the name of the macro.

2. Enter **suppresses headers, footers, pg. nos.** as the macro description; then press ⏎.

3. The suppress code needs to be the first thing on the current page so that WordPerfect will suppress that page's header. To make sure that you're at the very beginning of the page where you're using this macro, press Ctrl-Home (Go To) and insert a pause so that you can enter the page number. Press Ctrl-PgUp, type **P**, and press ⏎ twice. When you execute the macro, you'll enter the current page number here, even if the cursor is already in that page.

4. Press Shift-F8 (Format) and type **P U A** to suppress all headers, footers, and page numbering.

5. Press F7.

6. Press Ctrl-F10 again to stop recording the macro.

The final macro should resemble the one in Figure 7.26.

## USING THE MACRO

When you use the macro, WordPerfect will pause for you to enter the page number of the page on which you're suppressing the formats. Even if you're already on that page, enter the page number (check the status line) and press ⏎. This makes sure that the suppress code will appear as the first item on the page.

If there are other pages in your document—section openings, for instance, or full-page tables and figures—on which you do not want to have headers, footers, and page numbers, use the macro on these pages as well. It works only on the page you specify when you execute the macro; headers, footers, and page numbers will appear on the next page, as long as you have defined them.

---

Define your headers, footers, and page-numbering system at the beginning of the document; then suppress them on any pages where you don't want them. That way, you'll know that the codes are in the correct position at the very beginning of the document to operate on all the pages.

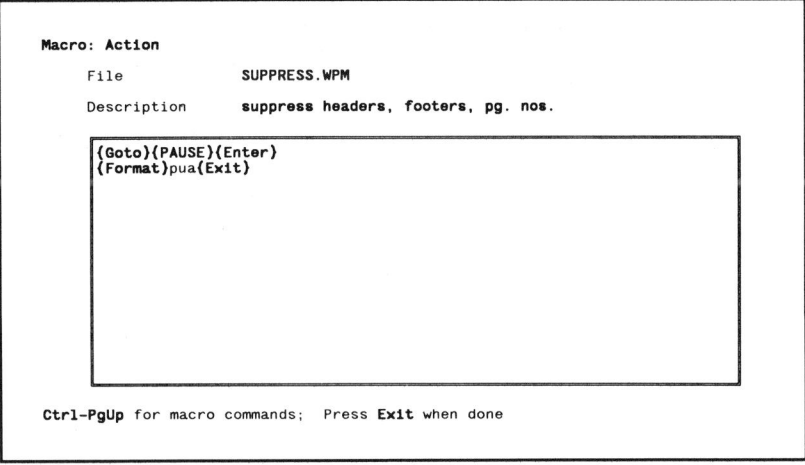

*Figure 7.26:* The **suppress** macro suppresses special page formatting for the current page.

## SWITCHING TO SINGLE OR DOUBLE SPACING

This macro, named **space**, pauses to let you indicate whether you want to use single, double, or triple line spacing, space-and-a-half, or whatever. If you use it often, you can reassign it to Alt-S or assign it to a Ctrl key on a soft keyboard.

### RECORDING THE MACRO

To record the macro, take the following steps:

1. Turn on the macro recorder by pressing Ctrl-F10 or choosing Macro from the Tools menu and then choosing Define. Enter **space** as the name of the macro.

2. Enter **changes line spacing** as the macro description; then press ⏎.

3. Press Shift-F8 (Format) and type **L S** for Line Spacing.

4. Insert a pause by pressing Ctrl-PgUp, typing **P**, and pressing ⏎.

5. Press ⏎ three times to return to your document.
6. Press Ctrl-F10 again to stop recording the macro.

The final macro should resemble the one in Figure 7.27.

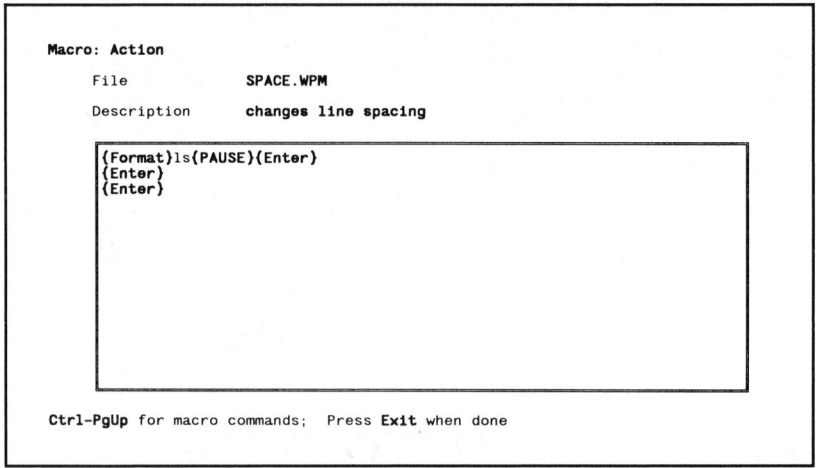

*Figure 7.27:* The **space** macro lets you indicate the spacing you want to use, so you don't need separate macros for single and double spacing.

## USING THE MACRO

When you use the macro, WordPerfect will pause and wait for you to enter a number. Entering 1 indicates single spacing, 1.5 is space-and-a-half, 2 is double spacing, and so forth. WordPerfect will multiply the number you enter by the line height of the font you're using to create the new line spacing.

After you enter the number and press ⏎, you'll be returned to your document, and the new line spacing will be in effect from the cursor's position on.

## OTHER USES

You may want to add a {BELL} command just before the pause so that the program will beep when it's ready for your input. See Chapter 3 for instructions on adding the beep.

## SETTING UP A COLUMN FORMAT: NEWSPAPER COLUMNS

WordPerfect is preset to give you two equally spaced newspaper columns. Newspaper columns, which are also called *snaking* or *winding* columns, are used whenever it doesn't matter where the material in the column ends, because the program automatically wraps text to the top of the next column. You may not know, however, that you can create a column definition at the beginning of your document and then simply turn columns on and off as you need them. This allows you to make your design decisions at the beginning of a document and then not have to worry about exactly which settings you used each time you want to turn columns on.

This macro, named **news**, will set up a newspaper-style column definition for two 3-inch columns, the first beginning at the left margin (the 1-inch position) and the second beginning at the 4½-inch mark and extending to the right margin, so there is ½ inch of space between columns. When you record the macro, you can change these values for different-sized columns.

After you've used this macro, you can then use the next macro, named **on**, to turn on the Columns feature whenever you want text in a document to be in columns. The **on** macro will turn Columns off if they're already on.

To copy or move a column definition so that you can use it again, put the cursor on the [Col Def] code for the definition you want to copy. Then press Del to delete it and respond **Y** to the prompt. Move to the new location and press F1 (Cancel); then type **R** for Restore. If you're copying it, restore it in its original position before you move the cursor. This works with math definitions, too.

### RECORDING THE MACRO

To record the macro, take the following steps:

1. Turn on the macro recorder by pressing Ctrl-F10 or choosing Macro from the Tools menu and then choosing Define. Enter **news** as the name of the macro.

2. Enter **sets newspaper column definition** as the macro description; then press ↵.

3. Press Alt-F7. In version 5.1, type **C** next for Columns.

4. Type **D** for Define; then press F7 twice to return to your document. If you want to set different column widths, enter those values while you see the Text Column Definition

screen. For example, typing **M** for Margins and changing the left and right margin settings to 1″ and 5″ for Column 1 and 5.5″ and 7.5″ for Column 2 will result in one 4-inch column on the left and one 2-inch column on the right.

5. Press Ctrl-F10 again to stop recording the macro.

Then, to record the **on** macro that will turn columns on (and off also, in version 5.0) as you need them, follow these steps:

> To end a newspaper column at a certain point, press Ctrl-⏎. WordPerfect will break the column there and start a new one.

1. Turn on the macro recorder by pressing Ctrl-F10 or choosing Macro from the Tools menu and then choosing Define. Type **on** as the macro's name and press ⏎.

2. Type **turns columns on and off** as the description and press ⏎.

3. Press Alt-F7.

4. Type **C** for Column and **O** for On. In version 5.0, just type **C** for Column On/Off.

5. Press Ctrl-F10 to stop recording the macro.

If you're using version 5.1, you'll need to record an **off** macro, too. Just substitute F for the O in step 4. The final **news** macro should resemble the one in Figure 7.28 (version 5.1) or Figure 7.29 (version 5.0).

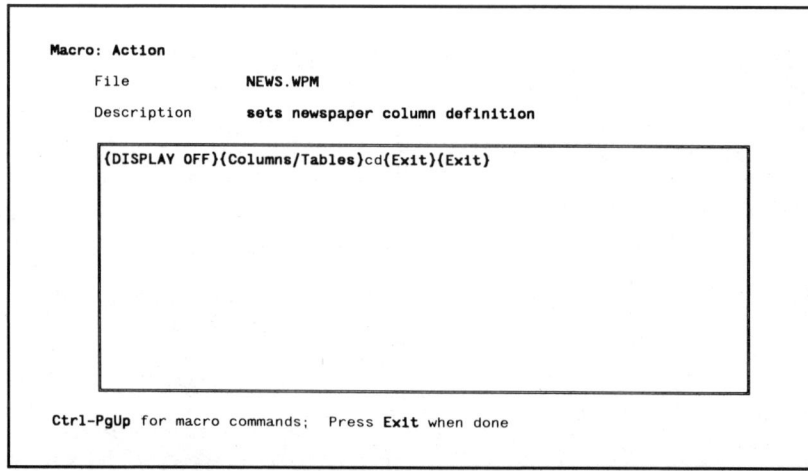

*Figure 7.28:* The version 5.1 **news** macro sets up newspaper-style columns, but it does not turn Columns on.

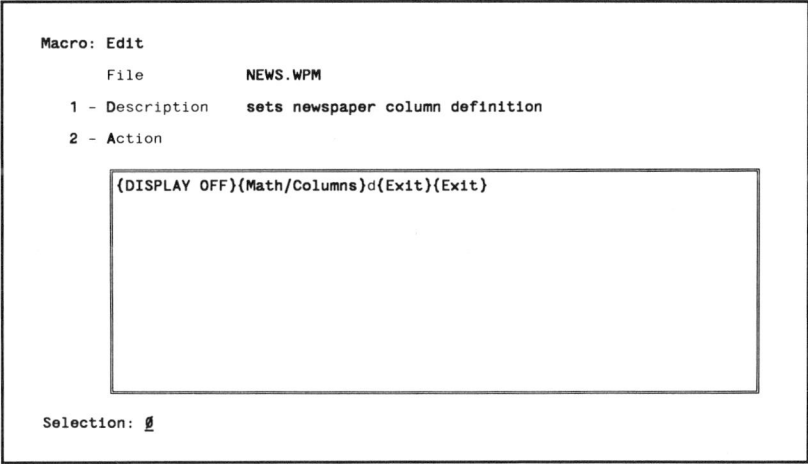

*Figure 7.29:* The version 5.0 **news** macro sets up newspaper-style columns, but it does not turn Columns on.

### USING THE MACRO

When you use the **news** macro, you define two equally spaced newspaper columns (unless you type new values into the Text Column Definition screen). The **on** macro turns the Columns feature on and off as you work in version 5.0; in version 5.1, you use the **on** and **off** macros. To record a macro for parallel columns, see the next macro.

## SETTING UP A COLUMN FORMAT: PARALLEL COLUMNS

You can have up to 24 columns on a page, but after three or four they get very narrow and hard to read unless you're using very small type.

Parallel columns are used whenever the material in the columns consists of items that should stay next to each other on the same page. Stage directions and dialog, for example, are often seen in parallel columns in scripts. Another common use for parallel columns is for agendas in which times and dates should stay parallel to events.

WordPerfect has two types of parallel columns: those that use block protection and those that don't. You're probably better off using the first kind, because it makes sure that if a page break occurs, the items won't be split between pages. The following macro sets up that kind of parallel column for you. (To turn these columns on and off, use the same **on** and **off** macros as in the previous example.)

This macro, named **par**, sets up a definition for two equal parallel columns. As in the **news** macro you just saw, if you don't want columns of equal size, just enter the left and right margin values for each column when you see the Text Column Definition screen.

### RECORDING THE MACRO

To record the macro, take the following steps:

> If you've just recorded the **news** macro and changed the column settings, you'll need to type **M** and enter 1″, 4″, 4.5″, and 7.5″ as the column margin settings to get two columns of equal size.

1. Turn on the macro recorder by pressing Ctrl-F10 or choosing Macro from the Tools menu and then choosing Define. Enter **par** as the name of the macro.

2. Enter **defines two equal parallel columns** as the macro description; then press ⏎.

3. Press Alt-F7 and type **C** for Columns (version 5.1), **D** for Define, and **T** for Type. (In version 5.0, you do not have to type the C.)

4. Type **B** for Parallel Columns with Block Protect.

5. Press F7 twice to return to your document.

6. Press Ctrl-F10 again to stop recording the macro.

The final version 5.1 macro should resemble the one in Figure 7.30.

### USING THE MACRO

When you use the macro, WordPerfect defines two equal parallel columns for you. To turn on the Columns feature so that the text you type will be entered in column format, use the **on** macro given previously. To indicate the end of a column and begin a new one, press Ctrl-⏎.

## TURNING ON PAGE NUMBERING

WordPerfect is preset for no page numbering. If you haven't used the Setup menu to change this setting so that page numbering will be

## MACROS FOR FORMATTING TEXT    255

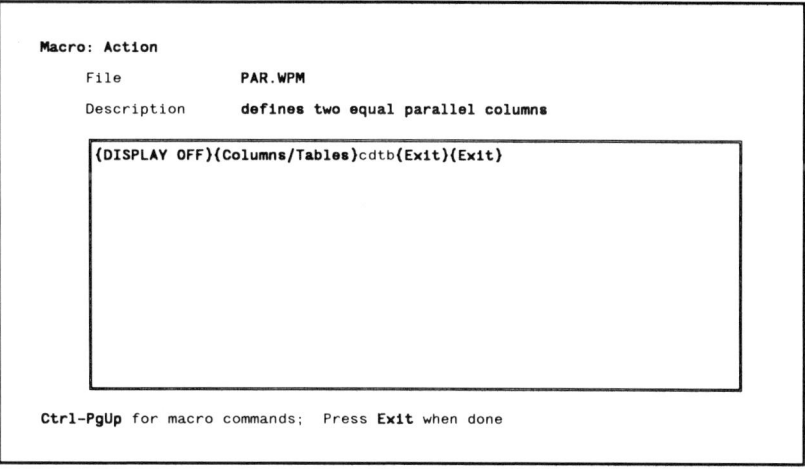

*Figure 7.30:* The **par** macro sets up parallel columns that use block protection so that they won't be broken between pages.

> You can also use this macro to turn off page numbering if it's been turned on. Just type **9** and press ← when the macro pauses.

on in all your documents, you may want to use a macro like this one to turn it on just in the pages where you want it. This macro, named **pgn**, displays the 'Format: Page Numbering' screen and pauses to let you choose a page-numbering option.

## *RECORDING THE MACRO*

To record the macro, take the following steps:

1. Turn on the macro recorder by pressing Ctrl-F10 or choosing Macro from the Tools menu and then choosing Define. Enter **pgn** as the name of the macro.

2. Enter **turns on page numbering** as the macro description; then press ←.

3. Press Shift-F8 (Format) and type **P** for Page; then type **P** (version 5.0) or **P N 4** (version 5.1) for Page numbering.

4. Insert a pause by pressing Ctrl-PgUp and typing **P**.

5. Press ← to resume the macro.

6. Press ← two times to return to your document.

7. Press Ctrl-F10 again to stop recording the macro.

### USING THE MACRO

When you use the macro, the program will pause for you to choose a page-numbering style. Type one of the following:

1. Page numbers in the upper-left corner of every page
2. Page numbers in the top center of every page
3. Page numbers in the upper-right corner of every page
4. Page numbers in the upper-left corner of even (left-hand) pages and in the upper-right corner of odd (right-hand) pages; this style is useful if you're printing a document on both sides of the paper and binding it
5. Page numbers in the lower-left corner of every page
6. Page numbers in the bottom center of every page
7. Page numbers in the lower-right corner of every page
8. Alternating page numbers like those in option 4, but they are placed in the lower-right and lower-left corners of odd and even pages
9. Turn off page numbering if it has been turned on

After you type the number and press ⏎, you will return to your document.

### OTHER USES

You may want to modify the macro so that it turns on page numbering and then immediately suppresses it for the current page. This is useful, for example, if you're turning on page numbering at the beginning of a document but want the first page to be a title page or a cover sheet with no page number. Likewise, a business letter usually has no page number on the first page but begins numbering with 2 on the second page.

## CHANGING THE ALIGNMENT CHARACTER

If you type equations that you want to align on the equals sign or write memos in which you want headings to align on a colon, you're probably often looking for the keystrokes to press to change the alignment character from the period to the = or :, or to something else. The command for changing the alignment character is on the Other submenu of the Format menu, but it's listed as Decimal Characters and can be hard to find. You can record this macro instead. It will pause for you to type the character that you want to use as the alignment character. For example, you can quickly set up memo headings that are aligned on the colon as follows:

SUBJECT:
  DATE:
     TO:

This macro, named **align**, lets you specify an alignment character.

## *RECORDING THE MACRO*

To record the macro, take the following steps:

1. Turn on the macro recorder by pressing Ctrl-F10 or choosing Macro from the Tools menu and then choosing Define. Enter **align** as the name of the macro.

2. Enter **change alignment character** as the macro description; then press ←⎯.

3. Press Shift-F8 (Format) and type **O** for Other.

4. Type **D** for Decimal/Alignment Character; then insert a pause (Ctrl-PgUp **P**).

5. Resume the macro by pressing ←⎯.

6. Press F7 to return to your document.

7. Press Ctrl-F10 again to stop recording the macro.

The final macro should resemble the one in Figure 7.31.

## *USING THE MACRO*

When you use the macro, WordPerfect will pause for you to type a character that will be used as the new alignment character in that document only, until you change it. Then, when you're ready to type

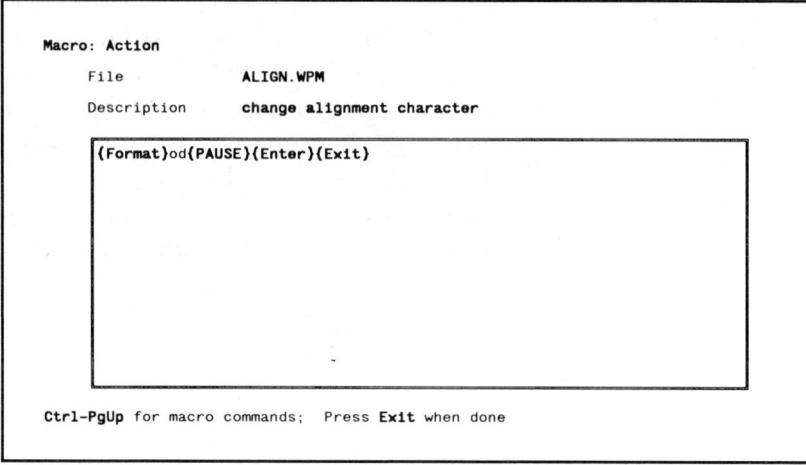

*Figure 7.31:* The **align** macro lets you choose a different alignment character.

text that should align on that character, press Ctrl-F6 (Tab Align). The cursor will move to the next tab stop, and the message 'Align char = .' will appear in the lower-left corner of the screen (the period will be replaced by your new alignment character). Text that you type moves to the left of the cursor until you type whatever character you have set as the decimal/alignment character. After you type that character, text is inserted normally.

As you type your text, it will be entered from right to left, just as it is when you use a right-justified or decimal tab. As soon as you type the alignment character, the 'Align Char = .' message disappears, and any text you then type is entered from left to right as though you were using a left-justified tab.

A few words of caution about the Tab Align command: when you use it, make sure that you have left enough space to enter all of the text that precedes the alignment character before WordPerfect reaches the left margin. If you haven't, and your text is longer than can be accommodated, WordPerfect will activate the margin release when it reaches the left margin, and your text will disappear off the screen. If you continue entering characters after the line has reached the left edge of the page, the text will begin to be entered from the alignment tab position to the right.

When you need to edit the text on a line that has been aligned with the Tab Align command, use the Reveal Codes window to place the cursor between alignment codes before inserting or deleting any text. To do this, press Alt-F3 and locate the [Align] and [C/A/Flrt] codes surrounding the text. Then move the cursor somewhere within these codes, press Alt-F3 to return to the document, and edit the text. Be careful not to insert more text than can be accommodated between the tab stop where the alignment character is entered and the left margin. When you insert new text, remember that text is entered from right to left, just the opposite of the way you are used to seeing it appear on the screen as you type.

To return text aligned with the Tab Align command to the previous tab stop, open the Reveal Codes window and delete either the [Align] or the [C/A/Flrt] formatting code. If you want the text flush with the left margin, also delete the [Tab] code.

## *STANDARDIZING SPACING BETWEEN SENTENCES*

If you're sloppy like me, sometimes you have one space between sentences, and sometimes you have two. If you're preparing material for publication, though, you can't afford to be that sloppy. Instead of going through your document line by line to check the spacing between sentences, use this macro instead. It searches for each occurrence of a period, exclamation point, or question mark, and makes sure that each one is followed by only one space.

### *BEFORE YOU BEGIN*

Before you begin to record the macro:

- You should have a document containing several sentences on the screen.

### *RECORDING THE MACRO*

To record the macro, take the following steps:

1. Turn on the macro recorder by pressing Ctrl-F10 or choosing Macro from the Tools menu and then choosing Define. Enter **spaces** as the name of the macro.

2. Enter **standardizes spacing between sentences** as the macro description; then press ⏎.

3. Press Home Home ↑ to move to the beginning of the document; then press Alt-F2 (Replace).

4. Press ⏎ to replace without confirming.

5. Type a period and press the Spacebar twice to search for any sentences that end in periods plus two spaces.

6. Press F2; then type a period and one space to replace those occurrences with a period and one space. Press F2 again.

7. Press Home Home ↑ to move to the beginning of the document; then press Alt-F2 (Replace).

8. Press ⏎ to replace without confirming.

9. Type an exclamation point and press the Spacebar twice to search for any sentences that end in exclamation points plus two spaces.

10. Press F2; then type an exclamation point and one space to replace those occurrences with an exclamation point and one space. Press F2 again.

11. Press Home Home ↑ to move to the beginning of the document; then press Alt-F2 (Replace).

12. Press ⏎ to replace without confirming.

13. Type a question mark and press the Spacebar twice to search for any sentences that end in question marks plus two spaces.

14. Press F2; then type a question mark and one space to replace those occurrences with a question mark and one space. Press F2 again.

15. As a finishing touch, press Home Home ↑ again so that you return to the beginning of the document when the macro is done.

16. Press Ctrl-F10 again to stop recording the macro.

The final macro should resemble the one in Figure 7.32.

```
Macro: Action
    File           SPACES.WPM
    Description    standardizes spacing between sentences

    {DISPLAY OFF}{Home}{Home}{Up}
    {Replace}{Enter}
    .··{Search}.·{Search}{Home}{Home}{Up}
    {Replace}{Enter}
    !··{Search}!·{Search}{Home}{Home}{Up}
    {Replace}{Enter}
    ?··{Search}?·{Search}{Home}{Home}{Up}

Ctrl-PgUp for macro commands;   Press Exit when done
```

*Figure 7.32:* The **spaces** macro standardizes the spacing between sentences for you.

### USING THE MACRO

When you use the macro, WordPerfect searches for the ending punctuation you have specified and replaces any places where you may have used two spaces with the symbol plus only one space.

## SUMMARY

By recording a selection of the macros in this chapter, you've added a few of the most often used formats to your macro library. Now you can explore the more specialized macros in Chapter 8. If you use graphics in your work or do desktop publishing, you will probably find uses for macros such as those that create presentation graphics, draw organization charts, create sidebars, and provide special figure borders. As people who do desktop publishing often also use WordPerfect's Styles feature, which allows you to quickly change the style of various text elements in a document, I've also included a few macros for working with styles in Chapter 8.

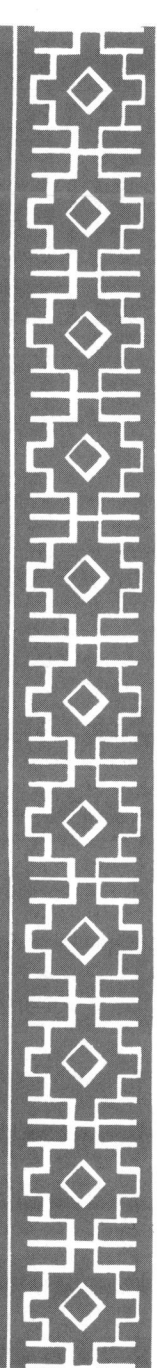

# *Graphics and Style Macros*

CHAPTER

8

# CHAPTER 8

In this chapter, you'll find all sorts of macros ranging from those that change fonts to those that automate the process of creating graphics boxes. If you use either the Styles or the Graphics features of WordPerfect, you'll find macros here that can speed up your work.

In particular, you'll find many macros that will be of use if you do desktop publishing. For example, if you use Ventura Publisher with WordPerfect, you know that you have to use a different set of codes for changing print attributes and styles in that program. A macro in this chapter shows you how you can have WordPerfect convert its codes to those of Ventura Publisher automatically. Another macro demonstrates how to use WordPerfect to create mastheads, sidebars, and shaded figure boxes that use special borders, all of which can enhance your publications.

Other macros in this chapter illustrate how you can easily use WordPerfect to create presentation graphics. You'll find macros that create a border for your transparency master and set up a skeleton outline form within it, so that all you have to do is fill in the points of your outline. Another macro creates a standard organization chart for you, and another shows you how you can have automatic writing on the screen so that your message appears suddenly, giving the appearance of animation. And, if you present slide-show demonstrations, you'll find a useful macro that presents each "slide" automatically.

Finally, macros for working with text styles show you how to use different ones for different types of headings with no retyping, how to automatically change text elements to different fonts and then back again to your text font quickly, and how to turn styles on and off.

## CONVERTING WORDPERFECT CODES TO VENTURA PUBLISHER

If you use WordPerfect with another desktop publishing program, you know that you have to convert the WordPerfect codes to the ones used by that program. This is not always as simple as it sounds, because WordPerfect uses two codes, such as [UND][und], to turn on and off an effect in your text. To convert the codes correctly, you need to change the first one to an "On" code in the desktop publishing program and change the last one to an "Off" code. For example, Ventura Publisher uses the codes listed in Table 8.1. The code

*Table 8.1:* WordPerfect Attribute and Size Codes and Equivalent Codes in Ventura Publisher

| WORDPERFECT CODE | IN VENTURA |
|---|---|
| [BOLD] | \<B\> |
| [bold] | \<D\>* |
| [UND] | \<U\> |
| [und] | \<D\> |
| [OVERSTK] | \<O\> |
| [overstk] | \<D\> |
| [SUBSCPT] | \<v\> |
| [SUPRSCPT] | \<^\> |
| [FINE] | \<P06\>** |
| [SMALL] | \<P10\> |
| [LARGE] | \<P14\> |
| [VRY LARGE] | \<P18\> |
| [EXT LARGE] | \<P24\> |

\* In Ventura Publisher, \<D\> returns to normal type.
\*\* These codes assume your base or initial font is 12-point type. If you change the size of the base font, all other point sizes change.

<P10> turns on small type (10-point), and the code <P12> turns it off (back to 12-point type). If you tried to do a straightforward search-and-replace, you'd find that when you replaced all the [SMALL] codes with <P10>, you lost all the [small] codes that you need to change to <P12>.

This is because WordPerfect automatically deletes the second in a pair of style codes when you delete or change the first one. This macro, named **repsm** (for replace small), will replace the codes correctly for you. You will need to record it several times, each time with a different name indicating what is being replaced, for each instance of codes that you want to replace. For example, if you need to convert [BOLD][bold] codes, write a **repbd** (replace bold) macro; for [VRY LARGE][vry large] codes, write a **repvl** (replace very large) macro, and so forth.

## *BEFORE YOU BEGIN*

Before you begin to record the macro:

- You should have a document containing the kind of codes you want to replace on the screen. In this example, we will replace codes for small type in a document whose base or initial font is 12-point type, so small type will become 10-point type in Ventura Publisher.

## *RECORDING THE MACRO*

To record the macro, take the following steps:

1. Turn on the macro recorder by pressing Ctrl-F10 or choosing Macro from the Tools menu and then choosing Define. Enter **repsm** as the name of the macro.

2. Enter **replaces small codes for Ventura** as the macro description; then press ←┘.

3. Press Home Home ↓ to go to the end of the document.

4. Press Alt-F2 to search and replace; then press ←┘ to bypass having to confirm each replacement.

5. Press ↑ to search backward. Then press Ctrl-End to delete any codes that may already be at the prompt from a previous operation.

6. Press Ctrl-F8 (Font) and type **S S** to search for the [SMALL] code; then press F2.

7. Press Ctrl-F8 and type **S S** to generate another [SMALL] code. Type **<P10>** (or type the code your program needs to turn on the style). Your screen should have the line

    [SMALL]<P10>

    after the 'Replace with' prompt. This will replace all the [SMALL] codes with [SMALL]<P10>. Because you are adding a Ventura code, you can delete the WordPerfect code later after you have the other codes in place.

8. Press F2 to replace the codes.

9. When WordPerfect finishes replacing all the [SMALL] codes with [SMALL]<P10>, return to the end of your document by pressing Home Home ↓.

10. This time, you want to replace all the [small] codes with <P12>. Press Alt-F2, press ↵, and press ↑ to search backward. The [SMALL] code is at the prompt, so press Del; then press Ctrl-F8 and type **S S**. Do this twice to generate the [small] code.

11. Press ← and Backspace to delete the first [SMALL] code.

12. Press F2 and type **<P12>** (or type the code you need to turn off the style).

13. Press F2 to begin the search-and-replace operation.

Your final macro should resemble the one in Figure 8.1.

## *USING THE MACRO*

When WordPerfect finishes, all the [SMALL] codes will be replaced with <P10>, and all the [small] codes with <P12>.

## CH. 8

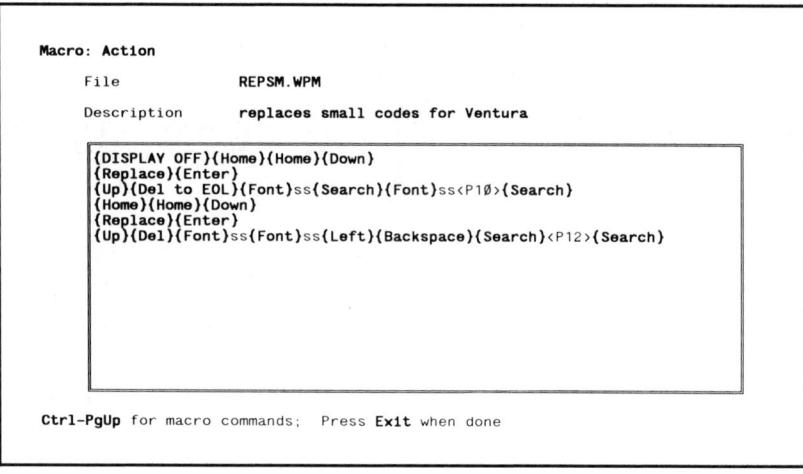

*Figure 8.1:* Use a macro that adds a character before it deletes one to get around WordPerfect's practice of deleting both codes of a pair.

### OTHER USES

> Any time you need to modify a macro slightly but keep the original intact, just use List Files (F5) to copy it under another name. You can then edit it as you wish.

You can use the same procedure to create macros for changing Bold codes to <B><D>, or Large codes to <P14><P12>, and so forth. Just use List Files (F5) to copy the macro: highlight the macro's name, type **C** to copy it, and edit the name that WordPerfect presents. When you press ⏎, WordPerfect will make a copy of the macro with the new name you have specified. You can copy a macro into a different directory by editing the path name. The new name of the macro will not immediately be displayed if you copy it within the same directory. However, it will be displayed when you start WordPerfect again or when you view the List Files screen again by pressing F5 ⏎. Although the new name isn't displayed, you can still retrieve the macro and edit it. Then copy it back into your macro directory and edit it for the specific codes you want to use.

### CREATING A MASTHEAD

This macro, named **mast**, creates the masthead shown in Figure 8.2. It is actually a text box. When you record the macro for yourself, substitute the text that you want to have in the masthead of

# GRAPHICS AND STYLE MACROS       269

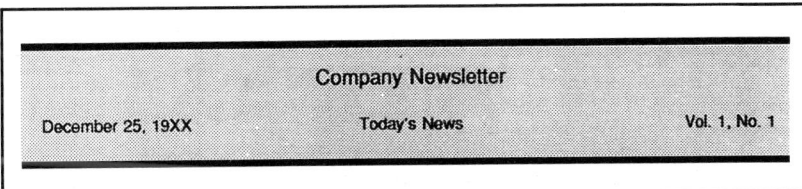

*Figure 8.2:* This shaded masthead was created by the **mast** macro.

your newsletter. You can also choose a different typeface. This macro uses 12-point Helvetica.

## *BEFORE YOU BEGIN*

Before you begin to record the macro:

- You should switch to single spacing if you are not already using it.

## *RECORDING THE MACRO*

To record the macro, take the following steps:

> Text boxes are automatically shaded with a 10-percent gray screen and thick borders at the top and bottom. If you don't want shading or thick borders, use a Figure box instead; it will have single rules on all four sides for borders and no shading.

1. Turn on the macro recorder by pressing Ctrl-F10 or choosing Macro from the Tools menu and then choosing Define. Enter **mast** as the name of the macro.

2. Enter **creates masthead** as the macro description; then press ⏎.

3. Press Alt-F9 (Graphics), then type **B** for Text Box.

4. Type **C** for Create; then choose Size (7 or S).

5. Choose Set Both (3 or B); then type **6.5** and press ⏎ to enter the width for a box that will extend from margin to margin, assuming you're using 1-inch left and right margins in the default unit of measurement (inches). If you aren't using inches, type " after the width and height (in the next step) to indicate inches.

6. For the height, type **1** and press ⏎.

7. Then type **E** to edit the graphics box.

8. To use a different font in the masthead, press Ctrl-F8 (Font); then type **F** for Base Font. Use Name Search to change the font to the one that you want to use with your printer by typing **N** and then the first few characters of the font's name. In this example, 12-point Helvetica was used on a laser printer. The keystrokes used to select a font on your printer will vary.

9. Press Shift-F6 (Center) and type **Company Newsletter** (or the name of your newsletter); then press ⏎.

10. To switch to a smaller size for the second line, press Ctrl-F8 (Font) and type **S S** for Size Small.

11. Then insert a pause so that you can type the current date when the macro executes. Press Ctrl-PgUp, type **P**, and press ⏎. You could insert either the date text or the date function here, but remember that WordPerfect will automatically update the date each time you retrieve the document if you use the Date function.

12. Press Shift-F6 (Center). Then type the text that you want to have centered on the second line ("Today's News" in the example).

13. Press Alt-F6 (Flush Right) and insert another pause (Ctrl-PgUp, **P**, ⏎). When you execute the macro, you would at this point type the text that you want to be flush right ("Vol. 1, No. 1" in the example).

14. Press F7 twice to return to your document.

15. Press Ctrl-F10 again to stop recording the macro.

Although you will not see the results on your screen, you can test-print the page or use the View Document feature to see the masthead that you have just created. The final macro should resemble the one in Figure 8.3.

## *USING THE MACRO*

When you use the macro, position the cursor at the top of the page. WordPerfect will then use its graphics abilities to create a 10-percent gray text box and position the text you typed within it, as in

Figure 8.2. It will pause for you to enter the date. After you type the date, press ⏎. The macro will pause again for you to enter the volume number.

## *OTHER USES*

If your newsletter uses a column format, you can include the instructions for defining columns and turning them on as part of the macro. In that way, you can immediately retrieve the text of your articles into columns, or start typing columns of text. For example, to define and turn on two equal-sized newspaper columns below the masthead, edit the macro to add the following steps at the end:

1. Press Alt-F7 (Math/Columns); type **C** (in version 5.1) and then type **D** to define the columns.

2. To accept the default settings of two equal newspaper columns, press F7.

3. Type **C** to turn on the Columns feature.

You may also want to add instructions for changing to a different font for the body of your newsletter.

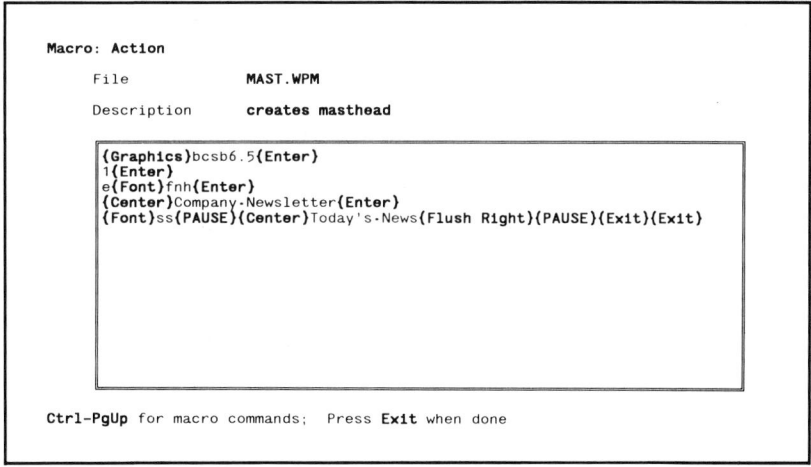

*Figure 8.3:* This macro creates a 1-inch shaded masthead containing the text you specify.

## CREATING PRESENTATION GRAPHICS

You don't need to purchase a separate presentation graphics program as long as you've got WordPerfect. Even without a source of graphic images, you can create bulleted outlines, organization charts, and—by using the Line Draw feature—graphs. The next few macros will show you how to create an empty text box that is the correct shape for transparency masters; how to create an outline with bulleted points in it; how to retrieve an already created organization chart; and how to put the whole thing together as a slide show in which each new slide appears when you press ↵. After you've assembled your slide show, in which each slide is on a separate page, you can simply print the document that contains it and you will have handouts for your audience.

This macro, named **border**, creates a full-page double border around a text box. You can use it as the basis for creating different types of presentation graphics, such as an outline of points to be made, graphs and charts, and so forth.

### BEFORE YOU BEGIN

Before you begin to record the macro:

- Clear the screen. If you're using version 5.1, check to see that you have a paper size defined for 11 by 8½ inch (wide) format, to be printed in Landscape mode. Press Shift-F8 (Format), type P for Page and S for Paper Size. You will be at the Format: Paper Size/Type screen, and you should see a line such as 'Standard–Wide 11 × 8.5''', and under Font Type should be 'Landscape.' This paper size comes with the program, but you or someone else may have deleted it. To recreate it if it's missing, while you're at the Format: Paper Size/Type screen, type A for Add, S for Standard, S for Size, T for Standard Landscape, F for Font Type, and L for Landscape, and press F7 until you return to your document.

*If you're creating presentation graphics for overhead transparencies, the ideal proportions are 3:4. The text box produced by this macro is 9 inches by 6½ inches, so it is best used for transparencies. For 35 mm slides, the best proportions are 2:3, which is a page of 9½ inches by 7½ inches. You can change the box size if you're making 35 mm slides.*

## RECORDING THE MACRO

To record the macro, take the following steps:

1. Turn on the macro recorder by pressing Ctrl-F10 or choosing Macro from the Tools menu and then choosing Define. Enter **border** as the name of the macro.

2. Enter **presentation graphic border** as the macro description; then press ⏎.

3. Press Shift-F8 (Format) and type **P** for Page.

Steps 4 and 5 will vary for versions 5.0 and 5.1 of the program.

4. In version 5.1: Type **S** for Paper Size; then press Ctrl-PgUp to enter a pause in the macro. Move the highlight cursor to the Standard–Wide entry with Landscape orientation and press ⏎ to resume the macro. In version 5.0: Type **S** for Paper Size; then type **T** for Standard Landscape.

5. In version 5.1: Type **S** to select Standard–Wide; then press F7. In version 5.0: Type **S** for Standard; then press F7. This instructs WordPerfect to print the page sideways, in Landscape orientation.

6. Now you can add the border options, because they must come before the code for the text box itself. Press Alt-F9 (Graphics), type **B** for Text Box, and type **O** for Options.

7. Type **B** for Border; then type **D** for a double rule four times.

8. Type **G** for Gray; then type **0**, press ⏎, and press F7 to exit.

9. Now you can create the text box. Press Alt-F9 (Graphics) and type **B** for Text Box.

10. Type **C** for Create, **T** for Anchor Type, **A** for Page, and **V** for Vertical Position.

11. Type **F** for Full Page.

12. Press F7 to exit.

13. Press Ctrl-F10 again to stop recording the macro.

Please note that when you use this macro, your screen will be blank during the pause that you entered (in version 5.1) unless you go into the macro editor and insert a {DISPLAY ON} command at the beginning of the macro. If you wish to do so here, or in other macros in which you get a blank pause, see Appendix A for more details on using {DISPLAY ON}.

You have now created an empty full-page text box. Although you can't see it on the screen, you can test-print the page or use View Document to see it. Figure 8.4 shows the results of printing the document, and Figures 8.5 and 8.6 illustrate the steps in the macro used to create it for versions 5.0 and 5.1, where it's named **border2**.

### USING THE MACRO

In version 5.1, select Standard-Wide when the macro pauses.

To add contents to the box when you use the macro, press Alt-F9, type **B** for text box, type **E** for Edit, and enter the number of the text box you want to edit. When the Definition: Text Box screen appears, you can type **E** for Edit, and then enter text, or type **F** for Filename and retrieve an existing graphic. If you enter text, you may want to change to a different typeface and size from the initial font that you normally use.

> If you can print in different fonts, you may want to choose a different font for your presentation graphics by moving to the beginning of the document that is going to hold them and then pressing Ctrl-F8 (Font) and selecting your typeface and size. All the text in the graphics you prepare in that document will then use the font you have chosen.

## PRESENTATION GRAPHICS: CREATING A BULLETED OUTLINE

This macro, named **outl**, creates the skeleton of a bulleted outline inside the graphics box you just created. You can simply edit the outline to delete the text that is being used as a placeholder and enter the text of your major and subordinate points. The outline uses the Indent key so that text that is longer than one line will wrap and indent correctly, as Figure 8.7 shows.

There are quite a few steps in this macro, but if you create outlines for presentation graphics frequently, it can save you a lot of time. You don't have to keep setting up the exact spacing or defining the outline style.

*Figure 8.4:* The **border** macro produces a full-page empty text box like this one (it will actually be printed in Landscape mode).

```
Macro: Action
    File            BORDER2.WPM
    Description     presentation graphic border
    ┌─────────────────────────────────────────────────────────┐
    │ {Format}ps{PAUSE}s{Exit}{Graphics}bobddddg0{Enter}{Exit}{Graphics}
    │ bcta0{Enter}vf{Exit}                                     │
    │                                                          │
    └─────────────────────────────────────────────────────────┘
Ctrl-PgUp for macro commands;  Press Exit when done
```

*Figure 8.5:* To create the **border2** macro, these steps are required (version 5.1).

```
Macro: Edit
        File            BORDER.WPM
    1 - Description     creates presentation graphic border
    2 - Action
        ┌─────────────────────────────────────────────────────┐
        │ {DISPLAY OFF}{Format}psts{Exit}{Graphics}bobddddg0{Enter}
        │ {Exit}{Graphics}bctavf{Exit}                         │
        └─────────────────────────────────────────────────────┘

Selection: 0
```

*Figure 8.6:* To create the **border** macro, these steps are required (version 5.0).

## *BEFORE YOU BEGIN*

Before you begin to record the macro:

- You should have recorded and executed the previous **border** or **border2** macro.

```
                          TITLE

     ● First Major Point
         -  Subordinate point
         -  Subordinate point
     ● Second Major Point
         -  Subordinate point
         -  Subordinate point
             *  Third level
             *  Third level. Because text is indented, it will wrap and align correctly when you
                get to the last line of each item
     ●Third Major Point
         -  Subordinate point
         -  Subordinate point
```

*Figure 8.7:* The **outl** macro creates the skeleton of an outline that you can change later.

- You should either change Units of Measure to inches, or remember to enter all units in the steps of the macro with the ″ indicator.

## *RECORDING THE MACRO*

To record the macro, take the following steps:

1. Turn on the macro recorder by pressing Ctrl-F10 or choosing Macro from the Tools menu and then choosing Define. Enter **outl** as the name of the macro.

2. Enter **creates outline for graphics** as the macro description; then press ⏎.

3. Press Alt-F9 (Graphics) and type **B** for Text Box.

4. Type **E** for Edit; then pause the macro by pressing PgUp, typing **P**, and pressing ⏎. You will enter the number of the text box you want to edit and then press ⏎ when you use the macro. Normally, this will be text box 1 unless you have other text boxes in your document.

5. Set line spacing to double spacing by pressing Shift-F8 (Format), typing **L** for Line, typing **S** for Spacing, typing **2**, and pressing ⏎ three times.

6. Press ⏎ twice more to add space at the top of your outline.

7. Press Shift-F6 (Center). Then, to use Large type for the main head, press Ctrl-F8 (Font), type **S** for Size, and type **L** for Large.

8. As you are only creating placeholding text here, type **TITLE**. Then press Ctrl-F8 and type **N** for Normal to return to normal- sized type for the rest of the outline.

9. Press ⏎ twice to add space between the title and the body of the outline.

10. Now you can set tabs so that the outline will be indented correctly. Press Shift-F8, type **L** for Line, and type **T** for Tab Set.

11. Press Home-← to move to the beginning of the tab line.

12. Press Ctrl-End to delete all tabs.

13. Type **1.5,.25** to set the first tab at the 1.5″ mark and set tab intervals of .25″.

14. Press ⏎; then press F7 twice.

15. Now you need to define the style that you will be using. Bullets are popular for presentation graphics; press Shift-F5 (Date/Outline), type **D** for Define, and type **5** for Bullets. Then press ⏎ twice.

16. Press Tab. Then press Shift-F5 and type **P** for Paragraph Numbering (Outline works erratically in graphics).
17. Press ⏎.
18. Press F4 (Indent); then type **First Major Point**.
19. Press ⏎; then press Tab twice.
20. Press Shift-F5, type **P**, and press ⏎. Press F4 (Indent) and type **Subordinate point**.
21. Press ⏎; then press Tab twice.
22. Press Shift-F5, type **P**, and press ⏎. Press F4 and type **Subordinate point**.
23. Press ⏎; then press Tab.
24. Press Shift-F5, type **P**, and press ⏎. Press F4 and type **Second Major Point**.
25. Press ⏎; then press Tab twice.
26. Press Shift-F5, type **P**, and press ⏎.
27. Press F4 and type **Subordinate point**.
28. Press ⏎; then press Tab twice.
29. Press Shift-F5, type **P**, and press ⏎.
30. Press F4 and type **Subordinate point**.
31. Press ⏎; then press Tab three times.
32. This time, you will choose the asterisk (level 5) as the bullet style. Press Shift-F5, type **P**, type **5**, press ⏎, and press F4.
33. Type **Third level**.
34. Press ⏎; then press Tab three times.
35. Press Shift-F5, type **P**, type **5**, press ⏎, and press F4.
36. To fill out the rest of the outline skeleton, you can add the rest of the points illustrated in Figure 8.7. Type **Third level. Because text is indented, it will wrap and align correctly when you get to the last line of each item**. Then press ⏎ and Tab.
37. Press Shift-F5, type **P**, and press ⏎. Press F4 and type **Third Major Point**.

38. Press ⏎; then press Tab twice.
39. Press Shift-F5, type **P**, and press ⏎.
40. Press F4 and type **Subordinate point**.
41. Press ⏎; then press Tab twice.
42. Press Shift-F5, type **P**, and press ⏎.
43. Press F4 and type **Subordinate point**.
44. Now, because when you use the macro you want to start by editing the title, you position the cursor next to it before you quit recording. Press Shift-F2 (Reverse Search), press Ctrl-F8 (Font), type **S** for Size and **L** for Large. Then press F2 to search for the Large code at the beginning of the word TITLE.
45. Press Ctrl-F10 again to stop recording the macro.

The final macro should resemble the one in Figures 8.8A–8.8C.

A more elegant way is to edit the macro so that it will execute the **border2** macro and prompt you for the box number. You can change

```
Macro: Action
     File            OUTL.WPM
     Description     creates outline for graphics

     {Graphics}be{PAUSE}{Enter}
     e{Format}ls2{Enter}
     {Enter}
     {Enter}
     {Enter}
     {Center}{Font}slTITLE{Font}n{Enter}
     {Enter}
     {Format}lt{Home}{Left}{Del to EOL}1.5,.25{Enter}
     {Exit}{Exit}{Date/Outline}d5{Enter}{Enter}
     {Tab}{Date/Outline}p{Enter}
     {Indent}First-Major-Point{Enter}
     {Tab}{Tab}{Date/Outline}p{Enter}
     {Indent}Subordinate-point{Enter}
     {Tab}{Tab}{Date/Outline}p{Enter}
     {Indent}Subordinate-point{Enter}

Ctrl-PgUp for macro commands;   Press Exit when done
```

*Figure 8.8A:* The **outl** macro created the outline structure (indents will be slightly different in versions 5.0 and 5.1).

```
Macro: Action
    File           OUTL.WPM
    Description    creates outline for graphics

    {Tab}{Tab}{Date/Outline}p{Enter}
    {Indent}Subordinate·point{Enter}
    {Tab}{Date/Outline}p{Enter}
    {Indent}Second·Major·Point{Enter}
    {Tab}{Tab}{Date/Outline}p{Enter}
    {Indent}Subordinate·point{Enter}
    {Tab}{Tab}{Date/Outline}p{Enter}
    {Indent}Subordinate·point{Enter}
    {Tab}{Tab}{Tab}{Date/Outline}p5{Enter}
    {Indent}Third·level{Enter}
    {Tab}{Tab}{Tab}{Date/Outline}p5{Enter}
    {Indent}Third·level.·Because·text·is·indented,·it·will·wrap·and·align·
    correctly·when·you·get·to·the·last·line·of·each·item{Enter}
    {Tab}{Date/Outline}p{Enter}
    {Indent}Third·Major·Point{Enter}

Ctrl-PgUp for macro commands;  Press Exit when done
```

*Figure 8.8B:* The **outl** macro (continued). To help you keep your place, the top lines of Figure 8.8B repeat the bottom lines of the preceding figure.

```
Macro: Action
    File           OUTL.WPM
    Description    creates outline for graphics

    {Tab}{Tab}{Tab}{Date/Outline}p5{Enter}
    {Indent}Third·level{Enter}
    {Tab}{Tab}{Tab}{Date/Outline}p5{Enter}
    {Indent}Third·level.·Because·text·is·indented,·it·will·wrap·and·align·
    correctly·when·you·get·to·the·last·line·of·each·item{Enter}
    {Tab}{Date/Outline}p{Enter}
    {Indent}Third·Major·Point{Enter}
    {Tab}{Tab}{Date/Outline}p{Enter}
    {Indent}Subordinate·point{Enter}
    {Tab}{Tab}{Date/Outline}p{Enter}
    {Indent}Subordinate·point{Search Left}{Font}sl{Search}

Ctrl-PgUp for macro commands;  Press Exit when done
```

*Figure 8.8C:* The **outl** macro (concluded). To help you keep your place, the top lines of Figure 8.8C repeat the bottom lines of the preceding figure.

the first line as follows in the macro editor:

{NEST}border ~ {Graphics}be{BELL}{PROMPT}Select box number ~ {PAUSE}{Enter}

## USING THE MACRO

When you use the macro, it will pause for you to enter the number of the text box you want to edit. After you enter it and press ← (or just press ← if the correct number is displayed), you can freely edit the text in the outline. To add new subordinate points, just copy the ones already there into the positions where you want them. You can delete any placeholder points that you don't need in your outline.

When you finish editing the outline to create your own outline, press F7 to exit. If you have used more text than can fit on one page, WordPerfect will prompt you that you can't exceed one page when you press F7 to exit. If this happens, you can either edit the text so that it is less than one page, or you can split the outline in two, change the line spacing, or switch to a smaller font if necessary.

If you're creating presentation graphics, remember that each one should be on a separate page, so press Ctrl-← to insert a hard page break after you have finished the outline and left the text box.

> To create a transparency, print the document. Then use a copier to copy the page onto a sheet of clear acetate.

## OTHER USES

Instead of using this macro within a text box, you can also modify it so that you can use it to create a skeleton outline of bulleted points in any other kind of document. Just delete the instructions that call the graphics box in steps 3 through 5 above.

## CREATING A SLIDE SHOW FOR YOUR PRESENTATION GRAPHICS

This macro, named **show**, is supplied with version 5.0, but it works in 5.1, too. It's on the Learning disk, but in case you've misplaced that disk, here are the steps required to recreate it. (You may also want to edit it so that it will display more than three slides. The macro automatically pauses to display each presentation graphic and then displays the next graphic when you press ←.)

# GRAPHICS AND STYLE MACROS

## BEFORE YOU BEGIN

> If you have access to a large-screen monitor, you can create a slide show with WordPerfect by using this macro.

Before you begin to record the macro:

- You should have created your presentation graphics and separated each one with a hard page break. Actually, you can record the macro with any series of pages separated by hard page breaks; they can contain any kind of text, not just graphics, that you want to display a page at a time.

- You should have saved the "slides" for the show in a document named SLIDES. It should be stored in the directory where WordPerfect automatically looks for documents (WP50 or WP51, unless you have specified a different directory for your documents by using the Setup menu). If you use a name other than SLIDES, edit the macro to use that name.

- You should save any document that you have on the screen, because the macro will automatically clear the screen.

## RECORDING THE MACRO

To record the macro, take the following steps:

1. Turn on the macro recorder by pressing Ctrl-F10 or choosing Macro from the Tools menu and then choosing Define. Enter **show** as the name of the macro.

2. Enter **automatic slide show** as the macro description; then press ←.

3. Press F7 (Exit), type **N**, and press ←. This clears the screen of whatever you may have been working on.

4. Press Shift-F10 (Retrieve), enter **slides** (or the name of the document containing your slide show), and press ←.

5. Press Shift-F7 (Print), type **6** (or **V**) for View Document, and type **1** for 100%.

6. Press ↓; then press → to adjust the display.

7. Press Ctrl-F10 to stop recording the macro.

At this point, you need to use the macro editor to insert special commands that sound a beep when the graphics display is ready. In version 5.1, press Home, press Ctrl-F10, enter **show**, and press ⏎ twice. In version 5.0, press Ctrl-F10 and enter **show** (the name of the macro you just recorded); then type **E** for Edit and **A** for action.

8. Move to the end of the macro by pressing Home Home ↓. The next steps will sound a beep and pause the macro each time a slide is displayed. If you are displaying a slide that contains more than half a screen of information, you can use the pause to press ↓ and view the other half of it. (Pressing PgDn will take you to the next slide.)

9. Press Ctrl-PgUp and move the cursor to {DISPLAY ON} on the menu box. Then press ⏎ to insert that command in the macro.

10. Press Ctrl-PgUp and move the cursor to {BELL}, and press ⏎.

11. Press Ctrl-PgUp, move the cursor to {PAUSE}, and press ⏎.

12. Press Ctrl-PgUp, move the cursor to {DISPLAY OFF}, and press ⏎.

13. Press Ctrl-F10. Then press PgDn, press ↓, and press →. Press Ctrl-F10 again.

14. Insert a {DISPLAY ON}, a {BELL}, a {PAUSE}, and a {DISPLAY OFF}.

15. Press Ctrl-F10. Then press PgDn, press ↓ twice, and press →. Press Ctrl-F10 again.

16. Insert a {DISPLAY ON}, a {BELL}, a {PAUSE}, and a {DISPLAY OFF}.

17. Repeat steps 14 through 17 for as many slides as you have in your slide show. It's better to have too many than not enough, because you can always stop the macro when you've viewed all the slides. The **show** macro illustrated in Figures 8.8A–8.8C has enough steps to display three slides.

> This macro displays text in reverse video—"black" on "white." To display it as "white" on "black," press Shift-F3 (Switch) when the slide is being displayed on the screen.

18. As the final steps in the macro, press Ctrl-V F7 Ctrl-V F7. Then type **N N** in response to the prompts about saving the document and exiting WordPerfect. When you execute the macro, the screen will clear at the end of the slide show, and you will still be in WordPerfect.

19. Press F7 (twice in version 5.0) to exit from the macro editor.

The final macro should resemble the one in Figure 8.9.

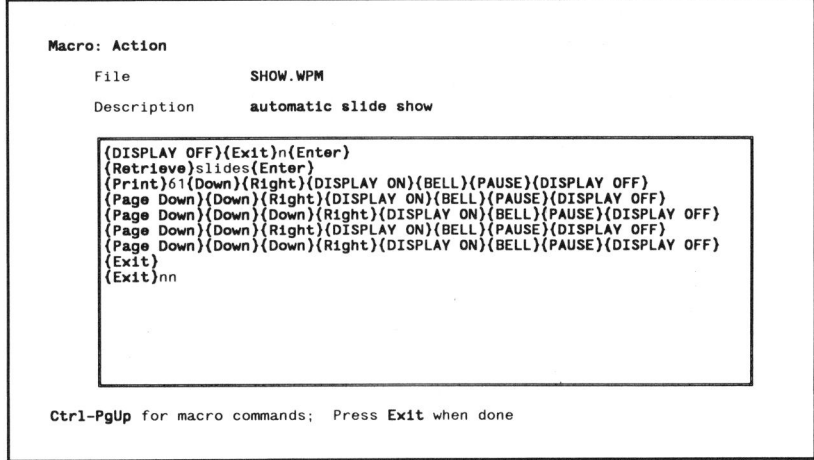

*Figure 8.9:* The **show** macro is provided with the program, but you may want to edit it.

## USING THE MACRO

When you use the macro, WordPerfect will beep and pause as each slide is displayed. You can use the arrow keys to move around on the page to see more than is displayed on the screen.

## CREATING AN ORGANIZATION CHART (VERSION 5.0)

This macro is not really a macro at all but a tip. WordPerfect 5.0 has already created and supplied an organization chart for you on the

Learning disk. Most organizations use a similar hierarchical structure. So, unless you are illustrating a dual management reporting system—one in which each function reports to two or more superior managers—you'll probably be able to modify WordPerfect's chart for your own uses and not have to create a chart from scratch.

Figure 8.10 illustrates this basic chart, slightly revised (the text of the first box and the font have been changed). Retrieve it as CHART.WKB and select your printer (it comes with the Standard Printer selected).

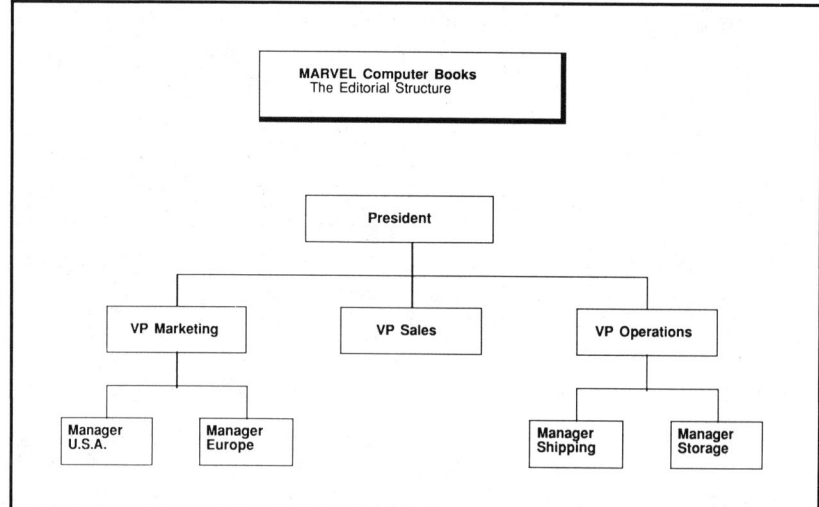

*Figure 8.10:* This basic organization chart is on the Learning disk for version 5.0.

You won't see anything on the screen at first, but if you move the cursor through the document, a series of highlighted rectangles will appear. These are text boxes, and you can see their contents either by printing the whole document, using View Document, or by choosing to edit each text box separately.

## CHANGING THE CHART BOXES

If you use Reveal Codes on the document, you will see that all the text boxes are positioned by using spaces, tabs, and hard returns. They are character boxes, which makes it easy to move them around on the page. To delete a box, just delete its [Text Box] code and delete the [HLine] and [VLine] codes that connect it to other boxes. To change the contents of a box, press Alt-F9 (Graphics), select Text Box (option 3), select Edit (option 2), enter the text box number, press ↵, and choose Edit (option 8). To create a new box, you should copy an existing one, delete it, immediately restore it with F1 (Cancel), move to the new location, and restore it again. Then edit it to change its text.

You'll probably also want to change the font that the chart uses. To change the font for the entire chart, be sure to position the cursor at the very beginning of the document, before the code for the first text box. If you just press Home Home ↑ to go to the beginning of the document, your cursor will not be before the first text box code.

If you are using a proportionally spaced font, in which each character occupies a different amount of space, you will probably find, after you've changed the font and test-printed the document, that the text inside each box needs to be adjusted. Rather than try to adjust the spacing with the Spacebar, you may find it faster to delete the contents of each text box and then press Shift-F6 (Center) to center each new line of type.

> If you change the font to a larger or smaller size (10-point is used in the chart), you may also have to change the vertical lines that connect the boxes.

## *ADDING NEW LINES*

If you need to create new vertical or horizontal lines, just position the cursor where you want the new line to start and make a note of the line number (in inches). Then position the cursor where you want the line to end and note the number of that line also. You can then use the first line number as the vertical position of the line and subtract the first from the second to get the line length. These measurements are approximate, though, so you may need to test-print or view the document at 100 percent to get the lines exactly right.

## *CREATING NEW CHARTS*

If you find that you can't adapt CHART.WPG for your uses, or if you have only version 5.1, which doesn't have CHART.WKB, you can create a new chart from scratch by using the following general procedure. First, create and position the text boxes that you're going to use. Remember to make them character-style boxes so that they can easily be positioned with the Spacebar, the Tab key, and hard returns.

Then create your horizontal lines, using the method discussed above to determine their position. Finally, create the vertical lines that join the boxes.

## CREATING BOXES WITH LINE DRAW

WordPerfect's Line Draw feature also lets you create boxes for organization charts and position text in them. This macro, named **smbox**, creates a small rectangle, shown in actual size in Figure 8.11. It's suitable for use in charts that contain two relatively short lines of text, such as a person's first initial, name, and title. You can quickly create several of these and use Line Draw to link them with vertical or horizontal lines.

*Figure 8.11:* The **smbox** rectangle creates a rectangle 4 spaces high by 15 spaces wide.

However, in Line Draw you should be aware that the rectangles you see on your screen don't have the same proportions as printed rectangles. The cursor moves a greater distance vertically than it does horizontally. Boxes that look square on the screen may not be square when printed. Also, different types of printers use different vertical-to-horizontal ratios. For example, an Epson FX-85 dot-matrix printer prints as a square a box that is five spaces wide by three spaces deep, but it doesn't look like a square on the screen. Test-print the rectangles you create with Line Draw to see if they are the size you want.

## BEFORE YOU BEGIN

Before you begin to record the macro:

- Clear the screen. Line Draw works in Typeover mode, so it may disrupt the alignment of whatever is on the screen.
- Set single line spacing if you haven't already.
- Choose a nonproportional font such as Courier or Pica. Line drawings don't print correctly with proportionally spaced text.

## RECORDING THE MACRO

To record the macro, take the following steps:

1. Turn on the macro recorder by pressing Ctrl-F10 or choosing Macro from the Tools menu and then choosing Define. Enter **smbox** as the name of the macro.
2. Enter **creates small rectangle** as the macro description; then press ⏎.
3. Press Ctrl-F3 (Line Draw) and type **L** for Line Draw.
4. Press Esc, type **4**, and press ↓.
5. Press Esc, type **15**, and press →.
6. Press Esc, type **4**, and press ↑.
7. Press Esc, type **15**, and press ←.
8. Press F7 to exit from Line Draw mode.
9. Press Ctrl-F10 again to stop recording the macro.

> Line Draw doesn't work on many laser printers, including the Apple LaserWriter and other PostScript printers. Check the Printer Help screen for your printer (Shift-F7 **S H**) or test-print a document with line drawings in it before you invest a great deal of time in creating graphics with Line Draw.

The final macro should resemble the one in Figure 8.12.

## USING THE MACRO

When you use the macro, WordPerfect creates a rectangle at the cursor's position. If you're using any spacing other than single, the vertical rules will not join.

To insert text in boxes that you've created with Line Draw, press the Ins key to go into Typeover mode. If you stay in Insert mode,

```
Macro: Action
    File            SMBOX.WPM
    Description     creates small rectangle

    {DISPLAY OFF}{Screen}1{Esc}4
    {Down}{Esc}15{Right}
    {Esc}4{Up}
    {Esc}15{Left}
    {Exit}




Ctrl-PgUp for macro commands;  Press Exit when done
```

*Figure 8.12:* This macro creates a small rectangle.

lines will be pushed to the right as you type, and pressing ↵, Tab, or the Spacebar will insert spaces in your drawings. You may find it faster to type the text first and then create the boxes in position. Just position the cursor where you want the upper-left corner of the box to be before you execute the macro or draw the box manually.

### OTHER USES

To create larger or smaller rectangles and rectangles of other proportions, use numbers other than 4 and 15 in the macro.

## FIGURE BORDER MACROS: DOUBLE BORDERS

In WordPerfect, each type of graphics box—Figure, Table, Text Box, or User-Defined Box—uses a slightly different set of default settings as options.

- Figure boxes are bordered on all four sides with a thin rule.
- Text boxes are bordered at the top and bottom with a thick rule and are shaded 10-percent gray.

- Table boxes are bordered at the top and bottom with a thick rule but are not shaded.
- User-defined boxes have no borders and are not shaded.

However, if you want to change graphics options for the borders, the change takes effect from the cursor position forward—which means that you must remember to change the graphics options before you create the graphics box. It's easy to forget to do this, so the following graphics macros will set graphics options for you and put you in the Definition screen. We're only using figure boxes and text boxes in these macros. But they are similar enough for you to find it easy, once you get the pattern, to set up macros like these for whatever styles of graphics box you use most frequently.

These macros don't attempt to second-guess what you want to *do* with your graphics boxes, since the range of applications is so varied—anything from a newsletter to a report to a garage sale notice. The macros stop for you to complete the definition of the graphics box in the Definition screen, where you can choose Filename and retrieve a graphic, choose Edit and type text, choose Size and set a size, specify whether text is to wrap around the graphic, and so forth.

This macro, named **dblfig**, creates a double border around a figure box. An example of its style in a 2-inch by 2-inch box is illustrated in Figure 8.13.

## BEFORE YOU BEGIN

Before you begin to record the macro:

- Clear the screen so that you can see the results of the macro more clearly.

## RECORDING THE MACRO

To record the macro, take the following steps:

1. Turn on the macro recorder by pressing Ctrl-F10 or choosing Macro from the Tools menu and then choosing Define. Enter **dblfig** as the name of the macro.

---

Graphics options also control the numbering style. Figure boxes, text boxes, and user-defined boxes use numbers (Figure 1, Table 1), but table boxes use Roman numerals (Table I). If you're keeping lists of graphics, you may want to edit any of these macros to specify a different numbering style (Figure 1-1, Table 1-a).

You can quickly see the effects of any of these graphics boxes by using the View Document feature (Shift-F7 V). To make sure you're looking at the correct graphic, have only one in each editing screen as you view them.

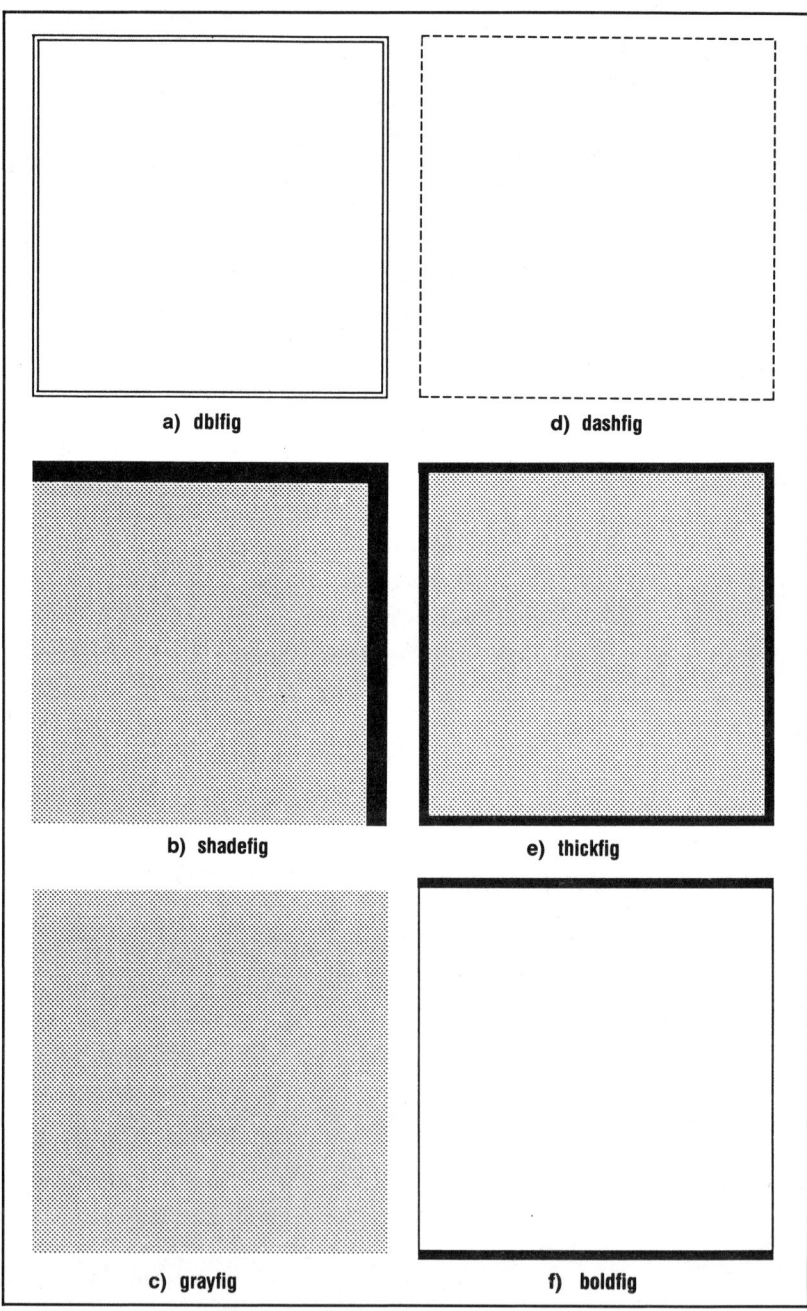

*Figure 8.13:* The graphics macros in the next few sections create different types of figure boxes.

2. Enter **creates double-bordered figure box** as the macro description; then press ←.

3. Press Alt-F9 (Graphics) and type **F** for Figure and **O** for Options.

4. Type **B** for Borders; then type **D D D D** for Double.

5. In case you've used shading earlier, have the macro clear that setting. Type **G 0** and press ←. Press F7.

6. Press Alt-F9 (Graphics); then type **F** for Figure.

7. Type **C** for Create.

8. Press Ctrl-F10 again to stop recording the macro.

The final macro should resemble the one in Figure 8.14.

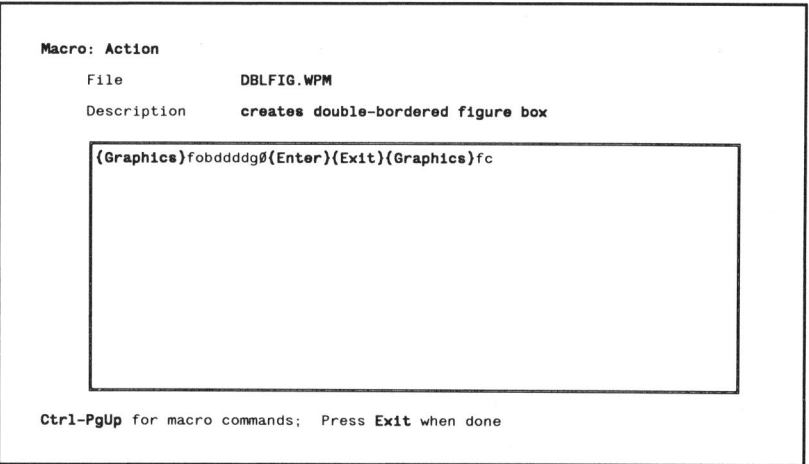

*Figure 8.14:* The steps used in the **dblfig** macro are similar to those in the following border macros.

## *USING THE MACRO*

When you use the macro, WordPerfect will stop at the Definition: Figure screen for you to enter the rest of the specifications for your graphic. You can retrieve a graphic image from another source or choose Edit and type text for the graphic, even though it is a figure box.

The type of graphics box you use doesn't really matter as far as the type of graphic you use is concerned; it only matters if you want WordPerfect to automatically maintain lists of its graphics boxes. If you want to have the program create an automatic list of figures and tables, you should be careful to place the right kinds of graphics in the correct types of boxes so that those lists will be accurate.

### OTHER USES

As you'll see in the next few macros, you can edit the **dblfig** macro or record new macros that set different styles for your graphics boxes.

## FIGURE BORDER MACROS: SHADED FIGURES

This macro, named **shadefig**, creates a three-dimensional style border around a figure box that contains 10-percent gray shading. An example of its style in a 2-inch by 2-inch box is illustrated in Figure 8.13.

> Don't use more than a 10-percent screen (shading) if you want text and graphics to be legible. Use the heavier screens for special effects in your documents, such as decorative borders, but don't try to put text in them.

### BEFORE YOU BEGIN

Before you begin to record the macro:

- Clear the screen so that you can see the results of the macro more clearly.

### RECORDING THE MACRO

To record the macro, take the following steps:

1. Turn on the macro recorder by pressing Ctrl-F10 or choosing Macro from the Tools menu and then choosing Define. Enter **shadefig** as the name of the macro.

2. Enter **creates 3-d bordered shaded box** as the macro description; then press ↵.

# GRAPHICS AND STYLE MACROS    295

3. Press Alt-F9 (Graphics) and type **F** for Figure and **O** for Options.

4. Type **B** for Borders; then type **N E E N**.

5. Type **G** for Gray; then type **10**, press ↵, and press F7.

6. Press Alt-F9 (Graphics); then type **F** for Figure.

7. Type **C** for Create.

8. Press Ctrl-F10 again to stop recording the macro.

The final macro should resemble the one in Figure 8.15.

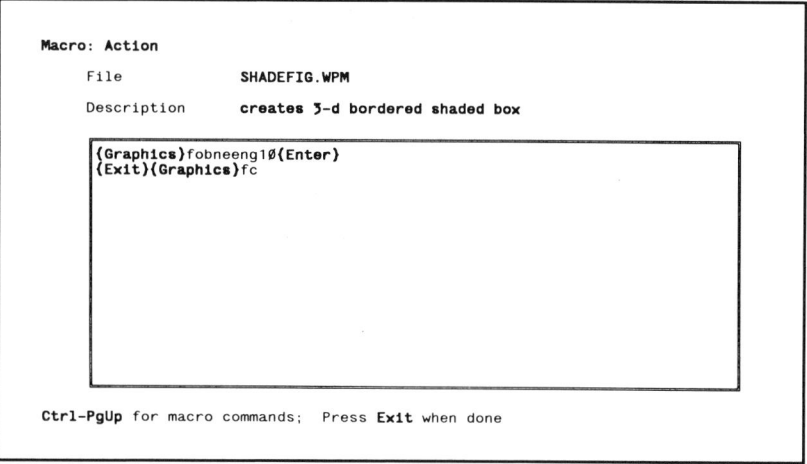

*Figure 8.15:* The steps used in the **shadefig** macro differ from those used in **dblfig**.

## USING THE MACRO

When you use the macro, WordPerfect will stop at the Definition: Figure screen for you to enter the rest of the specifications for your graphic. You can retrieve a graphic image from another source or choose Edit and type text for the graphic, even though it's a figure box.

## FIGURE BORDER MACROS: BORDERLESS SHADED FIGURES

This macro, named **grayfig**, creates a borderless figure box that contains 10-percent gray shading. An example of its style in a 2-inch by 2-inch box is illustrated in Figure 8.13.

### BEFORE YOU BEGIN

Before you begin to record the macro:

- Clear the screen so that you can see the results of the macro more clearly.

### RECORDING THE MACRO

To record the macro, take the following steps:

1. Turn on the macro recorder by pressing Ctrl-F10 or choosing Macro from the Tools menu and then choosing Define. Enter **grayfig** as the name of the macro.
2. Enter **creates borderless shaded figure box** as the macro description; then press ←.
3. Press Alt-F9 (Graphics) and type **F** for Figure and **O** for Options.
4. Type **B** for Borders; then type **N N N N**.
5. Type **G** for Gray; then type **10**, press ←, and press F7.
6. Press Alt-F9 (Graphics); then type **F** for Figure.
7. Type **C** for Create.
8. Press Ctrl-F10 again to stop recording the macro.

The final macro should resemble the one in Figure 8.16.

### USING THE MACRO

When you use the macro, WordPerfect will stop at the Definition: Figure screen for you to enter the rest of the specifications for your

## GRAPHICS AND STYLE MACROS 297

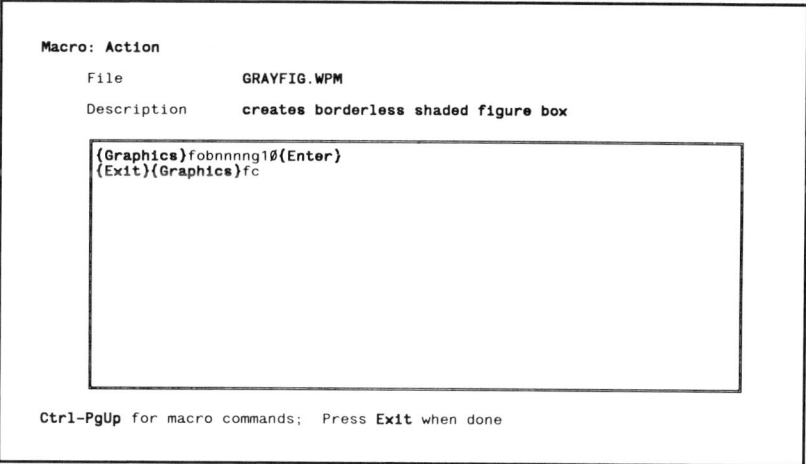

*Figure 8.16:* The steps used in the **grayfig** macro differ slightly from those used in **dblfig**.

graphic. You can retrieve a graphic image from another source or choose Edit and type text for the graphic, even though it is a figure box.

## FIGURE BORDER MACROS: DASHED FIGURE BORDERS

This macro, named **dashfig**, creates a figure box that uses dashed lines as borders. An example of its style in a 2-inch by 2-inch box is illustrated in Figure 8.13.

### BEFORE YOU BEGIN

Before you begin to record the macro:

- Clear the screen so that you can see the results of the macro more clearly.

### RECORDING THE MACRO

To record the macro, take the following steps:

1. Turn on the macro recorder by pressing Ctrl-F10 or choosing Macro from the Tools menu and then choosing Define. Enter **dashfig** as the name of the macro.

2. Enter **creates dash border for figure box** as the macro description; then press ⏎.

3. Press Alt-F9 (Graphics) and type **F** for Figure and **O** for Options.

4. Type **B** for Borders; then type **A A A A**.

5. In case you have used shading previously, clear the settings by typing **G 0** and pressing ⏎.

6. Press Alt-F9 (Graphics); then type **F** for Figure.

7. Type **C** for Create.

8. Press Ctrl-F10 again to stop recording the macro.

The final macro should resemble the one in Figure 8.17.

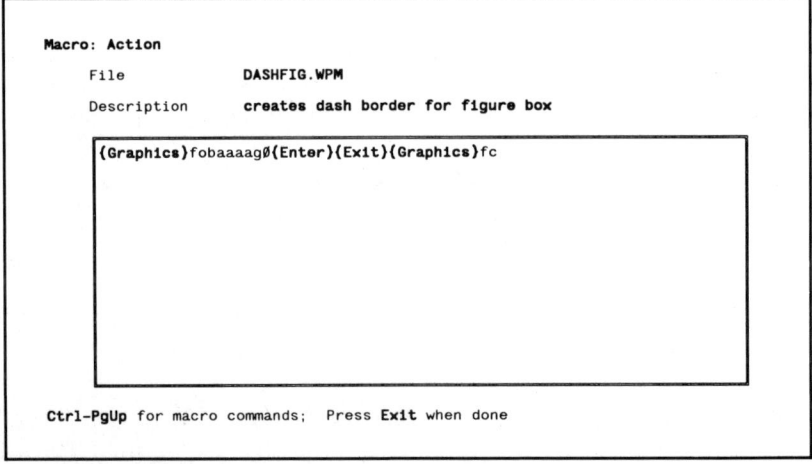

*Figure 8.17:* The steps used for the **dashfig** box follow the same pattern as those for the other border macros.

## *USING THE MACRO*

When you use the macro, WordPerfect will stop at the Definition: Figure screen for you to enter the rest of the specifications for your graphic. You can retrieve a graphic image from another source or choose Edit and type text for the graphic, even though it is a figure box.

# FIGURE BORDER MACROS: THICK BORDERS FOR FIGURES

This macro, named **thickfig**, creates thick borders all around a shaded figure. An example of its style in a 2-inch by 2-inch box is illustrated in Figure 8.13.

## BEFORE YOU BEGIN

Before you begin to record the macro:

- Clear the screen so that you can see the results of the macro more clearly.

## RECORDING THE MACRO

To record the macro, take the following steps:

1. Turn on the macro recorder by pressing Ctrl-F10 or choosing Macro from the Tools menu and then choosing Define. Enter **thickfig** as the name of the macro.

2. Enter **creates thick figure box border** as the macro description; then press ←.

3. Press Alt-F9 (Graphics) and type **F** for Figure and **O** for Options.

4. Type **B** for Borders; then type **T T T T**.

5. Press Alt-F9 (Graphics); then type **F** for Figure.

6. Type **C** for Create.

7. Press Ctrl-F10 again to stop recording the macro.

The final macro should resemble the one in Figure 8.18.

## USING THE MACRO

When you use the macro, WordPerfect will stop at the Definition: Figure screen for you to enter the rest of the specifications for your graphic. You can retrieve a graphic image from another source or choose Edit and type text for the graphic, even though it is a figure box.

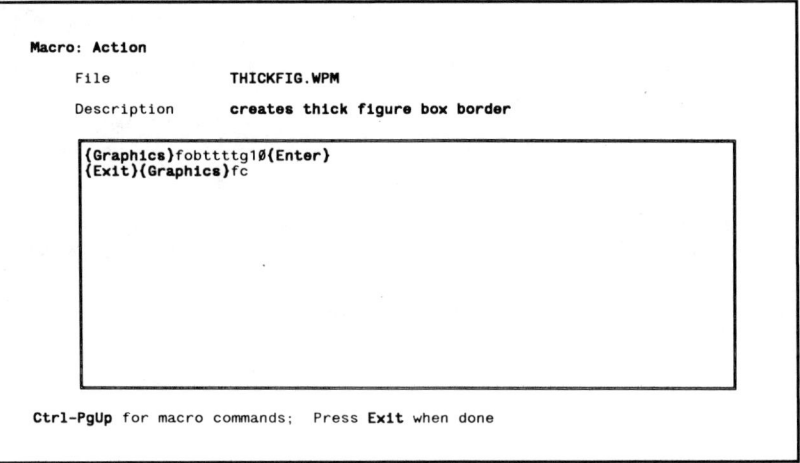

*Figure 8.18:* The steps used in the **thickfig** macro create thick borders.

## FIGURE BORDER MACROS: BORDERS OF VARYING SIZES

This macro, named **boldfig**, creates a figure with thick top borders and thin side borders. An example of its style in a 2-inch by 2-inch box is illustrated in Figure 8.13.

### BEFORE YOU BEGIN

Before you begin to record the macro:

- Clear the screen so that you can see the results of the macro more clearly.

### RECORDING THE MACRO

To record the macro, take the following steps:

1. Turn on the macro recorder by pressing Ctrl-F10 or choosing Macro from the Tools menu and then choosing Define. Enter **boldfig** as the name of the macro.

2. Enter **creates bold top and bottom border** as the macro description; then press ↵.

3. Press Alt-F9 (Graphics) and type **F** for Figure and **O** for Options.

4. Type **B** for Borders; then type **S S T T**.

5. To remove any previous shading setting, type **G 0** and press ↵. Press F7.

6. Press Alt-F9 (Graphics); then type **F** for Figure.

7. Type **C** for Create.

8. Press Ctrl-F10 again to stop recording the macro.

The final macro should resemble the one in Figure 8.19.

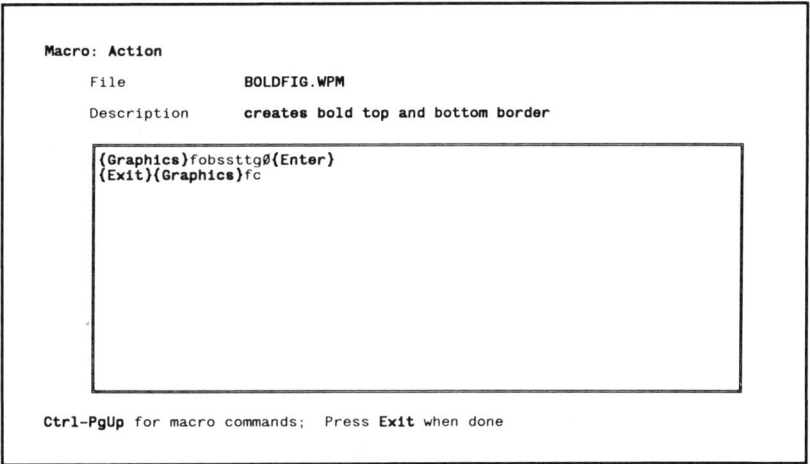

*Figure 8.19:* The **boldfig** macro uses slightly different steps, but you can edit any of the other border macros to create it.

## USING THE MACRO

When you use the macro, WordPerfect will stop at the Definition: Figure screen for you to enter the rest of the specifications for your graphic. You can retrieve a graphic image from another source or choose Edit and type text for the graphic, even though it is a figure box.

## CREATING SIDEBARS AND DISPLAYED QUOTATIONS

This macro, named **textbars**, creates a shaded text box with thick borders above and below it. Text boxes are preset to use the 10-percent gray shading, as Figure 8.20 shows, but you can record a macro so that no shading will be used. This effect is also illustrated in Figure 8.13.

> *This sample sidebar was set in 10-point Helvetica Bold Oblique using double spacing. (The textbars macro produces the box, not the text.) The size of the box was changed to 3.25" by 1.75".*

*Figure 8.20:* The **textbars** macro creates a box like this one.

### RECORDING THE MACRO

> When you use a text box, you'll often want to fit text closely within it. Record the text that the box is going to contain as a macro (include any font change or size or appearance change codes). You can then experiment freely with different sizes of boxes and different options and just retrieve the stored text.

To record the macro, take the following steps:

1. Turn on the macro recorder by pressing Ctrl-F10 or choosing Macro from the Tools menu and then choosing Define. Enter **textbars** as the name of the macro.

2. Enter **creates nonshaded text box** as the macro description; then press ↵.

3. Press Alt-F9 (Graphics); then type **B** for Text Box and **O** for Options.

4. Type **G** for Gray Shading; then type **0** and press ↵.

5. Press F7; then press Alt-F9 (Graphics), type **B** for Text Box, and type **C** for Create.

6. Press Ctrl-F10 again to stop recording the macro.

The final macro should resemble the one in Figure 8.21.

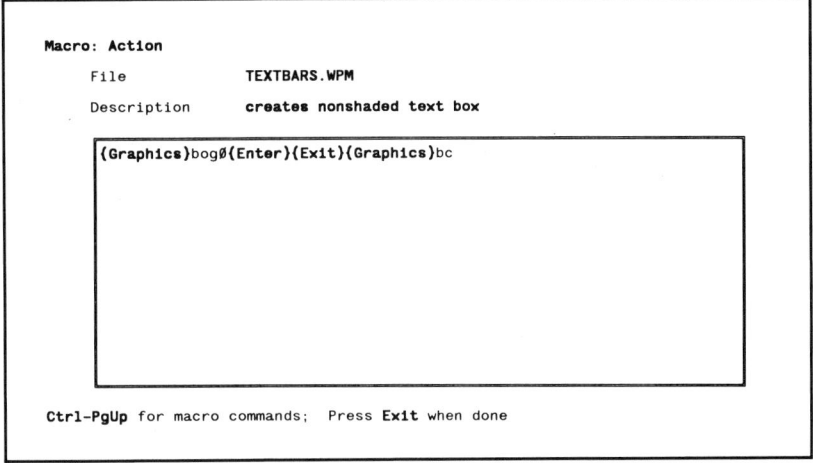

*Figure 8.21:* The **textbars** macro, like the figure boxes macro, can be edited to produce many different styles.

## USING THE MACRO

When you use the macro, WordPerfect will stop at the Definition: Text Box screen for you to finish defining the text box. You can set a size, specify the position of the box on the page, type the text the box is to contain, and so forth.

You can also fine-tune the placement of text in a graphics box by typing it just after the box and then using Advance Up to move it *n.nn* inches (or points or centimeters) into the box. (Advance is on the Other Format menu.) For example, if you've got a text box that's 1 inch deep and you want text to begin exactly in the middle of it (at the ½-inch mark), create the box, press ↵ to start the text on the line immediately following, advance the text up ½ inch, and type the text.

## AUTOMATIC WRITING ON THE SCREEN

> For other ideas on onscreen demonstrations with WordPerfect, see the automatic slide show macro shown earlier in the chapter.

You can create macros for onscreen demonstrations at sales presentations or status meetings. For example, you may want to record a macro that will draw a box slowly across the screen and then present your message within the box. This macro, named **draw**, is one that shows you how to create a short demonstration of automatic drawing. A sample of its output is shown in Figure 8.22 but to get its effect you really have to see this macro in action as it draws the box and then goes on to present the message on the screen. These onscreen demonstrations can be particularly effective if you have a large-screen projector.

*Figure 8.22:* Sample produced by the **draw** macro; the macros you create will contain your own message.

### BEFORE YOU BEGIN

- Clear the screen.
- Make sure single spacing is in effect.

### RECORDING THE MACRO

> If you want to print the output of your onscreen demonstrations, be sure to use a nonproportional typeface. Line Draw produces erratic results with proportional fonts, as each character occupies a different amount of space.

1. Turn on the macro recorder by pressing Ctrl-F10 or choosing Macro from the Tools menu and then choosing Define.

Name the macro **draw**, and enter **automatic drawing** as the description.

2. Press Ctrl-F3 and choose option 2 to start Line Draw.
3. Choose option 2 for the double rule.
4. Press Esc, type **20**, and press →.
5. Press Esc, type **10**, and press ↓.
6. Press Esc, type **20**, and press ←.
7. Press Esc, type **10**, and press ↑.
8. Press F7; then turn on Typeover mode by pressing Ins.
9. Press → seven times and ↓ four times; then type **Your**.
10. Press ↓; then press ← four times. Type **Name**.
11. Press ↓; then press ← four times. Type **Here**. If you make a mistake and have to edit the macro later to correct the spacing, press Ctrl-V before you press an arrow key. Otherwise, pressing an arrow key will simply move the cursor in the macro editor.
12. Press Ins again to turn off Typeover mode.
13. Press Ctrl-F10 to stop recording the macro.

The final macro should resemble the one in Figure 8.23.

## *USING THE MACRO*

Switch to a blank screen. Then, to execute the macro, press Alt-F10 and enter **draw**. You will see the box being drawn; then your name will appear instantly. You can create interesting visual effects by using Line Draw in this way, as you can have graphics drawn on the screen by an invisible hand.

If you're using a fast computer, you may want to slow the macro down by editing it to put a {SPEED} command at the beginning of the macro. {SPEED}100~ executes the macro's steps one second at a time, {SPEED}50~ executes it a half-second at a time, and so forth.

```
Macro: Action
    File            DRAW.WPM
    Description     automatic drawing

┌─────────────────────────────────────────────────┐
│ {DISPLAY OFF}{Screen}22                         │
│ {Esc}20{Right}                                  │
│ {Esc}10{Down}                                   │
│ {Esc}20{Left}                                   │
│ {Esc}10{Up}                                     │
│ {Exit}{Typeover}{Right}{Right}{Right}{Right}{Right}{Right} │
│ {Down}{Down}{Down}{Down}                        │
│ Your{Down}{Left}{Left}{Left}{Left}              │
│ Name{Down}{Left}{Left}{Left}{Left}              │
│ Here{Typeover}                                  │
└─────────────────────────────────────────────────┘

Ctrl-PgUp for macro commands;    Press Exit when done
```

*Figure 8.23:* The **draw** macro creates automatic writing on the screen.

## CHANGING HEADINGS TO BOLDFACE

Instead of using WordPerfect's Styles feature, which can be time-consuming, you can use macros to change the styles of elements in your text. The only thing you have to do in advance is remember to mark each element with some unique identifying characteristic—a symbol that can be deleted, for example, or a format code like [UND] or [SMALL]. It doesn't take any longer to do this than to go through your document and mark it for styles; actually, in many cases it's much faster to use macros.

I find that styles are best used if you're formatting a complex document and you want to be able to change the format of various elements over and over again. But I also find that it's tedious and time-consuming to set them up, remember to save them, mark each element in the document, retrieve the styles, apply the styles, and so forth.

You can use macros instead of styles to do some relatively complex formatting changes. However, let's start with the simple task of changing headings to boldface, which almost everybody can do no matter what type of printer is being used.

This macro, named **heads**, changes all the headings in your document to boldface type, so that you can type along without having to press F6 to turn bold on and F6 again to turn it off. The only thing you have to do in advance is mark each heading with a unique character—one that isn't used anywhere else in your document—as you type. The macro then searches for that character, deletes it, and marks the line it's on in boldface type.

## *BEFORE YOU BEGIN*

Before you begin to record the macro:

- You should have used a unique character at the beginning of each heading line, as illustrated in Figure 8.24.

- You should have some text on the screen for the macro to work on.

---

*First-Level Heading

    Depending on which printer you are using, you may want to use different type styles (attributes) in draft reports. Many people print draft reports on one printer and final reports on a higher-quality printer with that has more fonts.

*Second-Level Heading

    After writing regular text, you can switch to a different style for displayed quotations. Displayed material often looks better if it is indented from the right and left margins.

*First-Level Heading

    You may want the format for a draft report to have wider margins to leave space for others to write their comments. You may also want to use double spacing for the same reason.

---

*Figure 8.24:* To use the macro, mark all your headings with an identifier as you type.

## *RECORDING THE MACRO*

To record the macro, take the following steps:

1. Turn on the macro recorder by pressing Ctrl-F10 or choosing Macro from the Tools menu and then choosing Define. Enter **heads** as the name of the macro.

2. Enter **changes heads to bold** as the macro description; then press ⏎.

3. Press Home Home ↑, then press F2 (Search).

4. Type an asterisk (or whatever symbol you're using).

5. Press F2 again. When WordPerfect locates the first asterisk, press Backspace to delete it.

6. Press Alt-F4 (Block); then press End to highlight to the end of the line.

7. Press F6 (Bold).

8. Press Alt-F10 (Macro) and chain the macro to itself by typing **heads** and pressing ⏎.

9. Press Ctrl-F10 again to stop recording the macro.

The final macro should resemble the one in Figure 8.25.

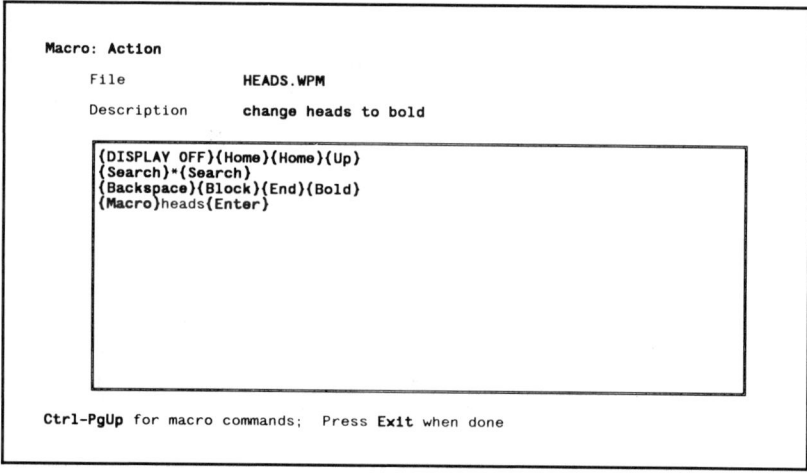

*Figure 8.25:* The **heads** macro changes all your headings to boldface.

## USING THE MACRO

To use the macro after you've entered your document, move to the beginning of the document (Home Home ↑) so that you catch all occurrences of headings, press Alt-F10, and enter **heads**. WordPerfect will move to the beginning of the document and search for each occurrence of the symbol that you used in the macro (in this case, *), delete it, and mark the line for boldface type.

If your headings are longer than one line, you can edit the macro so that it will pause for you to indicate what should be put in boldface type each time the macro locates a heading, that is, an occurrence of the symbol. Figure 8.26 illustrates the effects of using this macro and printing a document.

> **First-Level Heading**
>
> Depending on which printer you are using, you may want to use different type styles (attributes) in draft reports. Many people print draft reports on one printer and final reports on a higher-quality printer with that has more fonts.
>
> **Second-Level Heading**
>
> After writing regular text, you can switch to a different style for displayed quotations. Displayed material often looks better if it is indented from the right and left margins.
>
> **First-Level Heading**
>
> You may want the format for a draft report to have wider margins to leave space for others to write their comments. You may also want to use double spacing for the same reason.

*Figure 8.26:* This sample was printed after the **heads** macro was run on the text shown in Figure 8.24.

## CHANGING SEVERAL ATTRIBUTES IN HEADINGS

This macro, named **heads2**, changes both the size and the appearance of headings that have been marked with an identifier—again, with the asterisk. The change is to bold small caps. The procedure is slightly different from the one used in the previous macro. You can use this macro as a model for other macros that change both the size and appearance of text.

### BEFORE YOU BEGIN

Before you begin to record the macro:

- You should have used a unique character at the beginning of each heading line, as illustrated with the asterisks in Figure 8.24.

- You should have some text on the screen for the macro to work on.

### RECORDING THE MACRO

To record the macro, take the following steps:

1. Turn on the macro recorder by pressing Ctrl-F10 or choosing Macro from the Tools menu and then choosing Define. Enter **heads2** as the name of the macro.
2. Enter **change heads to bold small caps** as the macro description; then press ←.
3. Press F2 (Search), type an asterisk (*), and press F2 to begin the search.
4. When WordPerfect locates the first asterisk, press Backspace to delete it.
5. Press Alt-F4; then press End to highlight the line.
6. Press Ctrl-F8 (Font); then type **A** for Appearance and **C** for small caps.
7. Press Home ← to move back to the beginning of the line.
8. Press Alt-F4 and End again to rehighlight the line.
9. Press F6 (Bold).
10. Press Alt-F10 (Macro), type **heads2**, and press ← to chain the macro to itself so that it will repeat.
11. Turn off the macro recorder by pressing Ctrl-F10 or choosing Macro from the Tools menu and then choosing Define.

The final macro should resemble the one in Figure 8.27.

### USING THE MACRO

When you use the macro, WordPerfect changes the headings that you have identified with an asterisk. In this case, it marks them for both boldface and small caps.

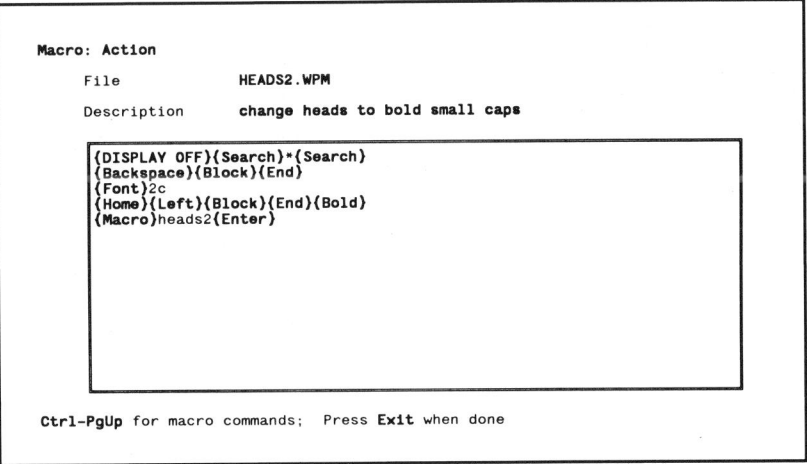

*Figure 8.27:* The **heads2** macro changes two different appearances, small caps and bold.

You could use a similar macro to change the size as well as the appearance of the text. The only trick is to rehighlight the line for each size or appearance change you want to make. You can choose boldface, italics, underlining, double underlining, outline, shadow, or small caps, and you can pick Fine, Small, Large, Very Large, and Extra Large. (The actual point size you get depends on the base or initial font you're using.)

WordPerfect will only let you change the size and appearance of blocked text, so you can't switch to a different font by using this macro. However, you can use the next macro to change the fonts in your headings.

## *CHANGING FONTS WITH MACROS*

This macro, named **chheads**, first changes the font that is being used in each heading (which you have previously marked with an *) and then switches back to the font you were using for the body of your text. It contains a very clever trick (steps 6–9) that deletes the code for the current font and then retrieves it at the appropriate place.

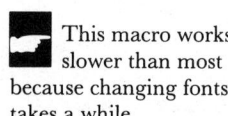
This macro works slower than most because changing fonts takes a while.

## BEFORE YOU BEGIN

Before you begin to record the macro:

- You should have used a unique character at the beginning of each heading line, as illustrated in Figure 8.24.
- You should have some text on the screen for the macro to work on.
- Close the Reveal Codes window, if it is open. This macro won't work correctly with Reveal Codes open.

## RECORDING THE MACRO

To record the macro, take the following steps:

1. Turn on the macro recorder by pressing Ctrl-F10 or choosing Macro from the Tools menu and then choosing Define. Enter **chheads** as the name of the macro.

2. Enter **change heads & text to different font** as the macro description; then press ←.

3. Press F2 (Search), type *, and press F2 again.

4. Press Backspace to delete the asterisk.

5. Press Ctrl-F8 (Font) and type **F** for Base Font. Press ← once (or twice if you must select the size also) to select the font you are using and then press Backspace and type **Y** to delete it immediately.

6. Press Ctrl-F8 and type **F** again. You will now go through the keystrokes required to choose the font you want to use for the headings (in steps 6 and 7). These keystrokes may vary with the type of printer you are using and the fonts available with it. In this example, we are using a QMS PSJet II printer and choosing 12-point Helvetica for the heads.

7. To switch to 12-point Helvetica for the headings, type **N** for Name Search; then type **H** for Helvetica. Press ← twice; then type **12** for 12-point type and press ← again.

8. Press End to move to the end of the line.
9. Press F1 (Cancel) and type **R** to return your original font.
10. Chain the macro to itself by pressing Alt-F10 (Macro), typing **chheads**, and pressing ←.
11. Turn off the macro recorder by pressing Ctrl-F10 or choosing Macro from the Tools menu and then choosing Define.

The final macro should resemble the one in Figure 8.28.

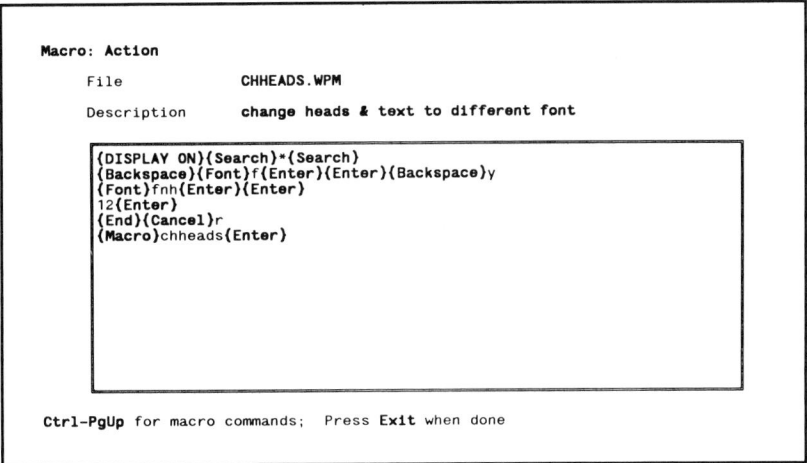

*Figure 8.28:* The **chheads** macro changes all headings to a typeface that you specify.

## USING THE MACRO

When you use the macro, WordPerfect will insert font change codes at the beginning and end of each line that was marked with an asterisk. The first font change code will change the typeface to the heading font, and the second one will change the typeface to the font that's being used for text.

This macro won't work correctly if you change to a printer other than the one that was selected when you recorded the macro.

## STYLING DIFFERENT LEVELS OF HEADINGS

The macros you've just been looking at work fine as long as you've got only one level of heading in your text. But what if you've got more than one? After you've run the **chheads** macro, headings of all levels will be in the same typeface, since you only selected one for them.

Just mark each level with its own unique identifying character as you type, as shown in Figure 8.29, and record a macro for each level of heading. For example, in the figure, * indicates level-1 headings and *# indicates level-2 headings. You could use *@ to indicate level-3 headings, and so forth. (You mark them all with an asterisk so that the first macro, **chheads**, will change all the headings to the same font.) You can then record a macro that searches for the # headings and specifies a size or attribute change (the * will have been removed by the first macro), and another macro that searches for the @ headings. For example, you could change level-2 headings to italics and level-3 headings to Small. Here's an example of how it's done.

This macro, named **chfont2**, changes the size of level-2 headings (marked originally with *#) to Small. Figure 8.30 illustrates a sample document printed after the macro was run.

> Note, by comparing Figures 8.24, 8.29, and 8.30, that the amount of text that fits on each line changes as you change fonts.

### BEFORE YOU BEGIN

Before you begin to record the macro:

- You should have used a unique character at the beginning of each heading line, as illustrated in Figure 8.29.
- You should have some text on the screen for the macro to work on.

### RECORDING THE MACRO

To record the macro, take the following steps:

1. Turn on the macro recorder by pressing Ctrl-F10 or choosing Macro from the Tools menu and then choosing Define. Enter **chfont2** as the name of the macro.

```
*First-Level Heading

    Depending on which printer you are
using, you may want to use different type
styles (attributes) in draft reports. Many
people print draft reports on one printer
and final reports on a higher-quality
printer with that has more fonts.

*#Second-level heading

    After writing regular text, you can
switch to a different style for displayed
quotations. Displayed material often looks
better if it is indented from the right
and left margins.

*First-Level Heading

    You may want the format for a draft
report to have wider margins to leave
space for others to write their comments.
You may also want to use double spacing
for the same reason.

*#Second-level heading

    Macros can substitute for
WordPerfect's Styles feature in many ways,
and they can often be easier to use than
styles.
```

*Figure 8.29:* For different levels of headings, create a unique identifying symbol system.

2. Enter **change font size for level 2 heads** as the macro description; then press ⏎.

3. Press Home Home ↑ to go to the beginning of the document.

4. Press F2, type #, and press F2 again.

---

> **First-Level Heading**
>
> Depending on which printer you are using, you may want to use different type styles (attributes) in draft reports. Many people print draft reports on one printer and final reports on a higher-quality printer with that has more fonts.
>
> **Second-level heading**
>
> After writing regular text, you can switch to a different style for displayed quotations. Displayed material often looks better if it is indented from the right and left margins.
>
> **First-Level Heading**
>
> You may want the format for a draft report to have wider margins to leave space for others to write their comments. You may also want to use double spacing for the same reason.
>
> **Second-level heading**
>
> Macros can substitute for WordPerfect's Styles feature in many ways, and they can often be easier to use than styles.

*Figure 8.30:* This document was produced by using the **chheads** and **chfont2** macros.

5. Press Backspace to delete the #.
6. Press Alt-F4 End to highlight the line.
7. Press Ctrl-F8 and type **S S**.
8. Press Alt-F10, type **chfont2**, and press ⏎ to chain the macro to itself.
9. Press Ctrl-F10 again to stop recording the macro.

The final macro should resemble the one in Figure 8.31.

## USING THE MACRO

When you use this macro, you can first use the **chheads** macro to switch your headings to whatever font you want. Then execute **chfont2**. It will go to the beginning of the document, search for each #, and mark the line that it's on for Small type.

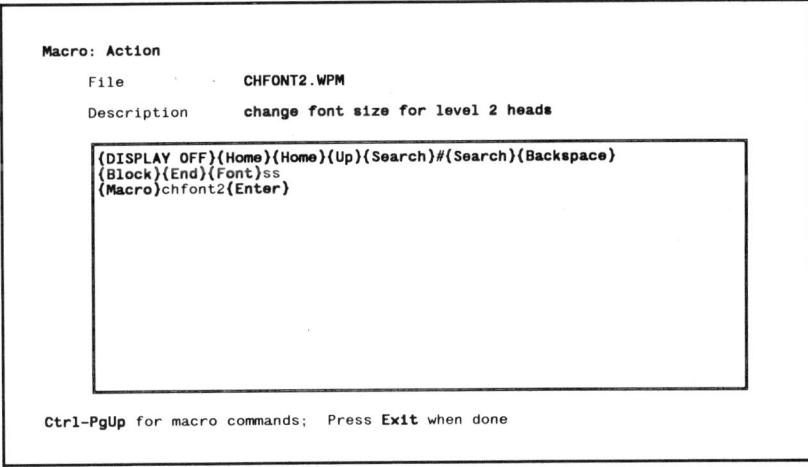

*Figure 8.31:* This **chfont2** macro changes all lines that are marked with # to Small type.

You can rename the macro **chfont3**, edit it to search for each @ (or whatever you use to indicate level-3 headings), and change them to whatever you like.

## TURNING STYLES ON/OFF

Turning a predefined style on and off in WordPerfect takes quite a few keystrokes. With a macro, you can decrease these keystrokes to two (if you assign the macro to an Alt- or Ctrl-key combination). The only trick to using such macros is to use the Search feature (F2) to locate the exact style name in the list of styles that you have defined. This macro, named **1h**, turns on the style for a level-1 heading.

### BEFORE YOU BEGIN

Before you begin to record the macro:

- You should have defined the style that you want the macro to turn on. In this case, it is a style for a level-1 heading, as illustrated in Figure 8.32.

If you have a large number of styles, instead of recording a macro for each one, record a macro that takes you to the Style menu with Search turned on (Alt-F8 F2). If you begin each style with a number, such as 1head, 2head, or 3head, you can just type **1**, **2**, or **3** to position the highlight on the style you want to use. This can save you a lot of time if you have a large number of styles.

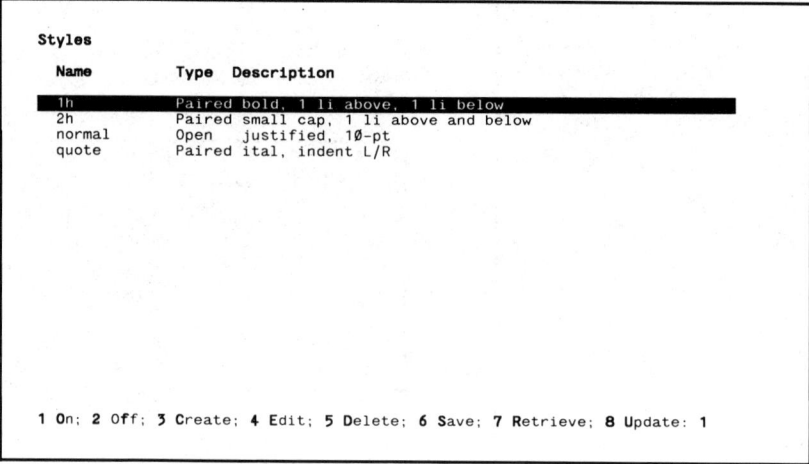

*Figure 8.32:* Before you can turn styles off and on with macros, you must define the styles first, such as the ones illustrated here.

## RECORDING THE MACRO

To record the macro, take the following steps:

1. Turn on the macro recorder by pressing Ctrl-F10 or choosing Macro from the Tools menu and then choosing Define. Enter **1h** as the name of the macro. If you plan to use it frequently, assign it to an Alt key, such as Alt-H, or map it to a Ctrl or Alt key on a soft keyboard.

2. Enter **turns on style for level-1 heading** as the macro description; then press ⏎.

3. Press Alt-F8 (Style) to display the menu of styles you have created.

4. Press F2 (Search) and enter **1h**.

5. Press ⏎ twice to select the highlighted style.

6. Press Ctrl-F10 again to stop recording the macro.

The final macro should resemble the one in Figure 8.33.

```
Macro: Action
    File            1H.WPM
    Description     turns on style for level-1 heading

    {DISPLAY OFF}{Style}{Search}1h{Enter}{Enter}




Ctrl-PgUp for macro commands;  Press Exit when done
```

*Figure 8.33:* This macro turns on the level-1 heading style.

## USING THE MACRO

When you use the macro, WordPerfect will select the 1h style from the list you have defined and turn it on in your text. If you have highlighted text before you used the macro, that text will be in the 1h style, surrounded by the [Style On:] and [Style Off:] codes. If you use the macro without having highlighted text first, the style will be turned on, and the [Style Off:] code will be pushed along in front of the cursor. To turn off the style when you have finished typing the text that is to appear in that style, just press → to move over the [Style Off:] code. (If you have set up your style so that pressing ↵ turns the style off, do that instead.) If you try to apply this style in the middle of existing text, without having highlighted any text first, it won't work; you'll simply get a blank line because there's no text to change to boldface. Delete the style codes and start over, or use Block Move to copy the text into the style.

> You can send an error message when the search is unsuccessful in any macro that uses the Search or Name Search feature—one that selects a printer, for instance.

## OTHER USES

If you haven't retrieved the style sheet that has the style that you want to use, or if you have deleted the style that this macro turns on, WordPerfect will select the style that's closest alphabetically to the style you intended. This can cause problems, because you often don't see the effects of a style on the screen unless you have a special graphics card that will display small caps and so forth. To protect yourself against such errors, you can use Macro Command Language to send yourself an error message if the style cannot be located. To do this, you would set up the macro as illustrated in Figure 8.34, using the Ctrl-PgUp key to insert the {ON NOT FOUND}, {GO}, {LABEL}, and {PROMPT} commands.

Note that there are two tildes after the '{GO}end ~ ~ .' See Appendix A for a description of WordPerfect's Macro Command Language and the notation used in the macro.

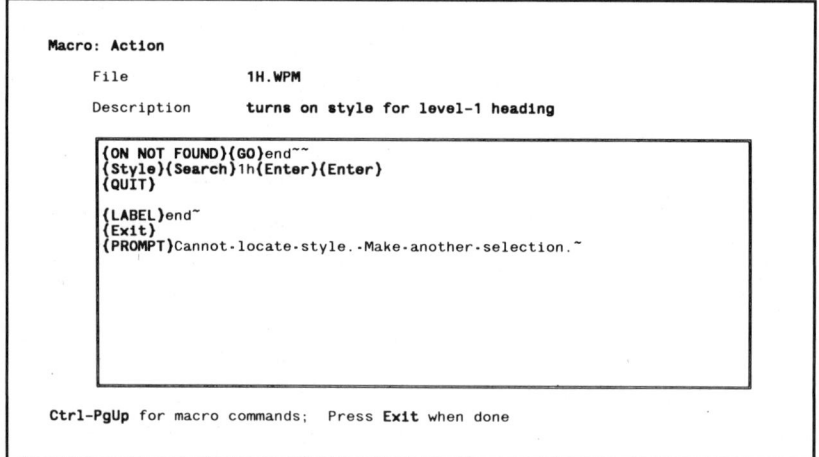

*Figure 8.34:* By using Macro Command Language, you can provide for an error message to appear if the style cannot be located.

## SUMMARY

This chapter has explored various types of macros that you can use for creating professional-looking publications and presentation graphics. Many of the specialized macros have shown you how to create graphic elements for publications, such as mastheads, figure boxes, and sidebars. Even if you don't do any desktop publishing but only need to create a chart or two for a department meeting, you will have found some useful macros here.

Chapter 9 contains a variety of macros that will streamline the printing process for you. In particular, there are macros for starting and stopping the printer, canceling print jobs, changing print quality, printing document comments (which normally don't print), and printing pages in reverse order, which with some laser printers lets you avoid having to restack your documents. As almost everyone who uses WordPerfect sooner or later prints documents, in Chapter 9 there will almost certainly be several macros of interest to you.

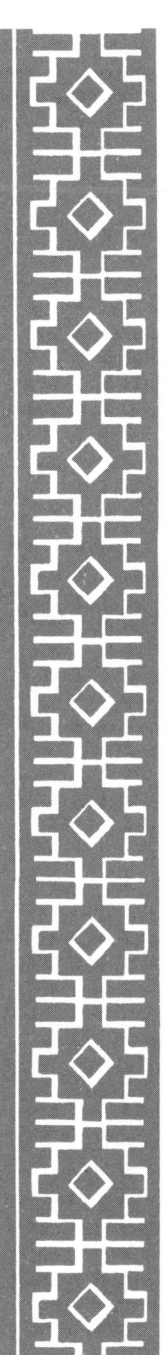

# *Printing Macros*

CHAPTER

9

# CHAPTER 9

Macros can come in handy for many everyday printing tasks, from stopping the printer immediately when there's a paper jam to formatting specific sizes of mailing labels and envelopes. The macros in this chapter will speed up your printing chores. You'll find macros that can be used both with dot-matrix and with laser printers.

The exact keystrokes in some of these macros may vary, depending on the type of printer you're using. WordPerfect keeps track of the capabilities of the printer you have selected and presents appropriate messages for that printer on the Control Printer screen when you pause or stop the printer. Therefore, the confirming prompts may differ from those used in these macros. Just follow the messages you see on your screen as you record the macros and you should have no trouble.

There are a few things you should keep in mind as you add the printing macros in this chapter to your macro library. First, because most printing macros, as just mentioned, are specific to the type of printer, you may need to record the same macro with variations for each printer you're using. For example, if you're printing on a dot-matrix printer, you will receive an extra 'Y/N?' prompt when you cancel a print job. If you're using a laser printer, you may not get this prompt.

Second, most of the printing macros will work correctly only when the printer they're recorded for is selected. If you switch to a laser printer for your final output but use a macro you recorded for a dot-matrix printer, the macro may not operate properly because the keystrokes are slightly different. If you use more than one printer, be sure to identify the macros that are for each one. You can use numbers in macro names, so you may want to name your macros accordingly—**1print** and **2print**, for example.

Third, you'll find that many macros in this chapter select different fonts for you. Be careful always to use Name Search, as the macros in this chapter do, when you record a macro that selects fonts, because the fonts that are available on each different printer also differ. If you simply press the arrow keys to highlight the font's name, WordPerfect records the relative position of the typeface as it is listed in the list of fonts, not the exact name of the font you want to use.

With these hints in mind, you can select many useful printing macros from the collection in this chapter. There are macros for routine printing chores, for previewing the document before you print, for printing envelopes, for changing the base font, for using subscripts and superscripts, for printing in reverse order so that your output is collated correctly, and for many more tasks related to printing.

## CANCELING A PRINT JOB

This macro, named **Alt-C** (for cancel), stops your printer and cancels the current job. It can be very useful, because without it you have to type **Shift-F7 C C ← C Y** (on a dot-matrix printer).

### BEFORE YOU BEGIN

Before you begin to record the macro:

- You must be currently sending a document to the printer, but the printer does not have to be turned on.

### RECORDING THE MACRO

To record the macro, take the following steps:

1. Turn on the macro recorder by pressing Ctrl-F10 or choosing Macro from the Tools menu and then choosing Define. Then press **Alt-C**.
2. Enter **Cancels current print job immediately** as the macro description; then press ←.
3. Press Shift-F7 (Print) and type **C** to choose Printer Control.
4. Type **C** to cancel the current job; then press ←.
5. Type **C** to cancel (if the prompt comes up); then type **Y** in response to the prompt.

6. Press F7 (Exit) to return to your document.
7. Press Ctrl-F10 again to stop recording the macro.

The final macro should resemble the one in Figure 9.1.

### USING THE MACRO

When you use the macro, WordPerfect will stop sending data to the printer immediately (and printing will stop when the print buffer is empty). You will need to reset the paper to the top of the form. If you are using a laser printer, you will need to reinitialize it before you can continue printing. Your sequence of keystrokes may also be slightly different, depending on which printer you are using.

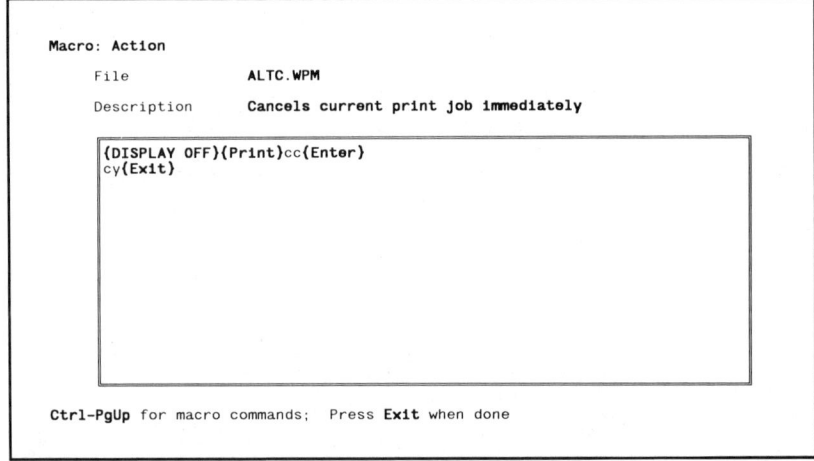

*Figure 9.1:* The **Alt-C** macro cancels the current print job.

## STOPPING THE PRINTER

When the paper is jamming or the ribbon isn't positioned correctly, it's nice to be able to stop printing quickly without thinking about which keys you have to press. This macro, named **Alt-S** (for stop), stops printing without canceling the current print job.

## BEFORE YOU BEGIN

Before you begin to record the macro:

- You should be sending a document to the printer, but the printer does not have to be turned on.

## RECORDING THE MACRO

To record the macro, take the following steps:

1. Turn on the macro recorder by pressing Ctrl-F10 or choosing Macro from the Tools menu and then choosing Define. Press **Alt-S** as the name of the macro.
2. Enter **stops printer** as the macro description; then press ⏎.
3. Press Shift-F7 (Print); then type **C** to choose Printer Control.
4. Type **S** to stop the printer; then type **Y** in response to the prompt (if you receive one with your printer).
5. Press Ctrl-F10 again to stop recording the macro. You will still be at the Control Printer screen, where you can read any messages WordPerfect gives about restarting your printer.

The final macro should resemble the one in Figure 9.2.

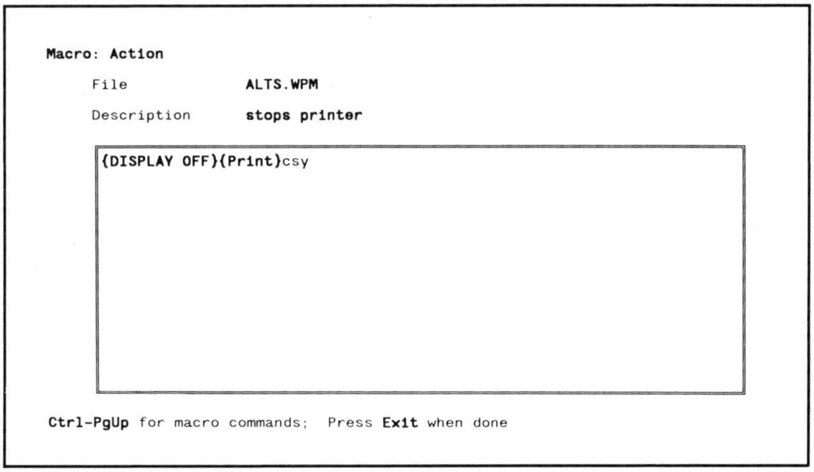

```
Macro: Action
    File           ALTS.WPM
    Description    stops printer

    {DISPLAY OFF}{Print}csy




Ctrl-PgUp for macro commands;   Press Exit when done
```

*Figure 9.2:* This **Alt-S** macro stops printing without canceling the print job.

### USING THE MACRO

When you use this macro, the printer will stop when the current print buffer is empty. To resume printing after you have fixed whatever was causing the problem, adjust the paper in the printer and type **G** to restart the printer or type **C** to cancel the print job. You may also need to reset the printer by turning it off and on, depending on the type of printer you are using. The Control Printer screen will indicate whether you need to do this. When you type **G**, the printer will not advance the paper to a new page but will begin printing where it left off.

If your printer has a large print buffer, stopping printing may take a little time. Use the **Alt-C** macro to cancel the job if you want to stop the printer right away. You can then finish printing the document from disk, beginning on the page where the problem was.

## CANCELING ALL PRINT JOBS

It's noon, and everybody else is waiting in the hall for you to go to lunch. This macro, named **cancel**, cancels all the print jobs that you are currently running.

### BEFORE YOU BEGIN

Before you begin to record the macro:

- You should have a print job running and another in the queue behind it.

### RECORDING THE MACRO

To record the macro, take the following steps:

1. Turn on the macro recorder by pressing Ctrl-F10 or choosing Macro from the Tools menu and then choosing Define. Enter **cancel** as the name of the macro.

2. Enter **Cancels all print jobs** as the macro description; then press ⏎.

3. Press Shift-F7 (Print); then type **C** to choose Printer Control.
4. Type **C** to cancel printing; then type * (pressing the asterisk key is easier than using the shifted symbol on the upper row of keys).
5. Type **Y** in response to the prompt.
6. Press Ctrl-F10 again to stop recording the macro.

The final macro should resemble the one in Figure 9.3.

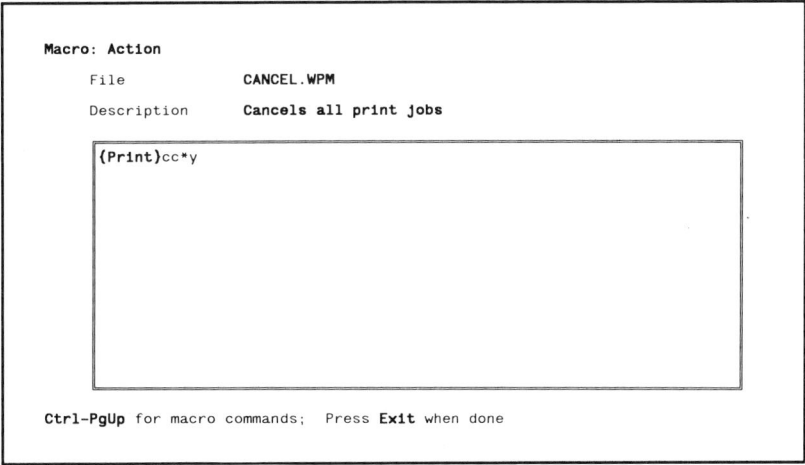

*Figure 9.3:* Canceling all print jobs can be handy when you're in a hurry to do something else.

### USING THE MACRO

When you use the macro (by pressing Alt-F10, typing **cancel**, and pressing ⏎), all the print jobs in the queue will be canceled. You can then exit WordPerfect and be on your way.

## PREVIEWING THE DOCUMENT

This macro, named **Alt-V**, shows you the current page as it will appear when printed, with page numbers, headers, footnotes, and so forth. If you do not have a graphics monitor, you will see a screen very similar to the normal editing screen, but it will show you the elements on the page that are not normally visible on the editing screen (top and bottom margins, justification, headers, and so forth). This macro is very useful when you are doing complex page layouts such as multicolumn layouts or pages that mix text and graphics. Although the macro saves you relatively few keystrokes, it's nice to be able just to press Alt-V to view your page.

You can also see how your document would look if it were printed on another printer, even if that printer isn't attached to your computer. For example, you may be working at home on a document that you're going to print on a laser printer at work. You can install that printer, even though it's not connected to your computer, and then just select it and view the document.

### *BEFORE YOU BEGIN*

Before you begin to record the macro:

- You should be working with a document on the screen. Ideally, so that you can see some of the things that you can't see otherwise, it should contain footnotes or a header or footer, but that's not essential.

### *RECORDING THE MACRO*

To record the macro, take the following steps:

1. Turn on the macro recorder by pressing Ctrl-F10 or choosing Macro from the Tools menu and then choosing Define. Press **Alt-V**.

2. Enter **view current page** as the macro description; then press ↵.

3. Press Shift-F7 and type **V**.

4. Press Ctrl-F10 again to stop recording the macro.

## USING THE MACRO

When you use the macro, you will see a full-screen view of the page you are working on, assuming that you have a graphics monitor. You can choose to see the text either 100 percent or 200 percent closer up, or choose Facing Pages to see the current page plus its facing page. (WordPerfect assumes that all odd-numbered pages are right-hand pages and all even-numbered pages are left-hand pages.)

You can see more of your document by pressing PgUp, PgDn, Screen Up (Gray −), or Screen Down (Gray +). You can also use the arrow keys to scroll. To view another page, press Ctrl-Home and enter the page number. You can also go to the beginning of the document with Home Home ↑ and to the end with Home Home ↓. Press Shift-F3 (Switch) to see the display in reverse video ("black" on "white").

Press F7 to return to your document. You will be returned to the page you were viewing. Pressing F1 (Cancel) or the Spacebar returns you to the Print menu.

> WordPerfect uses only three fonts in the View Document screen. It substitutes the closest match for the exact font you've specified, so you may not see the exact font that you're using.

## OTHER USES

You may want to edit the macro so that you can go to a certain page and view it instead of viewing the page that the cursor is on. To do this, add the following to the macro before step 4 above:

- Press Ctrl-Home; then press Ctrl-PgUp and choose Pause so that the macro will pause for you to enter a page number. Then press ⏎.

Then, when you execute the macro by pressing Alt-V, WordPerfect will pause for you to enter the number of the page you want to view.

## PRINTING TWO COPIES OF A DOCUMENT

> Version 5.1 lets you set a default number of copies for printing from the Setup menu. Choose Initial Settings; then Print Options.

This macro, named **print2**, prints two copies of the document on the screen. If you habitually need two copies, you can use it instead of the print macro described earlier.

## BEFORE YOU BEGIN

Before you begin to record the macro:

- You should have a previously saved document on the screen.

## RECORDING THE MACRO

To record the macro, take the following steps:

1. Turn on the macro recorder by pressing Ctrl-F10 or choosing Macro from the Tools menu and then choosing Define. Enter **print2** as the name of the macro.

2. Enter **Prints N copies** (or **Prints two copies**) as the macro description; then press ⏎.

3. Press F10 (Save); then press ⏎.

4. Type **Y** in response to the prompt.

5. Press Shift-F7 (Print) and type **N** for Number of Copies. Enter **2** and press ⏎.

6. Choose Full Document (option 1).

7. To reset the Print menu so that two copies will not be printed the next time you print the document, press Shift-F7, type **N** and **1**; then press F7 twice to return to your document.

8. Press Ctrl-F10 again to stop recording the macro.

The final macro should resemble the one in Figure 9.4.

## USING THE MACRO

When you use this macro or another one containing it, WordPerfect will print one complete copy of your document and then immediately begin printing a second. In either case, you should make sure that your printer is on and that paper is loaded in it correctly.

## OTHER USES

You could also have the macro pause for you to type in any number of copies you want. To do this, edit the macro to insert a pause, as follows:

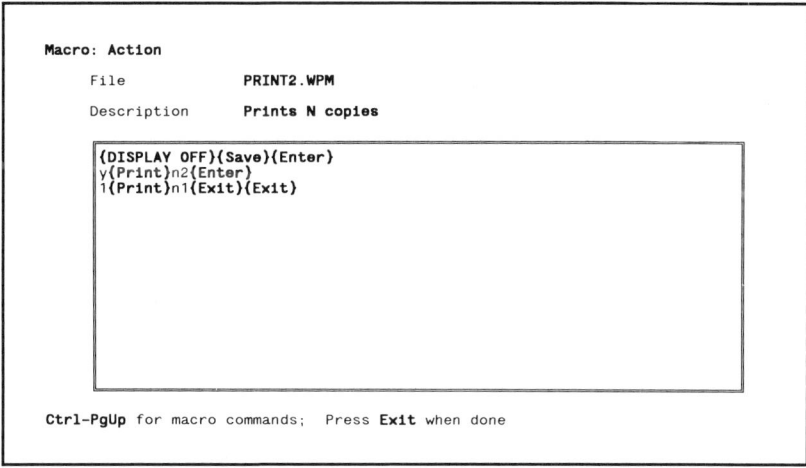

*Figure 9.4:* This macro prints two copies of your document.

1. Press Ctrl-F10 and enter **print2** as the name of the macro; then choose option 2 to edit it.

2. If necessary, change the the description to read **Prints N copies**. In version 5.1, select *3* to edit the description.

3. Insert a {DISPLAY ON} command by pressing Ctrl-PgUp and selecting {DISPLAY ON}. Delete the {DISPLAY OFF} command. In version 5.0, type **2** to change the action of the macro; in version 5.1, you are ready to edit it. Position the cursor on the *2* and press Del to delete the *2*.

4. Press Ctrl-PgUp and type **pau** (just **P** will do in version 5.0) to move the highlight to the {PAUSE} command.

5. Press ← to insert the pause.

6. When your screen resembles the one in Figure 9.5, press F7 to exit the edited macro.

## SENDING A "GO" TO THE PRINTER

There are many times when you will need to indicate to WordPerfect that you have corrected a print problem and are ready to start printing again. This macro, named **go**, sends the printer a Go without your having to use the Printer Control screen.

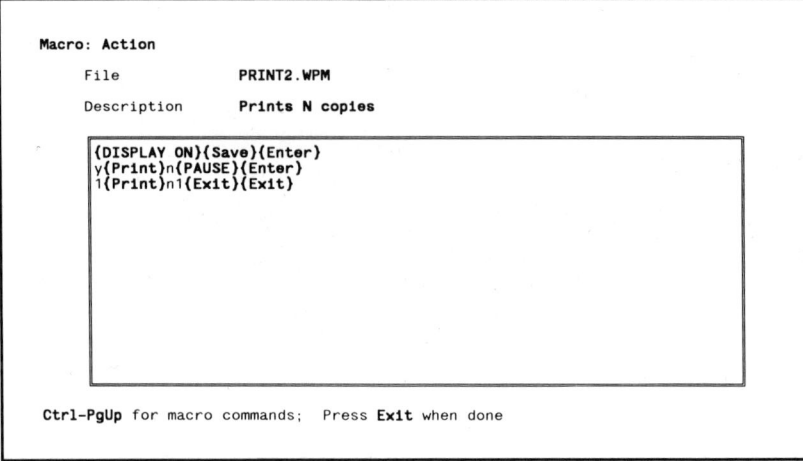

*Figure 9.5:* This macro allows you to enter the number of copies of your document you want to print.

If you find that you use it often, you may want to call it **Alt-G** instead.

## BEFORE YOU BEGIN

Before you begin to record the macro:

- You must have installed a printer.

## RECORDING THE MACRO

To record the macro, take the following steps:

1. Turn on the macro recorder by pressing Ctrl-F10 or choosing Macro from the Tools menu and then choosing Define. Enter **go** as the name of the macro.

2. Enter **sends a Go to the printer** as the macro description; then press ⏎.

3. Press Shift-F7 (Print), type **C** for Control Printer, and type **G**.

4. Press F7 to return to your document.

5. Press Ctrl-F10 again to stop recording the macro.

PRINTING MACROS   *335*

### USING THE MACRO

To send a Go to the printer if you are not viewing the Control Printer screen, just press Alt-F10, type **go**, and press ←⎯.

## CHANGING PRINT QUALITY

This macro, named **qual**, changes from the default text quality of High to Medium. If you have a laser printer, you will have no use for this macro, as there is no difference in print qualities. However, if you use a dot-matrix printer, you will probably want to use Medium quality most of the time, unless you are printing the final version.

### RECORDING THE MACRO

To record the macro, take the following steps:

1. Turn on the macro recorder by pressing Ctrl-F10 or choosing Macro from the Tools menu and then choosing Define. Enter **qual** as the name of the macro.
2. Enter **set print quality to medium** as the macro description; then press ←⎯.
3. Press Shift-F7 (Print); then type **T** for Text Quality.
4. Type **M** for Medium; then press F7.
5. Press Ctrl-F10 again to stop recording the macro.

The final macro should resemble the one in Figure 9.6.

> ■ In version 5.1, you can change the default print quality for both text and graphics on the Setup menu. Choose Initial Settings; then Print Options. In version 5.0, there isn't any way to set your default print quality by using the Setup key (Shift-F1). So, if you know you want to print with Medium quality during an entire session with WordPerfect 5.0, use **qual** as a startup macro. Start WordPerfect with the command **wp/m-qual**.

### USING THE MACRO

When you use the macro, you will be switched to medium quality and then returned to your document. You will then need to execute the **Alt-P** macro or use the Print menu to print your document.

### OTHER USES

You can include this macro in other print macros to change the print quality. After you have changed the print quality for a

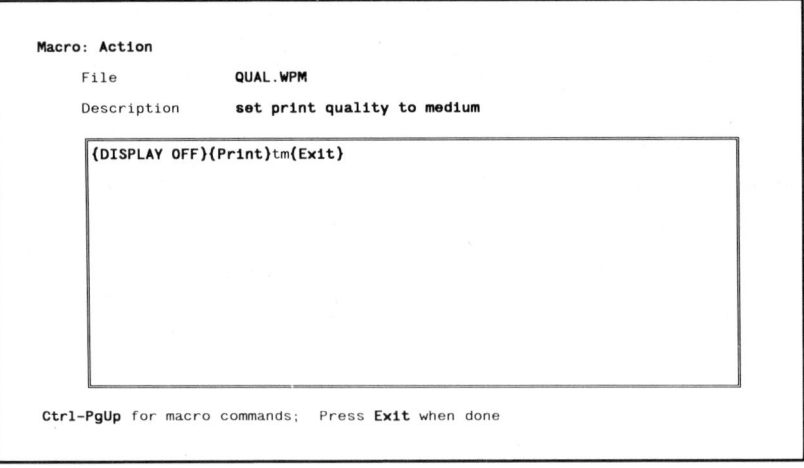

*Figure 9.6:* This macro switches print quality to medium for dot-matrix printers.

document, that setting is saved with the document so that, the next time you print it, it will be set for medium quality.

## SELECTING A NEW INITIAL FONT

This macro, named **fontch**, changes the initial font used in the document. It pauses to allow you to select another font, which then becomes the initial font only in the document you are creating.

If you change the initial font for the *printer* by using the Initial Font option on the Printer Edit menu, your fellow workers may be surprised when they use your computer and printer and discover that you have chosen a new initial font for your printer. To avoid such problems, use the Initial Font option on the Document Format menu, as this macro does, to change the default font only for the current *document*. Use the Initial Font option on the Printer Edit menu only when you really aren't satisfied with the font selected by WordPerfect for your printer.

When you change the initial font, WordPerfect doesn't insert any hidden codes in the document, so there is no way to tell that a different initial font is in use even if you look at the Reveal Codes screen. The only way you might suspect that the initial font has been

When you want to change just the *type size* or *type style* (as from roman to italic) but retain the *typeface* designated as the initial font, use the Size and Appearance options on the Font menu (Ctrl-F8). When you want to intermix different typefaces, use the Base Font option on the Font menu.

changed is if you notice a change in the line length, which occurs if the new font happens to accommodate a different number of characters per line from the font you were using.

## *BEFORE YOU BEGIN*

Before you begin to record the macro:

- You should have installed the printer that you are planning to use and have set up any additional cartridges and fonts that contain the font you want to use.

## *RECORDING THE MACRO*

To record the macro, take the following steps:

1. Turn on the macro recorder by pressing Ctrl-F10 or choosing Macro from the Tools menu and then choosing Define. Enter **fontch** as the name of the macro.

2. Enter **Changes document default font** as the macro description; then press ⏎.

3. Press Shift-F8 (Format); then type **D** for Document.

4. Type **F** for Initial Font.

5. You will see a full-screen listing of all the available fonts. The highlight bar will be on the current initial font and its name will be preceded by an asterisk (*). Press Ctrl-PgUp to insert a pause; then type **P** for Pause and press ⏎.

6. Press ⏎ three times to return to the document editing screen.

7. Press Ctrl-F10 again to stop recording the macro.

The final macro should resemble the one in Figure 9.7. In version 5.1, you can use the macro editor to insert a pause and an {Enter} after the first {Enter} so that you can pick a point size in addition to the typeface.

```
Macro: Action
    File            FONTCH.WPM
    Description     Changes document default font

    ┌─────────────────────────────────────────────────┐
    │ {Format}df{PAUSE}{Enter}                        │
    │ {Enter}                                         │
    │ {Enter}                                         │
    │                                                 │
    │                                                 │
    │                                                 │
    │                                                 │
    └─────────────────────────────────────────────────┘

Ctrl-PgUp for macro commands;  Press Exit when done
```

*Figure 9.7:* You can use this **fontch** macro to change the initial font for the document you are working on.

### USING THE MACRO

When you use the macro, WordPerfect will pause for you to select the new font. Move the highlight bar to the name of the font you want to make the initial one in the document you are creating, and press ←. You can use Name Search (**N** or F2) to quickly locate a particular font in a long list. After you select a new initial font, you are returned to the Document Format menu.

## USING SUBSCRIPTS AND SUPERSCRIPTS

This macro, named **Alt-U** (for up), marks for superscripting text that you have previously typed. You will probably find it faster to type out text and then return to it to mark it for appearance and size changes, as in this macro and the next few macros, rather than switch to the appearance change you want, type the text, and switch back to the Normal font again.

## BEFORE YOU BEGIN

Before you begin to record the macro:

- You must have typed a character or a few characters that you can superscript.

## RECORDING THE MACRO

To record the macro, take the following steps:

1. Turn on the macro recorder by pressing Ctrl-F10 or choosing Macro from the Tools menu and then choosing Define. Press **Alt-U** as the name of the macro.
2. Enter **Converts typed text to superscript** as the macro description; then press ←.
3. Press Alt-F4. Then insert a pause by pressing Ctrl-PgUp and typing **P**. Press ←.
4. Press Ctrl-F8 (Font), type **S** for Size, and **P** for Superscript.
5. Press Ctrl-F10 again to stop recording the macro.

The final macro should resemble the one in Figure 9.8.

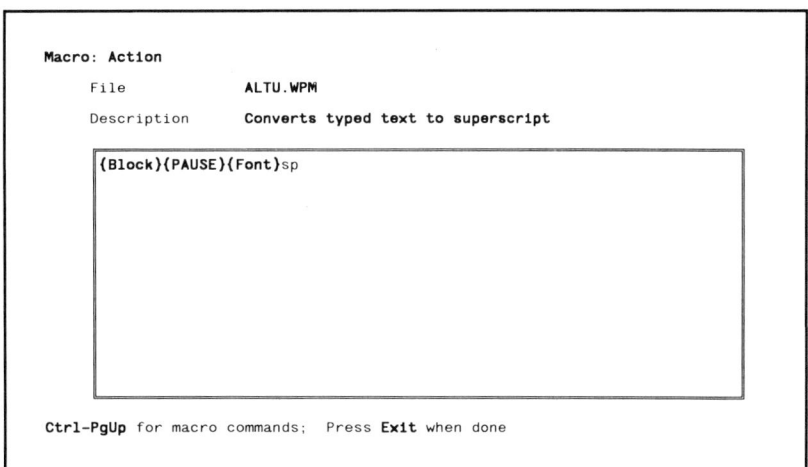

*Figure 9.8:* You will find that macros like this one speed up your typing, as you do not have to switch back and forth between appearance changes and normal text.

### USING THE MACRO

When you use the macro, first position the cursor at the beginning of the text you want to change to superscript. WordPerfect will pause for you to highlight the character or characters to be superscripted. When they are highlighted, press ↵. WordPerfect will insert the [SUPRSCPT] and [suprscpt] codes around the highlighted text and return you to the normal font.

### OTHER USES

You can easily record a similar macro named **Alt-D** (for down) that converts text to subscripts: just type **B** instead of P in step 4.

## PRINTING PAGES IN REVERSE

This macro, named **rprint**, prints from the last page to the first. This is useful if your printer is one of the laser printers that doesn't have a reverse-print option, such as the original HP LaserJet. With this macro, sheets come out of the printer from last to first, so you don't have to rearrange them.

### BEFORE YOU BEGIN

Before you begin to record the macro:

- You should have a document longer than one page on the screen.
- You should have the correct printer selected and ready.

The **rprint** macro prints one page at a time and uses PgUp to move to the previous page. The macro repeats as many times as there are pages in your document. Unfortunately, there is no way for WordPerfect to know this number automatically, so you have to provide it.

## RECORDING THE MACRO

To record the macro, take the following steps:

1. Turn on the macro recorder by pressing Ctrl-F10 or choosing Macro from the Tools menu and then choosing Define. Enter **rprint** as the name of the macro.
2. Enter **prints page and moves back** as the macro description.
3. Press Shift-F7 (Print) and type **P**.
4. Press PgUp.
5. Press Ctrl-F10 to stop recording the macro.

The final macro should resemble the one in Figure 9.9.

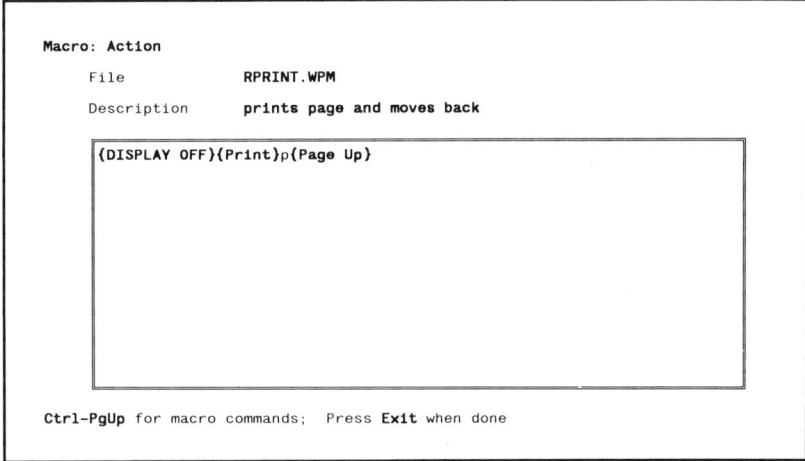

*Figure 9.9:* The **rprint** macro prints each page in the document from the end to the beginning.

## USING THE MACRO

When you use the macro, move to the end of your document (Home Home ↓) and make a note of the last page number; then press Esc, enter that number, and execute the **rprint** macro immediately. The macro will then execute as many times as there are pages in your document, printing one page at a time from the last to the first.

## PREVIEWING PAGE BREAKS

This macro, named **pgbreak**, pauses to let you preview each page break in a document. It's useful for letting you see where page breaks are occurring, especially if there is material in your document that shouldn't be broken between pages—such as tables or lists—and you haven't used block protection on it to make sure it stays together.

To avoid bad page breaks, by the way, use the Widow/Orphan Protection command as one of your default settings. Press Shift-F1 (Setup); then type **I C** for Initial Settings and Initial Codes. Press Shift-F8 (Format); then type **L W Y** to turn on Widow/Orphan Protection. Then press ⏎ twice and F7 twice to return to the document. This will prevent stray lines from occurring at the tops and bottoms of pages. It won't solve all your page-break problems, though, so this macro will still be useful.

### BEFORE YOU BEGIN

Before you begin to record the macro:

- You should have a document that is several pages long on the screen.
- You should have selected the printer you're going to print the document with, because that's the one for which it'll be formatted.

### RECORDING THE MACRO

To record the macro, take the following steps:

1. Turn on the macro recorder by pressing Ctrl-F10 or choosing Macro from the Tools menu and then choosing Define. Enter **pgbreak** as the name of the macro.

2. Enter **previews page breaks** as the macro description; then press ⏎.

3. Press Shift-F7 (Print); then type **V** for View Document.

4. Type **4** to view facing pages.

5. Press Ctrl-F10 to stop recording the macro.

## USING THE MACRO

> What's the difference between Block Protect and Conditional End of Page? You can edit text in a block-protected block and the whole block will still be protected. With Conditional End of Page, only the number of lines you specify will be kept together.

If you want to preview all of the page breaks in your document, move to the beginning of the document first (Home Home ↑). Then execute the macro. You may see the first page repeated quickly, because if you have been viewing a page at 100 percent, that setting will still be in effect, and the macro contains the command to view facing pages. The macro will then show you the facing pages (or the first page alone, if you are at the beginning of the document). Press PgDn to view the next set of pages. If you want a closer look, type **1** to view them at 100%, **2** for an enlarged (200%) view, or **3** to view only one page. When you are ready to go to the next set of pages, press PgDn.

If you spot a problem, press F7 to return to that page in your document and fix the problem by using one of the page-break commands such as Conditional End of Page or Block Protect. Or you can use the brute-force method: either edit the page or insert a hard page break. Then start the **pgbreak** macro again. It will pick up at the page you are currently on.

## PRINTING ENVELOPES OR MAILING LABELS

Once you've created a merge file, it's useful to be able to print envelopes from the names and addresses in your letters. The macros in this section format a business envelope in the Doc 2 window and then take the address block from the letter and copy it there. The macro pauses so that you can indicate the address block in each letter, because no matter how well you plan, there's almost never the same number of lines in each address.

You can also use these macros effectively if you're in the habit of saving your letters in a letter archive file that consists of all the letters you write. Retrieve your letter archive file into the Doc 1 window; then use these macros to copy the addresses into the Doc 2 window for the envelopes.

The first macro, named **busenv**, formats the business-sized envelope. The second, called **address**, puts the addresses on the envelope.

## BEFORE YOU BEGIN

- If you're using version 5.1 and haven't set up an envelope format, you will need to set up an envelope paper size first. For a standard business-sized envelope format, press Format (Shift-F8), type **P** for Page and **S** for Paper Size/Type. Then type **A** for Add, **E** for Envelope, **S** for Size, and **E** for Envelope again. If you're using a laser printer, type **F** for Font Type; then choose Landscape, because most laser printers load envelopes from the end instead of from the top. If you're using a dot-matrix printer, leave the Font Type set as Portrait. Since envelopes are usually loaded manually, type **R** for Prompt to Load and **Y** for Yes; then type **L** for Location and **M** for Manual. Press ↵ when your screen looks like Figure 9.10 (for a dot-matrix printer). Then press F7 (Exit) to return to your document.

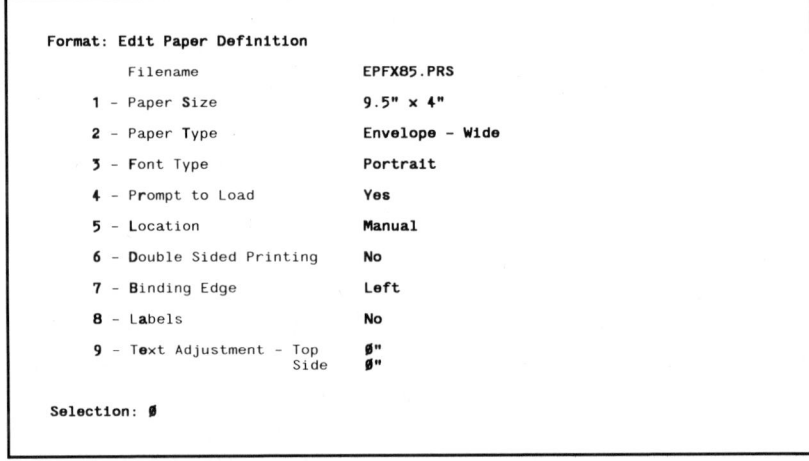

*Figure 9.10:* To set up a format for a dot-matrix printer to print business envelopes in version 5.1, your screen should look like this one.

- Clear the screen in both windows; then type an address block (name; street address; city, state, and zip) in the Doc 1 window (or retrieve a document that has an address block).

- Move to the Doc 1 window, if you're not already there, by pressing Shift-F3.

## RECORDING THE MACRO

To record the first macro, take the following steps:

1. Turn on the macro recorder by pressing Ctrl-F10 or choosing Macro from the Tools menu and then choosing Define. Enter **busenv** as the name of the macro.

2. Enter **formats a business envelope** as the macro description; then press ←.

3. Press Shift-F3 (Switch) to go to the Doc 2 window.

4. The steps at this point are different in versions 5.0 and 5.1. In version 5.1, press Shift-F8 (Format); then type **P** for Page, **S** for Paper Size, **N** for Name Search, **E** for Envelope, and press ←. Type **S** to select the envelope format. In version 5.0, press Shift-F8 (Format); then type **P** for Page, **S** for Paper Size, **E** for Envelope, and then **E** for Envelope again.

5. Type **M 0** and press ← three times. This sets the top margin to 0 or as close to 0 as possible.

6. To change the margins to sizes that are appropriate for a business (legal-size) envelope, type **L M 4** and press ← four times. This sets the left margin to four inches.

7. Press Shift-F3 (Switch) to return to Doc 1.

8. Press Alt-F10, type **address**, and press ←. This calls the address macro that you will create in the next steps.

9. Press Ctrl-F10 to stop recording the macro.

Now you can record the macro that copies the addresses from the letters:

1. Turn on the macro recorder by pressing Ctrl-F10 or choosing Macro from the Tools menu and then choosing Define. Enter **address** as the name of the macro; then press ←.

2. Enter **copies addresses into envelopes** as the description and press ←.

3. Pause the macro so that you can move to the first line in the address block: press Ctrl-PgUp, type **P**, and press ←.

4. Press Alt-F4 to turn on block marking; then pause the macro again: press Ctrl-PgUp, type **P**, and press ⏎.

5. Press Ctrl-F4 (Move) and type **B** for Block and **C** for Copy.

6. Switch to Doc 2 by pressing Shift-F3; then press ⏎ to paste the copied address block.

7. Press Home Home ↓ to move to the end of the address block.

8. Press Ctrl-⏎ to insert a hard page break.

9. Press Shift-F3 to return to the Doc 1 window.

10. Press Alt-F10 and type **address** so that the macro will call itself and you can indicate another address block; then press ⏎.

11. Turn off the macro recorder by pressing Ctrl-F10.

The final macros should resemble those represented in Figures 9.11, 9.12, and 9.13.

### *USING THE MACRO*

When you use the macro, first retrieve your merge file or letter archive file into the Doc 1 window. Go to the top of the file if you're

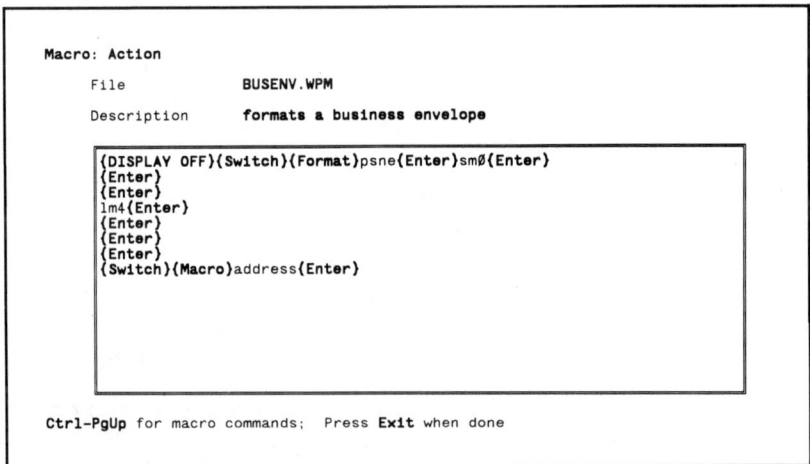

*Figure 9.11:* The **busenv** macro formats a page as a legal-sized envelope (version 5.1).

```
Macro: Edit

        File            BUSENV.WPM
  1 - Description       formats a business envelope
  2 - Action

        ┌─────────────────────────────────────────────┐
        │ {DISPLAY OFF}{Switch}{Format}pseem0{Enter}  │
        │ {Enter}                                     │
        │ {Enter}                                     │
        │ lm4{Enter}                                  │
        │ {Enter}                                     │
        │ {Enter}                                     │
        │ {Enter}                                     │
        │ {Switch}{Macro}address{Enter}               │
        │                                             │
        └─────────────────────────────────────────────┘

Selection: 0
```

*Figure 9.12:* The **busenv** macro formats a page as a legal-sized envelope (version 5.0).

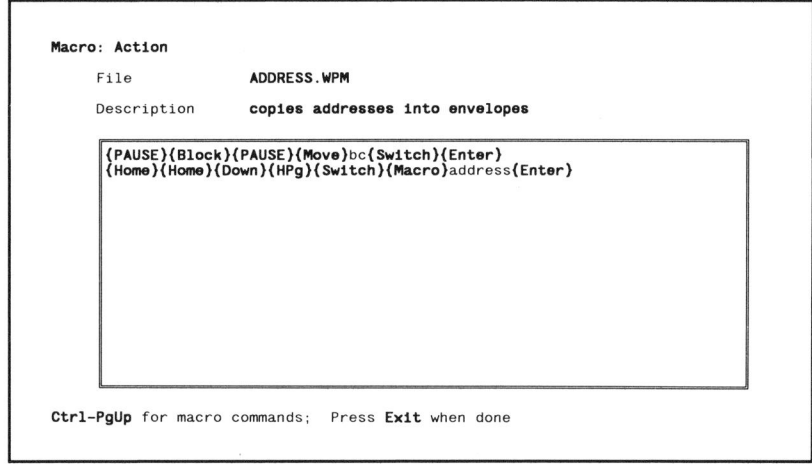

*Figure 9.13:* The **address** macro allows you to copy each address block into an envelope page.

not already there by pressing Home Home ↑. Then start the **busenv** macro. When it pauses, put the cursor on the first character in the first address block and press ↵. When it pauses again, highlight the address block and press ↵. Keep on going until you have copied all the addresses you want to use. To stop the macro, press F1 (Cancel).

> You can press PgDn or any of the arrow keys during a macro pause; pressing ⏎ starts the macro again.

When you've copied all the addresses you want to use on envelopes, switch to the Doc 2 window. There you'll find that each address has been formatted as a separate page, ready to be printed on an envelope. Insert an envelope in your printer and position it where you want the address to start; then press Shift-F7 and type **P** to print that page. Press PgDn to go to the next address, load another envelope in the printer, and print that page, until you've printed all the addresses.

### OTHER USES

> Version 5.1 comes with a macro named LABELS.WPM that makes it easy to create mailing labels.

You can edit the version 5.0 **busenv** macro—or copy, rename, and edit it if you want to have both an envelope-printing and a label-printing macro—so that it will print mailing labels instead. All you have to do is determine the size of the "page" that you want to use for the mailing labels. As this page size will vary, depending on the size of mailing labels you're using, you'll probably need to measure the labels first and do a little test-printing to get the right size of font for the longest line, and so forth. (See "Generating Mailing Labels" in Chapter 7 for an explanation of how to estimate page size for labels and a step-by-step discussion of how to set up a page for 4 inch by 1½ inch labels.)

To make the macro more useful for other users, you may want to use WordPerfect's Macro Command Language to insert a {BELL} command, which produces a beep, before each pause to remind you that the macro has paused and that you must take an action and press ⏎. Figure 9.14 illustrates how you could edit the macro to do this and also provide prompts for the user at each step. (See Appendix A for details on how to use Macro Command Language.)

## PRINTING SELECTED PAGES (VERSION 5.0)

This macro, named **pages**, allows you to print selected pages of a document in version 5.0. In that version of WordPerfect, to print selected pages, you must have saved a document first. The macro takes you to the List Files screen in the directory you specify and

```
Macro: Action
    File            ADDRESS.WPM
    Description     copies addresses into envelopes

    {DISPLAY ON}{BELL}{PROMPT}Put·cursor·at·beginning·of·first·line·in·addr
    Then·press·Enter:~
    {WAIT}20~
    {PAUSE}{Block}{BELL}{PROMPT}Put·cursor·at·end·of·last·line·in·address·b
    Then·press·Enter:~
    {PAUSE}{Move}bc{Switch}{Enter}
    {Home}{Home}{Down}{HPg}{Switch}{Macro}address{Enter}

Ctrl-PgUp for macro commands;   Press Exit when done
```

*Figure 9.14:* You can edit the **address** macro to provide prompts for the user.

pauses for you to highlight a document file name. It then prompts you to enter the selected pages.

Version 5.1 of WordPerfect allows you to print selected pages of the document that is on the screen, even if it hasn't been saved, so no macro is given for that version. (The option is called Multiple Pages in version 5.1.)

## *RECORDING THE MACRO*

To record the macro, take the following steps:

1. Turn on the macro recorder by pressing Ctrl-F10 or choosing Macro from the Tools menu and then choosing Define. Enter **pages** as the name of the macro.

2. Enter **print selected pages** as the macro description; then press ⏎.

3. Press F5 (List Files); then press End to take the cursor to the end of the path name.

4. Insert a pause so that you can edit the path name of the desired directory when you use the macro. Press Ctrl-PgUp and type **P**.

5. Press ⏎ twice; then immediately insert a pause again so that you can highlight the desired document's name in the List Files screen.

6. Type **P** for Print; then insert another pause and press ⏎ twice.

7. Press Ctrl-F10 again to stop recording the macro.

The final macro should resemble the one in Figure 9.15.

```
Macro: Edit
        File            PAGES.WPM
    1 - Description     print selected pages
    2 - Action

        {List Files}{End}{PAUSE}{Enter}
        {PAUSE}
        p{PAUSE}{Enter}




Selection: 0
```

*Figure 9.15:* The **pages** macro (version 5.0) lets you indicate which pages in a document you want to print.

## USING THE MACRO

When you use the macro, WordPerfect pauses after it displays the path name of the current directory. You can edit the path name to the directory that contains the document you want to print. For example, if the program displays

   Dir C:\5\*.*

when you press ⏎, you will display the contents of the directory named 5. To view the contents of a subdirectory named BOOK, for example, you would edit the path name to

   Dir C:\5\BOOK

by using the Backspace key to delete the *.* and replace it with BOOK. WordPerfect assumes that you want to see all the files in a directory (*.*) unless you specify another pattern. For example, editing the line to

Dir C:\5\BOOK\*.ltr

would get you a listing of only the files with the extension .LTR in the directory.

After the path name is correct, press ↵. When the List Files screen appears, highlight the document that has the pages you want to print; then press ↵. You will see a

Pages: (All)

prompt. To print all of the pages in the document, simply press ↵. To print selected pages, enter the page numbers. To print a range of pages, separate the page numbers with a hyphen. To print separate pages, separate them with a comma. For example:

| ENTERING | PRINTS |
| --- | --- |
| 6-12 | pages 6 through 12 |
| 6,12 | pages 6 and 12 |
| 6,8-12 | page 6 plus pages 8 through 12 |
| -6 | from the beginning of the document through page 6 |
| 6- | from page 6 to the end of the document |

You should know which pages you want to print before you start. When you use the Look option in List Files, page numbers aren't indicated. Also, be aware that if you've saved the document with Fast Save on, you won't be able to print it from the List Files screen. If you don't know in advance which pages you want to print (or if you've used Fast Save), retrieve the document, check the page numbers, and then print it.

## SWITCHING TO ITALICS

If you often want to switch to italics as you type—for example, if you often type equations with unknowns or italicize words or phrases in your text—you can use this macro instead of the rather cumbersome key sequence Ctrl-F8 A I. By assigning those keystrokes to **Alt-I** (for Italics), you can cut them in half.

You can also use this macro on text that you've already typed and blocked instead of using it as you type. When you use it on blocked text, the final [italc] code is put in position at the end of the block, so you don't have to worry about turning off Italics.

> This macro uses italics, but you could just as well record it for any of the other size or appearance changes on the Font key (Ctrl-F8).

### RECORDING THE MACRO

To record the macro, take the following steps:

1. Turn on the macro recorder by pressing Ctrl-F10 or choosing Macro from the Tools menu and then choosing Define. Press **Alt-I** to assign the macro to **Alt-I**.

2. Enter **switches to italics** as the macro description; then press ↵.

3. Press Ctrl-F8 (Font).

4. Type **A I** for Appearance and Italics.

5. Press Ctrl-F10 again to stop recording the macro.

The final macro should resemble the one in Figure 9.16. A variation of the macro, one that italicizes only the word the cursor is on or the word to its immediate right, is shown in Figure 9.17.

### USING THE MACRO

When you use the macro, simply press Alt-I and the next text you type will be in italics until you press Alt-I again. Or you can press → once to move over the final [italc] code that is being pushed along in front of the cursor. Remember, in any case, to turn Italics off once you've turned it on, or the rest of your document will be italicized. To make sure that Italics doesn't get turned on and never turned off again, block text and then italicize it instead of italicizing it as you type it.

```
Macro: Action

     File              ALTI.WPM

     Description       switches to italics

          {DISPLAY OFF}{Font}ai

Ctrl-PgUp for macro commands;  Press Exit when done
```

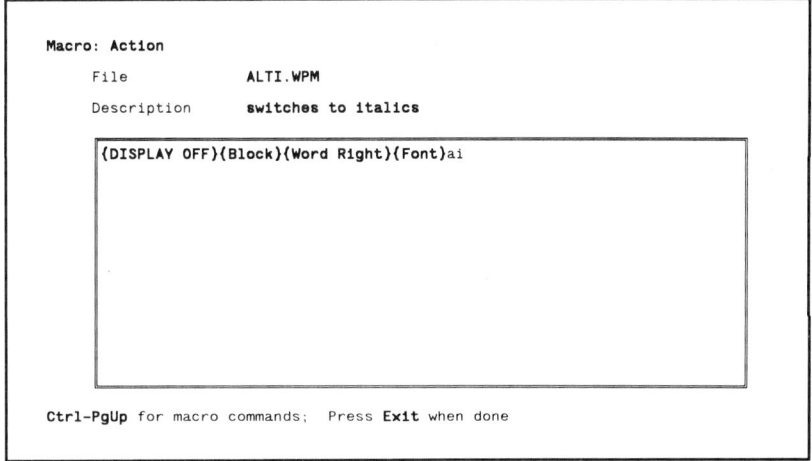

*Figure 9.16:* This macro quickly switches the appearance of the font to italics.

```
Macro: Action

     File              ALTI.WPM

     Description       switches to italics

          {DISPLAY OFF}{Block}{Word Right}{Font}ai

Ctrl-PgUp for macro commands;  Press Exit when done
```

*Figure 9.17:* You can use a variation of the **Alt-I** macro to italicize the word the cursor is on.

If you've run out of Alt key combinations at this point, consider setting up a soft keyboard that gives you 26 Alt combinations plus 26 Ctrl combinations. See Chapter 4 for details. Also see Chapter 3 for details about how to set up two-keystroke Alt-key macros.

## *OTHER USES*

If there are other appearance changes you make frequently in documents, such as underlining, using boldface, or marking text for redline or strikeout, record macros for them also, using this one as a pattern. You can also use it as a pattern for size change macros if, for example, you often switch to Large or Small type. Just type the letter of the option you want in place of the **I** for Italics. If you're recording a size change macro, type **S** and the option letter instead of **A** and the option letter. Name the macros with an Alt combination that helps you remember what they do: for example, Alt-L for Large.

## *RETURNING TO NORMAL TYPE*

The macro you just looked at automatically returns you to Normal type the second time you use it. However, if you're making size and appearance changes without using macros, you have to tell WordPerfect to return to Normal type after you've switched to a different appearance (such as Small Caps or Italics) or changed sizes (as to Superscript or Subscript).

This macro, named **Alt-N**, quickly returns you to Normal text without your having to use the menu system. It's very simple, but it saves keystrokes.

### *RECORDING THE MACRO*

To record the macro, take the following steps:

1. Turn on the macro recorder by pressing Ctrl-F10 or choosing Macro from the Tools menu and then choosing Define. Press **Alt-N** to assign the macro to **Alt-N**.

2. Enter **returns to normal text** as the macro description; then press ⏎.

3. Press Ctrl-F8 (Font) and type **N** for Normal.

4. Press Ctrl-F10 again to stop recording the macro.

### *USING THE MACRO*

When you use the macro, just press Alt-N after you've finished typing text in a different size or appearance.

## DRAFT PRINTING

If you only occasionally print at Draft quality and want to leave your print quality set to High, use this macro. It changes print quality to Medium temporarily and then switches back to High quality for the next print job. You will need to use Macro Command Language to insert one instruction in this macro.

This macro, named **draftp**, prints one copy of the document that's on the screen in draft quality and then switches back to High quality.

### BEFORE YOU BEGIN

Before you begin to record the macro:

- You should have a document on the screen.
- Your printer should be on.

### RECORDING THE MACRO

To record the macro, take the following steps:

1. Turn on the macro recorder by pressing Ctrl-F10 or choosing Macro from the Tools menu and then choosing Define. Enter **draftp** as the name of the macro.

2. Enter **prints draft of document** as the macro description; then press ↵.

3. Press Shift-F7 (Print) and type **T D** for Text Quality and Draft.

4. Type **F** for Full Document.

5. Press Ctrl-F10 to stop recording the macro. Your printer will probably be running at this point. You can cancel the job quickly by using the **Alt-C** macro given at the beginning of this chapter.

6. Retrieve the macro into the editor by pressing Ctrl-F10, entering **draft**, pressing ↵, and typing **E** for Edit (type **A** for Action if you have version 5.0).

CH. 9

7. Press End to move to the end of the macro.
8. Press Ctrl-PgUp (Macro Commands) and type **W**. Press ↵ to insert a {WAIT} instruction in the macro.
9. Type **30 ~** to insert a wait of three seconds. Remember to type the tilde.
10. Press Shift-F7 (Print) and type **T H** to return print quality to High. Press Ctrl-V and then F7.
11. Press F7 (twice in version 5.0) to return to your document.

The final macro should resemble the one in Figure 9.18.

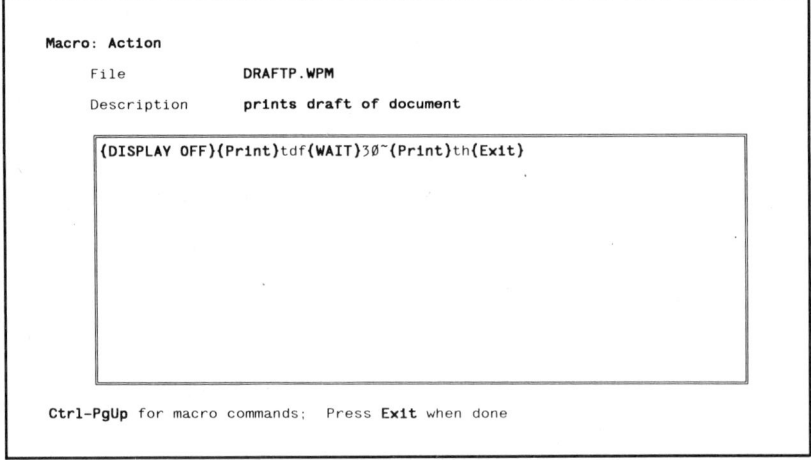

*Figure 9.18:* The **draftp** macro prints one copy in Draft quality **and** then switches back to High quality.

### USING THE MACRO

When you use the macro, WordPerfect prints one copy of your document in Draft quality (assuming that your printer's on). It waits until that information has been sent to the printer and then switches back to High quality.

To see the results that Draft quality gives on your printer, turn it on and print a page or so with the macro. You may decide that you'd rather do draft printing in Medium quality instead.

▬ Laser printers print in High quality only.

## PRINTING DOCUMENT COMMENTS

This macro, named **printcom**, prints any normally nonprinting document comments that are in your document. It converts them to text first.

However, if you simply convert document comments to text and then print the document, there is no way to distinguish the comments from the text. This macro therefore also converts the comments to italics.

*This macro illustrates nesting and chaining with a search macro.*

For this macro, you will need to record three macros: One, named **convert**, carries out the steps required to search for each [Comment] code, surround it with [ITALC][italc] codes, and convert the comment to text. The second, named **printit**, simply prints the document. (You may substitute your general-purpose print macro here, if you've already recorded one.) Finally, the **printcom** macro moves to the beginning of the document before any format codes and calls the other macros, repeating **convert** until no more instances of comment boxes can be found.

### BEFORE YOU BEGIN

Before you begin to record the macro:

- You should have a document on the screen, and it should contain one or more comments. To insert a comment, press Ctrl-F5 (Text In/Out), and type **C C** for Comment Create. Then type the text of the comment and press F7 (Exit).

### RECORDING THE MACRO

To record the **convert** macro, take the following steps:

1. Turn on the macro recorder by pressing Ctrl-F10 or choosing Macro from the Tools menu and then choosing Define. Type **convert** as the macro's name and press ⏎.

2. Type **converts comments to text** as the description and press ⏎.

3. In version 5.0, press F2 (Search); then press Ctrl-F5 (Text In/Out) to search for the [Comment] code. In version 5.1, type **C** for Comment.

4. Press F2 to start the search.

5. When the program locates the [Comment] code, it positions the cursor after it. Press ← to move the cursor onto the code; then press Alt-F4 (Block) and press → to highlight it.

6. Press Ctrl-F8 (Font) and type **A I** for Appearance Italics.

7. Press Ctrl-F5 (Text In/Out) and type **C T** to convert the comment to text. The text will then be surrounded by [ITALC][italc] codes so that you can tell it from normal text when the document is printed.

8. Press Alt-F10 (Macro), type **convert**, and press ↵ to chain the macro to itself.

9. Press Ctrl-F10 to stop recording the macro.

To record the **printit** macro, simply include the keystrokes Shift-F7 **F** in a macro. If you already have a print macro, use it here instead of recording a new one.

To record the **printcom** macro, take the following steps:

1. Turn on the macro recorder by pressing Ctrl-F10 or choosing Macro from the Tools menu and then choosing Define. Enter **printcom** as the name of the macro.

2. Enter **print document comments** as the macro description; then press ↵.

3. Move to the beginning of the document by pressing Home Home Home ↑. This moves the cursor to the very beginning of the document, before any format codes that may be before the text.

4. Press Alt-F10 (Macro) and enter **convert**. Then press ↵. This calls the **convert** macro, which repeats itself until all comments are converted to italics.

5. Press Ctrl-F10 to stop recording the macro, as the next step is done in the editor.

6. Retrieve the **printcom** macro into the editor. Type **A** for Action if you're using version 5.0.

7. Move the cursor to the end of the macro.

8. Nest the **printit** macro that will print the document by pressing Ctrl-PgUp, typing **N**, pressing ←, and typing **printit** ~

9. Exit from the macro editor by pressing F7 twice.

The final **convert** and **printcom** macros should resemble the ones in Figures 9.19 and 9.20. Figure 9.21 illustrates how the comments would appear if printed on a dot-matrix printer.

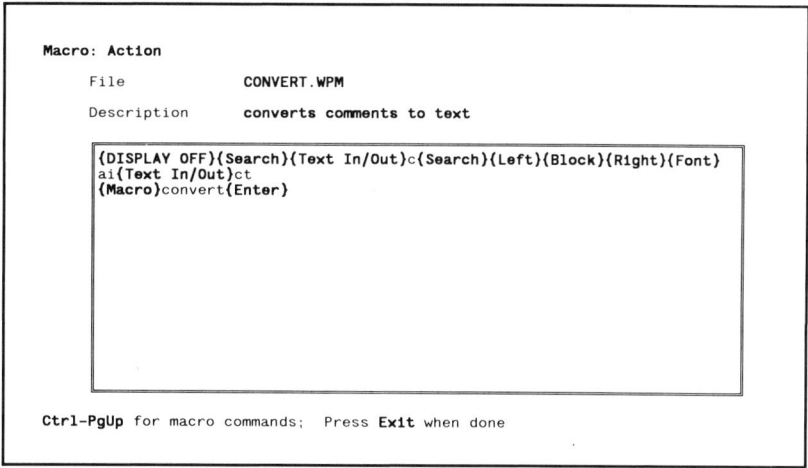

*Figure 9.19:* The **convert** macro (version 5.1) converts comments to italic text.

## USING THE MACRO

When you use the macro, it will go to the beginning of your document first. WordPerfect searches for any nonprinting document comments in your document and converts them to text; it then prints the full document.

If you are using italics elsewhere in your document, you can record the macro so that it uses a different appearance code for comments (which one depends on your printer's capabilities). For example, if your printer can produce small caps, you could use those for comments instead by changing the **I** in step 6 of the **convert** macro to **C**. If

```
Macro: Action
    File            PRINTCOM.WPM
    Description     print document comments

    {DISPLAY OFF}{Home}{Home}{Up}
    {Macro}convert{Enter}
    {NEST}printit~




Ctrl-PgUp for macro commands;   Press Exit when done
```

*Figure 9.20:* The **printcom** macro chains the **convert** macro and nests the **printit** macro.

```
      When  you  start   WordPerfect,  the  program  automatically
assigns specific  word  processing commands  to  each  of  the  10
function keys. Mention the enhanced keyboard with 12 function keys? If
you have the  IBM enhanced keyboard,  you have 12  function keys.
Each of these keys can be used alone  and in combination with the
Ctrl, Shift, and Alt keys. Along with these standard function key
assignments, the  program  assigns its  own  cursor movement  and
deletion functions to the keys on  the numeric pad Mention separate
cursor pad? (or cursor pad,  if it is separate on  your keyboard),
used alone and in combination with the Ctrl  key. In addition, it
uses the ASCII  code system to  assign the correct values  to the
number, letter, and symbol keys on keyboard.
```

*Figure 9.21:* This sample paragraph contained two comments, which are printed in italics.

you can't produce small caps with your printer, try changing to Small type (and uppercase) instead by substituting the **S S** (Size Small) for **A I** in step 6.

## SUMMARY

Now that you've rounded out your macro library by recording printing macros that speed up your printing chores, you can take a look at the specialized macros in Chapter 10 and see if any of them will be of use to you. These macros deal primarily with reference aids, such as footnotes, endnotes, tables of contents, and bibliographies. However, you'll also find macros for managing lists, numbering lines, outlining, and creating special symbols. These are tasks that you probably don't do every day, so it's nice to have macros that remember an often complex set of keystrokes for these relatively infrequent jobs.

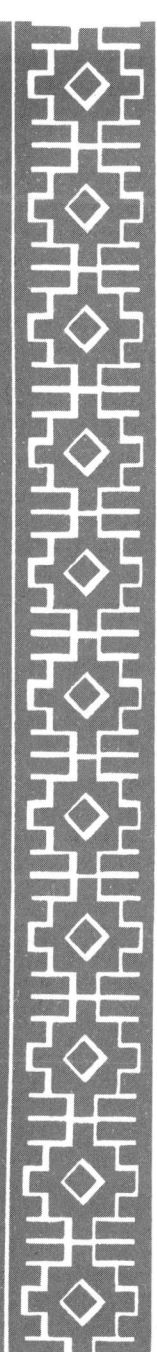

# *Specialized Macros*

CHAPTER

# 10

# CHAPTER 10

The title of this chapter, specialized macros, gives you a clue to the fact that there are all different kinds of macros in here. Many of them are useful for specialized tasks that you probably don't have to do very often but that can be tedious to remember exactly how to set up, such as creating tables of contents or changing endnotes to footnotes. In addition, you'll find several macros that deal with reference aids, such as bibliographies and indexes.

Also included in this chapter are macros for mathematical typing and creating special symbols. If you do much of this sort of typing, you may find these macros especially useful in your work. You'll also see macros for marking text with strikeout and redlining, which can save you a lot of time if you work with contracts and other legal documents.

Other macros in this hodgepodge chapter deal with outlining, paragraph numbering, and managing lists in WordPerfect. Undoubtedly you will find many macros in here that you will want to record or adapt for your own purposes; others you may have no use for at present, but who knows? Someday you may need to create a bibliography or do a paragraph sort. Good hunting!

## CHANGING THE OUTLINE FORMAT

WordPerfect's default outlining style uses the eight-level system detailed below:

> ◉ WordPerfect uses the default outlining style for *paragraph* numbering unless you change it, and this can be confusing.

    I.
        A.
            1.
                a.
                    (1)

(a)

i)

a)

> WordPerfect uses the nearest preceding [Par Num Def] code when it does automatic outlining or numbering. This means that you can switch styles within a document. For instance, if you've used an outline near the beginning of a document, you can define a new style and use bullets in a list later in the document.

You can choose paragraph-numbering style—1., a., i., (1), (a), (i), 1), a)—or legal style—1., 1.1, 1.1.1, 1.1.1.1, and so forth. In addition, you can choose to use a system of bullets or to set your own style.

This macro, named **parout**, changes the outline format from the default outlining style to the paragraph style and turns on paragraph numbering. You can record similar macros to switch to bullets or legal numbering, if you prefer.

## RECORDING THE MACRO

To record the macro, take the following steps:

1. Turn on the macro recorder by pressing Ctrl-F10 or choosing Macro from the Tools menu and then choosing Define. Enter **parout** as the name of the macro.
2. Enter **switches to paragraph numbering style** as the macro description; then press ←.
3. Press Shift-F5 (Date/Outline) and type **D P**. This defines the style as paragraph numbering.
4. Press F7 to exit from the Paragraph Number Definition screen.
5. To insert a paragraph number, type **P**.
6. Press Ctrl-F10 to stop recording the macro.
7. Press ← to start automatic paragraph numbering, or enter a level number.

The final macro should resemble the one in Figure 10.1.

## USING THE MACRO

When you use the macro, WordPerfect changes the numbering style to paragraph numbering, turns on paragraph numbering, and

```
Macro: Action
    File            PAROUT.WPM
    Description     switches to paragraph numbering style

    {Date/Outline}dp{Exit}p




Ctrl-PgUp for macro commands;   Press Exit when done
```

*Figure 10.1:* This macro switches to paragraph-numbering style and inserts a paragraph number.

prompts you to enter a paragraph level. Pressing ⏎ inserts a paragraph number in the style defined for that level (tab stop). If the cursor is at the left margin, you get a level-1 style number; if it is at the first tab stop, you get a level-2 style number, and so forth. Figure 10.2 illustrates the built-in styles for each level. For example, if the cursor were on the second tab stop when you saw the prompt, you would get a paragraph numbered as i. (or ii., or iii.) if you pressed ⏎. Inserting a [Tab] code before that number will change it to the next level.

If you want paragraphs to be numbered in a particular style no matter where the cursor is, you can enter a level number. For example, to number all paragraphs as a), b), c), and so forth, no matter where the cursor is positioned, you would enter **8** and press ⏎. If you enter a level number, you can insert tabs freely and the numbering style will not change.

## *OTHER USES*

As mentioned earlier, you can edit this macro so that it will use either legal or bullet style. Simply enter the correct letter in step 3 (**L** for Legal, **B** for Bullets).

```
Outline Style (the default)
Level 1   2    3    4    5    6    7    8
       I.  A.   1.   a.  (1)  (a)  1)   a)
Paragraph Style
Level 1   2    3    4    5    6    7    8
       1.  a.   i.  (1)  (a)  (i)  1)   a)
Legal Style
Level 1   2    3    4    5    6    7    8
       1   .1   .1   .1   .1   .1   .1   .1
Bullets
Level 1   2    3    4    5    6    7    8
       •   o    -    ■    *    +    ·    x


C:\5\MB\FIG10-2                          Doc 1 Pg 1 Ln 1" Pos 1"
```

*Figure 10.2:* WordPerfect uses these styles for its outline and paragraph numbering.

## AUTOMATIC PARAGRAPH/OUTLINE NUMBERING

This macro, named **number** (you will probably want to change it to an Alt macro if you use it so that it will be quicker), automatically turns on outlining and inserts the number—normally a four- or five-step process. After you enter the text and press ←, it turns off Outline mode. It also formats the entry for you so that the number is aligned on the period instead of with WordPerfect's usual alignment, which is

    I. Text
    II. Text
    III. Text

After you use the macro, the entry will be aligned as

      I. Text
     II. Text
    III. Text

## RECORDING THE MACRO

To record the macro, take the following steps:

1. Turn on the macro recorder by pressing Ctrl-F10 or choosing Macro from the Tools menu and then choosing Define. Enter **number** as the name of the macro.
2. Enter **automatic outlining/formatting** as the macro description; then press ←.
3. Press Shift-F5 (Date/Outline) and type **O** for Outline and **O** for On (in version 5.0, just type **O** for Outline). Then press ←.
4. To align the numbers on the period, press ← to move to the left of the [Par Num:Auto] code; then press Ctrl-F6 (Tab Align).
5. Press → to move the cursor to the right of the [Par Num:Auto] code; then press F4 (Indent) to create a hanging indent.
6. Press Ctrl-PgUp and type **P** to insert a pause; then press ←.
7. Press Shift-F5 and type **O** to turn off Outline mode after you have finished making the entry. In version 5.1, type **F** to turn Outline mode off.
8. Press ← to move the cursor to the next line.
9. Press Ctrl-F10 again to stop recording the macro.

The final macro should resemble the one in Figure 10.3.

## USING THE MACRO

When you use the macro, WordPerfect automatically numbers the entry you are making according to the last outline number you used. It then pauses for you to enter the text of the item. If your item is longer than one line, an indent like this one will be created:

> I. If the text of your item is longer than one line, WordPerfect will wrap the next line to create a hanging indent instead of taking the line back to the left margin.

*SPECIALIZED MACROS* **369**

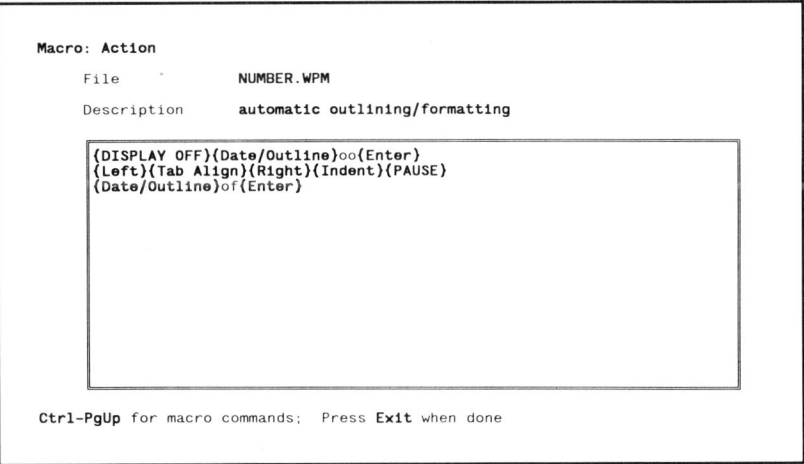

*Figure 10.3:* This automatic outlining macro (version 5.1) also formats your entries as hanging indents.

As soon as you press ←, Outline mode is turned off, and you are returned to a new line where you can enter normal text or use the macro again to make a new outline entry.

If the outline number isn't at the level you want to use—maybe you want an *(a)* entry instead of an *I.* entry, for example—just position the cursor to the left of the outline number (and to the left of the [Align] code) after you've created the entry, and press Tab until you're at the level you want. When you move the cursor down through the outline, the numbers will automatically change to reflect the new levels.

### *OTHER USES*

Although automatic paragraph numbering works a little differently from outlining, you can edit this macro for use with outlining. For example, to change the macro so that it will number paragraphs with arabic numerals (1., 2., 3., and so forth), change the keystrokes in steps 3 through 5 to Shift-F5 **P 3** ← F4 and delete the keystrokes in step 7. This tells WordPerfect to use fixed numbering and—since you are assumed not to have changed the default numbering style—to use arabic numbers with periods (the level-3 style of outline numbering) and to create a hanging indent. Paragraph numbering is turned off automatically.

## USING AN OUTLINE STYLE

In version 5.1, you can also create styles for your outlines by using the Outline Style Name option on the Paragraph Number Definition menu. It allows you to create a style for each numbering level and to maintain a library of those styles that you can choose from at any time.

You can use this feature to set up a particular style of outlining that will be in effect wherever you turn Outline mode on. In this macro, outline items will be in boldface, but you can edit the macro later so that they will be in italics, or you may want to have them in smaller type or even in a different font altogether. In addition, you'll set this macro up so that the entries will be formatted and aligned on the period after the number and text that wraps to the next line will be aligned with the line above. As a final touch, you'll see how to set up outlining so that WordPerfect will pick up numbering wherever it left off, so that you can intersperse outline text with the rest of your document and have it numbered consecutively.

If that isn't enough, you'll then record two short Alt macros that turn Outline mode on and off quickly, so that you can intersperse outline entries with regular document text.

Once you do all this, though, you'll have a nicely formatted style that you can use without thinking about whenever you create an outline. Figure 10.4 shows a printed sample. (When you see the steps involved to format it, you will see what I mean.)

### BEFORE YOU BEGIN

Before you begin to record the macro:

- Clear the screen.

### RECORDING THE MACRO

1. Press Ctrl-F10 (Macro Define) or choose Macro from the Tools menu and then choose Define. Enter **out** as the name of the macro.

2. Enter **sets up outline style** as the macro description.

> I. INTRODUCTION
>
> Under a project funded by the SEC, a two-wavelength LIDAR system has been successfully constructed and demonstrated.
>
>     I.A.    **Task 1: Improve Wavelength Sensitivity**
>
> While the infrared wavelength is of primary importance, operation of the model may be advantageous during certain atmospheric conditions.
>
>     I.B.    **Task 2: Improve LIDAR Performance for Remote Measurement of Gas Concentrations**
>
> The SEC funded this system design as a separate project to define capability and cost before the project began. If sufficient sensitivity is obtained, gas concentration profile information may be derived by analysis of the aerosol samples.

*Figure 10.4:* A printed sample of the outline created with the **out** macro.

3. Press Shift-F5 (Date/Outline) and type **D** for Define.

4. Type **N** for Outline Style Name.

5. If you aren't using any other styles, you may see a line showing that no style is being used and that pressing Enter inserts paragraph numbers only. Type **C** to create a new style.

6. You will see the screen shown in Figure 10.5; you can define a format for each of the eight outline levels. Here we'll define only three.

7. Type **N** for Name; then type **bold indent** as the style name; then press ←⎦. Once you have named an outline style and selected it, its name will appear on the Paragraph Number Definition screen as the outline style name.

8. Type **D** for Description and enter **bold indented style** and press ←⎦.

9. Now you can define a format for level-1 outlining. The cursor should be highlighting level 1. Because you want the style to turn off when you are done (that is, to have a Style On and Style Off code), type **T** for Type and **P** for Paired. (If you didn't make this a paired style, you would turn on boldface for the rest of your document.)

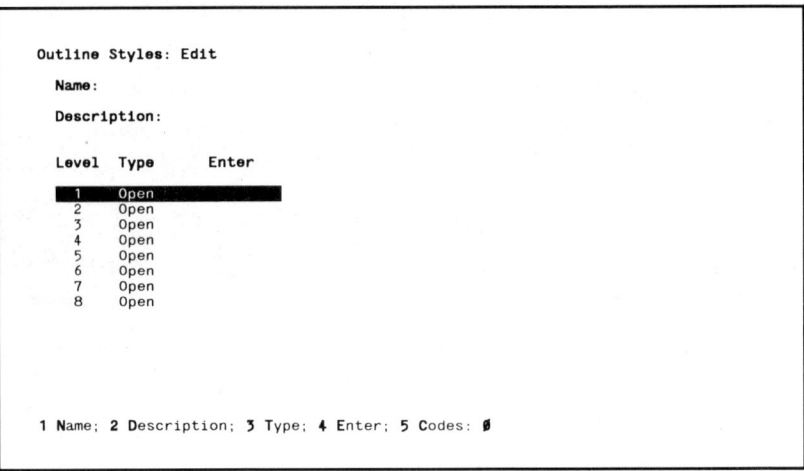

*Figure 10.5:* You can access this screen either from the Date/Outline menu (Shift-F5) or from the Styles menu (Alt-F8).

10. So that the style will turn off when you press the Enter key, type **E** for Enter and **F** for Off.

11. Then, to insert the codes for the style that turn on boldfacing and create the hanging indent for level-1 entries, type **C** for Codes.

12. Press F6 (Bold); then press Ctrl-F6 (Tab Align). This will produce a [DEC TAB] code so that the level-1 numbers will align on the decimal points. (WordPerfect will normally produce level-1 entries flush left on the left margin, so the decimal points will not align.)

13. Press the → key to move over the [Par Num: 1] code, and then press F4 (Indent) to create the hanging indent. When your screen resembles the one in Figure 10.6, press F7 to return to the Outline Styles: Edit screen.

14. Now you can create a format for level-2 outline entries. Press ↓ to move the highlight cursor to level 2. Type **T P E F C**.

15. This time, for the codes, press F6 (Bold); then press Tab so that your level-2 entries will be indented one tab stop from level-1 entries; press F4 (Indent) and then Ctrl-F6 (Dec Tab)

*SPECIALIZED MACROS* **373**

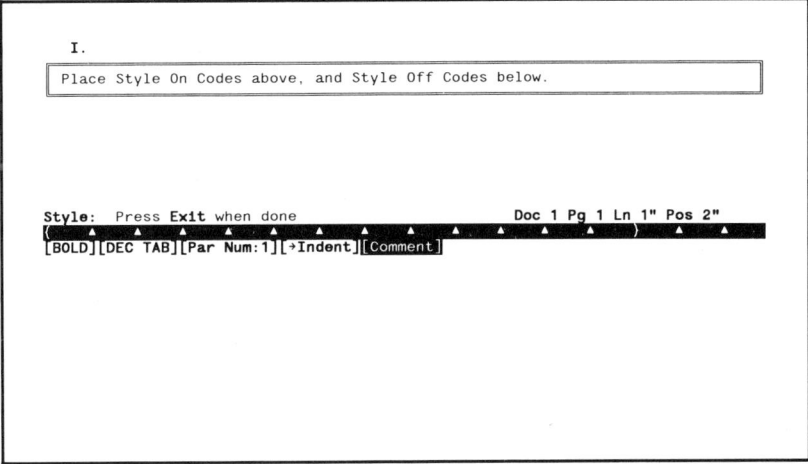

***Figure 10.6:*** Inserting the codes for the outline style. These codes turn on boldfacing and create a hanging indent, with the entries aligned on the decimal point.

so that the numbers will be aligned, then press →, and press F4 so that the text will be aligned. When the codes read

**[BOLD][Tab][->Indent][DEC TAB][Par Num: 2] [->Indent][Comment]**

press F7 to return to the Outline Styles: Edit screen.

16. Press ↓ to move to level 3. Then type **T P E F C**. Press F6 (Bold); then press Tab twice so that the level-3 entries will be further indented from the level-2 entries. Press F4 (Indent), press Ctrl-F6 (Dec Tab), press →, and press F4. The codes should resemble these:

    **[BOLD][Tab][Tab][->Indent][DEC TAB][Par Num: 3] [->Indent][Comment]**

    If you define additional levels, press Tab three times for level 4, four times for level 5, and so on.

17. Press F7 twice to exit. You can now insert a pause so that the macro will pause to let you select a style when you execute it.

18. Press Ctrl-PgUp, type **P**, and press ↵. When you execute the macro, you will highlight the style you want and press ↵.

> If you're doing legal-style numbering and don't want your outline levels to be successively indented, define the formats for each level with the same number of tab stops.

19. Then move the highlight to the bold indented style (it should be on it) and type **L** to select the style.

20. So that WordPerfect will automatically keep numbering where it left off, type **S** and then type **?.?.?.** (If you are using more than three levels, type as many **?.** sequences as the number of levels you're defining.)

21. So that the program will automatically keep you at the level you are currently entering when you make successive entries, type **A Y** for Automatically Adjust to Current Level and Yes. This saves you on keystrokes a bit because when this feature is off, WordPerfect will wrap the text back to the left margin when you press ⏎ to stop making an entry. This way, the program will position the cursor ready for you to make an entry at the *same* level. It won't be obvious when you're doing level-1 entries, because you are already at the left margin, but when you're indented three or four tab stops for a level-3 or level-4 entry, it saves you from having to press Tab three or four times to get back to the right place.

22. If you want the macro to number outline entries with their full "path name"—that is, I.A.1. instead of just 1., add these final keystrokes to the macro: **U** ⏎ ↓ **Y Y Y**. This tells WordPerfect to "attach" the previous levels. If you're writing a document in which outline numbers are interspersed with text, they may be few and far between; it's a good idea to do this so that your readers can keep track of where they are in the outline.

23. Press F7 twice; then type **O O** to turn outline mode on. Press ⏎ so that the macro will automatically begin numbering. Your finished macro should resemble the one in Figure 10.7. You can use this style as a way to automatically number the headings in your document. After you've executed the **out** macro, each time you turn underlining on, the text you type will be numbered automatically according to the last number you used and will be in boldface type.

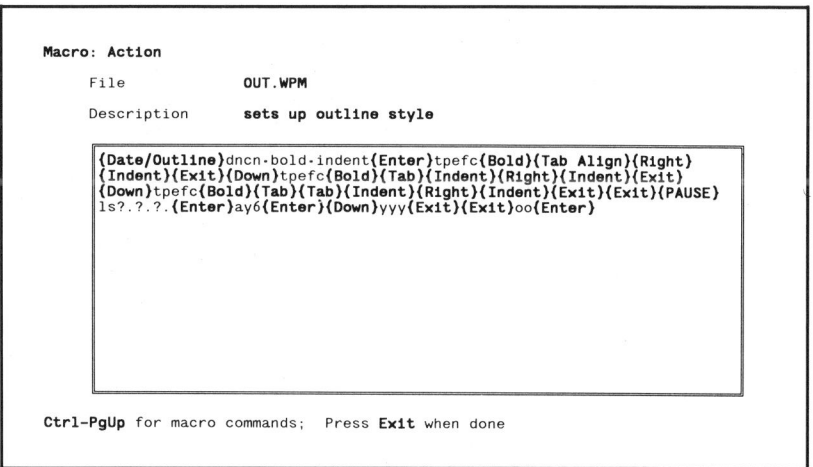

*Figure 10.7:* The completed **out** macro

Now you can record two simple Alt macros that will quickly turn Outline mode on and off: Record Alt-O (for On) as Shift-F5 **O O** and Alt-F (for Off) as Shift-F5 **O F**.

## USING THE MACRO

You only have to use the **out** macro once in a document to set up the style and turn it on. When you execute the **out** macro, Word-Perfect sets up the outline style you have laboriously just defined and pauses for you to select the style you want to use. If you're in a document in which you haven't used any other styles or haven't retrieved a style library, this style will be the only one listed. You can simply press ← to select it. Otherwise, move the cursor to its name and press ← to select it.

You'll then immediately be placed in Outline mode where you can type the text of your outline entries. Because you've assigned the Enter key to Off, you can press ← once to turn off the boldfacing or press ← twice to begin the next entry. To turn off Outline mode and type regular document text, press Alt-F. To turn it back on again and keep on writing your outline where you left off, press Alt-O. To turn it off and go back to writing text, press Alt-F.

## OTHER USES

You can use this macro as a way to number headings consecutively throughout a document. In fact, you can change it so that it will mark headings as entries for the table of contents so that all you have to do is define the contents page and generate it (and there's a **create** macro later in this chapter that will do that for you).

To have the macro automatically mark headings (outline entries) for the contents page, add these steps to it: after each C for Codes, press Alt-F4 to turn on block marking; then press Alt-F5 (Mark Text) and type **C** for ToC. Then enter the level number you're defining and press ⏎. A finished example of an entry for a level-1 head would look like this:

[Mark:ToC,1][Bold][DEC TAB][Par Num:1]
[->Indent][Comment][End Mark:ToC,1]

# NUMBERING ITEMS IN A LIST

Instead of numbering items as you type them, you may find that it's faster to type out a list and then number it. This macro, named **itemize**, uses the program's built-in paragraph-numbering system to automatically number the items in a list that you have already created. It also formats the entries aligned on the period, with a hanging indent.

*This is another macro that you'll want to assign to an Alt or Ctrl key if you use it frequently.*

## BEFORE YOU BEGIN

- You should have a list on the screen, with each item separated by a hard return, as illustrated in Figure 10.8. (Double spacing is being used in this figure.) The first item in the list has a hard return on the line before it.

- Move to the beginning of the list, before the first hard return.

*SPECIALIZED MACROS* 377

```
Press Ctrl-F10 to turn on the macro recorder.
Press the keys that carry out the task that you want to perform.
Press Ctrl-F10 to turn off the macro recorder.
Press Alt-F10 and enter the macro's name to execute the macro.




                                                    Doc 1 Pg 1 Ln 1" Pos 1"
```

*Figure 10.8:* You will need some sample text like this to record the **itemize** macro.

## RECORDING THE MACRO

To record the macro, take the following steps:

1. Turn on the macro recorder by pressing Ctrl-F10 or choosing Macro from the Tools menu and then choosing Define. Enter **itemize** as the name of the macro.

2. Enter **numbers list** as the macro description; then press ←⏎.

3. Press F2 (Search), press ←⏎, and press F2 again so that the macro will search for the hard return separating the items.

4. Press Shift-F5 (Date/Outline) and type **P** for Para Num.

5. Press ←⏎ to use automatic numbering.

6. Press ←; then press Ctrl-F6 to align the numbers on the period.

7. Press →; then press F4 to create a hanging indent.

8. Press Ctrl-F10 again to stop recording the macro.

The final macro should resemble the one in Figure 10.9.

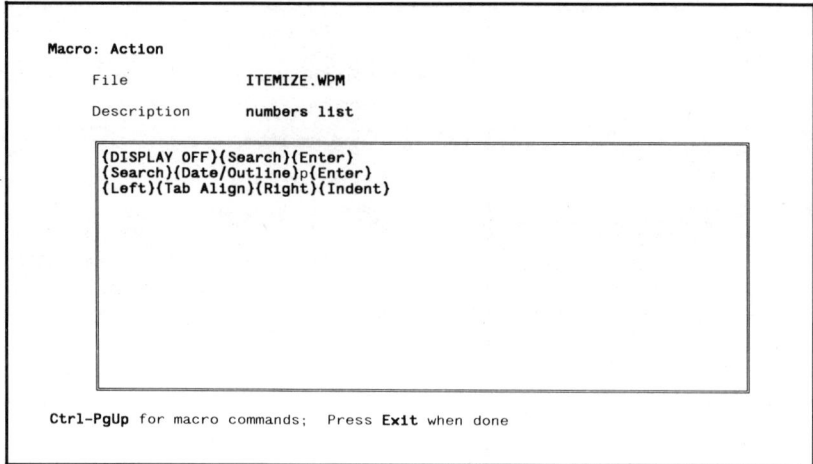

*Figure 10.9:* The **itemize** macro will number items in a list.

The sample list numbered by using the macro is illustrated in Figure 10.10. As outline style is the default, roman numerals are used. To use arabic numbers instead, change the numbering style to paragraph by using the **parout** macro (Figure 10.1) before you use the **itemize** macro.

*Figure 10.10:* After you've used the macro on the list shown in Figure 10.8, it will resemble this one.

## USING THE MACRO

When you use the **itemize** macro, move to the beginning of your list, count the number of items you want to number (remember, each must be separated by a hard return), press Esc, and enter that number. Then immediately press Alt-F10 and execute the macro. WordPerfect will repeat the macro the number of times you have indicated after pressing Esc.

The macro will number each line (or set of lines) that ends in a hard return. However, it will also number blank lines since they end in a hard return, so if you want to number paragraphs that have blank lines between them, use two [HRt] codes in step 3 to have the macro search for two hard returns.

# TURNING LINE NUMBERING ON AND OFF

WordPerfect has a built-in line-numbering feature that numbers lines when the document is printed; you don't see the line numbers on the screen unless you use the View Document feature. The program automatically starts over with line 1 each time it begins a new page, but you can change this so that the lines are numbered consecutively throughout a document. The line-numbering feature works with the spacing you've set, whether it's single, double, or something else. Blank lines (those created by pressing ←, not blank lines in double-spaced documents) are normally counted unless you specify them not to be.

This macro, named **num**, turns on line numbering whenever you use it. Once you turn line numbering off, the numbering system will start with line 1 the next time you use it.

## RECORDING THE MACRO

To record the macro, take the following steps:

1. Turn on the macro recorder by pressing Ctrl-F10 or choosing Macro from the Tools menu and then choosing Define. Enter **num** as the name of the macro.

2. Enter **turns on line numbering** as the macro description; then press ↵.

3. Press Shift-F8 (Format) and type **L N Y** for Line Numbering Yes.

4. Insert a pause by pressing Ctrl-PgUp, typing **P**, and pressing ↵.

5. Press F7 to return to your document.

6. Press Ctrl-F10 again to stop recording the macro.

The final macro should resemble the one in Figure 10.11.

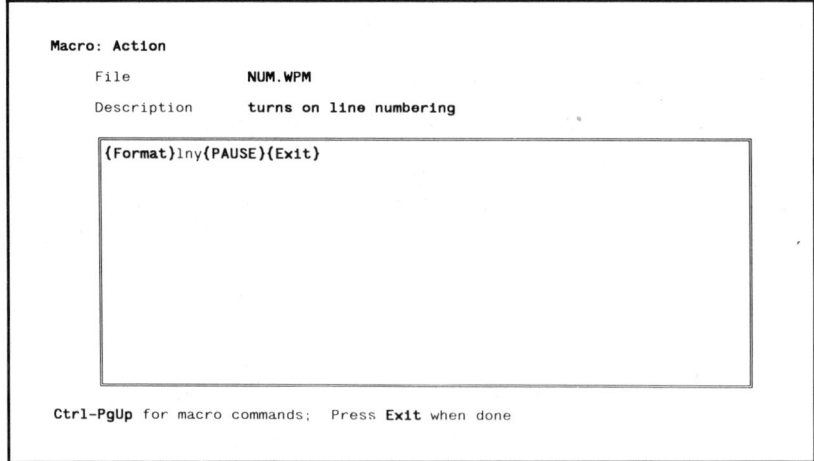

*Figure 10.11:* This macro turns on line numbering at the cursor's position.

## USING THE MACRO

When you use the macro, WordPerfect will pause and let you select any options that you want to use with the line-numbering feature. You can choose to have only every *n* lines numbered, to count blank lines, to choose a starting number, or to number pages cumulatively. When you press ↵, lines will be numbered beginning with 1 at the cursor's position. Footnote lines will be numbered, but header and footer lines will not be.

## OTHER USES

You can record a similar macro that turns off line numbering: Just substitute **N** for **Y** in step 3 and remove the pause. You don't see line numbering on the screen, so remembering to turn it off is especially important if you are only numbering a certain section of lines in a document. If you use line numbering often, you will want to assign these macros to Alt or Ctrl keys.

You can use this macro to count the number of lines in a document. First, move to the beginning of the document (press Home Home ↑) and execute the **num** macro. When it pauses, type **R N** so that lines will be numbered consecutively to the end of the the document; then press ⏎. Move to the end of the document (Home Home ↓) and print the last page (Shift-F7 **P**). (You won't be able to determine the last line number by using the View Document feature, because it doesn't display consecutive numbers.) When the page is printed, the last numbered line is the total number of lines in the document. If you don't want the line numbers to be printed in the final document, go back to the beginning of it and delete the [Ln Num:On] code before you print.

# CHANGING ENDNOTES TO FOOTNOTES

It's easy to change footnotes to endnotes. Because WordPerfect won't let you have footnotes in columns, to switch footnotes to endnotes you just turn on Columns, move to the end of your document, and then go back and delete the [Col On] code. However, switching endnotes to footnotes once you've created them is slightly more complex. You have to choose to edit each note, block its text and move it, delete the note, create a footnote, and paste the moved text. This macro, named **endfoot**, changes endnotes to footnotes for you automatically.

## BEFORE YOU BEGIN

Before you begin to record the macro:

- You should have a document on the screen, and it should contain at least one endnote.

## RECORDING THE MACRO

To record the macro, take the following steps:

1. Turn on the macro recorder by pressing Ctrl-F10 or choosing Macro from the Tools menu and then choosing Define. Enter **endfoot** as the name of the macro.

2. Enter **changes endnotes to footnotes** as the macro description; then press ⏎.

3. Press Ctrl-F7 (Footnote) and type **E E** for Endnote Edit.

4. Press ⏎ to edit the next endnote.

5. Press → to move over the note code when the editing screen appears.

6. Press Alt-F4 (Block); then press Home Home ↓ to block the entire text of the note.

7. Press Ctrl-F4 (Move); then type **B M** to move the block.

8. Press F7 to exit from the note editing screen.

9. Press Backspace and type **Y** to delete the note.

10. Press Ctrl-F7 and type **F C** to create a new footnote.

11. Press ⏎ to paste the text of the former endnote; then press F7 to exit.

12. Press Alt-F10 (Macro), enter **endfoot**, and press ⏎ to chain the macro to itself so that all the notes will be located and changed.

13. Press Ctrl-F10 again to stop recording the macro.

The final macro should resemble the one in Figure 10.12.

## USING THE MACRO

When you use the macro, move to the beginning of the document before you execute it so that you'll be sure to catch all the endnotes.

---

You can mix endnotes and footnotes in a document. For example, footnotes can be used to clarify what's on a page, and endnotes can be used for suggested readings. If you mix the two, though, be sure to use a different numbering system for each so that your readers don't get completely confused. WordPerfect will use numerals for both unless you use Options to tell it to use letters for one.

```
Macro: Action
    File            ENDFOOT.WPM
    Description     changes endnotes to footnotes

    {DISPLAY OFF}{Footnote}ee{Enter}
    {Right}{Block}{Home}{Home}{Down}{Move}bm{Exit}{Backspace}y{Footnote}fc
    {Enter}
    {Exit}{Macro}endfoot{Enter}




Ctrl-PgUp for macro commands;  Press Exit when done
```

*Figure 10.12:* This **endfoot** macro converts endnotes to footnotes.

## CHANGING FOOTNOTE MARGINS

WordPerfect doesn't automatically change the margins in your footnotes if you change them in your document after you've typed it. In version 4.2, there were shortcuts for automatically updating note margins (you could do a word count through the Speller or do an extended search for a nonexistent code), but these shortcuts don't work in versions 5.0 and 5.1. (There is a way around this, though, as you'll see in the next macro.) So here's a macro that will take care of footnote margin changes for you. This macro, named **fmarg**, will automatically update your footnote margins once you've determined which margin setting you're going to use.

### *BEFORE YOU BEGIN*

Before you begin to record the macro:

- You need to have a document containing a footnote on the screen.

- You need to change a margin setting in the document. Move to the beginning of the document, press Ctrl-F8 (Format), choose Line (1 or L), and then type **M** for Margins. For this example, type **2″** to change the left margin to two inches; then press F7 three times to return to the document.

- Before you start to record the macro, press Home Home ↑ to go to the beginning of the document.

## *RECORDING THE MACRO*

▰ This macro calls a nested macro, so you need to record the Alt macro first.

Before you can record the master macro, **fmarg**, you will need to record the Alt macro that will update the margins. It will be nested inside the **fmarg** macro. The margin settings you use in the Alt macro, which we'll call **Alt-V** in this example, should be the ones you changed your document to. If you need to check what those margin settings are, you can search for the [L/R Mar] codes in your document: Press F2; then press Shift-F8 (Format) and type **L M** to choose Line Margin. Press Alt-F3 to view the codes, and make a note of the margin settings.

To record the **Alt-V** macro, once you've determined what margin settings to use (this one uses a two-inch left margin):

1. Turn on the macro recorder by pressing Ctrl-F10 or choosing Macro from the Tools menu and then choosing Define. Press Alt-V to name the macro.

2. Enter **sets left margin to 2″** as the description.

3. Press Shift-F8 (Format); then type **L** for Line and **M** for Margins.

4. Type **2″** for the left margin; then press ⏎ four times. (The last ⏎ is necessary to return you to the document when you use the macro.)

5. Press Ctrl-F10 to stop recording the macro.

To record the main macro, take the following steps:

1. Turn on the macro recorder. Enter **fmarg** as the name of the macro. Enter **updates margins in footnotes** as the macro description; then press ⏎.

2. Press F2 (Search); then press Ctrl-F7 and type **F N** to search for the first footnote code. Press F2 again to start the search.

3. When WordPerfect locates the first footnote, press ← to move over the note code.
4. Press Ctrl-F7 (Footnote), then type **F E** and press ↵ to edit the first footnote.
5. You will be in the footnote editing screen. Press Alt-V to nest the margin-change macro here.
6. Press F7 to exit from the footnote editing screen.
7. Chain the **fmarg** macro to itself by pressing Alt-F10 and typing **fmarg**, then pressing ↵.
8. Press Ctrl-F10 to stop recording the macro.

The final macro should resemble the one in Figure 10.13.

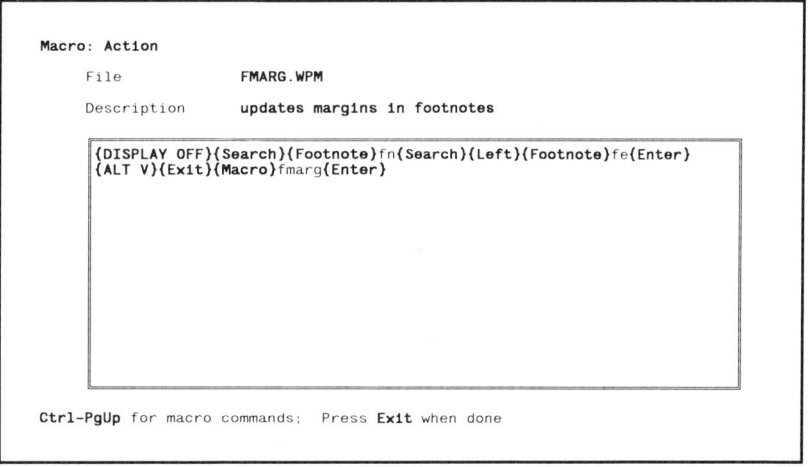

*Figure 10.13:* This macro will correct footnote margins for you so that they match those of your document.

## *USING THE MACRO*

When you use the macro, WordPerfect will search for each footnote, open it for editing, and insert the margin change you specified in the **Alt-V** macro. Once you have recorded an **Alt-V** macro, you can edit it to reflect the margin change that you want to use.

# RESETTING MARGINS

There is a way to reset margins in your document to make sure that everything—footnotes, endnotes, headers, footers, and so forth—has the same margins, no matter how many times you have changed your mind as you were typing the document. This macro, named **margins**, searches for any and all margin changes you may have made and handily strips them all out. It then takes you to the Initial Codes menu, where you can enter margin settings and have them take effect for the entire document.

## BEFORE YOU BEGIN

Before you begin to record the macro:

- You should have a document on the screen with at least one margin change in it. To do this quickly, retrieve any short document; then move to the middle of a line, press Shift-F8 (Format), type **L M 2″**, and press ⏎ four times to return to your document.

## RECORDING THE MACRO

> Use an extended search-and-replace in your macros to strip out all occurrences of something by replacing it with nothing, even in your headers and footers. Just press F2 at the 'Replace with' prompt, as in this macro.

To record the macro, take the following steps:

1. Turn on the macro recorder by pressing Ctrl-F10 or choosing Macro from the Tools menu and then choosing Define. Enter **margins** as the name of the macro.

2. Enter **removes all margin changes** as the macro description; then press ⏎.

3. Press Home Home ↑ to move to the very beginning of the document.

4. Press Alt-F2 (Replace) and press ⏎ to replace without confirming the selection.

5. Press Shift-F8 (Format); then type **L M** to search for the [L/R Mar] codes.

6. Press F2. Then press F2 again to replace the [L/R Mar] codes with nothing, effectively removing them.

7. Press Home Home ↑ once again to go to the beginning of the document.

8. Press Shift-F8 (Format) and type **D C** to change the document's initial codes.

9. Press Ctrl-F10 again to stop recording the macro.

The final macro should resemble the one in Figure 10.14.

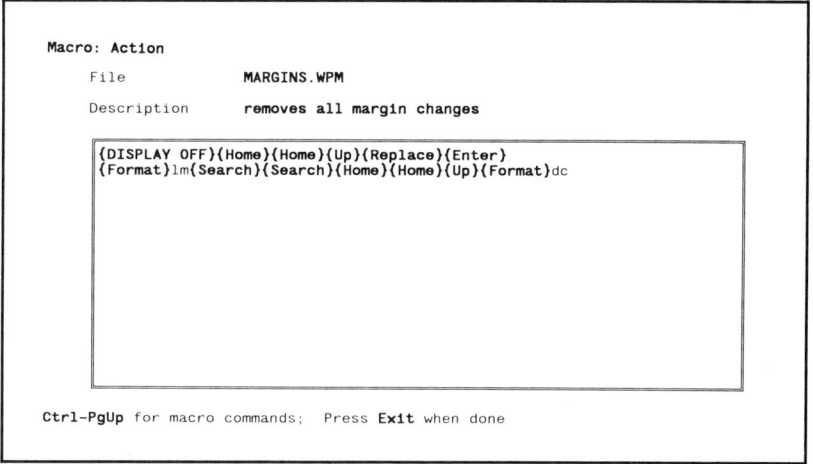

*Figure 10.14:* The **margins** macro strips out all margin changes and lets you set a default margin for the document.

## *USING THE MACRO*

When you use the macro, any margin settings you may have made will be removed. You will then be able to enter default margin settings. These settings will take effect in all footnotes, endnotes, and headers, so you don't have to worry about having inconsistent margins in your document. (If you just moved to the beginning of your document and changed the margins, the new settings wouldn't affect any subsequent settings. And if you just removed all the old [L/R Mar] codes and put in new settings at the beginning of the document, the new settings wouldn't affect your footnotes, headers, and footers.)

When the macro pauses, the codes you enter will be used as the document's initial codes. Press Shift-F8, type **L M**, and enter new right and left margin settings. While you are in that screen, you can also turn on any other features you want to use as the document defaults, such as Widow/Orphan Protection or Justification. Press F7 until you return to your document.

## *AUTOMATIC BIBLIOGRAPHY: AUTHOR-DATE METHOD (NATURAL SCIENCES)*

This macro, named **bib**, copies a short reference in the form (*Smith, 1988*) from a master bibliography that you maintain separately. Each time you see an article or book that you may want to use as a reference, add it to the master bibliography in the correct format, being careful to get all the punctuation and styling right, because you'll never have to type that entry again. You should separate the entries with blank lines, as shown in Figure 10.15, but you don't have to keep them in alphabetical order.

> This macro is very punctilious about punctuation. You should be, too, when you make each entry in your master bibliography. If there are typos in it, such as a period where there should be a comma, you may get incomplete citations. If this happens, proofread the entry that's causing trouble.

```
Cassirer, E., 1944. An Essay on Man. New Haven: Yale University
Press.

Darling, F., 1934. A Herd of Red Deer. London: Oxford University
Press.

Hallowell, A., 1945. "Sociopsychological Aspects of
Acculturation," in Linton, R. (ed.), The Science of Man in the
World Crisis. New York: Columbia University Press.

Hilgard, E., 1956. Theories of Learning. New York: Appleton-
Century-Crofts.




                                              Doc 2 Pg 1 Ln 1" Pos 1"
```

*Figure 10.15:* A sample master bibliography using the author-date style of reference

Then, when you write a paper, you simply retrieve your master bibliography into the Doc 2 window and, when you're ready to make an entry, execute the **bib** macro. The macro pauses to let you select the reference you want to use at that point; then it copies the full entry at the end of the document you're working on.

## *BEFORE YOU BEGIN*

Before you begin to record the macro:

- You should have created the bibliography to which you want to refer. A sample is shown in Figure 10.15. It should be retrieved into the Doc 2 window.

- You should have some text on the screen so that you can see the effects of the macro. A sample is shown in Figure 10.16.

- You should also create a blank page at the end of your document for the bibliography (press Home Home ↓ Ctrl-⏎). Otherwise, the first entry will appear just after the text of your paper ends.

```
        Within the family, for example, different members may occupy
such positions as father, mother, son, or daughter. Since each
position ("status") within the group is associated with one
(Hilgard, E., 1956) or more (Hallowell, A., 1945) sets of
activities ("roles"), each institution may be broken down into
its constituent roles




C:\5\BIBENTRY                              Doc 1 Pg 1 Ln 2.66" Pos 3.1"
```

*Figure 10.16:* In this sample text, you're ready to cite a reference at the end of the text.

You'll record two macros. The master macro is **bib**; it calls another macro, named **entry**, that creates the full bibliographic reference at the end of your paper.

> Another advantage of this macro is that you can write your paper first and then go back and insert your references later.

## *RECORDING THE MACRO*

To record the **bib** macro, take the following steps:

1. Turn on the macro recorder by pressing Ctrl-F10 or choosing Macro from the Tools menu and then choosing Define. Enter **bib** as the name of the macro.

2. Enter **author-date bibliography** as the macro description; then press ⏎.

3. Type ( (a left parenthesis); then press ⏎ and ←. This opens the line so that you can make entries in the middle of an already typed line of text. Press Shift-F3 (Switch). You will have retrieved your master bibliography into the Doc 2 window before you begin to use the macro, and this step switches you to it.

4. Insert a pause (Ctrl-PgUp **P** ⏎).

5. Press Alt-F4 to turn on blocking; then press F2 to search.

6. Type . (period) and press the Spacebar once to search for the end of the author-date portion of the bibliographic entry.

7. Press F2 to start the search; then press ← twice to move back over the final punctuation at the end.

8. Press Ctrl-F4 (Move) and type **1 2** (or **B C**) to copy the highlighted block.

9. Press Shift-F3 to switch back to the Doc 1 window, which holds the paper you're writing.

10. Press ⏎ to paste the author and date.

11. Press End to move to the end of the entry; then type ) (a right parenthesis) and press Del to close up the line.

12. Press Alt-F10 (Macro), type **entry**, and press ⏎. This will call the entry macro, which you'll create in the next set of steps.

13. Press Ctrl-F10 again to stop recording the macro.

Now you can create the **entry** macro that copies the full reference to the end of your paper each time you make a reference.

1. Turn on the macro recorder by pressing Ctrl-F10 or choosing Macro from the Tools menu and then choosing Define. Enter **entry** as the name of the macro.
2. Enter **copies full reference** as the macro description; then press ←.
3. Type #. This marks your place so that you can return here later. The macro will delete the # automatically. (If you've used this sign elsewhere in your document, substitute here another symbol that you haven't already used.)
4. Press Shift-F3 to switch to the Doc 2 window.
5. Press Home Home ← to move to the beginning of the line.
6. Press Alt-F4 to turn on block marking; then press F2 ← F2 to search for the next [HRt] and highlight the entry.
7. Press Ctrl-F4 (Move) and type **1 2** to copy the block.
8. Press Shift-F3 to switch back to Doc 1.
9. Press Home Home ↓ to go to the end of the document; then press ← to paste the copied reference.
10. Press Shift-F2 (Reverse Search) and type # to search for this sign (or use the symbol you selected earlier).
11. Press F2 to start the search; then press Backspace to delete the #.
12. Press Ctrl-F10 to stop recording the macro.

The final macros should resemble the one in Figures 10.17 and 10.18. Figure 10.19 illustrates the sample paper after the **bib** macro has been used to make the references. As you can see, the full references are at the end of the paper, separated by a hard page break.

## *USING THE MACRO*

When you write a paper, retrieve your master bibliography into the Doc 2 window. Each time you want to create a citation, use the

```
Macro: Action
    File         BIB.WPM
    Description  author-date bibliography
    ({Enter}{Left}{Switch}{PAUSE}{Block}{Search}..{Search}{Left}{Left}
    {Move}12{Switch}{Enter}{End}){Del}{Macro}entry{Enter}




Ctrl-PgUp for macro commands;   Press Exit when done
```

*Figure 10.17:* The **bib** macro lets you maintain one, and only one, master bibliography, from which you select entries each time you write a paper.

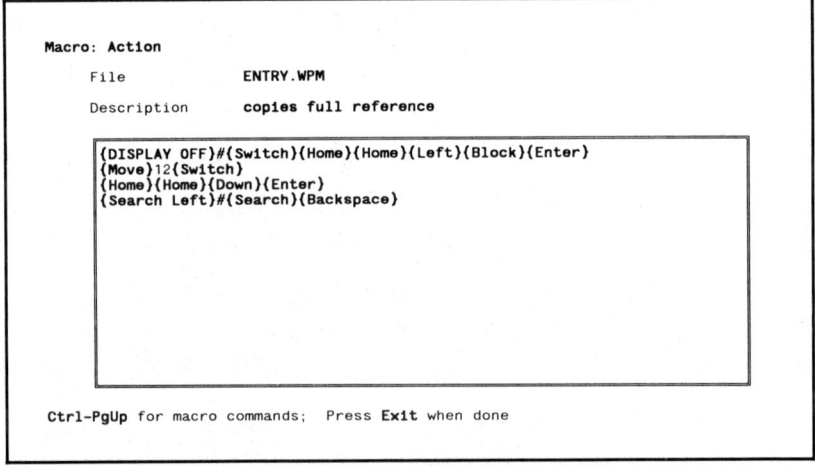

*Figure 10.18:* The **entry** macro is part of the **bib** macro; it copies the full reference to the end of your paper.

**bib** macro. WordPerfect will pause for you to move the cursor to the beginning of the bibliographic entry you want to reference. When you press ⏎, it copies the short form (the author and the date) into the document in the Doc 1 window, puts parentheses

```
        Within the family, for example, different members may occupy
    such positions as father, mother, son, or daughter. Since each
    position ("status") within the group is associated with each one
    (Hilgard, E., 1956) or more (Hallowell, A., 1945) sets of
    activities ("roles"), each institution may be broken down into
    its consituent roles (Cassirer, E., 1944)
    ================================================================
    Hilgard, E., 1956. Theories of Learning. New York: Appleton-
    Century-Crofts.
    Hallowell, A., 1945. "Sociopsychological Aspects of
    Acculturation," in Linton, R. (ed.), The Science of Man in the
    World Crisis. New York: Columbia University Press.
    Cassirer, E., 1944. An Essay on Man. New Haven: Yale University
C:\5\BIBENTRY                                    Doc 1 Pg 1 Ln 2.66" Pos 5.1"
```

*Figure 10.19:* This shows the sample paper during the reference process; the full entries are being created at the end of the paper.

around it, switches back to the Doc 2 window and gets the full reference, then switches back again to Doc 1 and copies the full reference at the end of the document. You'll have to go through the references at the end and eliminate any duplicates, but you can do that quickly with a search for author names. It certainly beats the old way of typing out each reference each time it's used.

One other benefit of using a macro like this is that you can maintain a separate master bibliography for each subject area you write in. In fact, you don't even have to maintain the master bibliography in alphabetic order unless you want to, because you can use the next macro to sort your bibliographic entries for each paper you write.

## *ALPHABETIZING A BIBLIOGRAPHY*

This macro, named **alpha**, will alphabetize any list that contains items separated by two hard returns (one blank line). Basically, it does an alphanumeric paragraph sort, so you can use it on bibliographies, lists of key words, or even phone lists.

## BEFORE YOU BEGIN

Before you begin to record the macro:

- You should have a list on the screen, and each entry should be separated by two hard returns. If you're using this macro on a bibliography created by the **bib** macro, be sure that each entry is separated by two hard returns, not just by double spacing. Remember, you can mark text as a block and replace all occurrences of one [HRt] with two [HRt]s to generate these codes quickly.

## RECORDING THE MACRO

To record the macro, take the following steps:

1. Turn on the macro recorder by pressing Ctrl-F10 or choosing Macro from the Tools menu and then choosing Define. Enter **alpha** as the name of the macro.
2. Enter **paragraph sort** as the macro description; then press ↵.
3. Press Ctrl-F9 (Merge/Sort); then type **S** for Sort and press ↵ twice to sort the contents of the screen.
4. Type **T** for Type; then **P** for Paragraph.
5. Type **3** or **K** for Keys; then press → seven times.
6. Type **2**. This tells WordPerfect to sort on the second word after it sorts on the first word.
7. Press F7; then type **P** for Perform Action.
8. Press Ctrl-F10 again to stop recording the macro.

The final macro should resemble the one in Figure 10.20.

## USING THE MACRO

When you use the macro, WordPerfect will sort the list on the screen first on the first word and then on the second word or initial.

For example, Figures 10.21 and 10.22 show a sample bibliography before and after the **alpha** macro was used to sort it. As you can see, the Hilgard entries have been alphabetized by the author's initial as well as last name.

```
Macro: Action
    File              ALPHA.WPM
    Description       paragraph sort

    {DISPLAY OFF}{Merge/Sort}s{Enter}
    {Enter}
    tp3{Right}{Right}{Right}{Right}{Right}{Right}2{Exit}p




Ctrl-PgUp for macro commands;   Press Exit when done
```

*Figure 10.20:* The **alpha** macro sorts any list in which the items are separated by two hard returns.

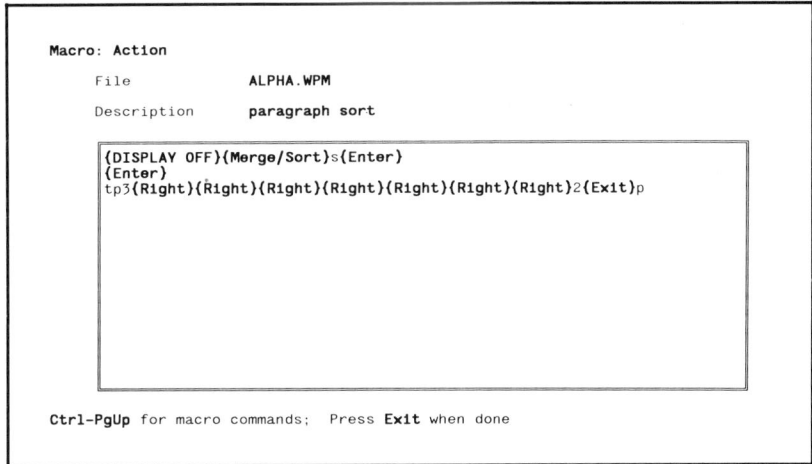

*Figure 10.21:* The bibliography before the sort

```
┌─────────────────────────────────────────────────────────────┐
│                                                             │
│    Cassirer, E., 1944. An Essay on Man. New Haven: Yale University
│    Press.                                                   │
│                                                             │
│    Darling, F., 1934. A Herd of Red Deer. London: Oxford University
│    Press.                                                   │
│                                                             │
│    Hallowell, A., 1945. "Sociopsychological Aspects of      │
│    Acculturation," in Linton, R. (ed.), The Science of Man in the
│    World Crisis. New York: Columbia University Press.       │
│                                                             │
│    Hilgard, E., 1956. Theories of Learning. New York: Appleton-
│    Century-Crofts.                                          │
│                                                             │
│    Hilgard, R., 1956. Learning Theories. New York: Appleton-Century-
│    Crofts.                                                  │
│                                                             │
│                                                             │
│                                                             │
│                                                             │
│    C:\5\BIBLIO                          Doc 2 Pg 1 Ln 1" Pos 1"
│                                                             │
└─────────────────────────────────────────────────────────────┘
```

*Figure 10.22:* After the sort—entries are sorted both on last name and first name or initial.

If you only want to sort a block of text instead of the entire document on the screen, mark the text as a block and move it into another document window. Then execute the macro and move the sorted text back into the original document.

## AUTOMATICALLY NUMBERING EQUATIONS

This macro, named **auto**, automatically numbers the equations in your document according to their equation box number. Many scientific papers require equation numbers so that complex equations may be referenced by number within the paper.

When you use this macro, equation numbers will be in boldface within parentheses at the right margin of the page, like this:

$$\lim_{n \to \infty} v_n^{(1)} = v^{(1)} \qquad\qquad (1)$$

### BEFORE YOU BEGIN

Before you begin to record this macro:

- You must have created at least one equation in the document that is on the screen.

- The cursor should be at the top of the document before the first equation box code (Home Home Home ↑).

## RECORDING THE MACRO

1. Press Ctrl-F10 (Macro Define), or choose Macro from the Tools menu and then choose Define; enter **auto** as the name of the macro.
2. Enter **automatically numbers equations** as the macro description; then press ←.
3. Press Alt-F9 (Graphics) and type **E** for Equation and **E** for Edit; then press ← to edit Equation 1.
4. Type **C** for Caption. This inserts a bold number in parentheses in the right margin next to your equation, although you won't see it on the document screen.
5. Press F7 twice to exit to your document.
6. Now edit the macro by pressing Ctrl-F10, entering **auto** and choosing **E** for Edit.
7. In the macro editor, press Home Home ↓ to move to the end of the macro, then press Ctrl-PgUp.
8. Type **ch** to move to the {CHAIN}macroname ~ command. Press ← to insert it in the macro; then type **auto** ~ to chain the macro to itself so that it will repeat until no more equation boxes are found in the document.

When you have finished, your screen should resemble Figure 10.23.

## USING THE MACRO

When you use the macro you've just recorded, all the equations in your document will be numbered according to the equation box numbers they have. You can see how they will look if you use the View Document feature on them (Shift-F7 **1**).

To make sure that you number all the equations, be sure to move the cursor to the very beginning of the document (Home Home Home ↑) before you execute it. If you'd rather not remember to do that, you can use the macro editor to create a slightly different version of this macro. Just record a macro named **numb** that consists of the Home Home Home ↑ keystrokes and chain the **auto** macro to it (Figure 10.24).

```
Macro: Action
    File            AUTO.WPM
    Description     automatically numbers equations
    ┌─────────────────────────────────────────────────┐
    │ {DISPLAY OFF}{Graphics}ee{Enter}                │
    │ c{Exit}{Exit}                                   │
    │ {CHAIN}auto~                                    │
    │                                                 │
    └─────────────────────────────────────────────────┘
Ctrl-PgUp for macro commands;  Press Exit when done
```

*Figure 10.23:* The **auto** macro automatically numbers the equations in a document.

```
Macro: Action
    File            NUMB.WPM
    Description
    ┌─────────────────────────────────────────────────┐
    │ {DISPLAY OFF}{Home}{Home}{Home}{Up}{CHAIN}auto~ │
    │                                                 │
    └─────────────────────────────────────────────────┘
Ctrl-PgUp for macro commands;  Press Exit when done
```

*Figure 10.24:* The **numb** macro simply calls the **auto** macro, but ensures that you are at the beginning of your document.

## OTHER USES

The next macro, **chnum**, will show you how you can specify a chapter number to be used with these numbers.

## SPECIFYING A CHAPTER NUMBER FOR EQUATION NUMBERING

This macro, named **chnum**, pauses to allow you to insert a chapter or section number to be used with your equation box numbering system.

> If you want to number equations with a number other than the one for their graphics boxes, press Alt-F9 and type **E** or choose Equation from the Graphics menu. Then choose New Number (3 or N). Subsequent equation boxes will be numbered sequentially from the number you specified.

### BEFORE YOU BEGIN

Before you begin to record the macro:

- You will need to have recorded the previous **auto** macro.
- Save your document in case you make an error.

### RECORDING THE MACRO

To record the macro, take the following steps:

1. Press Ctrl-F10 (Macro Define) or choose Macro from the Tools menu and then choose Define. Enter **chnum** as the name of the macro.

2. Enter **specify chapter number for equations** as the macro description; then press ←⎯.

3. Press Home Home Home ↑; then press Alt-F9 (Graphics).

4. Type **E O C** for Equations, Options, and Caption Style; then press → twice to position the cursor on the equation box number.

5. To insert a pause here, press Ctrl-PgUp and type **P**; then press ←⎯ twice.

6. Press F7 (Exit) to return to your document.

7. Then, to chain the **auto** macro you recorded earlier so that it will number the equations in the style you have just specified,

press Ctrl-F10 to end macro recording. Press Ctrl-F10, enter **chnum** as the name of the macro, and type **E** to edit it.

8. In the macro editor, press Home Home ↓ to move to the end of the macro; then press Ctrl-PgUp, type **ch** and press ↵.

9. Then type **auto~** and press F7 to exit.

Your screen should look like Figure 10.25.

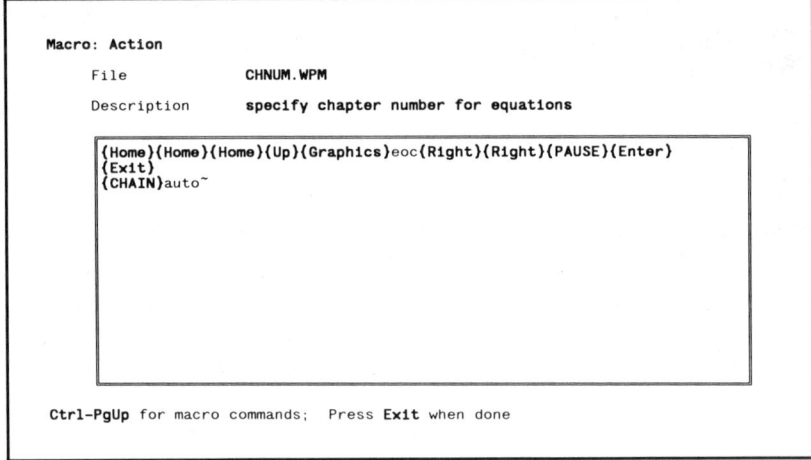

*Figure 10.25:* The **chnum** macro allows you to specify a section or chapter to be used in equation numbering.

## USING THE MACRO

When you use the macro, WordPerfect will pause for you to type a section or chapter number plus any punctuation you want to use (such as 6. or 8-); it will then execute the **auto** macro until it finds no more equation boxes in the document, numbering each equation according to the numbering style you set.

Figure 10.26 shows a printed sample of the new style.

## OTHER USES

If you'd rather have equations numbered in italics instead of boldface, delete the [Bold] codes and change them to [Ital] in step 4 (Ctrl-F8 A I) of the **chnum** macro.

> The macro named chnum allows you to number equations by chapter or section number:
>
> $$x = \sqrt[3]{-\frac{144}{5}} \qquad (6.1)$$
>
> Even though large sections of text may come between equations, the program will keep track of the correct numbers:
>
> $$y = \frac{d}{dx}\tan^2(x) \qquad (6.2)$$

*Figure 10.26:* A printed sample of an equation numbered in the new style

## CHANGING THE FONT USED FOR EQUATIONS

This macro, named **eqns**, allows you to specify a different font to be used for the equations in a document. It also allows you to change the point size.

Normally, WordPerfect will print equations as graphics in the same point size as the text of your document, in either Helvetica, Times Roman, or Courier, whichever is closest to the base font of your document. However, you can print equations as text, and if WordPerfect can't find a symbol in the font you specify, it will create that symbol graphically. You may find that printing equations as text produces better results, depending on two conditions: 1) that your equations are not overly complex and 2) that you have a sophisticated printer, such as a laser printer, that has a wide range of symbols in its fonts. Figure 10.27 compares the same equation printed as text and as graphics.

No matter whether you are printing equations as graphics or printing them as text, you will need to specify a point size when you specify a different font. However, if you're printing equations as graphics, WordPerfect will ignore this point size and will use the point size (or the default setting) specified as the Graphical Point Size on the Equations Setup menu (Shift-F1 I E).

> This equation was printed as graphics:
>
> $$\frac{\partial^2 x}{\partial x^2} = c^2 e^{cx+b}$$
>
> And this one was printed as text, in 12-point Palatino:
>
> $$\frac{\partial^2 x}{\partial x^2} = c^2 e^{cx+b}$$

*Figure 10.27:* Here, the top equation was printed as graphics and the bottom one as text.

## *BEFORE YOU BEGIN*

Before you begin to record the macro:

- You must have a document on the screen with an equation in it if you plan to test this macro once you've recorded it.

- If you are printing equations as graphics, which is the program's default setting, press Shift-F1 (Setup); then type **I E G S** for Initial Settings, Equations, Graphical Font Size, and Set Point Size. Enter a point size and press ⏎ until you return to your document screen.

## *RECORDING THE MACRO*

To record the macro, take the following steps:

1. Press Ctrl-F10 (Macro Define) or choose Macro from the Tools menu and then choose Define. Enter **eqns** as the name of the macro.

2. Enter **change equation font** as the macro description; then press ⏎.

3. Press Home Home Home ↑ to move to the top of the document before any codes.

## SPECIALIZED MACROS 403

> To change the font size for only the equation you're working on, if you're printing equations as graphics, press Shift-F1 while you are in the equation editor and choose Graphical Font Size; then choose Set Point Size. Enter a point size and press ←.

4. Press Alt-F9 (Graphics) and type **E O S** for Equation, Options, Second Level Numbering Method; then press F7 to exit. (This step doesn't do anything except insert an [Eqn Opt] code in your document, but WordPerfect needs that code to produce the font change.)

5. Press ← to move over the equations options code; then press Ctrl-F8 (Font) and type **F** for Base Font.

6. Insert a pause for specifying the font by pressing Ctrl-PgUp, typing **P**, and pressing ← twice.

7. Insert a pause for specifying the point size by pressing Ctrl-PgUp, typing **P**, and pressing ← twice. Then press →.

8. Press → to move over the equations options code; then press Ctrl-F8 (Font) and type **F** for Base Font.

9. Insert a pause for specifying the font for the text of your document by pressing Ctrl-PgUp, typing **P**, and pressing ← twice.

10. Insert a pause for specifying the point size by pressing Ctrl-PgUp, typing **P**, and pressing ← twice.

11. Press Ctrl-F10 again to stop recording the macro.

The final macro should resemble the one in Figure 10.28.

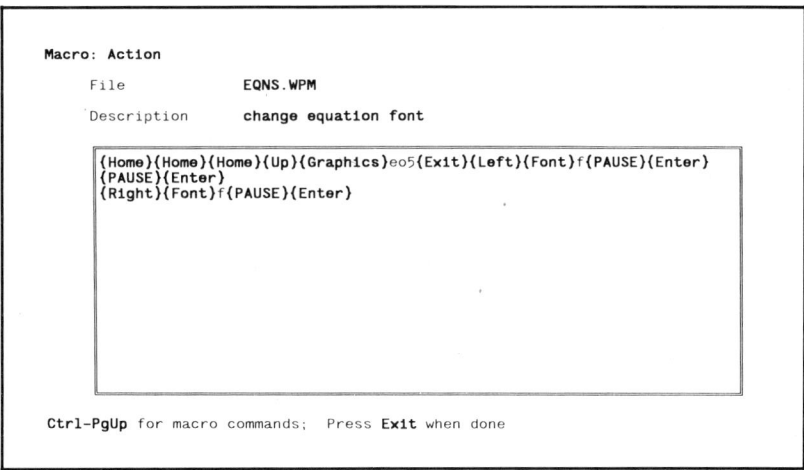

*Figure 10.28:* The **eqns** macro allows you to use one font for your equations and another for the text of your document.

### USING THE MACRO

When you use the macro, WordPerfect pauses for you to specify a font and a point size to be used for equations. It then pauses to let you specify a font and point size for the text of your document.

### OTHER USES

You can also print equation captions in a different font. A caption will normally be printed in the same font as the equation, but you can press Ctrl-F8 (Font) and choose Base Font (4 or F) before you begin typing the text of the caption in the Equation Definition screen. (Equations don't generally use captions, but in the equation numbering macros above, you can see that you use the Caption option to turn on the numbering system, so this feature will let you print equation numbers in a different font.)

> If you write complex equations, you may find that a point size two points larger than your text font is best for your document. For example, if your text is in 12-point type, try using 14-point for your equations. Subscripts, superscripts, limits, and so forth, will be easier to read.

## CREATING AN AREA FOR EQUATIONS (VERSION 5.0)

If you have to type equations in your work, you know that WordPerfect doesn't always display everything on the screen as you'd like it to, unless you have a Hercules RAMFont card or an EGA/VGA color system. You can't see subscripts and superscripts as you type, and it can be awkward to correct your equations.

This macro, named **eqn**, creates an area in which you can freely write multilevel equations. It sets WordPerfect to half-line spacing so that you can see each level of the equation you're writing. It also puts you in Typeover mode so that you can move the cursor around by using the arrow keys and the Spacebar without changing the spacing of the other characters.

### BEFORE YOU BEGIN

Before you begin to record the macro:

- Clear the screen, or go to the end of your document.

## RECORDING THE MACRO

> Change to a non-proportional font such as Courier before you work in Line Draw. You will get unexpected results in Line Draw with proportional fonts, because each character occupies a different amount of space. If you have to use a proportional font, use the Advance feature to create equations.

To record the macro, take the following steps:

1. Turn on the macro recorder by pressing Ctrl-F10 or choosing Macro from the Tools menu and then choosing Define. Enter **eqn** as the name of the macro.
2. Enter **creates equation area for line draw** as the macro description; then press ↵.
3. Press Shift-F8 (Format) and type **L** for Line.
4. Type **S** for Spacing; then type **.5** for half-line spacing.
5. Press ↵.
6. Type **J** for Justification and **N** for No. Press F7.
7. Press Esc, type **65**, and press the Spacebar to insert a line 65 characters wide.
8. Press Ctrl-F3 (Screen), type **L** for Line Draw, and type **M** for Move.
9. Press Esc, type **15**, and press ↓ to insert 15 blank half lines of space into your document. You will see the Ln indicator change in the lower-right corner of the screen.
10. Press F7 to return to your document; then press Ins to enter Typeover mode.
11. Turn off the macro recorder by pressing Ctrl-F10.

The final macro should resemble the one in Figure 10.29.

## USING THE MACRO

When you use the macro, WordPerfect sets up an area that is 16 half lines deep and 65 characters wide in the font you're using. You can type equations in this area and be able to see each level on the screen. For example, to create the equation

$$x^2 = \frac{(n-1)^n}{a_2}$$

```
Macro: Edit

        File            EQN.WPM

    1 - Description     creates equation area for line draw

    2 - Action

        ┌─────────────────────────────────────────────────┐
        │ {DISPLAY OFF}{Format}ls.5{Enter}                │
        │ jn{Exit}{Esc}65-{Screen}lm{Esc}15{Down}{Exit}{Typeover} │
        │                                                 │
        │                                                 │
        │                                                 │
        │                                                 │
        └─────────────────────────────────────────────────┘

    Selection: 0
```

*Figure 10.29:* The **eqn** macro sets up an area 65 characters wide and 16 half lines deep in which you can create equations.

> For typing equations, you may be more comfortable with WordPerfect 4.2 units, so that you can see the position number of what you're typing, than with inches, which can be confusing when you're trying to count spaces. To change to WordPerfect 4.2 units, press Shift-F1, type **U D U S U**, and press F7.

you would execute the macro, move the cursor to the top of the equation area, and take the following steps:

1. First, you will enter all the characters that are to be superscripted on the first line of the centered equation. Press Shift-F6 (Center), press the Spacebar twice, and type **2**. Then press the Spacebar 11 times, type **n**, and press ⏎.

2. Now, you will enter the characters that appear on the second line. Press Shift-F6, type **x**, press the Spacebar twice, type = , press the Spacebar once again, and then type **(n − 1)**.

3. Press ← seven times to move the cursor back to the beginning of the (n − 1), press Alt-F4 to mark it as a block, and press → seven times to extend the block to the right parenthesis. Then press F8 (Underline) to create the line. After the line appears, press ⏎.

4. Press Shift-F6, and press the Spacebar four times; then type **a** and press ⏎ to move to the next half line.

5. Press Shift-F6, and press the Spacebar six times; then type **2** for the subscript and press ⏎.

*SPECIALIZED MACROS* **407**

When you're through, your screen should resemble the one in Figure 10.30. As you can see, all the different levels are represented on the screen so that you can see what you're doing as you type. You can then delete any extra hard returns that remain and resume typing the text of your document.

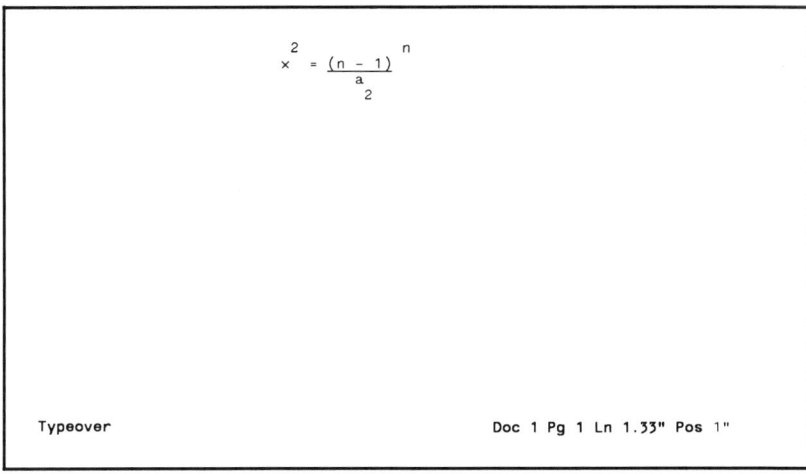

*Figure 10.30:* This equation was created within a space defined by the **eqn** macro.

You can change the number of characters that the macro inserts from 65, as it's given in the macro, to whatever number of characters you need in the font you're using. You can also change to more or fewer half lines of spacing. If you find that you don't need any of the extra space below the equation after you've created it, just press Alt-F3 (Reveal Codes) and delete any extra [HRt] codes and spaces that may be there. You can then resume typing your document normally.

If you're not using Line Draw, you can use the Horizontal Line option on the Graphics key (Alt-F9 L H) to draw the rules in equations. First, make sure that the cursor is at the place on the line where you want the horizontal rule to begin. Then select the Horizontal Position option (1 or H), choose the Set Position option (S) on its menu, and press ⏎ to accept the measurement supplied by Word-Perfect. Then select the Length of Line option (2 or L) and enter its measurement. You'll need to use the View Document feature (Shift-F7 V) at 100% or 200% to preview the positioning of the elements in a formula or equation before you print it.

While you're within the equation area, you can use the Compose key (Ctrl-2) to create special characters and symbols. The next macro will suggest a few that you may need in mathematical typing; which ones you choose depends on your needs and your printer's capabilities, as not all printers can produce all the characters in WordPerfect's character sets.

## CREATING SPECIAL SYMBOLS WITH MACROS

This macro, named **inf** (for infinity), creates the infinity symbol (∞) at the cursor's position.

### RECORDING THE MACRO

To record the macro, take the following steps:

1. Turn on the macro recorder by pressing Ctrl-F10 or choosing Macro from the Tools menu and then choosing Define. Enter **inf** as the name of the macro.

2. Enter **creates infinity symbol** as the macro description; then press ←.

3. Press Ctrl-2.

4. Type **6,19**. These are the character set numbers for the ∞ symbol.

5. Press ←.

6. Press Ctrl-F10 again to stop recording the macro.

### USING THE MACRO

When you use the macro, WordPerfect creates the infinity symbol (∞) at the cursor's position.

> To view Word-Perfect's character sets, retrieve the document CHARACTR.DOC (on the Learning disk) and scroll through it. A solid rectangle represents a character that can't be displayed on the screen, but that your printer may be able to print. You won't know unless you try.

## *OTHER USES*

You may want to create macros for other mathematical symbols that your printer can produce, such as the summation symbol, the integral, greater than, less than, and so forth. First, test-print the symbol on your printer; then record a macro to create it, using its character-set numbers as in the **inf** macro just given.

After you have recorded macros for special mathematical or foreign-language symbols, you can map them on a special MATH (or FRENCH, GERMAN, or ITALIAN) keyboard. You can also put the macros that change to subscripting, superscripting, italics, and so forth, on this keyboard. See Chapter 4 for how to set up such a keyboard.

# *MARKING TEXT FOR STRIKEOUT AND REDLINE*

*Redlining* is useful for drawing readers' attention to revised sections in a document. When you redline text, a vertical bar normally appears in the printed version on one side of the material that has been changed. With *strikeout*, on most printers, a dashed line is placed through the text you have marked for deletion. (You can change how the text appears by pressing Shift-F8 and typing D R.) This feature is often used in contracts where clauses that have been dropped must be initialed by the parties involved.

This macro, named **strike**, marks text for strikeout. It's a modification of some other macros that you've already seen, and you can easily modify it to redline text instead. Since redlining and strikeout are most often used on text that's already been typed, the macro pauses to let you highlight the text you want to strike out. When you highlight the text and press ⏎, it inserts the [STKOUT][stkout] codes around it.

## *BEFORE YOU BEGIN*

Before you begin to record the macro:

- You should have some text on the screen.

## RECORDING THE MACRO

To record the macro, take the following steps:

1. Turn on the macro recorder by pressing Ctrl-F10 or choosing Macro from the Tools menu and then choosing Define. Enter **strike** as the name of the macro.

2. Enter **marks text for strikeout** as the macro description; then press ⏎.

3. Press Alt-F4 to turn on block marking; then insert a pause (press Ctrl-PgUp and type **P**).

4. So that the macro will have something to work on, highlight a couple of lines of text; then press ⏎.

5. Press Ctrl-F8 (Font).

6. Type **A** for Appearance and **S** for Strikeout.

7. Press Ctrl-F10 again to stop recording the macro.

The final macro should resemble the one in Figure 10.31.

## USING THE MACRO

When you use the macro, WordPerfect will pause with Block on for you to indicate the text that is to be struck out. As soon as you press ⏎, the text will be struck out. You can use the Setup menu's Display Colors/Fonts/Attributes options to select a method of viewing struck-out text. Otherwise, you may need to use Reveal Codes to see the [STKOUT][stkout] codes on the screen.

To edit this macro so that it redlines text instead, simply change the **S** in step 6 to **R** for Redline.

When the final version of your document is ready, you'll probably want to remove the redlining and delete any struck-out text. To do so, press Alt-F5 (Mark Text) and select option 6 or G (Generate). Select option 1 or R (Remove Redline Markings and Strikeout Text from Document); then type **Y** to confirm. Redline markings *and text that has been struck out* will be deleted from your document. Not just the markings, the text itself.

```
Macro: Action
    File            STRIKE.WPM
    Description     marks text for strikeout

    {Block}{PAUSE}{Font}as




Ctrl-PgUp for macro commands;   Press Exit when done
```

*Figure 10.31:* The **strike** macro marks text for strikeout.

## *MARKING A WORD OR PHRASE FOR AN INDEX*

This macro, named **index**, simply pauses to let you highlight a word or phrase and then brings up the 'Index Heading' prompt when you press ←. If you mark a lot of entries for an index, you'll find that you can save quite a bit of time by using it instead of the usual keystrokes. To save even more time, name it **Alt-I**.

You can use this macro at any time while you're preparing a document, but be sure to generate the index only when your document is in final form and ready to print. If you make any changes that affect pagination in the original document after you generate the index, the page numbers in the index entries won't be accurate.

### *BEFORE YOU BEGIN*

Before you begin to record the macro:

- You should have some text on the screen.

## RECORDING THE MACRO

To record the macro, take the following steps:

1. Turn on the macro recorder by pressing Ctrl-F10 or choosing Macro from the Tools menu and then choosing Define. Enter **index** or **Alt-I** as the name of the macro.
2. Enter **marks index entry** as the macro description; then press ↵.
3. Turn on block marking by pressing Alt-F4.
4. Insert a pause by pressing Ctrl-PgUp and typing **P**.
5. To give the macro something to work on, highlight a couple of words; then press ↵. The macro will resume recording.
6. Press Alt-F5 (Mark Text) and type **3** or **I** for Index.
7. Press Ctrl-F10 to stop recording the macro.

The final macro should resemble the one in Figure 10.32. It's named **index** in the figure, but assigning it to Alt-I will make it easier to execute as you work.

## USING THE MACRO

When you use the macro, place the cursor at the beginning of the word or phrase you want to index. Then press Alt-F10 to execute the **index** macro. You can extend the highlighting to several words, if you're indexing a phrase. When you press ↵, the highlighted word or phrase will appear as your index heading. If you don't want to use it exactly as it appears—for example, you may want to change *John Doe* to *Doe, John*—you can edit it. Press ↵ or Tab when you've finished editing it, and you'll be prompted for a subheading. Press ↵ or Tab again if you don't want to use a subheading.

You can also set up a search macro that will search for all occurrences of a given word or phrase and mark them as index entries. But we won't go into that macro here, for two reasons: 1) Creating an index often requires a judgment to be made (as in the *John Doe* example); 2) You can use WordPerfect's Concordance feature to accomplish the same thing for *all* the words and phrases you want to index.

> You can use more than one set of index codes at the same place in your text, so you can index a phrase under several different headings. Just repeat the macro and enter a different heading for the entry.

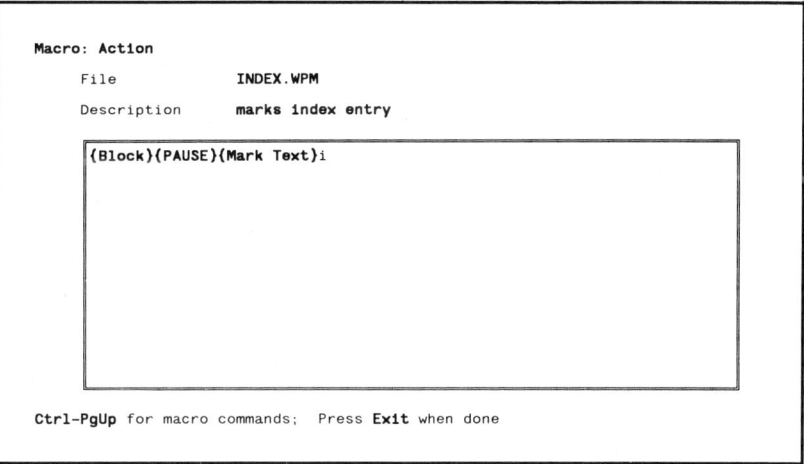

*Figure 10.32:* This index-marking macro can speed up the process of creating an index.

To use the Concordance feature, you create a file containing all the words and phrases that you want to index, each separated by hard returns. Then, when you define the style of the index, you specify the name of this concordance file. When WordPerfect generates the index, it searches the document, locates each word or phrase that you've specified, and marks it for the index.

## *STYLING AND GENERATING AN INDEX*

This macro, named **doindex**, creates an index page with a heading at the end of the document, defines the style of the index and issues the commands and prompts necessary to create the index from the entries you've marked. Why have a macro for this? Because it's easy to forget to do it, and unless you define the index's style and generate it, you'll be left wondering why your index didn't print.

### *BEFORE YOU BEGIN*

Before you begin to record the macro:

- You should have at least one item marked as an index entry in a document on the screen.

### RECORDING THE MACRO

To record the macro, take the following steps:

1. Turn on the macro recorder by pressing Ctrl-F10 or choosing Macro from the Tools menu and then choosing Define. Enter **doindex** as the name of the macro.

2. Enter **creates index from entries** as the macro description; then press ⏎.

3. Press Home Home ↓ to move to the end of the document.

4. Press Ctrl-⏎ to create a hard page break.

5. Press Shift-F6 (Center), press F6 (Bold), and type **Index** to create a bold, centered heading for the index page. Press F6 again to turn off boldface.

6. Press ⏎ twice to insert a blank line between the heading and the first index entry.

7. Press Alt-F5 and type **D I** to define the index.

8. Insert a pause so that you can enter a concordance file name if you're using one: Press Ctrl-PgUp, type **P**, and press ⏎ twice.

9. To define the index so that page numbers follow the entries, type **P**.

10. Press Alt-F5 and type **G G Y** to generate the index.

11. Turn off the macro recorder by pressing Ctrl-F10.

> If you have both an index and endnotes in a document, guess which gets printed last? The endnotes. To avoid this, use the Endnote Placement feature to specify that the endnotes be created on the page before the first page of the index.

The final macro should resemble the one in Figure 10.33.

### USING THE MACRO

When you use the macro, WordPerfect will pause for you to enter a concordance file name. If you're not using one, just press ⏎. The macro will then generate your index at the end of the document, on a separate page with an "Index" heading.

```
Macro: Action
    File            DOINDEX.WPM
    Description     creates index from entries

    {DISPLAY OFF}{Home}{Home}{Down}{HPg}{Center}{Bold}Index{Bold}{Enter}
    {Enter}
    {Mark Text}di{PAUSE}{Enter}
    p{Mark Text}ggy




Ctrl-PgUp for macro commands;  Press Exit when done
```

*Figure 10.33:* The **doindex** macro creates an index at the end of your document.

You'll get an index that looks like this:

> Edward the Confessor  567
> Geographical factors  548
> Norse approach  558
> Saxon invasion
>     Sources  548
>     Traditions  549

Subheadings are indented one tab stop.

You can edit the macro to use another style for the index. For example, you can use no page numbers, have page numbers in parentheses, or have page numbers flush right on the page, with or without dot leaders. If you want a comma between an index entry and the page number, you'll have to type it as you're marking your index entries when the 'Index Heading' prompt comes up; for example, you'd type *Doe, John*.

## USING SMALL TYPE FOR FOOTNOTES

Footnotes often appear in type that's slightly smaller than the body of a document. However, if you forget to switch to small type some of the times you create footnotes, some of your notes will be one size and some of them will be another. This macro, named **note**, automatically switches you to small type before you start writing a footnote.

You'll find that the **index** macro for italicizing several words will come in handy here if you're typing titles of works in footnote text. Just type out the note and then go back and italicize the titles.

## *RECORDING THE MACRO*

To record the macro, take the following steps:

1. Turn on the macro recorder by pressing Ctrl-F10 or choosing Macro from the Tools menu and then choosing Define. Enter **note** as the name of the macro.

2. Enter **uses Small type for footnotes** as the macro description; then press ⏎.

3. Press Ctrl-F7 (Footnote) and type **F** for Footnote.

4. Type **C** for Create.

5. When the Note Editing screen appears, press Ctrl-F8 (Font) and type **S S** so that the footnote will appear in Small type (generally two points smaller than your base or initial font).

6. Press Ctrl-F10 to stop recording the macro.

The final macro should resemble the one in Figure 10.34.

## *USING THE MACRO*

When you use **note**, position your cursor where you want the footnote reference number to appear in your text. Then execute the macro. You'll be placed immediately in the note editing screen and you can begin typing the text of the note.

You can edit this macro so that it produces endnotes in small type instead. Just change the **F** in step 3 to **E**.

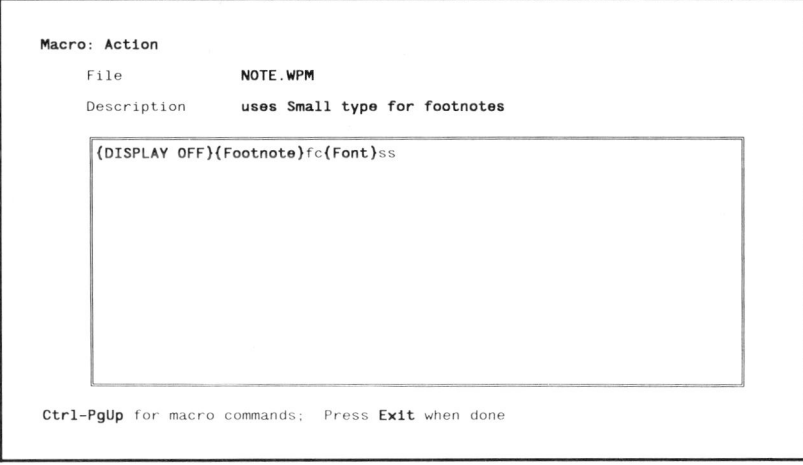

*Figure 10.34:* The **note** macro helps you remember to switch to Small type for footnotes.

## *MARKING ITEMS FOR A LIST*

WordPerfect has a built-in list-marking feature that will generate up to ten (nine in version 5.0) lists for you. For example, you might want the program to provide a list of all your figure captions. You simply mark all the figure captions to be included in the program's List 1; when you generate the list, the program prints all the figure captions you've marked.

You can automate the process of marking items that are to be included in a list by using a unique identifier on them as you type them. For example, you might begin each figure caption with the word **Figure** in boldface. You can write a macro like this **list1** that searches for each occurrence of **Figure** and marks the paragraph it's in to be included in List 1.

Keep in mind two things about setting up a document to use this macro: First, all your figure captions that you want to include in the list should be in separate paragraphs—that is, each should end with a hard return. Second, each figure caption should be in boldface type. As you can see in Figure 10.35, text intervenes between each of the captions, and only the captions themselves are bold.

Don't confuse this macro with the automatic lists of graphics boxes that WordPerfect maintains as Lists 6 (figure boxes), 7 (table boxes), 8 (text boxes), 9 (user-defined boxes), and 10 (equation boxes in version 5.1). This macro marks text in your document, not graphics boxes.

You can also edit this macro to search for any other unique identifier (a symbol such as @ or #, for example, as long as it's not used for any other purpose in your text), delete it, and mark the item it's on for inclusion in Lists 2 through 5.

Note that WordPerfect reserves Lists 6 through 10 for graphics boxes. You don't have to mark what's to be included in these lists, because the program automatically keeps track of box numbers and captions that you use with boxes of this type. To generate any of these lists, move to the place in your text where you want the list and then define it as List 6, 7, 8, 9, or 10. It will then be generated when you generate lists.

## *BEFORE YOU BEGIN*

Before you begin to record the macro:

- You should have some boldfaced figure captions on the screen, like those in Figure 10.35. Each should end in a hard return.
- You should move to the beginning of your document.

```
        When you use the macro, WordPerfect will sort the list on
the screen first on the first word and then on the second word or
initial. For example, Figures 10.17 and 10.18 show a sample
bibliography before and after the alpha macro was used to sort
it. As you can see, the Hilgard entries are alphabetic by the
author's first name within the last name.

Figure 10.17: The bibliography before the sort
Figure 10.18: After the sort, entries are sorted both on last
name and first name or initial

C:\5\MB\CHPT10                              Doc 2 Pg 33 Ln 8.66" Pos 1"
```

*Figure 10.35:* The **list1** macro marks figure captions in text for inclusion in List 1.

## RECORDING THE MACRO

To record the macro, take the following steps:

1. Turn on the macro recorder by pressing Ctrl-F10 or choosing Macro from the Tools menu and then choosing Define. Enter **list1** as the name of the macro.

2. Enter **marks bold figure captions for list 1** as the macro description; then press ←.

3. Press F2 (Search), press F6 (Bold), and type **Figure**.

4. Press F2 to start the search.

5. When WordPerfect locates the first caption, the cursor will be located after the word *Figure*. Press Ctrl-← to put the cursor under the **F**.

6. Press Alt-F4 to turn on block marking.

7. Press ← to highlight the paragraph.

8. Press Alt-F5 (Mark Text) and type **L** for List.

9. Type **1** and press ←.

10. Press Ctrl-F10 again to stop recording the macro.

The final macro should resemble the one in Figure 10.36.

```
Macro: Action
    File            LIST1.WPM
    Description     marks bold figure captions for list 1

    {DISPLAY OFF}{Search}{Bold}Figure{Search}{Word Left}{Block}{Enter}
    {Mark Text}11{Enter}




Ctrl-PgUp for macro commands;   Press Exit when done
```

*Figure 10.36:* This list-marking macro can automate marking items for a list.

## USING THE MACRO

When you use the macro, go to the beginning of your document (Home Home ↑). Then press Esc and enter a number that you know is larger than the number of items that are to be marked in your text—say, 100. Then press Alt-F10 and execute the **list1** macro.

The macro marks the paragraph that the word **Figure** is in. But you can have it mark the sentence, if your captions always end in periods; or you can have the macro pause so that you can mark only the words you want to include in the list.

If you usually create several lists in each document, such as lists of equations as well as figure captions, copy the **list1** macro after you've recorded it, rename the copy, and edit it to search for the identifier you use for List 2. Then mark those items for List 2, and so forth, until you have a macro for each list that you want.

When you've marked all the items that you want to include in your list, you'll still have to define the list and generate it, as you'll see in the next macro.

# DEFINING AND GENERATING A LIST

This macro, named **dolist**, creates a page at the end of the document for List 1, defines List 1 with no page numbers, and generates the list.

## BEFORE YOU BEGIN

Before you begin to record the macro:

- You have to have marked items for List 1 in order for the program to produce a list for you (see the previous macro).

## RECORDING THE MACRO

To record the macro, take the following steps:

1. Turn on the macro recorder by pressing Ctrl-F10 or choosing Macro from the Tools menu and then choosing Define. Enter **dolist** as the name of the macro.

2. Enter **defines and generates list** as the macro description; then press ↵.
3. To create the page for the list, press Home Home ↓ to go to the end of your document.
4. Press Ctrl-↵ to create a new page.
5. Press Alt-F5 (Mark Text) and type **D** for Define and **L** for List.
6. Type **1** for List 1, press ↵ (in 5.1 only), and type **N** for No Page Numbers.
7. Press Alt-F5 again and type **G G Y** to generate the list.
8. Press Ctrl-F10 again to stop recording the macro.

The final macro should resemble the one in Figure 10.37.

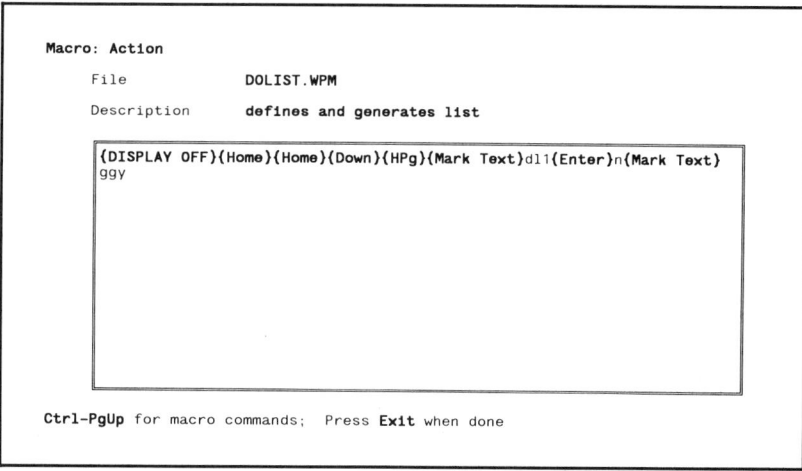

*Figure 10.37:* The **dolist** macro defines a list with no page numbers and generates it at the end of your document.

## *USING THE MACRO*

When you use the macro, WordPerfect searches for all the items that you've marked to be included in List 1 and creates the list on a blank page at the end of your document.

You can edit the macro so that your list will include the page number on which each item is located. Just select a different list style from the List Definition screen when it appears in step 6.

## SORTING BY PARAGRAPH

This macro, named **sortpar**, sorts any document in which the entries are separated by two hard returns or by a hard page break. It sorts first on the first word and then on the second, so it's very useful for situations in which you have subentries as part of the paragraph, as in the index sample that follows.

>   Indexes
>      alphabetizing, 66
>      creating, 72
>      marking headings in, 101

All the text here is considered to be within one paragraph, so the subentries stay with the main heading. If you sorted by line in this case, you would get unusable entries in your index, as the subentries would become separated from the main entry.

This macro is also useful for sorting name and address lists, as long as all their entries are contained within the same paragraph.

### BEFORE YOU BEGIN

Before you begin to record the macro:

- You should have several items on the screen, separated by two hard returns or a hard page break. Some sample text that you may wish to use is shown in Figure 10.38.

### RECORDING THE MACRO

To record the macro, take the following steps:

1. Turn on the macro recorder by pressing Ctrl-F10 or choosing Macro from the Tools menu and then choosing Define. Enter **sortpar** as the name of the macro.

---

⊙ Always save before you sort, just in case the results aren't exactly what you want. You can then retrieve the unsorted document if you make a mistake.

```
Explorer Traveler
Its optional fold-up case makes this model a favorite with
vacationers and travelers.
Scout
This is our most compact and economical compass, preferred by
backpackers and hikers.
Sierra
Slightly larger and with an easier-to read dial, this compass is
suitable for the most rugged terrains.
Explorer Extra
With its automatically lighted dial, this compass proves its
worth on dark nights.




C:\5\SORTEX                                    Doc 1 Pg 1 Ln 1" Pos 1"
```

*Figure 10.38:* You can enter this sample text to prepare for recording the **sortpar** macro.

2. Enter **sorts by paragraph** as the macro description; then press ↵.

3. Press Ctrl-F9 (Merge/Sort) and type **S** for Sort.

4. Press ↵ twice to take input from the screen and sort to the screen. There will be a slight wait, after which you will see another screen.

5. Type **T** for Type; then type **P** for Paragraph.

6. Type **K** for Keys; then press → seven times.

7. Type **2** to indicate that the program should sort on word 2 after it finishes sorting on word 1.

8. Press F7 to exit from the Sort screen; then type **P** to perform the action.

9. Press Ctrl-F10 again to stop recording the macro.

The final macro should resemble the one in Figure 10.39.

> You may have to delete extra or misplaced hard returns between items after this type of sort.

## USING THE MACRO

When you use the macro, WordPerfect will sort by the first line in the entry—first by the first word and then by the second word—so that, for instance, Explorer Extra comes before Explorer Traveler, as in Figure 10.40.

## OTHER USES

This macro, which sorts by first word and second word on the first line of a paragraph, should handle most paragraph sorting. However,

```
Macro: Action
    File            SORTPAR.WPM
    Description     sorts by paragraph

{DISPLAY OFF}{Merge/Sort}s{Enter}
{Enter}
tpk{Right}{Right}{Right}{Right}{Right}{Right}
2{Exit}p
```

Ctrl-PgUp for macro commands;   Press Exit when done

*Figure 10.39:* This **sortpar** macro sorts items that are separated by two hard returns or by hard page breaks.

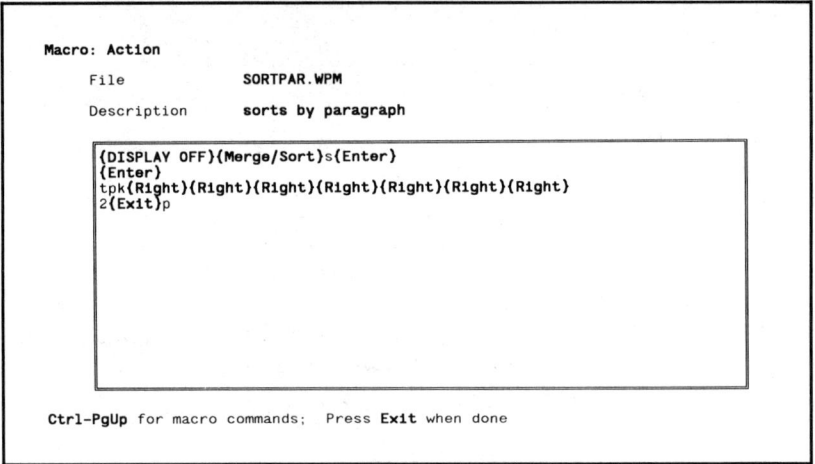

*Figure 10.40:* Results of using the **sortpar** macro show that it sorts first on the first word and then on the second word.

you can use paragraph-sorting macros to sort on specified lines any entries that are separated by paragraph breaks. For example, you may have records in which the first line is a company name but the second line is the name of the person at the company in first-name, last-name order, as Figure 10.41 illustrates. You can easily sort these records by the persons' names in last-name, first-name order (Figure 10.42). To record a macro for a sort like this, you specify line 2 as the line to sort on and word 2 as the first word to sort on

```
Roxy Industries
Malcolm Smith
(800) 555-1290

Princess Theatres
Linda Lebow
(415) 555-4400

View-In Drive-Ins
Charles Washington
(404) 555-1200




                                            Doc 1 Pg 1 Ln 1" Pos 1"
```

*Figure 10.41:* You can sort on different lines in paragraphs like these.

```
Princess Theatres
Linda Lebow
(415) 555-4400

Roxy Industries
Malcolm Smith
(800) 555-1290

View-In Drive-Ins
Charles Washington
(404) 555-1200




                                            Doc 1 Pg 1 Ln 1" Pos 1"
```

*Figure 10.42:* After you sort on line 2 and word 2, the items appear like this.

(assuming word 2 is always the person's last name), as shown in Figure 10.43. (Since fields are defined by tab settings and there are no tabs within paragraphs, the field number is always 1.)

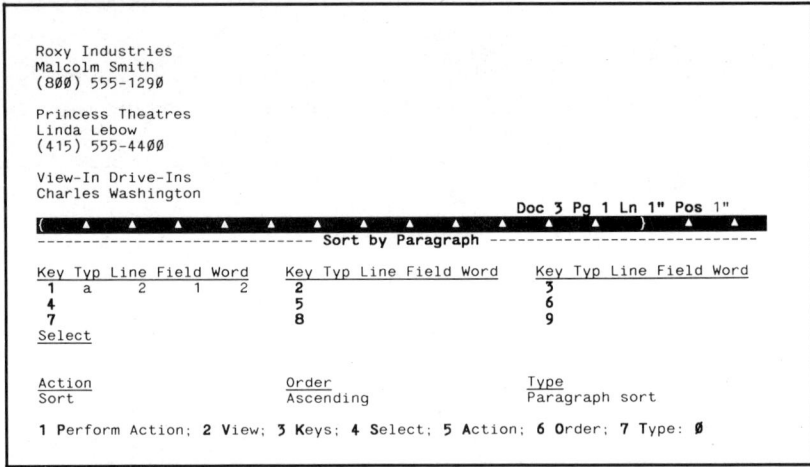

*Figure 10.43:* To set up a paragraph sort on line 2 of a paragraph, you would set up this Sort by Paragraph screen.

> When you sort, WordPerfect does not change the arrangement of the lines. It only changes the arrangement of the items you are sorting.

If you find that you often sort on different keys, you can record the macro to pause at the Sort screen so that you can manually indicate which keys you want to use. To do this, delete the instructions in steps 4, 5, and 6 and insert a pause instead. The screen you see when you use this modified macro will be the last one you used during your current work session; if you've previously sorted by paragraph, you'll see the Sort by Paragraph screen, for example.

If you are sorting an extremely large file, you may want to direct the output to a file instead of sorting to the screen, as this macro does in step 4. However, sorting to the screen does allow you to check the results of the sorting process: If you find that the file is not sorted as you want, you can clear the screen, retrieve the original document, and sort it again.

Don't forget that, when sorting, WordPerfect considers a *word* to be any item in a field that is separated by spaces (so watch out for initials and names like "de Groot"). A *field* is any information that is separated by tabs. A *line* is separated by a hard return, and a *paragraph* is separated by two hard returns or by a hard page break.

If you do an alphanumeric sort on numeric data, it must all be of equal length for the sort to be meaningful. This type of sort works fine on zip codes (if they are all the same length) and social security numbers. If you do a numeric sort, WordPerfect ignores currency symbols such as $. It also ignores commas. Use this type of sort on numeric information that is of unequal length.

## CREATING TABLES OF CONTENTS AUTOMATICALLY

You can also use some of the list-marking techniques you saw in previous macros to automate the often tedious process of creating a table of contents. The only additional steps you need to take are to mark each heading for the table of contents with a unique identifier, such as boldface type.

The following set of macros will automate the process of creating tables of contents. In WordPerfect, this is a two-step process: First you mark the text that is to be included, and then you define the style for the table and tell WordPerfect to generate the actual table. The macro named **contents** searches for each instance of boldface in your text and prompts you to indicate the level of that heading (up to three levels in this macro) in a table of contents. After all the headings have been marked, another macro named **create** creates a page for a table of contents at the beginning of your document and generates the table itself.

### BEFORE YOU BEGIN

Before you begin to record the macro:

- You should have a short document on the screen, such as the one in Figure 10.44. Boldface should be used only in the headings, nowhere else. Move the cursor to the beginning of the document, before any codes (Home Home Home ↑).

```
Level-1 Heading
    Although in a regular document you would probably have many
paragraphs between headings, this short document is enough to
record the macro.
Level-2 Heading
    Likewise, you would probably have several pages between
headings.
Level-3 Heading
    Although this macro defines styles for only three levels of
headings, you can use up to five.


                                         Doc 1 Pg 1 Ln 1" Pos 1"
```

*Figure 10.44:* You can create a short document like this one to use for recording the **contents** macro.

## RECORDING THE MACRO

To record the macro, take the following steps:

1. Turn on the macro recorder by pressing Ctrl-F10 or choosing Macro from the Tools menu and then choosing Define. Enter **contents** as the name of the macro.

2. Enter **mark text for toc** as the macro description; then press ↵.

3. Press F2 (Search); then press F6 (Bold) to search for the first occurrence of boldface in your text. Press F2 to begin the search. (If you are using a different unique identifier, such as small caps or italics, press the keys required to generate its code. You would press Ctrl-F8 and type **A I** to generate the code for italics, for example.)

4. When the program locates the first boldface text, press Alt-F4 to turn on block marking; then press End to block to the end of the line.

5. Press Alt-F5 (Mark Text) and type **C** for ToC. So that Word-Perfect will pause and let you enter the correct level, insert a

pause by pressing Ctrl-PgUp, typing **P**, and pressing ←.
(You may also want to insert a {DISPLAY ON} command at
the beginning of the macro so that the prompts will be
visible.)

6. Press Ctrl-F10 again to stop recording the macro. You will
   now chain it to itself by using the macro editor. Press F1 to
   turn off block marking.

7. In version 5.0, press Ctrl-F10 (Macro Def) and enter **contents** as the name of the macro. Type **2 2** to edit the macro
   you just created. In version 5.1, just press Home; enter
   **contents** and press ← twice.

8. The macro will resemble the one in Figure 10.45. Move to
   the end of the macro and press Ctrl-PgUp, then type **ch** and
   press ← to enter the {CHAIN} command in the macro.
   Type **contents** ~ as the name of the file to chain (don't forget
   the tilde).

9. Press F7 once or twice to exit to your document.

The **contents** macro should resemble the one in Figure 10.45 and,
after you've edited it, the one in Figure 10.46.

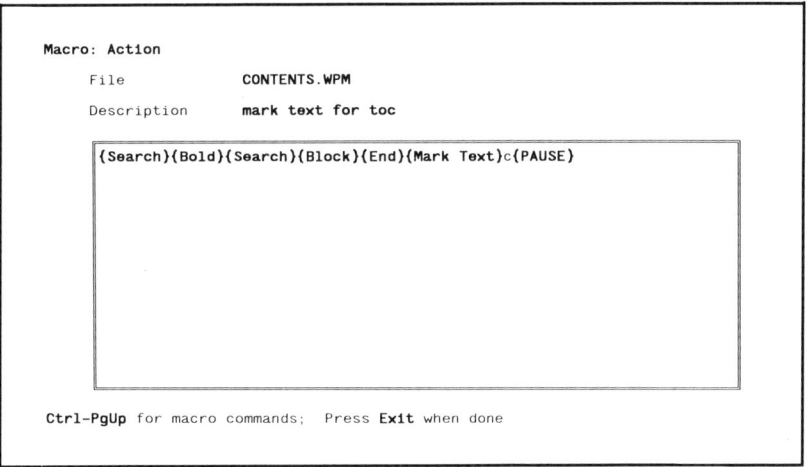

*Figure 10.45:* The **contents** macro before it is chained to itself

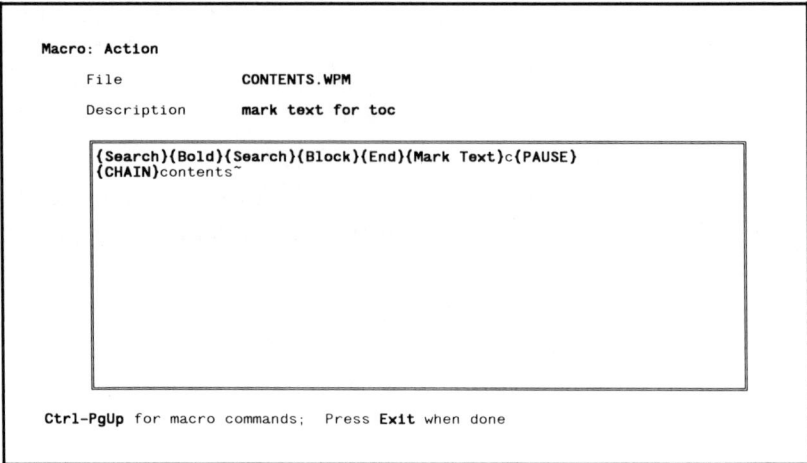

*Figure 10.46:* After the macro is chained to itself, it should resemble this one.

To record the second macro—the one that creates the contents page and generates the table of contents—take the following steps:

1. Turn on the macro recorder by pressing Ctrl-F10 or choosing Macro from the Tools menu and then choosing Define. Enter **create** as the name of the macro.

2. Enter **creates and generates contents page** as the macro description; then press ←.

3. Press Home Home ↑ to move the cursor to the beginning of the document; then press Ctrl-← to create a new page.

4. Press ↑ to move into the new blank page.

5. Press Shift-F6 (Center) and type **Contents** to create a heading for the contents page.

6. Press ← twice to insert a blank line between the heading and the table of contents that will appear.

7. Press Alt-F5 (Mark Text). Then, to define a three-level table of contents that uses dot leaders, type **D C N 3** and press F7 to exit. You can choose to use a different number of levels or a different style while you are at this screen.

# SPECIALIZED MACROS 431

8. Press Alt-F5 again and type **G G Y** to generate the table of contents.

9. Press Ctrl-F10 to stop recording the macro.

The final **create** macro should resemble the one in Figure 10.47. A sample table of contents created with the sample text is shown in Figure 10.48.

## USING THE MACROS

When you use the **contents** macro, move to the beginning of your document. WordPerfect will pause at each bold heading and prompt you for the level at which that heading should be in the final table of contents. Enter a number and press ↵. The program will then search for the next bold heading in your document until it can no longer locate any bold headings.

After you have marked all the headings for the table of contents, execute the **create** macro. You can execute it from any position in your text, even if you are on the last page of the document and have

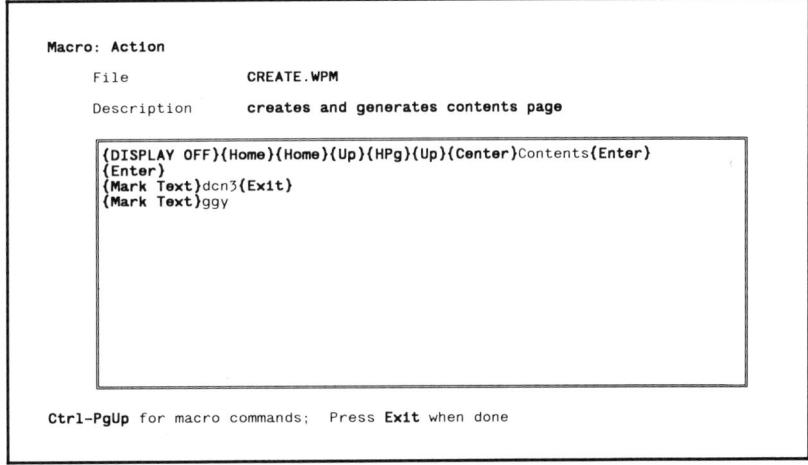

*Figure 10.47:* The final **create** macro creates and generates the table of contents.

```
                              Contents


        Level-1 Heading. . . . . . . . . . . . . . . . . . . . . . . 2

                 Level-2 Heading . . . . . . . . . . . . . . . . . . 2

                       Level-3 Heading. . . . . . . . . . . . . . . 2


        ===========================================================

        Level-1 Heading

              Although  in  a  regular  document  you  would  probably  have  many
        paragraphs  between  headings,  this  short  document  is  enough  to
        record the macro.
        C:\5\MB\TOC                                   Doc 1 Pg 1 Ln 1.66" Pos 1"
```

*Figure 10.48:* Using the sample text shown in Figure 10.44, the **create** macro created this short table of contents as a separate page at the beginning of the document.

finished using the **contents** macro. If you prefer, you can wait to generate the table of contents with the **create** macro until after you have made any last-minute changes that may affect page breaks.

One final warning: If you use the **create** macro to create a table of contents and there already is one in your document, you'll get two tables of contents—one for each [Def Mark:ToC] code that the program finds. To remove any extra [Def Mark:ToC] codes, go to the beginning of the document and search for them. Pressing F2 and then pressing Alt-F5 and typing **D D** will locate any that remain in your text.

## *SETTING UP A TABLE FORMAT*

WordPerfect 5.1's Table feature allows you to create beautifully formatted tables that will also do calculations the way a spreadsheet would. This macro, named **table**, sets up a three-column by six-row table with bold headings in the top column that is formatted to show a total at the bottom of each column (Figure 10.49 shows the table skeleton, and Figure 10.50 shows a printed table that has been filled in with sample data). The macro pauses for you to enter a table number, a title, or both, and then automatically moves to the first cell, where you can enter your first heading.

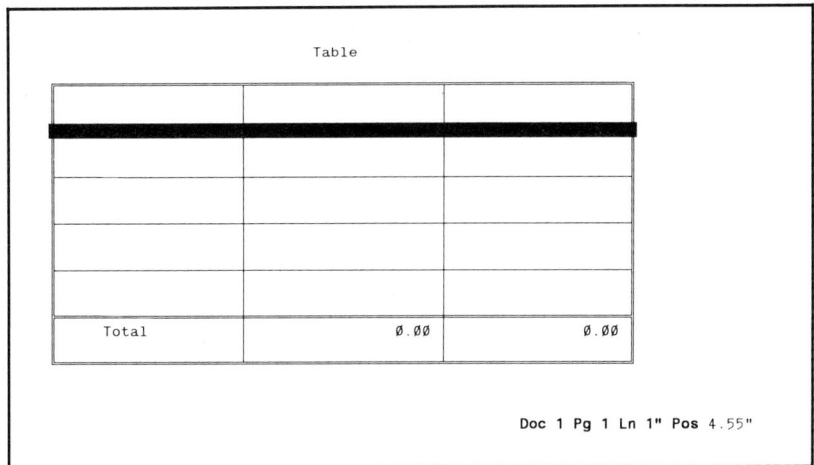

*Figure 10.49:* The form of the table before it has been filled in with the text you type

| Table 7: Output in Dollars and Per Capita, Selected Countries |||
|---|---|---|
| Country | Value of Output (Billions) | Value of Output Per Capita (Dollars) |
| United States | $730.75 | $3670.76 |
| West Germany | 104.80 | 1750.50 |
| Japan | 99.90 | 1000.00 |
| USSR | 235.50 | 970.28 |
| Total | 1,170.95 | 7,391.54 |

*Figure 10.50:* A printed sample of a filled-in table

## BEFORE YOU BEGIN

Before you begin to record the macro:

- Clear the screen.

## RECORDING THE MACRO

To record the macro, take the following steps:

1. Turn on the macro recorder by pressing Ctrl-F10 or choosing Macro from the Tools menu and then choosing Define. Enter **table** as the name of the macro.

2. Enter **set up table format** as the macro description; then press ↵.

3. Press Alt-F7 (Columns/Table); type **T** for Table and **C** for Create.

4. To create a three-column by six-row table, press ↵, type **6**, and press ↵ again.

5. Press Alt-F4 (Block); then press Home → to highlight the top row.

6. Type **L B T** (for Lines Bottom Thick) to add a thick rule between the top row and the body of the table. When you enter the text for the table, your column headings will go in this row. You won't see a thick rule on the screen; instead, you'll see a shaded line. If you look at your table with the View Document feature (Shift-F7 V), though, you can see the thick rule.

7. Press Alt-F4 (Block); then press Home ← to highlight the top row again.

8. Type **F C J C** (for Format Cell Justify Center) so that column headings will be centered in each cell.

9. Press Alt-F4 (Block); then press Home → to highlight the top row again. Press F6 (Bold) so that your headings will be in boldface type.

> Create a larger table than the size you think you're usually going to need; you can always delete unwanted rows after you enter the text for each table.

10. Press ↓; then press Alt-F4 and Home ↓ to highlight the rest of the column. Type **F C J D M** + . This formats the rest of the cells in the column to align on the decimal. In addition, it uses the Math feature to tell WordPerfect to calculate a subtotal ( + ) at the bottom of the column. You'll have to tell WordPerfect when you want the total calculated after you enter the text for the table; you'll see how later.

11. Press Alt-F4 Home ← to highlight the bottom row. Then type **L T D** (for Lines Top Double) so that the last row, which will contain the calculated totals for the table, will have a double rule separating it from the rest of the table, which is standard practice for a row that holds totals.

12. To shade that last row, press Alt-F4 Home → and type **L S O** (for Lines Shade On). You won't see the shading on the screen, but it's there. Use View Document to see it after you finish this macro.

13. Press ← and type **M** + so that a subtotal can be calculated at the bottom of the second column also.

14. Press Alt-F4; then press ↑ four times. Type **F C J D** to format those cells to align on the decimal point.

15. Press ← to move to the left column. Press Ctrl-Home (Go To); then press Home ↓. This moves the cursor to the last cell in the column.

16. Turn off the table editor by pressing Alt-F7. You can now enter the word *Total* for the last cell in the column. To indent it one tab stop, press Home Tab (pressing Tab alone would move you to the next cell in the table). Then type **Total**.

17. Now, to go to the top of the table, where you can enter a title, press Ctrl-Home Home Home ↑.

18. Press ↑; press ↵ to enter a hard return; then press ↑ again. This positions the cursor before the [Tbl Def] code, outside the table area.

19. Press Shift-F6 (Center) so that the table title will be centered over the table; then type **Table** and press the Spacebar.

> Ctrl-Home Home Home ↑ will take you to the first cell in a table. If you do a lot of table editing, you may want to define those keystrokes as a macro. Likewise, Ctrl-Home Home Home ↓ will take you to the last cell in a table. To go to the first or last cell in a column, use Ctrl-Home Home ↓ or ↑. To go to the first or last cell in a row, use Ctrl-Home Home ← or →.

20. To insert a pause so that you can type a table number and title, press Ctrl-PgUp; type **P**, and press ⏎.

21. To position the cursor in the first cell, ready for you to begin typing, press ↓ twice.

22. Press Ctrl-F10 to turn off the macro recorder.

Your screen should resemble the one in Figure 10.51.

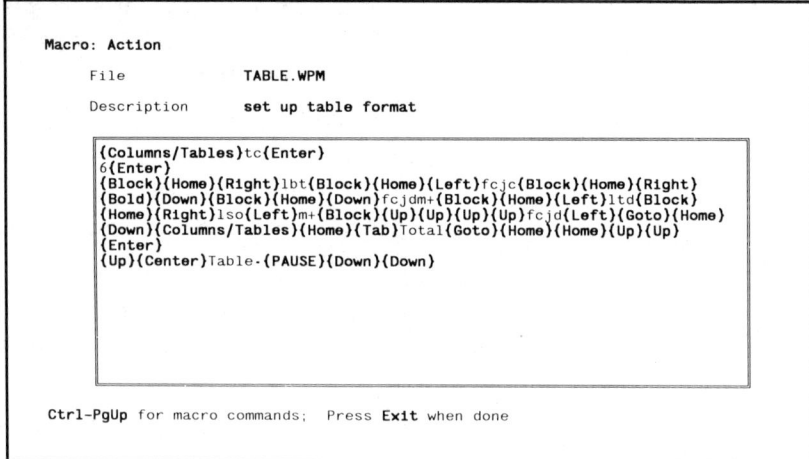

*Figure 10.51:* The **table** macro allows you to quickly create complex table formats.

## USING THE MACRO

When you use the macro, WordPerfect sets up the blank skeleton table shown in Figure 10.49. It pauses to let you enter a table number and title, such as *3: Estimated Exports for 1991*, and then moves to the first cell so that you can begin typing. Headings in the first row will be bold and centered.

Whenever you want to calculate the totals in the last row after you've entered the text for the table, move the cursor into the table, press Alt-F7 and type **M C**. If the cursor is outside of the table area, the totals won't be calculated.

If you set up a larger table than you need, just delete the extra rows when you're done by positioning the cursor in the first cell on the first row to be deleted. Then turn on the table editor (Alt-F7), press Del, type R for Rows, and enter the number of rows you want to delete. Don't delete the last row unless you don't want totals. Enter one row less than the number of blank rows remaining in the table.

As you enter text in the cells, WordPerfect will automatically expand their width to accommodate what you type. After you've inserted all the text for the table, you can adjust the size of the columns by placing the cursor in the column you want to change, pressing Alt-F7 to turn on the table editor, and pressing Ctrl-→ to widen it or Ctrl-← to narrow it.

Use the Options option (3 or P) on the Table Editor menu to change how the table is positioned on the page. It's preset to Left, but you can choose to have it centered between the margins; expand automatically to fill the space between the margins (Full); or appear at a set position.

If you don't want to see the table as it's formatting (it's very pretty, especially on a color monitor), edit it to turn the display off. In the macro editor, press Ctrl-PgUp, highlight {DISPLAY OFF}, and press ↵ to insert that as the first instruction in the macro.

## *OTHER USES*

You can set up a table very much like this one to use as an expense account form to calculate daily and weekly totals. Set up a seven-column table, one column for each business day of the week plus one for categories (far left) and one for totals (far right). Just put the + symbol in the left column to calculate across the rows (the weekly totals). Daily totals can be calculated down the columns.

You can set up tables to perform many other calculations. For example, to calculate sales tax of 6.5 percent on all the items in column B in this table, choose Math from the Table Editor menu, type F for Formal, and enter the formula as (B2+B3+B4+B5)*1.065 in cell B6 at the bottom of column B.

A similar table can be used to keep track of exam results for your students, or to use as an invoice.

> To turn off all the lines—if you're creating an invoice, for example—highlight each column when the table editor is on and type L A N (for Lines All None).

## CREATING AN INVOICE

This macro, named **invoice**, sets up a complex table format and creates a multipurpose invoice that will automatically calculate subtotals, sales tax, and a total for you.

### BEFORE YOU BEGIN

Before you begin to record the macro:

- Make sure line spacing is set to 1.

### RECORDING THE MACRO

To record the macro, take the following steps:

1. Press Ctrl-F10 (Macro Define) or choose Macro from the Tools menu and then choose Define. Enter **invoice** as the name of the macro.

2. Enter **creates invoice** as the macro description; then press ←⎯.

3. To create the logo shown at the top of the invoice (Figure 10.52), take the following steps. (You would, of course, substitute your own company name and address and use the fonts available on your printer. This logo is set in ITC Avant Garde Gothic Demi.) Press Ctrl-F8 (Font) and type **F** for Base Font. Then choose ITC Avant Garde Gothic Demi 14-point (or whichever font and size you want). Press Shift-F6 (Center) and type **Somebody's Supplies** (or the name of your company). Then press Home ←, turn on blocking with Alt-F4, and press End to highlight the line. Press Ctrl-F8 and type **A I** to italicize the line. Then, to switch to a smaller type size, press Ctrl-F8 and type **S S** for Small, then press ←⎯. Press Shift-F6 (Center), type **Retail Division** (or the next line of your own company's address), and press ←⎯. Press Shift-F6, type **55 West Eastern St.** (or your company's address), and press ←⎯. Press Shift-F6, type **San Diego, CA 92126**, and then press ←⎯. Press Shift-F6, type **(800) 555-1212**, press →,

SPECIALIZED MACROS    **439**

and press ← twice to add an extra line of space. If some labels seem not to align correctly, don't worry; they'll look okay when printed.

4. Then, to switch to 12-point type for the rest of the table, Press Ctrl-F8, type **F**, and choose a smaller size (in this case, 12-point ITC Avant Garde Gothic Book).

5. Next, you will create three tables, each one right above the other. On your screen, it will appear that the tables are separate, but they will be joined when the invoice is printed. Press Alt-F7 (Columns/Table) and type **T C**. Enter **2** as the number of columns and press ←. Press ← again to accept the default of one row.

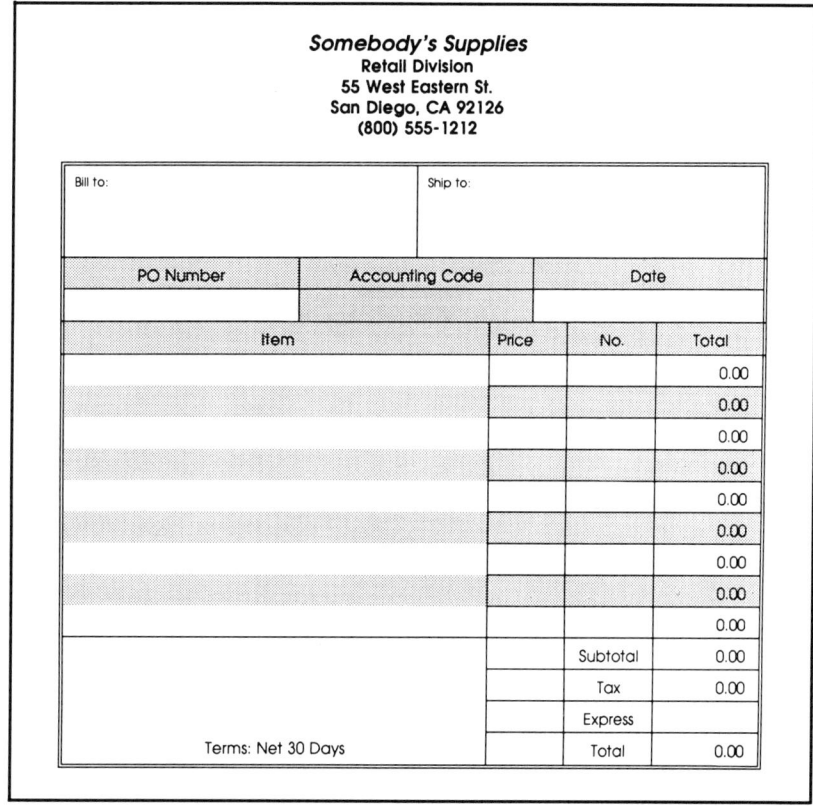

*Figure 10.52:* The completed invoice. The zeros indicate where results will be calculated.

6. To exit the table, press F7 and ↓. Then, to create the next table, press Alt-F7 and type **T C**. Enter **3** and press ←; enter **2** and press ←. Press F7 and ↓ twice.

7. To create the last table, which will hold the actual order information, press Alt-F7 and type **T C**. Enter **4** as the number of columns and **14** as the number of rows. You have now created the basic structure of the invoice.

8. To structure the last table, type **F L W** for Format Column Width, type **3.93**, and press ←.

9. Press Alt-F4; then press Home ↓. Type **L I N** for no inside lines. Then press ↑ three times and type **L T S** for a single line.

10. Press → and type **F L W .725** to format the column .725″ wide. Press ←; then type **F L J D** for decimal alignment, as this column will hold figures.

11. Press → to move into the next column; then type **F L W .825** and press ← to format the column width. Type **F L J C** for center justification.

12. Press → to move into the next column; then type **F L W 1.03** and press ←. Type **F L J D** for decimal alignment.

13. Press Home ← and type **F L W 3.93** and press ←. (For some reason the table reformats if you do not enter this measurement twice.)

14. Press End; then press Home ↓ to go to the last cell. Type **M F D 12 + D 13** and press ←. This indicates that the cells immediately above should be added.

15. Press ↑ twice; then type **M F D 11 * 1.065** and press ←. This calculates a 6.5% sales tax on the total that will appear in the cell above. Enter the tax rate in effect in your area.

16. Press ↑; then type **M +** for a total in that cell.

17. Press Home ↑; then press ↓ and type **M F B 2 * C 2** and press ←. This will multiply the price times the quantity.

18. To copy the formula down the column, type **M P D 8** and press ←.

19. Turn on blocking by pressing Alt-F4 and Home-←. Press ↑; then type **L T S** for a top single line.
20. Turn on blocking by pressing Alt-F4 and End. Type **L B S** for a bottom single line.
21. Turn on blocking again with Alt-F4; then press Home ← and type **L S O** for shading in that row.
22. Press ↓ twice; then Alt-F4 and End. Type **L S O**.
23. Press ↓ twice; then Alt-F4 and Home ←. Type **L S O**.
24. Press ↓ twice; then Alt-F4 and Home →. Type **L S O**.
25. Press ↓ twice; then Alt-F4 and Home ←. Type **L S O**.
26. Press Home ↑ and F7 to turn off the table editor.
27. Press ↑ twice to move into the next table; then press Alt-F7 to turn on the table editor again.
28. Press →; then type **L S O**. Press ↑ and ←.
29. Press Alt-F4 to turn on blocking. Press End and type **L S O**.
30. Press Alt-F4; then press Home ←. Type **L T S**.
31. Press Alt-F4; then press ↓ and End. Type **F L J C** for centered justification.
32. Press Alt-F4 and Home ←. Type **L B S** for a single bottom line.
33. Press F7 and ↑ three times to move into the next table. Type **Bill to:** and press Tab. Type **Ship to:** and press Shift-Tab. These cells will automatically expand as you enter addresses in them.
34. Press Alt-F7 to turn on the table editor. Press Alt-F4 and press →. Type **L B S** and press F7.
35. Press ↓ and →. Type **PO Number** and press →. Type **Accounting Code** and press →. Type **Date** and press ↓ twice.
36. Press →; then press Shift-F6. Type **Item** and press →. Press Alt-F7, type **F C J C**, and press F7.

37. Type **Price** and press →. Type **No.** and press →.
38. Type **Total** and press Esc. Type **6** and press ← to move the cursor left six times.
39. Press Esc and type **10**. Press ↓ ten times to move the cursor down.
40. Type **Subtotal** and press ↓. Type **Tax** and press ↓. Type **Express** and press ↓. Type **Total**, press Esc, type **7**, and press ←.
41. Press Shift-F6 and type **Terms: Net 30 Days.**
42. Press Home Home ↑ to go to the top of the document. Then, to search for the Table code so that the cursor will be positioned in the first cell when the macro executes, press F2 (Search) and press Alt-F7. Type **T** for Tables and press F2 again. Then press End and the Spacebar.
43. Press Ctrl-F10 to stop recording the macro.

The final macro should resemble the one in Figures 10.53A, B, C, and D.

```
Macro: Action
    File            INVOICE.WPM
    Description     creates invoice

    {DISPLAY OFF}{Font}fni{Down}{Down}{Enter}
    14{Enter}
    {Center}Somebody's Supplies{Home}{Left}{Block}{End}
    {Font}ai{Enter}
    {Font}ss{Center}Retail Division{Enter}
    {Center}55 West Eastern St.{Enter}
    {Center}San Diego, CA 92126{Enter}
    {Center}(800) 555-1212{Enter}
    {Enter}
    {Font}f{Up}{Up}{Enter}
    10{Enter}
    {Columns/Tables}tc2{Enter}
    {Enter}
    {Exit}{Down}{Columns/Tables}tc3{Enter}
    2{Enter}

Ctrl-PgUp for macro commands;  Press Exit when done
```

*Figure 10.53A:* The **invoice** macro automatically calculates an invoice for you.

```
Macro: Action

    File            INVOICE.WPM
    Description     creates invoice

    ┌─────────────────────────────────────────────────┐
    │ 2{Enter}                                        │
    │ {Exit}{Down}{Down}{Columns/Tables}tc4{Enter}    │
    │ 14{Enter}                                       │
    │ flw3.93{Enter}                                  │
    │ {Block}{Home}{Down}lin                          │
    │ {Up}{Up}{Up}lts{Right}flw.725{Enter}            │
    │ fljd{Right}flw.825{Enter}                       │
    │ fljc{Right}flw1.03{Enter}                       │
    │ fljd{Home}{Left}flw3.93{Enter}                  │
    │ {End}{Home}{Down}mfd12+d13{Enter}               │
    │ {Up}{Up}mfd11*1.065{Enter}                      │
    │ {Up}m+                                          │
    │ {Home}{Up}{Down}mfb2*c2{Enter}                  │
    │ mpd8{Enter}                                     │
    │ {Block}{Home}{Left}{Up}lts                      │
    └─────────────────────────────────────────────────┘

Ctrl-PgUp for macro commands;   Press Exit when done
```

*Figure 10.53B:* Lines in this macro have been broken into steps to make it easier for you to follow the text.

```
Macro: Action

    File            INVOICE.WPM
    Description     creates invoice

    ┌─────────────────────────────────────────────────────────┐
    │ {Block}{Home}{Left}{Up}lts                              │
    │ {Block}{End}lbs                                         │
    │ {Block}{Home}{Left}lso                                  │
    │ {Down}{Down}{Block}{End}lso                             │
    │ {Down}{Down}{Block}{Home}{Left}lso                      │
    │ {Down}{Down}{Block}{Home}{Right}lso                     │
    │ {Down}{Down}{Block}{Home}{Left}lso                      │
    │ {Home}{Up}{Exit}{Up}{Up}{Columns/Tables}{Right}lso{Up}{Left} │
    │ {Block}{End}lso                                         │
    │ {Block}{Home}{Left}lts                                  │
    │ {Block}{Down}{End}fljc                                  │
    │ {Block}{Home}{Left}lbs                                  │
    │ {Exit}{Up}{Up}{Up}Bill-to:{Tab}Ship-to:{Left Mar Rel}   │
    │ {Columns/Tables}{Block}{Right}{Right}lbs{Exit}          │
    │ {Down}{Right}PO-Number{Right}                           │
    └─────────────────────────────────────────────────────────┘

Ctrl-PgUp for macro commands;   Press Exit when done
```

*Figure 10.53C:* The first line repeats so that you can find your place.

## USING THE MACRO

When you use the macro, the cursor will be positioned in the 'Bill to:' box. Press Tab to move from cell to cell. To calculate the table, position the cursor in the lower part, the one containing the order amounts and prices, and press Alt-F7. Type **M C** for Math Calculate.

```
Macro: Action
    File            INVOICE.WPM
    Description     creates invoice

    {Block}{Down}{End}fljc
    {Block}{Home}{Left}lbs
    {Exit}{Up}{Up}{Up}Bill-to:{Tab}Ship-to:{Left Mar Rel}
    {Columns/Tables}{Block}{Right}{Right}lbs{Exit}
    {Down}{Right}PO-Number{Right}
    Accounting-Code{Right}
    Date{Down}{Down}
    {Right}{Center}Item{Right}
    Price{Right}No.{Right}
    Total{Esc}6{Left}
    {Esc}10{Down}
    Subtotal{Down}Tax{Down}Express{Down}Total{Esc}7{Left}
    {Center}Terms:-Net-30-Days
    {Home}{Home}{Up}{Search}{Columns/Tables}t{Search}{End}.

Ctrl-PgUp for macro commands;   Press Exit when done
```

*Figure 10.53D:* Several lines are repeated in this screen, which shows the end of the macro.

## OTHER USES

You can adapt this table to a variety of uses that require calculations in columns. By using Macro Command Language, you can also add prompts that will guide the user through filling out the form, such as presenting options for various accounting codes when the user reaches the special shaded cell. You can add your own messages for your customers, such as a special hotline telephone number or hours available for ordering, in the 'Terms: Net 30 Days' area.

## SUMMARY

We've come to the end of this cookbook of macros, but if you want to explore further into WordPerfect's Macro Command Language, you'll find that Appendix A describes all the commands and gives the syntax of each. If you've had a little experience with a programming language such as BASIC or Pascal, you should have no trouble using Macro Command Language to create custom applications for yourself or others.

# Using Macro Command Language

APPENDIX

# A

# APPENDIX A

> The discussions in this appendix assume that you are familiar with the macro editor, since most of the macro commands must be entered by using it. See Chapter 2 for a quick review of how it works.

WordPerfect 5's macro command language consists of special commands that you can insert into your macros by using the macro editor. To add one of these commands to a macro, you press Ctrl-PgUp in the editor, type the first few letters of the command's name (which automatically activates the Name Search feature), and press ↵.

Other commands are entered in the macro editor by pressing the appropriate keys. If the command you want does not appear, try pressing Ctrl-V first. Pressing Ctrl-V inserts the literal meaning of the next key that is pressed into the macro that is being created. You will need to press Ctrl-V first to insert the following commands in the macro editor: Tab, Enter, Delete, Cancel, Exit, and the cursor-movement commands—Right, Left, Up, and so forth.

Many commands require the use of variables, as explained in the following section.

## USING VARIABLES

A *variable* is (usually) the number or name assigned to the place where a value is stored in your computer's memory. Both WordPerfect 5.0 and 5.1 allow you to assign ten variables (0 through 9), but WordPerfect 5.1 also allows you to use named variables in its Macro Command Language.

To assign a value to one of the ten variables 0–9 in the editing screen, press Ctrl-PgUp, select Assign, and type the number you want the variable to have. At the 'Value' prompt you can type up to 129 characters as the text of the variable. If you block text before pressing Ctrl-PgUp, you can assign that text to a variable.

To insert the value of variables 0–9 anywhere in your document, press Alt plus the variable's number. In the macro editor, press Ctrl-V before you press Alt and the variable number.

In the 5.1 macro editor, you can use the {ASSIGN} command to assign a value to a named variable. First, you enter a name for the variable and follow it with what the variable is to contain. For example, to assign the name *Harold Brown* to a variable called *client*, you would enter

{ASSIGN} client ~ Harold Brown ~

A tilde ( ~ ) is used to indicate the end of a variable or other operand that a specific macro command requires, such as a label name or file name. It's easy to forget to type the tilde, but without the correct tildes, your macros won't operate as you intend. In addition, some commands require you to use two tildes when you use them with other commands that also require tildes. For example

{ON NOT FOUND}{GO}out ~ ~

requires two tildes at the end because the {ON NOT FOUND} and the {GO} commands both require tildes. In general, commands that use {CALL} or {GO} when a certain condition is met (commands such as {ON NOT FOUND}, {ON CANCEL}, {ON ERROR}, and the like) will require the use of two tildes.

Tildes are also required to indicate the end of text or of a value that a particular command may call for.

## USING MACRO CONTROL CHARACTERS IN DISPLAYS

Tables A.1 and A.2 show the control characters that you can use to manipulate the various text attributes, and Table A.1 shows the control characters you use to position the cursor on the screen.

For example, you might want to display a prompt in reverse video. To do this, you would enter the prompt in the form

{TEXT}0 ~ {^R}Enter your employee number: ~

As another example, to position the cursor in the following message so that it will be on the N in No, so that the user can simply press ⏎

*Table A.1:* Using Control Characters in a Message.

| Control Character | Effect |
|---|---|
| ^H | Moves cursor to upper-left corner of screen; displayed as {Home} in the macro |
| ^J | Inserts blank line and positions cursor at beginning of next line without moving the cursor; displayed as {Enter} in the macro |
| ^K | Clears to the end of the line; displayed as {Del to EOL} in the macro |
| L | Clears screen and displays cursor in upper-left corner; displayed as {Del to EOP} in macro |
| ^M | Moves cursor to beginning of line; displayed as {^M} in the macro |
| ^N | Turns on display attributes for text that follows; displayed as {^N} in the macro |
| ^O | Turns off display attributes for text that follows; displayed as {^O} in the macro |
| ^P | Plus ASCII character and code equivalent of column and row positions (Table A.3); displays cursor at a specific column and row position |
| ^Q | Turns off all display attributes; displayed as {^Q} in the macro |
| ^R | Turns on reverse video; displayed as {^R} in the macro |
| ^S | Turns off reverse video; displayed as {^S} in the macro |
| ^T | Turns on underlining; displayed as {^T} in the macro |
| ^U | Turns off underlining; displayed as {^U} in the macro |
| ^V | Turns on menu letter (mnemonic) attribute; displayed as {^V} in the macro; turned off with ^Q |

*Table A.1:* Using Control Characters in a Message (continued).

| Control Character | Effect |
|---|---|
| ^W | Moves cursor one line up; displayed as {Up} in the macro |
| ^X | Moves cursor one character right; displayed as {Right} in the macro |
| ^Y | Moves cursor one character left; displayed as {Left} in the macro |
| ^Z | Moves cursor one line down; displayed as {Down} in the macro |
| ^\ | Turns off bold; displayed as {^\} in the macro |
| ^] | Turns on bold; displayed as {^]} in the macro |

*Table A.2:* Using Control Characters to Display Print Attributes.

| Control Character | Print Attribute |
|---|---|
| ^A | Very large print; displayed as {^A} in the macro |
| ^B | Large print; displayed as {^B} in the macro |
| ^C | Small print; displayed as {^C} in the macro |
| ^D | Fine print; displayed as {^D} in the macro |
| ^E | Superscript; displayed as {^E} in the macro |
| ^F | Subscript; displayed as {^F} in the macro |
| ^G | Outline; displayed as {^G} in the macro |
| ^H | Italics; displayed as {Home} in the macro |
| ^I | Shadow; displayed as {Tab} in the macro |
| ^J | Redline; displayed as {Enter} in the macro |
| ^K | Double underline; displayed as {Del to EOL} in the macro |

*Table A.2:* Using Control Characters to Display Print Attributes (continued).

| Control Character | Print Attribute |
|---|---|
| ^L | Bold; displayed as {Del to EOP} in the macro |
| ^M | Strikeout; displayed as {^M} in the macro |
| ^N | Underline; displayed as {^N} in the macro |
| ^O | Small caps; displayed as {^O} in the macro |
| ^P | Blink; displayed as {^P} in the macro |
| ^Q | Reverse video; displayed as {^Q} in the macro |

*Note:* These characters must be entered after the Display Attribute On (^N) and Display Attribute Off (^O) characters. To enter {Del to EOP}, {Home}, {Enter}, or {Tab}, press Ctrl-V first.

for No, you would enter the message like this:

{TEXT}0 ~ Text will be deleted. Continue? (Y/N) No
{Left}{Left} ~

To move the cursor to the beginning of the line, you can use the ^M code, or to move it up or down one line, use the ^W or ^Z codes, respectively.

To position the cursor at a specific point on the screen, such as within a box that contains a menu, use the {^P} code followed by the column coordinate (0-79) and row coordinate (0-24 on most screens). To enter these coordinates, use the control characters shown in Table A.3. The screen positions begin with column 0 and row 0. For example, to position the cursor at the top-left corner of the screen, you would enter the message as

{TEXT}0 ~ Enter your employee number:{P}{A}{A}{Up}{Left}

You can also use the numeric keypad instead of entering the control characters. To do this, hold down the Alt key and type the coordinate position. For example, to position a message at column 20,

*Table A.3:* ASCII Character and Code Equivalents.

| Position Number | Enter As | Displayed As |
|---|---|---|
| 1 | ^A | {^A} |
| 2 | ^B | {^B} |
| 3 | ^C | {^C} |
| 4 | ^D | {^D} |
| 5 | ^E | {^E} |
| 6 | ^F | {^F} |
| 7 | ^G | {^G} |
| *8 | ^H | {Home} |
| *9 | ^I | {Tab} |
| *10 | ^J | {Enter} |
| *11 | ^K | {Del to EOL} |
| *12 | ^L | {Del to EOP} |
| 13 | ^M | {^M} |
| 14 | ^N | {^N} |
| 15 | ^O | {^O} |
| 16 | ^P | {^P} |
| 17 | ^Q | {^Q} |
| 18 | ^R | {^R} |
| 19 | ^S | {^S} |

*Note:* To enter asterisked position numbers, press Ctrl-V and then the Ctrl key combination. Otherwise, for numbers 1–29, press Ctrl and then type the character. To enter codes for position numbers 30–80, press and hold down Alt and type the number using the numeric keypad.

*Table A.3:* ASCII Character and Code Equivalents (continued).

| Position Number | Enter As | Displayed As |
|---|---|---|
| 20 | ^T | {^T} |
| 21 | ^U | {^U} |
| *22 | ^V | {^V} |
| *23 | ^W | {Up} |
| *24 | ^X | {Right} |
| *25 | ^Y | {Left} |
| *26 | ^Z | {Down} |
| *27 | ^[ | {Esc} |
| 28 | ^\ | {^\} |
| 29 | ^] | {^]} |
| 30 | Alt-30 | ▲ |
| 31 | Alt-31 | ▼ |
| 32 | Alt-32 | (space) |
| 33 | Alt-33 | ! |
| 34 | Alt-34 | " |
| 35 | Alt-35 | # |
| 36 | Alt-36 | $ |
| 37 | Alt-37 | % |
| 38 | Alt-38 | & |
| 39 | Alt-39 | ' (apostrophe) |
| 40 | Alt-40 | ( |

*Note:* To enter asterisked position numbers, press Ctrl-V and then the Ctrl key combination. Otherwise, for numbers 1–29, press Ctrl and then type the character. To enter codes for position numbers 30–80, press and hold down Alt and type the number using the numeric keypad.

*Table A.3:* ASCII Character and Code Equivalents (continued).

| POSITION NUMBER | ENTER AS | DISPLAYED AS |
|---|---|---|
| 41 | Alt-41 | ) |
| 42 | Alt-42 | * |
| 43 | Alt-43 | + |
| 44 | Alt-44 | , (comma) |
| 45 | Alt-45 | - |
| 46 | Alt-46 | . |
| 47 | Alt-47 | / |
| 48 | Alt-48 | 0 |
| 49 | Alt-49 | 1 |
| 50 | Alt-50 | 2 |
| 51 | Alt-51 | 3 |
| 52 | Alt-52 | 4 |
| 53 | Alt-53 | 5 |
| 54 | Alt-54 | 6 |
| 55 | Alt-55 | 7 |
| 56 | Alt-56 | 8 |
| 57 | Alt-57 | 9 |
| 58 | Alt-58 | : |
| 59 | Alt-59 | ; |

*Note:* To enter asterisked position numbers, press Ctrl-V and then the Ctrl key combination. Otherwise, for numbers 1–29, press Ctrl and then type the character. To enter codes for position numbers 30–80, press and hold down Alt and type the number using the numeric keypad.

*Table A.3:* ASCII Character and Code Equivalents (continued).

| Position Number | Enter As | Displayed As |
|---|---|---|
| 60 | Alt-60 | < |
| 61 | Alt-61 | = |
| 62 | Alt-62 | > |
| 63 | Alt-63 | ? |
| 64 | Alt-64 | @ |
| 65 | Alt-65 | A |
| 66 | Alt-66 | B |
| 67 | Alt-67 | C |
| 68 | Alt-68 | D |
| 69 | Alt-69 | E |
| 70 | Alt-70 | F |
| 71 | Alt-71 | G |
| 72 | Alt-72 | H |
| 73 | Alt-73 | I |
| 74 | Alt-74 | J |
| 75 | Alt-75 | K |
| 76 | Alt-76 | L |
| 77 | Alt-77 | M |
| 78 | Alt-78 | N |
| 79 | Alt-79 | O |
| 80 | Alt-80 | P |

*Note:* To enter asterisked position numbers, press Ctrl-V and then the Ctrl key combination. Otherwise, for numbers 1–29, press Ctrl and then type the character. To enter codes for position numbers 30–80, press and hold down Alt and type the number using the numeric keypad.

row 10, press Ctrl-P to insert the {^P}; then press Alt and type **20**. Press Alt again and type **10**. You won't see the numbers on the screen; instead, you'll see the ASCII equivalents, such as the paragraph symbol for Alt-20. (You have to use this method to enter coordinates above 26.)

To display a prompt in the top-left corner of the screen, you can also use a {Home} code:

{TEXT}0~{HOME}Enter your Social Security number: ~

> If you don't put the {Home} code at the beginning of the prompt, you will see the prompt at odd places on the screen.

To enter the {Home} code, press Ctrl-V and then press Ctrl-H.

To display a prompt in the middle of the screen, use this pattern:

{PROMPT}{Del to EOP}{^P}{Down}{Del to EOP}
{^R}Welcome to the menu system {Q} ~

The {^R} command displays the message in reverse video (or the same color combination used for blocked text, if you have a color monitor. The first {Del to EOP} command clears the screen, and the second, after the {^P} command, is used to position the message 12 lines from the top of the screen.

The message created by the {CHAR}, {TEXT}, {INPUT}, {PROMPT}, and {STATUS PROMPT} commands remains on the screen until the screen is rewritten. This happens each time the cursor is moved vertically, if {DISPLAY ON} is active. If {DISPLAY OFF} is on, the screen won't be rewritten until a {DISPLAY ON} command occurs in the macro. You may want to force a screen rewrite at points in a macro by inserting the commands {Screen}{Screen}, which is the same as pressing Ctrl-F3 twice to rewrite the screen. You can also use the {Del to EOP} command as shown in the previous example.

If the Reveal Codes screen is open when your macro displays a message, the message may not be visible if it is positioned in the lower half of the screen. You can use the {IF}{STATE} command to check to see whether the Reveal Codes screen is on and turn it off:

{IF}{STATE}&512~
    {Reveal Codes}
{END IF}

# THE MACRO COMMANDS

Commands marked with an asterisk are available only in version 5.1.

## {ASSIGN}

**Syntax:**

    {ASSIGN}variable~value~

Use the {ASSIGN} command to assign a value to a variable numbered 0 through 9 (in version 5.0) or to any combination of characters (in version 5.1). Once a value has been assigned to that variable, it can be used in another command (such as {IF EXISTS}) in a document or in a prompt. You may use text, integers, or an expression that evaluates to integers as the value to be assigned.

For example,

    {ASSIGN}1~5440~

assigns the value 5,440 to variable 1, while

    {ASSIGN}1~10/5~

assigns the value 2 to variable 1, and

    {ASSIGN}1~yourname~

assigns the string *yourname* to variable 1.

The command

    {ASSIGN}language~FR~

in version 5.1 would create the variable *language* and assign FR to it.

To cancel a variable's assignment, use the following syntax:

    {ASSIGN}variable~~

Table A.4 summarizes the various ways values may be used as arithmetic or logic expressions.

*Table A.4:* Valid Expressions of Values.

| OPERATOR | RESULT |
| --- | --- |
| value1 + value2 | Adds values and assigns sum to variable |
| value1 − value2 | Subtracts values and assigns difference to variable |
| value1*value2 | Multiplies values and assigns product to variable |
| value1/value2 | Divides values and assigns integer result to variable |
| value1%value2 | Divides values and assigns remainder to variable |
| −value | Assigns negative value to variable |
| !value | Returns logical NOT |
| value1&value2 | Returns logical AND |
| value1 \| value2 | Returns logical OR |
| value1 = value2 | Assigns −1 to variable if values are equal; otherwise, assigns 0 |
| value1! = value2 | Assigns −1 to variable if values are not equal; otherwise, assigns 0 |
| value1 >value2 | Assigns −1 to variable if value1 is greater than value2; otherwise, assigns 0 |
| value1 <value2 | Assigns −1 to value if value1 is less than value2; otherwise, assigns 0 |

## {BELL}

**Syntax:**

{BELL}

Use the Bell command to get the user's attention at a pause or when an error message is encountered. It makes the computer sound a beep.

If you use the {BELL} command with a pause, make sure it appears before the pause to get the user's attention, not after:

{BELL}{Pause}

## {BLOCK APPEND}, {BLOCK COPY}, {BLOCK MOVE}

*Syntax:*

{Block Append}, {Block Copy}, {Block Move}

You can use these commands within a macro instead of the individual instructions {Move}bc for Block Copy, and so forth. In addition, if you don't have a keyboard with an enhanced BIOS, you can assign these commands to an Alt- or Ctrl-key combination. For example, you might want to assign block move to Alt-X (for Cut). If you have a keyboard with an enhanced BIOS, Ctrl-Ins is Block Copy and Ctrl-Del is Block Move.

## {BREAK}

*Syntax:*

{BREAK}

Use the {BREAK} command to exit from an {IF} command and go to an {ENDIF} command, as in the following:

{IF}{VAR 9}<4~
{BREAK}
{ENDIF}

## {CALL}

*Syntax:*

{CALL}label~

Use the {CALL} command to direct a macro to a subroutine identified by a label. For example

    {CALL}more~

executes the instructions stored with the label *more*.

If a {RETURN}, {RETURN CANCEL}, {RETURN ERROR}, or {RETURN NOT FOUND} instruction is encountered after a {CALL} command executes, the macro will go back to the place where the {CALL} command was used and execute the next command at that location.

If you use a subroutine more than once within a macro, use the {CALL} command to execute it rather than typing out the steps of the subroutine each time you need to use it.

## *{CANCEL ON}, {CANCEL OFF}*

***Syntax:***

    {CANCEL ON}
    {CANCEL OFF}

Use the {CANCEL ON} command to allow the user to stop macro execution by pressing F1 (Cancel). The {CANCEL OFF} command prevents the user from stopping the macro by pressing F1, and can be used in subroutines that you want to prevent the user from stopping. For example, you may want to use {CANCEL OFF} to prevent text that is in a buffer, such as the buffer that holds moved or copied text, from being lost if the user presses F1.

## *{CASE}*

***Syntax:***

    {CASE}value~
    case1~ label1~
    case2~ label2~
    case*n*~ label*n*~ ~

Use the {CASE} command to branch to different subroutines in a macro that are identified by {LABEL} commands. Depending on what the value is, the appropriate subroutine is executed. Note the use of tildes following the last label.

For example,

{CASE}{VAR1}~ 1~ letters~ l~ letters~ L~ letters~
2~ contracts~ c~ contracts~ C~ contracts~

tells the macro to execute the subroutine named *letters* if the user types **1**, **l**, or **L**, and to go to the subroutine named *contracts* if the user types **2**, **c**, or **C**.

If no matches are found, the macro simply executes the next step that follows the {CASE} command.

### *{CASE CALL}*

**Syntax:**

{CASE CALL}value~
case1~ label1~
case2~ label2~
case*n*~ label*n*~

Use the {CASE CALL} command in the same way that you would a {CASE} command. The {CASE CALL} command branches to a subroutine, executes it, and then returns to execute the next statement after the {CASE CALL}. The statement after the {CASE CALL} is executed whether a match was found or not.

### *{CHAIN}*

**Syntax:**

{CHAIN}macro~

Use the {CHAIN} command to have a macro executed as soon as the current macro finishes. For example:

{CHAIN}save~

will execute the **save** macro when the macro that is running stops executing.

If {CHAIN} is used in a macro that contains a search, the macro will chain to the second macro only when the search is successful. You can use only one {CHAIN} command per macro.

## *{CHAR}*

***Syntax:***

   {CHAR}variable ~ message ~

Use the {CHAR} command to display a message. The {CHAR} command takes a single character that the user enters and assigns it to a variable.

For example, this command produces a message at the bottom of the screen and waits for the user to type a **Y** or **N** response, which is stored in variable 1:

   {CHAR}1 ~ Do you want to exit? (Y/N) ~

It can also be used to create menu lines at the bottom of the screen:

   {CHAR}1 ~ 1 Yes; 2 No ~

To wait for a keystroke without displaying a message, enter the command as

   {CHAR}1 ~ ~

If you use the {CHAR} command, you can use the {DISPLAY OFF} command with it to turn off the display after the menu's purpose has been served.

Tables A.1, A.2, and A.3 summarize the control characters and codes you can use to display messages with the {CHAR}, {TEXT}, and {PROMPT} commands. Table A.1 shows the codes you use to position the message (which is normally on the status line at the bottom of the screen) and display it in reverse video, with underlining, or with bold face. To use other display attributes, insert the codes given in Table A.2 within a pair of ^N (Display Attribute On) and ^O

(Display Attribute Off) codes. To position the message at a specific column and line, use the codes shown in Table A.3. You can specify line numbers from 1 to 24 and column numbers from 1 to 80. For examples, see the {PROMPT} command and refer to the section "Using Macro Control Characters in Displays" earlier in this appendix.

To insert most of these codes, you must be in Command Insert mode (Ctrl-V or Ctrl-F10).

## {;} {COMMENT}

**Syntax:**

    {;}comment ˜

Use the {;} command to insert your own comments into your macros. The text you type between the {;} and the tilde is ignored when WordPerfect executes the macro. Using comments is a good way to document what each step of a complex macro does. For example

    {Alt-F5}ggy       {;}Generates index ˜

explains that this step of the macro generates the index of a document.

## {DISPLAY OFF}, {DISPLAY ON}

**Syntax:**

    {DISPLAY ON}
    {DISPLAY OFF}

Use the {DISPLAY ON} command to make a macro execute visibly on the screen. Use the {DISPLAY OFF} command to have the macro execute invisibly. {DISPLAY OFF} is the default state. While a macro is executing with the display turned off, you see a *Please wait* message on the status line.

{DISPLAY ON} can be used to debug macros because you can see the steps the macro is taking as it executes.

## {ELSE}

*Syntax:*

{ELSE}

This is used with the {IF}, {IF BLANK}, {IF NOT BLANK}, {IF EXISTS}, {CASE}, and {CASE CALL} commands to indicate the commands that are to be carried out when the IF condition is false. See "{IF}/{ELSE}/{ENDIF}."

## *{END FOR}

*Syntax:*

{END FOR}

This indicates the end of a {FOR} or {FOR EACH} loop. See "{FOR}" and "{FOR EACH}."

## {END IF}

*Syntax:*

{END IF}

This terminates an IF structure. See "{IF}/{ELSE}/{ENDIF}."

## *{END WHILE}

*Syntax:*

{END WHILE}

This marks the end of a {WHILE} loop. See the section entitled "{WHILE}, {END WHILE}."

## *{FOR}

*Syntax:*

{FOR}*variable ~ start ~ stop ~ step ~*

Use this command to repeat a command the number of times you specify. For example, you could search for the third [Mark] marking text for a table of contents in a document:

```
{FOR}[Mark]1 ~ 3 ~ 1 ~
{Search}[Mark]{Search}
{END FOR}
```

## *{FOR EACH}

**Syntax:**

{FOR EACH}*variable ~ expression1 ~ ... ~ expressionN ~*

Use the {FOR EACH} command to repeat a process for each expression listed. When you use the command, a loop that repeats the commands between the {FOR EACH} and the {END FOR} is carried out. After each loop is completed, the *expression* arguments assign a new value to the variable.

## {GO}

**Syntax:**

{GO}label ~

Use the {GO} command to transfer control to a set of commands that has been identified by a label. It is similar to the GOTO command in BASIC.

For example:

{GO}doit ~

executes the commands stored as the label *doit*.

You must use a {LABEL} command to identify the set of commands to which you want to branch. The {LABEL} command may be placed elsewhere in the macro, because the macro will not execute commands that occur between the {GO} command and its associated {LABEL} command. If you want the macro to return to the original location of the {GO} command after the set of commands has been executed, use the {CALL} command in place of {GO}.

You can also use the {GO} command to execute a set of commands over and over until a search cannot locate the pattern it is searching for. For example,

{LABEL}delete~
{SEARCH}{HRt}{HRt}{SEARCH}
{Backspace}
{Left}
{GO}delete~

searches for all instances of two hard returns (ends of paragraphs) and deletes one of them.

If you have two commands, you need to use two tildes, one for each command. For example,

{ON ERROR}{GO}doit~ ~

tells the macro to execute the *doit* subroutine whenever an error is encountered.

## *{IF}/{ELSE}/{ENDIF}*

**Syntax:**

{IF}value~
<*commands to carry out if the condition is true*>
{END IF}

or

{IF}value~
<*commands to carry out if the condition is true*>
{ELSE}
<*commands to carry out if the condition is false*>
{END IF}

Use the {IF} and {ENDIF} commands to test for a condition and take an action, depending on the result of the test. The {ELSE} command can be used to specify that another action be taken.

The {IF} statement says: "If the value is not zero (true), perform the action; if the value is zero (false), do nothing, but if there is an {ELSE} command, do what it says to do." If you are using characters or WordPerfect codes as values, instead of numbers, you must enclose the variable as well as its equivalent in quotation marks:

```
{IF}"{VAR 1}" = "bye"~
    {GO}out~
```

{IF} statements may be nested.

The following lines, which are part of the **Alt-E** macro on the MACROS keyboard supplied with WordPerfect, show how {IF} and {ELSE} commands may be used to issue a series of instructions to WordPerfect by checking for possible states that the program may be in.

```
{LABEL}top~
{IF}{STATE}&4~
    {IF}{STATE}&8~
        {Exit}
    {ELSE}{IF}{STATE}&64~
        {^Q}
    {ELSE}{IF}{STATE}128~
        {Block}
    {ELSE}{IF}{STATE}&256~
        {Typeover}
    {ELSE}{IF}{STATE}&512~
        {Reveal Codes}
    {ELSE}
    {RETURN}
    {ENDIF}{ENDIF}{ENDIF}{ENDIF}{ENDIF}
{ELSE}
    {IF}{STATE}&1024~
    y
    {ELSE}
    {Cancel}
    {END IF}
{END IF}
{GO}top~
```

These commands take you to the main editing screen from any menu. If you are in any editing screen other than the main editing screen, you leave it. If a merge is active, it is terminated. If Block or Typeover are on, the macro turns them off. If the Reveal Codes window is displayed, you leave it. If a Yes/No question is being displayed ({STATE}&1024), the macro answers Y, and if a menu is being displayed, the menu is canceled. For additional information about the various states and how they are expressed, see the {STATE} entry.

## *{IF EXISTS}*

**Syntax:**

> {IF EXISTS}variable ~
> <commands to perform if variable exists>
> {END IF}

Use the {IF EXISTS} command to see whether a variable exists (has a value). If it does, the macro performs an action. This command is very similar to the {IF} command and uses the same syntax. For example, you could write a macro that verifies if a value has been entered at a prompt, and, if so, branch to a subroutine:

> {IF EXISTS}1 ~
> {ELSE}
>     {GO}out ~
> {END IF}

## *{INPUT}*

**Syntax:**

> {INPUT}message ~

The {INPUT} command in effect combines the {PROMPT} and {PAUSE} commands. It displays a message and pauses for the user to enter something. After the user presses ←┘, the macro continues.

To be able to press ←┘ without resuming the macro, use the {PAUSE KEY} command instead.

## *{ITEM DOWN}, {ITEM LEFT}, {ITEM RIGHT}, {ITEM UP}

*Syntax:*

    {Item Down}, {Item Left}, {Item Right}, {Item Up}

Use these commands to move the cursor one section in an outline, one column, or one cell in a table. For example:

    {Item Down}

will move the cursor from cell B4 in a table to cell B5, the next cell down. In an outline, the cursor would move to the next paragraph number of the same or preceding level.

On an enhanced keyboard, these commands are already defined as Alt-↓, Alt-←, Alt-→, and Alt-↑.

## *{KTON}, {NTOK}

*Syntax:*

    {KTON}*key*~

Use the {KTON} command to convert a keystroke to a unique number. If the key typed is a character, the {KTON} command returns a number from which the character set number can be calculated.

To convert a number to its keystroke equivalent, use the {NTOK} command.

## {LABEL}

*Syntax:*

    {LABEL}*value*~

Use the {LABEL} command to assign a name to a set of instructions. You can then execute those instructions by using the {CASE}, {CASE CALL}, {CALL}, and {GO} commands.

For example:

```
{LABEL}print ~
    {Print}f
```

identifies the command sequence Shift-F7 (Print) F (Full document) as the label *print*.

A label can be any number of characters (the program reads only the first 15), and may consist of either lowercase or uppercase letters. The program does not distinguish between upper- and lowercase.

## *{LEN}

**Syntax:**

{LEN}*variable* ~

Use the {LEN} command to return the length of a variable. For example, you may record a macro that fills in blank spaces on a form. You can use the {LEN} and {IF} commands to check that the user has not entered more characters than will fit; if he or she has, the macro can then display a prompt requesting that the text be reentered.

```
{LABEL}Month ~
    {TEXT}Month ~ Enter month as two digits. ~
    {IF}{LEN}Month ~ >2 ~
    {GO}Month ~
    {END IF}
```

This would repeat the prompt if the user entered a one-digit month.

## {LOOK}

**Syntax:**

{LOOK}*variable* ~

Use the {LOOK} command to check whether the user has typed a character. It is similar to {CHAR}, except the program does not wait for a keystroke from the user.

For example,

    {LOOK}3~

assigns the character the user types to variable 3.

When you use the {LOOK} command, you can combine it with the {IF EXISTS} and {GO} commands to branch the macro to various subroutines. For example, the lines

    {LABEL}goodbye~  
    {LOOK}5~  
    {IF EXISTS}5~  
    {GO}goodbye~  
    {END IF}

assign the user's keystroke to variable 5. If a value is present in variable 5, the macro branches to the *goodbye* subroutine.

## *{MENU OFF}, {MENU ON}

**Syntax:**

    {MENU OFF}, {MENU ON}

Use these commands to turn the WordPerfect menus off and on. For example, you may want a menu of your own making to be displayed instead of the regular WordPerfect menus.

## *{MID}

**Syntax:**

    {MID} *variable~ offset~ count~*

The {MID} command can extract a certain number of characters, so you can use it to control the length of a user's entry. For example, if the user entered **December,** you could extract the "Dec" (stored in a variable named *month*):

    {MID}{VARIABLE}month~~3

There is no offset, since you are extracting the first three characters.

## {NEST}

**Syntax:**

    {NEST}macro~

Use the {NEST} command to have a macro execute another macro as soon as it encounters the {NEST} command. The original macro will resume after the nested macro executes.

For example,

    {NEST}alta~

executes the Alt-A macro as soon as the instruction is encountered in the macro.

Unlike chained macros, which are executed only at the end of the macro they're in, nested macros don't have to be the last steps of a process.

Nesting macros is also helpful when you're creating the instructions that are called in macros as labels. Instead of typing out the instructions for the label, nest a macro that you've already created. For example, you may have already recorded macros named **primary** and **secondar** that carry out mail merge routines. Instead of typing the keystrokes for each set of instructions after the {LABEL}primary~ and {LABEL}secondary~ commands, nest the already created macros in this way:

    {LABEL}primary~{NEST}primary~
    {LABEL}secondary~{NEST}secondar~

Note that labels can be of any number of characters, but macro names are limited to eight. In fact, labels and nested macro names can be completely different:

{LABEL}return ~ {NEST}print ~

You can nest several macros in one macro, but a macro can only execute one chained macro.

## *{NEXT}

***Syntax:***

{NEXT}

Use the {NEXT} command in a {FOR} or {WHILE} loop to go to the next step in the loop (see "{FOR}" and "{WHILE}").

## {ON CANCEL}

***Syntax:***

{ON CANCEL}command ~

Use the {ON CANCEL} command to instruct the program what sequence of steps to take if the user presses F1 (Cancel). This command is needed only if you want the program to do something other than cancel the action.

The command that follows an {ON CANCEL} command can be any one of the following: {BREAK}, {CALL}, {GO}, {RESTART}, {RETURN}, {RETURN CANCEL}, {RETURN ERROR}, {RETURN NOT FOUND}, or {QUIT}.

If you use either the {GO} or {CALL} command, you must use a double tilde, because each of these commands requires one also. For example:

{ON CANCEL}{GO}bye ~ ~

Place any {ON CANCEL} commands that you use at the top of your macro so that they will be effective whenever the user presses F1 (Cancel) while executing that macro.

## {ON ERROR}

*Syntax:*

{ON ERROR}command~

Use the {ON ERROR} command to tell WordPerfect what to do if an error condition arises during macro execution.

The command that follows an {ON ERROR} command can be any one of the following: {BREAK}, {CALL}, {GO}, {RESTART}, {RETURN}, {RETURN CANCEL}, {RETURN ERROR}, {RETURN NOT FOUND}, or {QUIT}.

An error condition can arise, for example, when a user tries to change to a directory that does not exist or to print a file that has been fast-saved from disk.

Be sure to place the {ON ERROR} command before the point in the macro where the error condition may occur.

## {ON NOT FOUND}

*Syntax:*

{ON NOT FOUND}command~

Use the {ON NOT FOUND} command to tell the program what to do if a search pattern is not found. Normally, the program will stop if an unsuccessful search occurs, but you can use the {ON NOT FOUND} command to specify a different action.

The command that follows an {ON NOT FOUND} command can be any one of the following: {BREAK}, {CALL}, {GO}, {RESTART}, {RETURN}, {RETURN CANCEL}, {RETURN ERROR}, {RETURN NOT FOUND}, or {QUIT}.

For example,

{ON NOT FOUND}{GO}message~~

tells the program to go to the subroutine identified by the *message* label and execute the instructions it finds there.

Note that because each command requires a tilde, two tildes have been used. Also, be sure to place any {ON NOT FOUND} commands before the place where the not-found condition may occur.

When you want a particular set of instructions to be executed if a certain condition is met (other than a search failing), use the {IF} and {ELSE} commands instead.

### {ORIGINAL KEY}

*Syntax:*

{ORIGINAL KEY}

Use the {ORIGINAL KEY} command to return the original definition of the last key that was pressed, not any definition that you have assigned to that key by using the Keyboard Layout feature. This keystroke can be a key combination, such as Ctrl- End. Using {ORIGINAL KEY} can be useful in a macro that checks to see which key the user has pressed, no matter which keyboard definition is currently in use.

### *{PARA DOWN}, {PARA UP}

*Syntax:*

{Para Down}, {Para Up}

Use these commands to move the cursor to the beginning of the next paragraph ({Para Down}) or to the beginning of the current paragraph ({Para Up}). (If the cursor is already at the beginning of a paragraph, it moves to the beginning of the previous paragraph.) For example,

{Para Up} {Home} {Home} {Left}

positions the cursor at the beginning of the first line of the current paragraph.

### {PAUSE}

*Syntax:*

{PAUSE}

Use the {PAUSE} command to pause a macro so that it will wait for the user to provide a response. As soon as ↵ is pressed, the macro resumes.

The {PAUSE} command differs from the other interface commands because it does not store the user's input.

The {BELL} command can be used effectively before the {PAUSE} command to get the user's attention.

## *{PAUSE KEY}

*Syntax:*

{PAUSE KEY}*key* ~

The {PAUSE KEY} command allows you to specify the key used to continue a macro after it has been paused. It allows the user to press ↵ without resuming the macro. For example, the user may be required to enter a multiline entry such as an address. Normally, when the macro is paused, pressing ↵ will restart it instead of inserting a hard return into what the user is typing. For example:

{STATUS PROMPT} Press F1 when entry is complete. ~
{PAUSE KEY}{Cancel} ~

You will probably want to use the {STATUS PROMPT} commands to tell the user which key to press to resume the macro.

## {PROMPT}

*Syntax:*

{PROMPT}*message* ~

Use the {PROMPT} command to display messages on the status line. It is erased immediately unless you use a {WAIT} command to display the message long enough for the user to read it. You will also need to turn the display on if it is turned off. For example,

{DISPLAY ON}
{PROMPT}Now exiting from the Merge menu... ~
{WAIT}20 ~

presents the message "Now exiting from the Merge menu..." in boldface on the status line and pauses two seconds for the user to read it.

You can also have messages that are longer than one line. See Tables A.1 through A.3 for a summary of the control characters and codes that can be used with a message string.

For example,

    {PROMPT}{DEL TO EOP}{^N}{^P}Blinking prompt:~
    {WAIT}20~
    {DISPLAY OFF}

clears the screen and produces a blinking prompt in the upper-left corner for two seconds. Similarly,

    {PROMPT}{^P}{^C}{Del to EOL}Prompt:~
    {WAIT}30~
    {DISPLAY OFF}

produces a three-second prompt at the column 3, row 11 position. (To enter the ^K for row 11, as shown in Table A.3, you press Ctrl-V and then press Ctrl-K in the macro editor. The {Del to EOP} command results.) Finally,

    {PROMPT}{Home}{^V}Mnemonic-style prompt:~

uses whatever attribute you've specified on the Setup key for your letter menu choices and displays the message in the upper-left corner of the screen without clearing it. If your menu choices are displayed in bold, the prompt you create after the {^V} code will be bold; if they are underlined, the prompt will be underlined, and so forth. Prompts are displayed at the bottom of the screen unless you specify another location. The {DISPLAY OFF} command will clear the prompt from the screen.

## {QUIT}

***Syntax:***

    {QUIT}

Use the {QUIT} command to stop a macro. A common use for it is to terminate a macro when an {IF} command returns TRUE. It can also be used with the {ON ERROR} command to terminate a macro if an error condition occurs.

## {RESTART}

*Syntax:*

{RESTART}

Use the {RESTART} command to stop all macro execution at the end of a subroutine. For example, you might want to terminate the macro if an error condition occurs:

{ON ERROR}{RESTART}

If a nested macro contains the {RESTART} command, the nested macro will complete its execution but will not return to the main macro.

## {RETURN}

*Syntax:*

{RETURN}

Use the {RETURN} command to leave a macro or to exit from a subroutine. For example,

{CALL}subroutine~
{LABEL}subroutine~
{RETURN}

tells WordPerfect to execute the subroutine and then return to the line immediately following the {CALL} command.

## {RETURN CANCEL}

*Syntax:*

{RETURN CANCEL}

Use the {RETURN CANCEL} command to return from the subroutine that is currently executing and indicate a cancel condition to the macro, just as if the user had pressed the Cancel key.

## {RETURN ERROR}

*Syntax:*

{RETURN ERROR}

Use the {RETURN ERROR} command to indicate an error condition after a subroutine or macro has been executed.

## {RETURN NOT FOUND}

*Syntax:*

{RETURN NOT FOUND}

Use the {RETURN NOT FOUND} command to indicate a not-found condition to a macro. If you have used an {ON NOT FOUND} command in the same macro, its instructions will be carried out when the {RETURN NOT FOUND} command is encountered.

## *{SHELL MACRO}

*Syntax:*

{SHELL MACRO}*macroname*~

Use the {SHELL MACRO} command to start a Shell macro (version 2.1 or higher, used with the WordPerfect Office) from within WordPerfect. Shell macros are always chained, so control will not return to the master WordPerfect macro.

## {SPEED}

*Syntax:*

{SPEED}*100ths*~

Use the {SPEED} command to control the speed at which a macro executes. The speed you enter is in hundredths of a second. The macro will pause that length of time between steps in the macro.

For example,

{SPEED}100~

executes the macro's steps with a one second pause between each command. To resume normal speed, enter the command as

{SPEED}~

Using the {SPEED} command is a good way to debug macros because it allows you to see them as they execute. You can also use it with prompts to slow them down for the user to read.

## {STATE}

**Syntax:**

{STATE}&<code>

WordPerfect considers special screens such as List Files, Help, Thesaurus, Speller, and so forth, to be menus.

Use the {STATE} command to test for the current state of WordPerfect. Numeric codes are assigned to the different states that the program can be in (see Table A.5). More than one state can be active at any one time. If more than one state is active, the resulting state number is the sum of the individual states. For example, if a macro is marking a block in the Doc 2 window, the current state is 167; 3 (for Document 2), plus 4 (for the editing screen), plus 32 (for macro execution), plus 128 (for block active).

The {STATE} command can be used with the following commands: {ASSIGN}, {CASE}, {CASE CALL}, and {IF}. For example, if you want to have a macro carry out a set of commands only when a merge is active, you would enter the command as

{IF}{STATE}&64
   <commands>
{END IF}

*Table A.5:* States in WordPerfect.

| Number | State |
|---|---|
| 1,2,3 | Current document number |
| 4 | Main editing screen |
| 8 | Other editing screen (such as footnote or header editing screen) |
| 16 | Macro definition active |
| 32 | Macro execution (always active, because you can check state only from within a macro) |
| 64 | Merge execution active |
| 128 | Block on |
| 256 | Typeover on |
| 512 | Reveal Codes active |
| 1024 | Yes/No question active |
| 2048 | In a list |

The ampersand (&) indicates a logical AND to WordPerfect. For example, you can test to see whether the cursor is in the main editing screen; if it is not, the following macro will sound a beep and quit instead of branching to the next set of instructions.

```
{IF}{STATE}&4~
    {IF}{STATE}&8~
    {BELL}
    {QUIT}
    {END IF}
    {GO}subroutine~
{BELL}
{QUIT}
{END IF}
{LABEL}subroutine~
```

Here, the {IF}{STATE}&4~ commands test to see whether the cursor is in the main editing screen; if it is not (if you are in a menu, for example), the computer beeps and the macro quits. If you are in the main editing screen (if {IF}{STATE}&4~ is true), then the macro checks to see whether you are in a secondary editing screen, such as a header or footer editing screen. If {IF}{STATE}&4~ is true and {IF}{STATE}&8~ is false, the macro goes to the commands identified by the label *subroutine*.

## *{STATUS PROMPT}

**Syntax:**

{STATUS PROMPT}*message*~

Use the {STATUS PROMPT} command to display a message on the screen that does not disappear when the user starts typing, as messages displayed with the {PROMPT} command do. Messages displayed with the {STATUS PROMPT} command will only display when the status line normally displays.

## {STEP ON}, {STEP OFF}

**Syntax:**

{STEP ON}
{STEP OFF}

Use the {STEP ON} and {STEP OFF} commands to turn Step mode on and off. With Step mode on, the macro is executed one step at a time. As soon as you press ←┘, another step is executed, so you can see your macro executing step by step and spot where it may be going wrong. Comments in the macro are ignored.

When Step mode is on, WordPerfect displays information on the status line about the next step that will be executed. If the next step inserts a variable or starts an Alt macro, you will see 'VAR 1' and 'VAR 2' or 'Alt A,' 'Alt B,' and so forth. (The variable name will be shown if you are using a named variable in version 5.1.) If the next keystroke is a character, you will see the character itself. However, if the next step is either a WordPerfect command such as Shift-F8 (Format) or a macro command such as {ASSIGN}, either 'KEY CMD' or 'MACRO CMD' will appear on the status line, along with numbers that represent the different commands. For example, the message 'KEY CMD 51' represents the Format command (Shift-F8) and 'MACRO CMD 1' represents {ASSIGN}.

Tables A.6 and A.7 present the meanings of the codes that are displayed when Step mode is on.

*Table A.6:* KEY CMD Code Numbers.

| NUMBER | COMMAND |
|--------|---------|
| 1      | ^A      |
| 2      | ^B      |
| 3      | ^C      |
| 4      | ^D      |
| 5      | ^E      |
| 6      | ^F      |
| 7      | ^G      |
| 8      | ^H ({Home}) |
| 9      | ^I ({Tab}) |
| 10     | ^J ({Enter}) |
| 11     | ^K ({Del to EOL}) |
| 12     | ^L ({Del to EOP}) |
| 13     | ^M      |
| 14     | ^N      |
| 15     | ^O      |
| 16     | ^P      |
| 17     | ^Q      |
| 18     | ^R      |
| 19     | ^S      |

*Table A.6:* KEY CMD Code Numbers (continued).

| Number | Command |
|---|---|
| 20 | ^T |
| 21 | ^U |
| 22 | ^V |
| 23 | ^W ({Up}) |
| 24 | ^X ({Right}) |
| 25 | ^Y ({Left}) |
| 26 | ^Z ({Down}) |
| 27 | Esc |
| 28 | ^\ |
| 29 | ^] |
| 32 | F1 |
| 33 | F2 |
| 34 | F3 |
| 35 | F4 |
| 36 | F5 |
| 37 | F6 |
| 38 | F7 |
| 39 | F8 |
| 40 | F9 |
| 41 | F10 |
| 44 | Shift-F1 |
| 45 | Shift-F2 |
| 46 | Shift-F3 |

*Table A.6:* KEY CMD Code Numbers (continued).

| Number | Command |
|---|---|
| 47 | Shift-F4 |
| 48 | Shift-F5 |
| 49 | Shift-F6 |
| 50 | Shift-F7 |
| 51 | Shift-F8 |
| 52 | Shift-F9 |
| 53 | Shift-F10 |
| 56 | Alt-F1 |
| 57 | Alt-F2 |
| 58 | Alt-F3 |
| 59 | Alt-F4 |
| 60 | Alt-F5 |
| 61 | Alt-F6 |
| 62 | Alt-F7 |
| 63 | Alt-F8 |
| 64 | Alt-F9 |
| 65 | Alt-F10 |
| 68 | Ctrl-F1 |
| 69 | Ctrl-F2 |
| 70 | Ctrl-F3 |
| 71 | Ctrl-F4 |
| 72 | Ctrl-F5 |
| 73 | Ctrl-F6 |
| 74 | Ctrl-F7 |

*Table A.6:* KEY CMD Code Numbers (continued).

| Number | Command |
|---|---|
| 75 | Ctrl-F8 |
| 76 | Ctrl-F9 |
| 77 | Ctrl-F10 |
| 80 | Backspace |
| 81 | Del |
| 82 | Ctrl-Backspace |
| 83 | Ctrl-→ |
| 84 | Ctrl-← |
| 85 | End |
| 88 | Ctrl-Home |
| 89 | PgUp |
| 90 | PgDn |
| 91 | + (Gray) |
| 92 | − (Gray) |
| 93 | Ins |
| 94 | Shift-Tab |
| 95 | Ctrl-↵ |
| 96 | Ctrl-- (soft hyphen) |
| 97 | Home-- (hard hyphen) |
| 98 | Home Spacebar (hard space) |
| 99 | Para Up |
| 100 | Para Down |
| 101 | Item Left |

APP. A

*Table A.6:* KEY CMD Code Numbers (continued).

| Number | Command |
|---|---|
| 102 | Item Right |
| 103 | Item Up |
| 104 | Item Down |
| 105 | Alt-Home |
| 106 | Ctrl-Del (delete row) |
| 107 | Alt- = (menu bar) |
| 108 | Block Append |
| 109 | Block Move |
| 110 | Block Copy |

*Note:* Codes 1–29 may have different meanings, depending on whether they are being used in a message string. For example, code 10 may indicate an {Enter} command if it is not in a message string, or, if it is, a New Line command or a Redline attribute. Refer to Tables A.1 and A.2 for the interpretations of these control codes in message strings. Codes 98–110 are for version 5.1 only.

*Table A.7:* MACRO CMD Code Numbers.

| Number | Macro Command |
|---|---|
| 1 | {ASSIGN} |
| 2 | {BELL} |
| 3 | {BREAK} |

*Table A.7:* MACRO CMD Code Numbers (continued).

| Number | Macro Command |
|---|---|
| 4 | {CALL} |
| 5 | {CANCEL OFF} |
| 6 | {CANCEL ON} |
| 7 | {CASE} |
| 8 | {CASE CALL} |
| 9 | {CHAIN} |
| 10 | {CHAR} |
| 11 | {;} |
| 12 | {DISPLAY OFF} |
| 13 | {DISPLAY ON} |
| 14 | {ELSE} |
| 15 | {END FOR} |
| 16 | {END IF} |
| 17 | {END WHILE} |
| 18 | {FOR} |
| 19 | {FOR EACH} |
| 20 | {GO} |
| 21 | {IF} |
| 22 | {LABEL} |
| 23 | {LOOK} |
| 24 | {NEST} |
| 25 | {NEXT} |
| 26 | {SHELL MACRO} |
| 27 | {ON CANCEL} |
| 28 | {ON ERROR} |
| 29 | {ON NOT FOUND} |

*Table A.7:* MACRO CMD Code Numbers (continued).

| Number | Macro Command |
|---|---|
| 30 | {PAUSE} |
| 31 | {PROMPT} |
| 32 | {QUIT} |
| 33 | {RESTART} |
| 34 | {RETURN} |
| 35 | {RETURN CANCEL} |
| 36 | {RETURN ERROR} |
| 37 | {RETURN NOT FOUND} |
| 38 | {SPEED} |
| 39 | {STEP ON} |
| 40 | {TEXT} |
| 41 | {STATE} |
| 42 | {WAIT} |
| 43 | {WHILE} |
| 44 | {Macro Commands} |
| 45 | {STEP OFF} |
| 46 | {ORIGINAL KEY} |
| 47 | {IF EXISTS} |
| 48 | {MENU OFF} |
| 49 | {MENU ON} |
| 50 | {STATUS PROMPT} |
| 51 | {INPUT} |
| 52 | {VARIABLE} |
| 53 | {SYSTEM} |
| 54 | {MID} |
| 55 | {NTOK} |

*Table A.7:* MACRO CMD Code Numbers (continued).

| NUMBER | MACRO COMMAND |
|--------|---------------|
| 56     | {KTON}        |
| 57     | {LEN}         |
| 58     | {~}           |
| 59     | {PAUSE KEY}   |

*Note:* Codes 48–59 are for version 5.1 only.

## *{SYSTEM}

**Syntax:**

{SYSTEM}*variable* ~

Use the {SYSTEM} command to determine the state the program is currently in. If you write macros for others to use, this is a way to make them less prone to error conditions, because you can check to see whether the user is in a state that does not operate the same way as the editing screen.

## {TEXT}

**Syntax:**

{TEXT}*variable* ~ *message* ~

Use the {TEXT} command to prompt the user with a message. When the user responds to the message, the response (up to 129 characters) is stored in the specified variable. For example,

{TEXT}8 ~ Enter street address: ~

assigns the street address that the user types to variable 8.

The {TEXT} command is similar to the {CHAR} command, which allows for one-character responses. Use the {TEXT} command whenever a response must be more than one character.

See Tables A.1 through A.3 for a summary of the control characters and codes that can be used with a message string.

## *{VARIABLE}

**Syntax:**

{VARIABLE}*variable* ~

Use the {VARIABLE} command to examine the text of a variable. With the {IF} and {CASE} commands, you can instruct the program to carry out an action, depending on what the variable contains. For example:

{IF}"{VARIABLE}State~"="CA"~
   {GO}mail~
   {END IF}

If the content of the State variable is CA, the macro will go to the section identified by the label *mail*.

## {WAIT}

**Syntax:**

{WAIT}10ths~

Use the {WAIT} command to pause a macro for a certain number of tenths of a second so that messages and prompts can be read. For example,

{WAIT}10~

pauses the macro for one second.

## *{WHILE}, {END WHILE}

**Syntax:**

{WHILE}*expression*

.
.
.

{END WHILE}

Use the {WHILE} and {END WHILE} commands to test to see whether a condition is true, and, if so, to carry out the steps listed between the {WHILE} and {END WHILE} commands. If the condition is initially false, the macro will execute the first command following the {END WHILE} command.

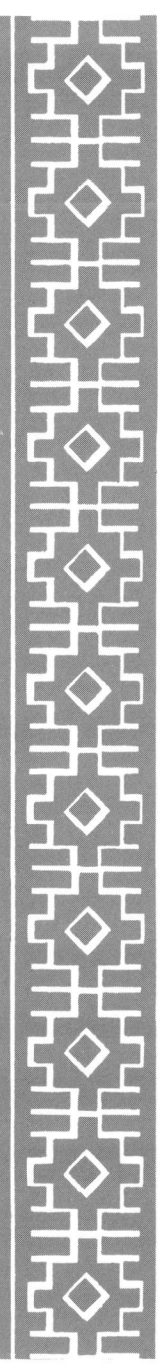

*WordPerfect's Reveal Codes*

APPENDIX

# B

# APPENDIX B

| Code | Meaning |
|---|---|
| ! | Formula Calculation |
| + | Calculate Subtotal |
| * | Calculate Grand Total |
| = | Calculate Total |
| _ | Cursor Position |
| - | Soft Hyphen |
| [ ] | Hard Space |
| [/] | Cancel Hyphenation |
| [-] | Hyphen |
| [Adv] | Advance |
| [AdvDn] | Advance Down |
| [AdvLft] | Advance Left |
| [AdvRgt] | Advance Right |
| [AdvToLn] | Advance to Line |
| [AdvToPos] | Advance to (Column) Position |
| [AdvUp] | Advance Up |
| [Align]* | Tab Align |
| [Bline] | Baseline Placement |
| [Block] | Beginning of Block |
| [Block Pro] | Block Protection |
| [BOLD] | Bold On |
| [bold] | Bold Off |

(* = Version 5.0 Code)

| CODE | MEANING |
|---|---|
| [Box Num] | Caption in Graphics Box (inserted inside of Box code) |
| [Brdr Opt]* | Border Options |
| [C/A/Flrt] | End of Tab Align or Flush Right |
| [Cell] | Table Cell |
| [Center] | Center |
| [Center Pg] | Center Page Top to Bottom |
| [Cndl EOP] | Conditional End of Page |
| [Cntr]* | Center |
| [Cntr Tab] | Centered Tab |
| [Col Def] | Column Definition |
| [Col Off] | End of Text Columns |
| [Col On] | Beginning of Text Columns |
| [Color] | Print Color |
| [Comment] | Document Comment |
| [Date] | Date/Time Function |
| [DBL UND] | Double Underline On |
| [dbl und] | Double Underline Off |
| [Dec Tab] | Decimal Tab |
| [DEC TAB] | Hard Decimal Tab |
| [Decml Algn Char] | Decimal Character or Thousands Separator |

(* = Version 5.0 Code)

APP. B

| Code | Meaning |
|---|---|
| [Def Mark:Index] | Index Definition |
| [Def Mark:List] | List Definition |
| [Def Mark:ToA] | Table of Authorities Definition |
| [Def Mark:ToC] | Table of Contents Definition |
| [Dorm HRt] | Dormant Hard Return |
| [DSRt] | Deletable Soft Return |
| [End Opt] | Endnote Options |
| [EndDef] | End of Index, List, or Table of Contents |
| [EndMark] | End of Marked Text |
| [Endnote] | Endnote |
| [Endnote Placement] | Endnote Placement |
| [Equ Box] | Equation Box |
| [Equ Opt] | Equation Box Options |
| [EXT LARGE] | Extra Large Print On |
| [ext large] | Extra Large Print Off |
| [Fig Box] | Figure Box |
| [Fig Opt] | Figure Box Options |
| [Figure]* | Figure Box |
| [FINE] | Fine Print On |
| [fine] | Fine Print Off |
| [Flsh Rgt] | Flush Right |

(* = Version 5.0 Code)

| Code | Meaning |
|---|---|
| [Flsh Rt]* | Flush Right |
| [Font] | Base Font |
| [Footer] | Footer |
| [Footnote] | Footnote |
| [Force] | Force Odd/Even Page |
| [Form]* | Form (Printer Selection) |
| [Form Typ]* | Form Type |
| [Ftn Opt] | Footnote/Endnote Options |
| [Full Form] | Table of Authorities, Full Form |
| [Header] | Header |
| [HLine] | Horizontal Line |
| [HPg] | Hard Page Break |
| [Hrd Row] | Hard Row |
| [HRt] | Hard Return |
| [HRt-SPg] | Hard Return – Soft Page |
| [Hyph Off] | Hyphenation Off |
| [Hyph On] | Hyphenation On |
| [HZone] | Hyphenation Zone |
| [→Indent] | Indent |
| [→Indent←] | Left/Right Indent |
| [Index] | Index Entry |
| [Insert Pg Num] | Insert Page Number |

(* = Version 5.0 Code)

| Code | Meaning |
|---|---|
| [ISRt] | Invisible Soft Return |
| [ITALC] | Italics On |
| [italc] | Italics Off |
| [Just] | Justification |
| [Just:Center] | Center Justification |
| [Just:Full] | Full Justification |
| [Just:Left] | Left Justification |
| [Just Lim] | Word/Letter Spacing Justification Limits |
| [Just Off]* | Left-Justified/Ragged-Right |
| [Just On]* | Right Justification |
| [Just:Right] | Right Justification |
| [Kern:Off] | Kerning Off |
| [Kern:On] | Kerning On |
| [Lang] | Language |
| [LARGE] | Large Print On |
| [large] | Large Print Off |
| [Leading Adj] | Leading Adjustment |
| [Line Height]* | Leading |
| [Link] | Spreadsheet Link |
| [Link End] | Spreadsheet Link End |
| [Ln Height] | Line Height |

(* = Version 5.0 Code)

# WORDPERFECT'S REVEAL CODES

| CODE | MEANING |
|---|---|
| [Ln Num] | Line Numbering |
| [Ln Spacing] | Line Spacing |
| [L/R Mar] | Left and Right Margins |
| [←Mar Rel] | Left Margin Release |
| [Mark:List] | List Entry |
| [Mark:ToA} | Table of Authorities Entry |
| [Mark:ToC] | Table of Contents Entry |
| [Math Def] | Definition of Math Columns |
| [Math Off] | End of Math |
| [Math On] | Beginning of Math |
| [N] | Negate |
| [New End Num] | New Endnote Number |
| [New Equ Num] | New Equation Box Number |
| [New Fig Num] | New Figure Box Number |
| [New Ftn Num] | New Footnote Number |
| [New Tab Num]* | New Table Box Number |
| [New Tbl Num] | New Table Box Number |
| [New Txt Num] | New Text Box Number |
| [New Usr Num] | New User-Defined Box Number |
| [Note Num] | Footnote/Endnote Reference (inserted inside of Footnote or Endnote code) |
| [Outline Lvl] | Outline Style |

(* = Version 5.0 Code)

| Code | Meaning |
|---|---|
| [Outline Off] | Outline Off |
| [Outline On] | Outline On |
| [OUTLN] | Outline Attribute On |
| [Outln] | Outline Attribute Off |
| [Ovrstk] | Overstrike Preceding Character |
| [Paper Sz/Typ] | Paper Size and Type |
| [Par Num] | Paragraph Number |
| [Par Num:Auto] | Paragraph Numbering and Outlining On |
| [Par Num Def] | Paragraph Numbering Definition |
| [Pg Num] | New Page Number |
| [Pg Num Style] | Page Number Style |
| [Pg Numbering] | Page Number Position |
| [Ptr Cmnd] | Printer Command |
| [REDLN] | Redline On |
| [redln] | Redline Off |
| [Ref] | Reference (Automatic Reference) |
| [RGT TAB] | Hard Right-Aligned Tab |
| [Rgt Tab] | Right-Aligned Tab |
| [Row] | Table Row |
| [SHADW] | Shadow On |
| [shadw] | Shadow Off |
| [Sm Cap] | Small Caps |
| [SM CAP]* | Small Caps |
| [SMALL] | Small Print On |

(* = Version 5.0 Code)

| CODE | MEANING |
| --- | --- |
| [small] | Small Print Off |
| [SPg] | Soft Page Break |
| [SRt] | Soft Return |
| [STKOUT] | Strikeout On |
| [stkout] | Strikeout Off |
| [Style Off] | Style Off |
| [Style On] | Style On |
| [Subdoc] | Subdocument (Master Documents) |
| [Subdoc End] | End of Subdocument |
| [Subdoc Start] | Beginning of Subdocument |
| [SUBSCRPT] | Subscript On |
| [subscrpt] | Subscript Off |
| [Suppress] | Suppress Page Format |
| [Suprscript] | Superscript |
| [SUPRSCRPT]* | Superscript |
| [T] | Total Entry |
| [t] | Subtotal Entry |
| [TAB] | Hard Left-Aligned Tab |
| [Tab] | Tab |
| [Tab Set] | Tab Set |
| [Table]* | Table Box |
| [Target( )] | Target (Auto Reference) |
| [T/B Mar] | Top and Bottom Margins |
| [Tbl Box] | Table Box |
| [Tbl Def] | Table Definition |
| [Tbl Off] | Table Off |
| [Tbl On] | Table On |
| [Tbl Opt] | Table Box Options |

(* = Version 5.0 Code)

| Code | Meaning |
| --- | --- |
| [Text Box] | Text Box |
| [ToA] | Table of Authorities Entry |
| [Txt Opt] | Text Box Options |
| [UND] | Underline On |
| [und] | Underline Off |
| [Usr Box] | User Box |
| [Usr Opt] | User Box Options |
| [VLine] | Vertical Line |
| [VRY LARGE] | Very Large Print On |
| [Vry Large] | Very Large Print Off |
| [W/O Off] | Widow/Orphan Off |
| [W/O On] | Widow/Orphan On |
| [Wrd/Ltr Spacing] | Word and Letter Spacing |

(* = Version 5.0 Code)

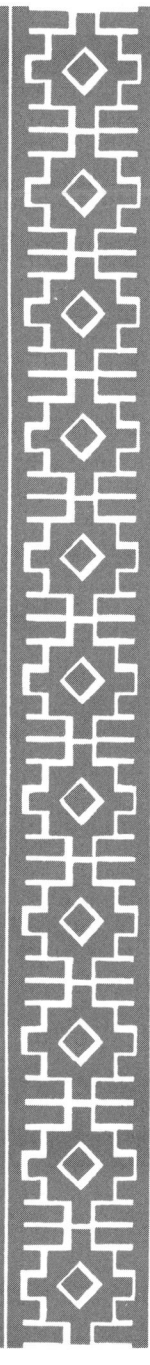

# *Converting Earlier Macros to WordPerfect 5.0 and 5.1*

APPENDIX

C

# APPENDIX C

If you have used earlier versions of WordPerfect, you may already have created macros that you would like to use with WordPerfect 5 (either 5.0 or 5.1). A macro conversion program provided on the Conversion disk called MACROCNV.EXE will convert 4.2 macros (with the extension .MAC) to version 5 format (.WPM). You will need DOS 2.0 or higher to run it.

However, not all parts of all macros can be converted successfully, since certain functions—in particular those that deal with font and pitch changes and printer numbers—operate differently in Word-Perfect 5. The macro conversion program will convert all of the macro that it can to the new format, and will then inform you of the parts that you will need to change by using the macro editor.

To run the macro conversion utility, type

   macrocnv *macroname*

at the DOS prompt. In place of *macroname*, type the name of the WordPerfect macro you want to convert.

You can convert several macros at once by using wildcard characters. For example, if you have a set of macros named S1.MAC, S10.MAC, and S300.MAC, you can convert them all at the same time by entering

   macrocnv s*.mac

Entering macrocnv *.mac will convert all the 4.2 macros in the current directory to their equivalents in WordPerfect 5. You don't have to enter the .MAC extension unless you're using wildcards to convert a group of macros.

Be sure to give the complete path name of the directory where your 4.2 macros are stored. For example, if a 4.2 macro named **Alt-P** that you want to convert is stored in a directory named C:\WP, you would change to the directory holding the MACROCNV utility and then enter the conversion command as

macrocnv c:\wp\altp

The utility will convert the 4.2 macro to the new format, automatically giving it the .WPM extension. After the macro is converted, a status report will show you the number of characters and functions processed (Figure C.1) and indicate how many of them will need a hand fix-up.

```
Version 1.5
Usage: C:\WP51\MACROCNV.EXE Macro-filename (/h,/o,/p)
Or, for Help: C:\WP51\MACROCNV.EXE /h

C:\WP51>macrocnv c:\5\head.mac

WP 4.2 to WP 5.0 Macro Conversion Utility.
Copyright (C) 1988 WordPerfect Corp., All Rights Reserved.
Version 1.5

Warning! File c:\5\head.wpm exists.
Ok to overwrite it? (Y/N) Yes

Done.  Conversion statistics for: c:\5\head.mac
          Number of characters processed: 7.
          Number of ctrl characters processed: 2.
          Number of functions processed: 5.

          This macro will not work properly without major modifications
          to 2 function(s) which require extensive hand fix-up.
          In the output macro these functions have been appended with the
          comment:{;}       BAD!      ~.

C:\WP51>
```

*Figure C.1:* When you convert 4.2 macros to version 5 format, you will receive a message that you must edit the macro manually if there are features that can't be directly converted.

If the macro you're converting is larger than 5K, the conversion utility will break it into macros that are named **macro1.wpm**, **macro2.wpm**, and so forth, and chain them.

If there are features in the macro that you are trying to convert that have no equivalents in WordPerfect 5, such as pitch changes or sheet-feeder bin numbers, you can return to WordPerfect 5.0 or 5.1 (by typing **exit** if you've exited to DOS temporarily) and retrieve the macro for editing. You can then delete the commands that are marked with a 'BAD!' comment (see Figure C.1) and insert the correct version 5 commands.

For example, Figure C.2 illustrates a **head** macro that changed fonts. The comment lines (beginning at ~ {;}) show the parts of the macro that could not be converted directly and indicate the keystrokes that must be edited to their version 5 equivalents.

```
Macro: Action
    File           HEAD.WPM
    Description    WP 4.2 Converted Macro:head.mac

    {DISPLAY OFF}{;}{;}<Chng-Font>~{;}  Bad!  ~108{Enter}
    {Exit}{End}{;}{;}<Chng-Font>~{;} Bad!   ~14*1{Enter}
    {Exit}




Ctrl-PgUp for macro commands;  Press Exit when done
```

*Figure C.2:* When you retrieve a converted macro into the macro editor, comment lines indicate the portions of the macro that you will need to edit to the appropriate version 5 commands.

Although you can convert some 4.2 macros without further editing, especially those that simply create boilerplate text, you will find that macros dealing with printing functions in 4.2 will require the type of manual editing specified in Figure C.2.

To get additional help on the use of the MACROCNV utility, enter its startup command as

   macrocnv.exe/h

at the DOS prompt.

# *WordPerfect Character Sets*

APPENDIX

# D

# APPENDIX D

### Character Set 0

|     | 0 | 1 | 2 | 3 | 4 | 5 | 6 | 7 | 8 | 9 | 0 | 1 | 2 | 3 | 4 | 5 | 6 | 7 | 8 | 9 |
|-----|---|---|---|---|---|---|---|---|---|---|---|---|---|---|---|---|---|---|---|---|
| 0   |   |   |   |   |   |   |   |   |   |   |   |   |   |   |   |   |   |   |   |   |
| 20  |   |   |   |   |   |   |   |   |   |   |   | ! | " | # | $ | % | & | ' |   |   |
| 40  | ( | ) | * | + | , | - | . | / | 0 | 1 | 2 | 3 | 4 | 5 | 6 | 7 | 8 | 9 | : | ; |
| 60  | < | = | > | ? | @ | A | B | C | D | E | F | G | H | I | J | K | L | M | N | O |
| 80  | P | Q | R | S | T | U | V | W | X | Y | Z | [ | \ | ] | ^ | _ | ` | a | b | c |
| 100 | d | e | f | g | h | i | j | k | l | m | n | o | p | q | r | s | t | u | v | w |
| 120 | x | y | z | { | \| | } | ~ |   |   |   |   |   |   |   |   |   |   |   |   |   |

### Character Set 1

|     | 0 | 1 | 2 | 3 | 4 | 5 | 6 | 7 | 8 | 9 | 0 | 1 | 2 | 3 | 4 | 5 | 6 | 7 | 8 | 9 |
|-----|---|---|---|---|---|---|---|---|---|---|---|---|---|---|---|---|---|---|---|---|
| 0   | ` | ˙ | ˜ | ˆ | ¯ | ´ | ˝ | ¨ | ¸ | ˛ | ʼ | ʻ |   | , | ˚ | . | ˝ |   | ˙ | ˋ |
| 20  | ˊ | ˉ | ˇ | ß | ı | ȷ | Á | á | Â | â | Ä | ä | À | à | Å | å | Æ | æ | Ç | ç |
| 40  | É | é | Ê | ê | Ë | ë | È | è | Í | í | Î | î | Ï | ï | Ì | ì | Ñ | ñ | Ó | ó |
| 60  | Ô | ô | Ö | ö | Ò | ò | Ú | ú | Û | û | Ü | ü | Ù | ù | Ÿ | ÿ | Ã | ã | Đ | đ |
| 80  | Ø | ø | Õ | õ | Ý | ý | Ð | ð | Þ | þ | Ă | ă | Ā | ā | Ą | ą | Ć | ć | Č | č |
| 100 | Ĉ | ĉ | Ċ | ċ | Ď | ď | Ĕ | ĕ | Ė | ė | Ē | ē | Ę | ę | Ğ | ğ | Ĝ | ĝ | Ǧ | ǧ |
| 120 | Ģ | ģ | Ĝ | ĝ | Ġ | ġ | Ĥ | ĥ | Ħ | ħ | Í | í | Ī | ī | Į | į | Ĭ | ĭ | Ĳ | ĳ |
| 140 | Ĵ | ĵ | Ķ | ķ | Ĺ | ĺ | Ľ | ľ | Ļ | ļ | Ŀ | ŀ | Ł | ł | Ń | ń | Ň | ň | Ñ | ň |
| 160 | Ņ | ņ | Ő | ő | Ō | ō | Œ | œ | Ŕ | ŕ | Ř | ř | Ŗ | ŗ | Ś | ś | Š | š | Ş | ş |
| 180 | Ŝ | ŝ | Ť | ť | Ţ | ţ | Ŧ | ŧ | Ŭ | ŭ | Ű | ű | Ū | ū | Ų | ų | Ů | ů | Ũ | ũ |
| 200 | Ŵ | ŵ | Ŷ | ŷ | Ź | ź | Ž | ž | Ż | ż | Ŋ | ŋ | Ð | đ | Ĺ | ĺ | Ñ | ñ | Ŕ | ŕ |
| 220 | Ś | ś | Ŧ | ŧ | Ў | ў | Ỳ | ỳ | D' | d' | O' | o' | U' | u' |   |   |   |   |   |   |

# WORDPERFECT CHARACTER SETS 509

## Character Set 2

|    | 0 | 1 | 2 | 3 | 4 | 5 | 6 | 7 | 8 | 9 | 10 | 11 | 12 | 13 | 14 | 15 | 16 | 17 | 18 | 19 |
|----|---|---|---|---|---|---|---|---|---|---|----|----|----|----|----|----|----|----|----|----|
| 0  | · | ·· | ° | ∘ | ’ | ˆ | = | − | ˇ | ˘ | ·  | ·  |    |    | ˛  | ˜  | ·  | ˷  | ’  | ’  |
| 20 | , | ˛ | ’ | ‘ | ˇ | ˘ | ´ | ˝ |   |   |    |    |    |    |    |    |    |    |    |    |

## Character Set 3

|    | 0 | 1 | 2 | 3 | 4 | 5 | 6 | 7 | 8 | 9 | 10 | 11 | 12 | 13 | 14 | 15 | 16 | 17 | 18 | 19 |
|----|---|---|---|---|---|---|---|---|---|---|----|----|----|----|----|----|----|----|----|----|
| 0  | ░ | ▒ | ▓ | █ | ▌ | ▄ | ▐ | ▀ | ─ | │ | ┌  | ┐  | ┘  | └  | ├  | ┬  | ┤  | ┴  | ┼  | =  |
| 20 | ║ | ╔ | ╗ | ╝ | ╚ | ╠ | ╦ | ╣ | ╩ | ╬ | ╒  | ╕  | ╛  | ╘  | ╞  | ╤  | ╗  | ╝  | ╚  | ╧  |
| 40 | ╡ | ╨ | ╟ | ╤ | ╢ | ╧ | ╫ | ╪ | - | ' | -  | ,  | =  | ‖  | =  | ‖  | ⊏  | ⊐  | ⊩  | Ұ  |
| 60 | ┝ | ┠ | ┞ | ┯ | ┰ | ┱ | ┲ | ┪ | ┩ | ┥ | ┷  | ┸  | ┹  | ╀  | ╁  | ╂  |    |    |    |    |
| 80 | ╈ | ╉ | ╇ | ╇ | ╅ | ╆ | ╄ | ╃ |   |   |    |    |    |    |    |    |    |    |    |    |

## Character Set 4

|    | 0 | 1 | 2 | 3 | 4 | 5 | 6 | 7 | 8 | 9 | 10 | 11 | 12 | 13 | 14 | 15 | 16 | 17 | 18 | 19 |
|----|---|---|---|---|---|---|---|---|---|---|----|----|----|----|----|----|----|----|----|----|
| 0  | • | ○ | ■ | · | ★ | ¶ | § | ¡ | ¿ | « | »  | £  | ¥  | ₧  | ƒ  | ª  | º  | ½  | ¼  | ¢  |
| 20 | ² | ⁿ | ® | © | ¤ | ¾ | ³ | ‘ | ’ | ‟ | "  | "  | –  | —  | ‹  | ›  | ○  | □  | †  |    |
| 40 | ‡ | ™ | ℠ | ₨ | ● | ○ | ■ | ▪ | □ | ▫ | –  | ff | ffi| ffl| fi | fl | …  | $  | ₣  | ₲  |
| 60 | ₠ | £ | , | „ | ⅓ | ⅔ | ⅛ | ⅜ | ⅝ | ⅞ | ☻  | ☺  | %  | ‰  | ‱  | №  | –  | ¹  |    |    |

## Character Set 5

|    | 0 | 1 | 2 | 3 | 4 | 5 | 6 | 7 | 8 | 9 | 10 | 11 | 12 | 13 | 14 | 15 | 16 | 17 | 18 | 19 |
|----|---|---|---|---|---|---|---|---|---|---|----|----|----|----|----|----|----|----|----|----|
| 0  | ♥ | ♦ | ♣ | ♠ | ♂ | ♀ | ☼ | ☻ | ● | ♪ | ♫  | ▬  | △  | ‼  | √  | ‡  | ⌐  | ⌐  | ◘  | ■  |
| 20 | ↵ |   |   | ✓ | □ | ⊠ | ⊗ | ♯ | ♭ | ♮ | ☎  | ⌚ | ✗  | ¢  | ⌴  |    |    |    |    |    |

## Character Set 6

|     | 0 | 1 | 2 | 3 | 4 | 5 | 6 | 7 | 8 | 9 | 10 | 11 | 12 | 13 | 14 | 15 | 16 | 17 | 18 | 19 |
|-----|---|---|---|---|---|---|---|---|---|---|----|----|----|----|----|----|----|----|----|----|
| 0   | − | ± | ≤ | ≥ | ∝ | / | / | \ | ÷ | \| | ⟨ | ⟩ | ~ | ≈ | ≡ | ∈ | ∩ | ‖ | Σ | ∞ |
| 20  | ¬ | → | ← | ↑ | ↓ | ↔ | ↕ | ▶ | ◀ | ▲ | ▼ | · | · | ∘ | • | Å | ° | μ | − | × |
| 40  | ∫ | ∏ | ∓ | ∇ | ∂ | ′ | ″ | → | ε | ℓ | ℏ | ℑ | ℜ | ℘ | ≠ | ≄ | ⇒ | ⇐ | ⇑ | ⇓ |
| 60  | ⇔ | ↕ | ↗ | ↘ | ↙ | ↖ | ∪ | ⊂ | ⊆ | ⊃ | ⊇ | ∋ | ∅ | ⌐ | ⌐ | ⌐ | ⌐ | ◀ | ▶ | ∠ |
| 80  | ⊗ | ⊕ | ⊖ | ⊙ | ∧ | ∨ | ⋁ | ⊤ | ⊥ | ⊢ | ⊣ | □ | ■ | ◇ | ◆ | [ | ] | ≠ |   |   |
| 100 | ≢ | ∵ | ∴ | ∷ | ∮ | ℒ | ℭ | ℨ | ℘ | ○ | △ | ◇ | ★ | ‴ | ∐ | ≃ | ≣ | ≺ | ≼ | ≻ |
| 120 | ≽ | ∃ | ∀ | ◄ | ► | ⊎ | ⊆ | ⊇ | ⊓ | ⊔ | ⊏ | ⊐ | ⊑ | ⊒ | ⊿ | ▽ | ◁ | ▷ |   |   |
| 140 | ⋈ | ⌣ | ⌢ | ◯ | → | ↤ | ↦ | ↼ | ↽ | ⇀ | ⇁ | ↰ | ↱ | ↿ | ↾ | ⇂ | ⇃ | ⇄ | ⇌ |   |
| 160 | ⌣ | ⌢ | ⊂ | ⊃ | ⊙ | ⊛ | ⊖ | Ʋ | ⋏ | ⋖ | ⋗ | △ | ▽ | + | + | ⋍ | ≠ | ○ | × |   |
| 180 | ⊨ | △ | ∤ | ⎱ | ★ | ✦ | ✧ | ✶ | ✴ | ✵ | ✦ | ✧ | ✩ | ✫ | ✬ | ✭ | ✮ | ∉ | ⊅ | ∢ |
| 200 | ⇸ | ⇷ | ⇶ | ⇵ | ✗ | ✘ | ∗ | ∄ | ∉ | ✧ | ℰ | ℱ | ℂ | 𝕀 | ℕ | ℝ | ² | ⌐ | ∃ |   |
| 220 | ⋯ | … | ⋮ | ⋰ | ⌐ |   | + | − | = | ∗ | / | // | // | ℋ | ℘ |   |   |   |   |   |

## WORDPERFECT CHARACTER SETS   511

*Character Set 7*

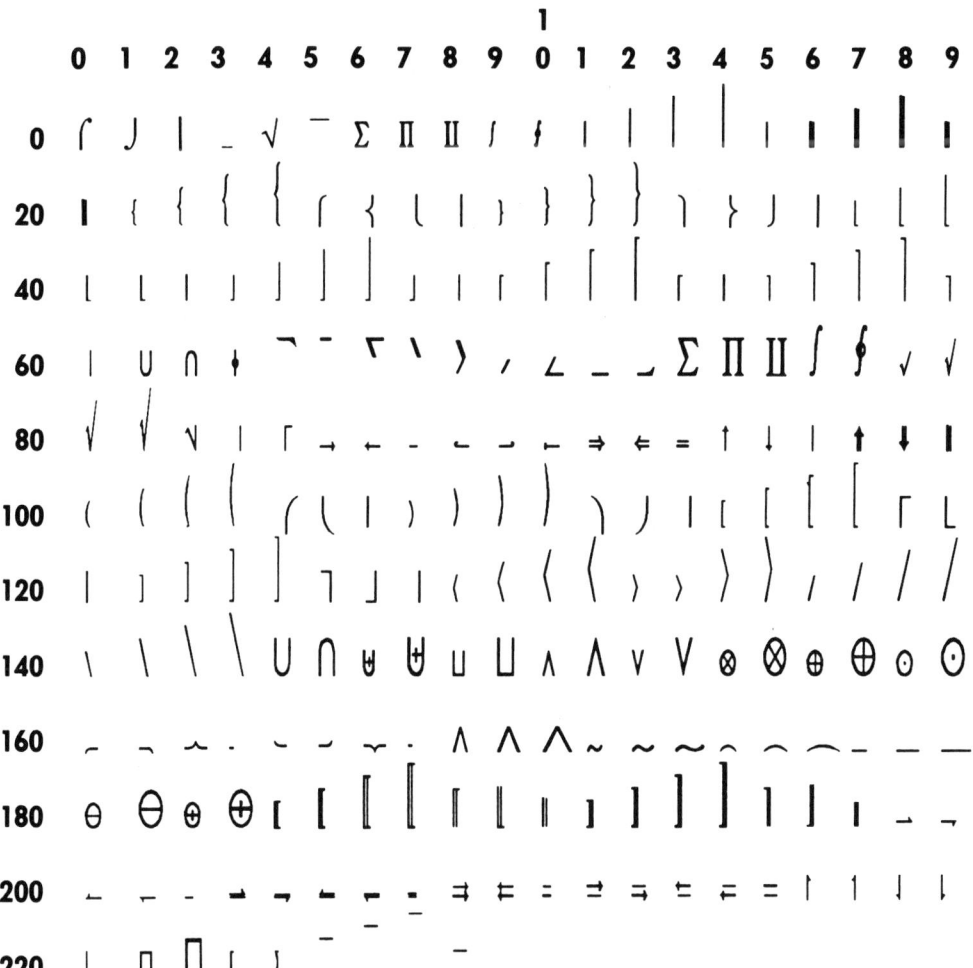

## Character Set 8

|     | 0 | 1 | 2 | 3 | 4 | 5 | 6 | 7 | 8 | 9 | 10 | 11 | 12 | 13 | 14 | 15 | 16 | 17 | 18 | 19 |
|-----|---|---|---|---|---|---|---|---|---|---|----|----|----|----|----|----|----|----|----|----|
| 0   | Α | α | Β | β | Β | б | Γ | γ | Δ | δ | Ε  | ε  | Ζ  | ζ  | Η  | η  | Θ  | θ  | Ι  | ι  |
| 20  | Κ | κ | Λ | λ | Μ | μ | Ν | ν | Ξ | ξ | Ο  | ο  | Π  | π  | Ρ  | ρ  | Σ  | σ  | Σ  | ς  |
| 40  | Τ | τ | Υ | υ | Φ | φ | Χ | χ | Ψ | ψ | Ω  | ω  | α  | έ  | η  | ί  | ι  | ύ  | υ  | ύ  |
| 60  | ώ | ε | ϑ | ϰ | ϛ | ϱ | ϒ | φ | ϖ | ; | ·  | ´  | ¨  | `  | ´  | ˆ  | ˜  | ¯  | ˘  | ˙  |
| 80  | ̔ | ̓ | ̑ | ̕ | ̣ | · | · | · | · | · | ·  | ·  | ·  | ·  | ·  | ·  | ·  | ·  | ά  | ά  |
| 100 | ά | ά | ά | ά | ά | ά | ά | ά | ά | ά | ά  | ά  | ά  | ά  | ά  | ά  | έ  | έ  | έ  | έ  |
| 120 | έ | έ | έ | ή | ή | ή | ή | ή | ή | ή | ή  | ή  | ή  | ή  | ή  | ή  | ή  | ή  | ή  | ή  |
| 140 | ή | ή | ή | ί | ί | ί | ί | ί | ί | ί | ί  | ί  | ί  | ί  | ί  | ί  | ό  | ό  | ό  | ό  |
| 160 | ό | ό | ύ | ύ | ύ | ύ | ύ | ύ | ύ | ύ | ύ  | ύ  | ύ  | ύ  | ύ  | ύ  | ώ  | ώ  | ώ  | ώ  |
| 180 | ώ | ώ | ώ | ώ | ώ | ώ | ώ | ώ | ώ | ώ | ώ  | ώ  | ϕ  | '  | ǀ  | ǀ  | ǀ  | ǀ  | ǀ  | ǀ  |
| 200 | Α | Ε | Η | Ι | Ο | Υ | Ω |   |   |   |    |    |    |    |    |    |    |    |    |    |

## Character Set 9

|    | 0 | 1 | 2 | 3 | 4 | 5 | 6 | 7 | 8 | 9 | 10 | 11 | 12 | 13 | 14 | 15 | 16 | 17 | 18 | 19 |
|----|---|---|---|---|---|---|---|---|---|---|----|----|----|----|----|----|----|----|----|----|
| 0  | א | ב | ג | ד | ה | ו | ז | ח | ט | י | ך  | כ  | ל  | ם  | מ  | ן  | נ  | ס  | ע  | ף  |
| 20 | פ | ץ | צ | ק | ר | ש | ת | ב | כ | פ |    |    |    |    |    |    |    |    |    |    |
| 20 |   |   |   |   |   |   |   |   |   |   | ׃  | ׃  | ׃  | ׃  | ָ  | ַ  | ֶ  | ֵ  | ִ  | ֹ  |
| 40 | ֻ |   | ֽ |   |   | ׳ |   |   |   |   |    |    |    |    |    |    |    |    |    |    |

# WORDPERFECT CHARACTER SETS 513

**Character Set 10**

|     | 0 | 1 | 2 | 3 | 4 | 5 | 6 | 7 | 8 | 9 | 10 | 11 | 12 | 13 | 14 | 15 | 16 | 17 | 18 | 19 |
|-----|---|---|---|---|---|---|---|---|---|---|----|----|----|----|----|----|----|----|----|----|
| 0   | А | а | Б | б | В | в | Г | г | Д | д | Е  | е  | Ё  | ё  | Ж  | ж  | З  | з  | И  | и  |
| 20  | Й | й | К | к | Л | л | М | м | Н | н | О  | о  | П  | п  | Р  | р  | С  | с  | Т  | т  |
| 40  | У | у | Ф | ф | Х | х | Ц | ц | Ч | ч | Ш  | ш  | Щ  | щ  | Ъ  | ъ  | Ы  | ы  | Ь  | ь  |
| 60  | Э | э | Ю | ю | Я | я | Ґ | ґ | Ђ | ђ | Ѓ  | ѓ  | Є  | є  | Ѕ  | ѕ  | І  | і  | Ї  | ї  |
| 80  | Ј | ј | Љ | љ | Њ | њ | Ћ | ћ | Ќ | ќ | Ў  | ў  | Џ  | џ  | Ѣ  | ѣ  | Ѳ  | ѳ  | Ѵ  | ѵ  |
| 100 | Ҳ | ҳ | Ҿ | ҿ | Ш̆| ш̆| Ӏ | ӏ | А́| а́| Е́ | е́ | Й́ | й́ | О́ | ó  | У́ | ý  |    |    |
| 120 | Ы́| ы́| Э́| э́| Ю́| ю́| Я́| я́| А̀| à | Ѐ  | è  | Ѐ  | ѐ  | Ѝ  | ѝ  | О̀ | ò  | У̀ | ỳ  |
| 140 | Ы̀| ы̀| Э̀| э̀| Ю̀| ю̀| Я̀| я̀|   |   |    |    |    |    |    |    |    |    |    |    |

**Character Set 11**

|     | 0 | 1 | 2 | 3 | 4 | 5 | 6 | 7 | 8 | 9 | 10 | 11 | 12 | 13 | 14 | 15 | 16 | 17 | 18 | 19 |
|-----|---|---|---|---|---|---|---|---|---|---|----|----|----|----|----|----|----|----|----|----|
| 0   | あ | い | う | え | お | っ | ゃ | ゅ | ょ | ヴ | か | き | あ | い | う | え | お | か | き | く |
| 20  | け | こ | が | ぎ | ぐ | げ | ご | さ | し | す | せ | そ | ざ | じ | ず | ぜ | ぞ | た | ち | つ |
| 40  | て | と | だ | ぢ | づ | で | ど | な | に | ぬ | ね | の | は | ひ | ふ | へ | ほ | ば | び | ぶ |
| 60  | べ | ぼ | ぱ | ぴ | ぷ | ぺ | ぽ | ま | み | む | め | も | や | ゆ | よ | ら | り | る | れ | ろ |
| 80  | わ | を | ん | 〔 | 〕 | 〔 | 〕 | 「 | 」 | 「 | 」 | 。 | ・ | ゛| ゝ | ゞ | ー | ・ | ・ |    |
| 100 | ア | イ | ウ | エ | オ | ッ | ャ | ュ | ョ | ヴ | カ | ケ | ア | イ | ウ | エ | オ | カ | キ | ク |
| 120 | ケ | コ | ガ | ギ | グ | ゲ | ゴ | サ | シ | ス | セ | ソ | ザ | ジ | ズ | ゼ | ゾ | タ | チ | ツ |
| 140 | テ | ト | ダ | ヂ | ヅ | デ | ド | ナ | ニ | ヌ | ネ | ノ | ハ | ヒ | フ | ヘ | ホ | バ | ビ | ブ |
| 160 | ベ | ボ | パ | ピ | プ | ペ | ポ | マ | ミ | ム | ヌ | モ | ヤ | ユ | ヨ | ラ | リ | ル | レ | ロ |
| 180 | フ | ヲ | ン | ヽ | ゞ |   |   |   |   |   |    |    |    |    |    |    |    |    |    |    |

**Character Set 12**

Character Set 12 is a user-defined character set.

# ❖ Index

**1h** macro (turns on style for level-1 heading), 318
24-hour time, 211
↵ key
  assigning a macro to, 6, 12–13
  in macro editor, 29
  to start macro after a pause, 31–32

## A

abbreviations, automatic, 173
absolute tabs, 206
**address** macro (copies addresses into envelopes), 345
Advance feature, 108, 303, 405
**alf** macro (alphabetic sort on second word), 153
**align** macro (changes alignment character), 257
aligning text, in outlines, 225
alignment character, changing, 227, 256–259
**alpha** macro (paragraph sort), 394
alphabetizing a list, 152
alphanumeric sorts, 155, 427
Alt key, for entering IBM Extended Characters, 94–96
Alt key macros, 5–6, 8–10, 20, 77, 84
  double-letter Alt macros, 77–78
  as key definitions, 100
  and menus, 130–133
  *vs* named macros, 15, 16
Alt macros (temporary), 13–14
**Alt-A** macro (master Alt-A macro), 77

**Alt-A** macro (sorts list alphabetically), 154
**Alt-B** macro (replaces @ for abbreviations), 173
**Alt-C** macro (cancels current print job immediately), 325
**Alt-D** macro (changes to small bold italics), 16–17
**Alt-D** macro (document comment), 185
**Alt-F** macro (searches for marker), 195
**Alt-G** macro (goes to specific page), 149
**Alt-I** macro (switches to italics), 167, 352
**Alt-K** macro (capitalizes current word), 161
**Alt-N** macro (returns to normal text), 354
**Alt-N** macro (underlines *n* words), 164
**Alt-O** macro (opens a new blank line), 181
**Alt-Q** macro (cuts text to Doc 2), 183
**Alt-R** macro (scrolls documents), 142
**Alt-S** macro (saves document) 9
**Alt-S** macro (saves document and starts Speller), 151–152
**Alt-S** macro (stops printer), 327
**Alt-T** macro (capitalizes first word in paragraph), 162
**Alt-U** macro (capitalizes current character), 18

**Alt-U** macro (converts typed text to superscript), 339
**Alt-V** macro (sets left margin to 2″), 384
**Alt-V** macro (view current page), 330
**Alt-W** macro (deletes current word), 179
**Alt-X** macro (saves and exits), 10
**Alt-Y** macro (transposes word to left), 187
ALTRNAT keyboard, 86
**altfoot** macro (alternating footer text), 244
ASCII characters
  character set, 104
  and code equivalents, 451-454
  entering, 451-455
**assemble** macro (displays document assembly menu), 119
ASSIGN command, 447, 456-457, 478, 481
attributes, changing text, 16
author-date bibliography, 388-393
automatic paragraph numbering, 223-227
automatic referencing, using for page numbers, 240-241
automatic writing, 37, 304-305

# B

Base Font option, 336
beep, sounding a, 39, 59-61. *See also* BELL command
beginning of document, going to, 58
BELL command, 39, 59, 61, 80, 250, 281, 284, 348, 457-458, 475
**bib** macro (author-date bibliography), 390
bibliography
  alphabetizing a, 393
  creating a, 388-393

block protection, 343
block, rehighlighting a, 16
Block Copy shortcut, 193
  without ENHANCED keyboard, 103-104
Block Move shortcut, 193
Block Protect *vs* Conditional End of Page, 343
BLOCK APPEND command, 458
BLOCK COPY command, 458
BLOCK MOVE command, 458
blocking, for temporary text macros, 14, 20
blocks
  cutting and pasting, 183-185, 193
  highlighting, 199
**bltr** macro (creates header for multiple-page letter), 234
boilerplate text
  menus, 117-130
  using for letters, 233
boldfacing, 13, 164-166
**boldfig** macro (creates double-bordered figure box), 291
**border** macro (presentation graphic border for 5.1), 273
**border2** macro (presentation graphic border for 5.0), 276
borders, in graphics boxes, 290-303
**bpp** macro (deletes to beginning of paragraph), 175
BREAK command, 458
breaking a document into sentences, 73
breaking columns, 252
**breakup** macro (breaks document into sentences), 73
bullet style, 366
bullet symbol, 109
bullets
  using, 223-227
  using in presentation graphics, 274-282

## INDEX 517

**busenv** macro (formats a business envelope), 345
business letter, formatting a, 231-232
**bye** macro (gives exit message), 128

## C

^C merge code, 130-132, 134
calculator, online, 89
CALL command, 447, 458, 460, 465
**cancel** macro (cancels all print jobs), 328
CANCEL ON/OFF commands, 459
canceling printing, 325-326, 328-329
**cap** macro (capitalizes first letter of word), 156
capitalizing a character, 18
capitalizing words, 156-164
**capn** macro (capitalizes *n* words), 158
captions
 changing fonts for, 404
 marking for a list, 417-420
case fractions, 110
CASE CALL command, 460, 468, 479
CASE command, 459, 468, 479
 for user input, 122, 134
catalog, creating a macro, 39
**cc** macro (copies selected text), 198
centering page top to bottom, 231-232
CHAIN command, 62-65, 429, 460
CHAIN MACRO command, 130-132, 134
chaining a macro, 29-30, 62, 170
changing directories, 12
command, 469
CHAR command, 78, 455, 461, 469

character sets, 508-511
 printing in version 5.1, 199
characters, transposing, 188-189
CHARACTR.DOC, 409
 using to test your printer, 104
**chheads** macro (changes heads and text to different font), 312
**chnum** macro (specifies chapter number for equations), 399
**cleanup** macro (inserts footer and fixes margins), 68
**clear** macro (clears all tabs), 205
clearing the screen, 13
**close** macro (signature block), 6
codes
 in Ventura, 265
 none for initial font, 336
 stripping out, 68-72
 used in WordPerfect, 494-502
[Col Def] code, searching for, 56-57
colon, aligning text on the, 227, 257
colon, using as alignment character
**colrev** macro (review column settings), 57
column definition, copying and moving, 251
columns
 in tables, 434-437
 reviewing settings for, 56-58
 setting up, 251-254
 using, 271
combining keys from soft keyboards, 100-101
combining macro commands, 44-47
COMMENT command, 38, 462
comments in macros, 37-38
Compose feature, 58, 80, 95, 103
 to create case fractions, 110
 to create bullets, 110
Concordance feature, 412-413
conditional macros, 72-76
Conditional End of Page *vs* Block Protect, 343

**contents** macro (marks text for toc), 428
control characters, using in messages, 448-449
**convert** macro (converts comments to text), 357
converting old macros to versions 5.0 and 5.1, 504-506
copies, number of, 331-333
copying a macro, 33-34, 78, 268
copying key definitions, 97, 113
copying text, 197-199
**copyl** macro (copies current line), 196
copyright symbol, 109
correcting macros, 4
counting lines, 379-381
**create** macro (creates and generates contents page), 430
Ctrl key macros, 353
Ctrl keys, mapping macros to, 84
Ctrl-2, to enter special characters, 58
Ctrl-6, to return to original keyboard, 89
Ctrl-B, to insert page number, 40
Ctrl-Backspace, to delete a word, 178
Ctrl-PgUp (Macro Commands key), 31, 48
**Ctrl-S** macro (character left), 92
Ctrl-V
  to enter macro instructions, 28, 48
  to insert commands in macro editor, 74-75
  to enter special characters, 58
  to enter special format codes, 176
cursor movement, in tables, 435
cursor movement, 42-43
cursor, positioning on the screen, 450-451, 455
cut text, retrieving, 194
cutting and pasting, 193
between windows, 183-185
cutting text, 194

## D

dagger symbol, 109-110
dash, creating a, 199-200
**dashfig** macro (creates dash border for figure box), 297
date format, changing the, 211
date, inserting the, 211
  in footer, 240, 242
Date Function feature, 212
Date Text feature, 212
**dblfig** macro (creates double-bordered figure box), 291
debugging macros, 37
defining a macro, 4-6, 9-10, 20
Del key, in macro editor, 29
delay, inserting in macros, 36-37, 48
deleted text
  restoring, 181
  retrieving, 194
deleting text, 15, 43-44, 175-181
**deltop** macro (deletes to top of page), 15
description of macro, 6
designing macros, 40-42
desktop publishing. *See* graphics boxes, presentation graphics, headings
directory
  seeing macros in, 7
  setting up for macros, 10-11, 20, 79
**display** macro (displays ruler), 143
display
  full screen, 145
  split screen, 141

## INDEX 519

DISPLAY OFF command, 25, 30, 44–45, 274, 462, 476
DISPLAY ON command, 44–45, 274, 462
displayed quotations, 302–303
displaying macros on screen, 305
distribution list, creating a, 229
Doc 1 and Doc 2
  cutting and pasting between, 183–185
  using, 140–146
document assembly menus, 117–130
document comments
  creating, 185
  printing, 357–360
document
  deleting to end of, 180
  viewing a, 329–331
documenting macros, 37–39
**doindex** macro (creates index from entries), 414
**dolist** macro (defines and generates list), 421
DOS, exiting to, 12
dot-matrix printers
  and text quality, 335
  and vertical to horizontal ratio, 288
  *vs* laser printers, 324
double spacing, switching to, 249–250
double-letter Alt macros, 77–78
draft format, 237–238
draft printing, 355–356
**draftp** macro (prints draft of document), 355
**draw** macro (automatic drawing), 304
**dt** macro (inserts 24-hour date and time), 211

## E

editing keyboard layouts, 94–95, 96–97
editing macros, 24–49

editing text with macros, 18, 140–201
ELSE command, 463. *See also* IF/ELSE/ENDIF
**em** macro (creates em dash), 199
em dashes, creating, 199–200
END FOR command, 463
END IF command, 463, 480. *See also* IF/ELSE/ENDIF
END WHILE command, 463, 491
**enddel** macro (deletes to end of document), 180
**endfoot** macro (changes endnotes to footnotes), 382
endless loops, 30
endnotes
  changing to footnotes, 381–382
  changing margins in, 387
  numbering, 382
  printing, 414
ENHANCED keyboard, 86
**entry** macro (copies full reference), 391
envelopes, printing, 343–348
**epp** macro (deletes to end of paragraph), 177
**eqn** macro (creates equation area), 405
**eqns** macro (changes equation font), 402
equation area, creating (version 5.0), 404–408
equation boxes, using, 396–401
EQUATION keyboard, 84, 86, 88–89
equations
  best font sizes for, 404
  changing font used for, 401–404
  numbering, 396
  numbering with chapter numbers, 399–401
Equations Setup menu, 401–402
error messages when using Search or Name Search in macros, 319
Esc key to repeat a macro, 18–19, 159

executing a macro, 4, 8, 20, 79
exiting WordPerfect, 10
expense account form, 437
Extended Search, 195

## F

F1 (Cancel) key
  in macro editor, 29
  to restore deleted text, 16
F5 (List Files) key, to get a list of macros, 7
F7 (Exit) key
  in macro editor, 29
  in designing macros, 41
figure boxes, default settings for, 269, 290
figure captions, marking for a list, 417-420
file names for keyboards, 85, 90-91
Find feature, 128
fixed paragraph numbering, 225
**fmarg** macro (updates margins in footnotes), 384
font *vs* type style, 336
Font menu, 336
**fontch** macro (changes document default font), 337
fonts
  changing to different, 311-313
  changing for document, 336-338
  changing in equations, 401-404
  changing in letterhead, 219
  changing for printer, 336
  changing size of, 171
  in Ventura Publisher, 265-268
  in View Document screen, 331
**foot** macro (inserts date and page number), 242
**footer** macro (chapter and page number footer), 40
footer code, position of, 237, 244

footers
  for chapter and page number, 40, 68
  and headers, alternating, 243-244
  and headers, multiple, 245-247
  and headers, suppressing, 247-249
  removing, 69
  setting up, 237-238, 240, 242
  viewing, 329
footnotes
  changing to endnotes, 381
  changing margins in, 383-385, 387
  numbering lines in, 380
  numbering, 382
  using small type in, 415-417
  viewing, 329
FOR command, 463
FOR EACH command, 464
foreign-language dictionaries, 106-107
foreign-language keyboards, 105-107
format codes
  as represented in macro editor, 28
  searching for, 26-27, 52-55, 80, 176
formatting text with macros, 16-17
fractions, case, 110
function keys, reassigning functions of, 85, 94-95

## G

^G merge code, 130-132, 134
generating a document, 241
generating an index, 413-415
German keyboard, 105-107
glossary macro, 27
**go** macro (sends a "Go" to the printer), 334
Go, sending to a printer, 328, 333-335

"Go To" macro, 149
Go To key (Ctrl-Home), 16
GO command, 73–74, 77–78, 80, 320, 447, 464, 468
**gopp** (goes to beginning of paragraph), 150
Graphical Font Size setting, 401–403
graphics boxes, 290–303
  using for equations, 397
  using numbering in, 399
graphics quality, changing the, 335
graphics, using horizontal lines in, 407
graphs, creating, 272
**grayfig** macro (creates borderless shaded figure box), 296

# H
half-line spacing, using, 404
**hang** macro (creates hanging indent), 220
hanging indents, 220, 368
**hdrs** macro (creates header A and header B), 245
header code, position of, 237, 244
header, for business letters, 234–235
headers and footers
  alternating, 243–244
  changing margins in, 245
  multiple, 245–247
  numbering lines in, 380
  suppressing, 247–249
  viewing, 329
headings
  changing to boldface, 306–309
  marking for table of contents, 59–62, 427–432
  styling different levels of, 314–317
**heads** macro (changes heads to bold), 307

**heads2** macro (changes heads to bold small caps, 309)
highlighting paragraphs, 199
horizontal lines, drawing, 407

# I
IBM Extended Character Set, 94–95, 104
IF BLANK command, 134
IF command, 455, 479
IF/ELSE/ENDIF command, 465–467
IF EXISTS command, 467
indenting text, 220–221
**index** macro (marks index entry), 412
index entries, sorting, 422
indexes
  generating, 413–415
  marking entries for, 411–413
  styling, 413–415
**inf** macro (creates infinity symbol), 408
infinity symbol, creating, 408
initial font
  changing the, 336–338
  for document *vs* for printer, 336
  and relative size of type, 173
INPUT command, 455, 467
**inquiry** macro (retrieves boilerplate text), 127, 129
**invoice** macro (creates invoice), 438
invoice, creating an, 438–444
italicizing, 166–171
**italics** macro (changes underlining to italics), 168
italics
  switching to, 352–354
  using in temporary macros, 13
ITEM DOWN/ITEM LEFT/ITEM RIGHT/ITEM UP commands, 468

**itemize** macro (numbers list), 377
items, marking for a list, 417

## K

key definitions
  editing, 96
  moving to another key, 97, 113
  *vs* macro assignments, 95
key, reassigning meaning of. *See* keyboards, key definitions
key words, alphabetizing lists of, 393
KEY CMD codes, 482–486
keyboards, 84–113
  creating from existing macros, 97–98
  creating new, 90–96
keyboard editor, 94
  recording a macro in, 98–99
keyboard, recording new macros for 98–99
Keyboard Edit screen, 91–92
Keyboard Layout feature, 84–113
KEYBOARD command, 130–132, 134
keys, using in a sort, 153
keys, defining. *See* keyboards, key definitions
KEYS.MRS, 85
KTON command, 469

## L

LABEL command, 73–74, 78, 80, 123, 320, 464, 468–469, 471–472
**labels** macro (generates mailing labels), 213
LABELS.WPM, 348
Language code, 106
**large** macro (changes small to large), 55

laser printers
  *vs* dot-matrix printers, 324
  and Line Draw, 289
last names, sorting, 426
left margin release, 220
legal style, 366, 373
LEN command, 469
letter archive file, using, 343–346
letter assembly menu, 124–130
letters
  formatting, 231–232
  macro for creating and printing, 45
**letterhd** macro (generates letterhead), 218
letterhead, creating, 218–219
**letters** macro (displays letter assembly menu), 127
library of macros, 62, 65, 69
ligatures, 110
line
  copying the current, 196
  deleting, 174
  going to beginning of, 196
  lowercasing, 159–161
line numbering, 379–381
line spacing, 249–250
Line Draw
  and nonproportional fonts, 289, 304
  and proportional fonts, 108, 405
  using, 288–290
  using for letterhead, 219
lines, in tables, 434
lists
  alphabetizing, 152–156
  creating, 184
  marking items for, 417
  numbering items in, 376–379
List Files
  creating a directory for macros with, 10–11

marking files in, 11
for copying and renaming macros, 28, 33-34, 78
using to see macros, 7
**list1** macro (marks bold figure captions), 419
lists
  defining and generating, 420-422
  of graphics boxes, 417-418
  numbering, 227
Location of Files option, 11
long dashes, 199-200
Look option, in List Files, 351
LOOK command, 469-470
**lower** macro (lowercases a line), 160
lowercase, changing to, 159-161
**lttr** macro (formats business letter), 231

## M

macro commands, combining, 44-47
macro control characters, using in displays, 447-455
macro, definition of, 4
macro description, 6, 20
macro editor, using, 24-49
macros
  assigning to keys, 97-98, 99-100
  converting, 504-506
  copying, 28, 33-34, 78, 268
  correcting, 4
  defining, 4-6, 9-10, 20
  executing from menus, 130-133
  executing from separate subdirectories, 79
  on soft keyboards, 95, 113
  organizing, 10-12
  recording in keyboard editor, 98-99
  renaming, 268
  repeating, 18-19, 21, 159
  running, 4, 8, 20, 79
  temporary, 13-14
  types of, 5-6
macros, list of:
  **1h** (turns on style for level-1 heading), 318
  **address** (copies addresses into envelopes), 345
  **alf** (alphabetic sort on second word), 153
  **align** (changes alignment character), 257
  **alpha** (paragraph sort), 394
  **Alt-A** (master Alt-A macro), 77
  **Alt-A** (sorts list alphabetically), 154
  **Alt-B** (replaces @ for abbreviations), 173
  **Alt-C** (cancels current print job immediately), 325
  **Alt-D** (changes to small bold italics), 16-17
  **Alt-D** (document comment), 185
  **Alt-F** (searches for marker), 195
  **Alt-G** (goes to specific page), 149
  **Alt-I** (switches to italics), 167, 352
  **Alt-K** (capitalizes current word), 161
  **Alt-N** (returns to normal text), 354
  **Alt-N** (underlines *n* words), 164
  **Alt-O** (opens a new blank line), 181
  **Alt-Q** (cuts text to Doc 2), 183
  **Alt-R** (scrolls documents), 142
  **Alt-S** (saves document), 9
  **Alt-S** (saves document and starts Speller), 151-152
  **Alt-S** (stops printer), 327
  **Alt-T** (capitalizes first word in paragraph), 162
  **Alt-U** (capitalizes current character), 18

**Alt-U** (converts typed text to superscript), 339
**Alt-V** (sets left margin to 2"), 384
**Alt-V** (view current page), 330
**Alt-W** (deletes current word), 179
**Alt-X** (saves and exits), 10
**Alt-Y** (transposes word to left), 187
**altfoot** (alternating footer text), 244
**assemble** (displays document assembly menu), 119
**bib** (author-date bibliography), 390
**bltr** (creates header for multiple-page letter), 234
**boldfig** (creates double-bordered figure box), 291
**border** (presentation graphic border for 5.1), 273
**border2** (presentation graphic border for 5.0), 276
**bpp** (deletes to beginning of paragraph), 175
**breakup** (breaks document into sentences), 73
**busenv** (formats a business envelope), 345
**bye** (gives exit message), 128
**cancel** (cancels all print jobs), 328
**cap** (capitalizes first letter of word), 156
**capn** (capitalizes *n* words), 158
**cc** (copies selected text), 198
**chheads** (changes heads and text to different font), 312
**chnum** (specifies chapter number for equations), 399
**cleanup** (inserts footer and fixes margins), 68
**clear** (clears all tabs), 205
**close** (signature block), 6
**colrev** (review column settings), 57
**contents** (marks text for toc), 428

**convert** (converts comments to text), 357
**copyl** (copies current line), 196
**create** (creates and generates contents page), 430
**Ctrl-PgUp** (Macro Commands key), 31, 48
**Ctrl-S** (character left), 92
**dashfig** (creates dash border for figure box), 297
**dblfig** (creates double-bordered figure box), 291
**deltop** (deletes to top of page), 15
**display** (displays ruler), 143
**doindex** (creates index from entries), 414
**dolist** (defines and generates list), 421
**draftp** (prints draft of document), 355
**draw** (automatic drawing), 304
**dt** (inserts 24-hour date and time, 211
**em** (creates em dash), 199
**enddel** (deletes to end of document), 180
**endfoot** (changes endnotes to footnotes), 382
**entry** (copies full reference), 391
**epp** (deletes to end of paragraph), 177
**eqn** (creates equation area), 405
**eqns** (changes equation font), 402
**fmarg** (updates margins in footnotes), 384
**fontch** (changes document default font), 337
**foot** (inserts date and page number), 242
**footer** (chapter and page number footer), 40
**go** (sends a "Go" to the printer), 334

# INDEX 525

**gopp** (goes to beginning of paragraph), 150
**grayfig** (creates borderless shaded figure box), 296
**hang** (creates hanging indent), 220
**hdrs** (creates header A and header B), 245
**heads** (changes heads to bold), 307
**heads2** (changes heads to bold small caps, 309)
**index** (marks index entry), 412
**inf** (creates infinity symbol), 408
**inquiry** (retrieves boilerplate text), 127, 129
**invoice** (creates invoice), 438
**italics** (changes underlining to italics), 168
**itemize** (numbers list), 377
**labels** (generates mailing labels), 213
**large** (changes small to large), 55
**letterhd** (generates letterhead), 218
**letters** (displays letter assembly menu), 127
**list1** (marks bold figure captions), 419
**lower** (lowercases a line), 160
**lttr** (formats business letter), 231
**margins** (removes all margin changes), 386
**mark1** (marks place), 195
**mast** (creates masthead), 268
**memo** (creates memo form), 227
**name** (signature), 4
**newpara** (types standard paragraph), 63
**news** (sets newspaper column definition), 251
**next** (view next screen), 147
**note** (uses Small type for footnotes), 416
**number** (automatic outlining/formatting), 368

**off** (turns columns off), 252
**oldtab** (restores tab settings), 207
**on** (turns columns on and off), 252
**oq** (creates open quote), 200
**out** (sets up outline style), 370
**outl** (creates outline for graphics), 277
**pages** (prints selected pages), 349
**parout** (switches to paragraph numbering style), 365
**pg#** (page *n* of *n*), 240
**pgbreak** (previews page breaks), 342
**pgn** (turns on page numbering), 255
**prev** (view preceding screen), 147
**print2** (prints two copies), 332
**printcom** (prints document comments), 358
**pstyle** (changes paragraph numbering style), 222
**qual** (sets print quality to medium), 335
**quote** (formats a displayed quote), 222
**repsm** (replaces small codes for Ventura), 266
**rmftr** (removes extra footer codes), 69
**rmmar** (removes extra margin change codes), 66
**rprint** (prints pages in reverse), 341
**shadefig** (creates 3-d bordered shaded box), 294
**show** (automatic slide show), 283
**sm** (moves sentence), 192
**small** (converts Large type to Small), 171
**sortpar** (sorts by paragraph), 423
**space** (changes line spacing), 249
**spaces** (standardizes spaces between sentences), 260

**suppress** (suppresses headers, footers, page numbers), 248
**tab** (sets tab at cursor position), 207
**table** (sets up table format), 434
**textbars** (creates nonshaded text box), 302
**thickfig** (creates thick figure box border), 299
**time** (inserts time), 209
**tr** (transposes characters), 188
**trsent** (transposes sentences), 190
**win1** (returns screen to one window), 145
**win2** (splits the screen), 140
**wrdlist** (creates word list), 34
Macro command, 29
Macro Command mode, 99
Macro Command Language and Map feature, 103
Macro Commands key (Ctrl-PgUp) 13, 31
Macro Define mode, 28
Macro key, 5
MACRO CMD code numbers, 486–489
MACROCNV utility, 504–506
MACROS keyboard, 86–88
  editing macros on, 189
mailing labels
  generating, 213–217
  printing, 343–348
Map feature, in version 5.1, 96, 101–104, 113
mapping key assignments, 101–104
mapping macros to keys, 84
margin settings
  and tabs, 206
  in columns, 251–254
**margins** macro (removes all margin changes), 386
margins
  changing, 66, 386–388
  in footnotes, 383–385

  in headers and footers, 245
  for mailing labels, 217
  resetting, 386–388
**mark1** macro (marks place), 195
marking headings for table of contents, 376
marking your place, 194–196
**mast** macro (creates masthead), 268
masthead, creating a, 268–271
math columns
  clearing tabs for, 206
  restoring tab settings for text, 207
math feature, using, 440–444
mathematical keyboard (version 5.0), 107–109
**memo** macro (creates memo form), 227
memo, creating a, 227–231
menu display, 130
menu
  for assembling letters, 124–130
  for document assembly, 117–130
menu options, searching for, 56–58
menu selections, as represented in macro editor, 28
menu systems, setting up, 116–135
MENU OFF/ON commands, 470
merge commands, using in menus, 130–134
merge files
  for addressing envelopes, 343–346
  for mailing labels, 213–217
merge keyboard, 110–112
Merge Command Language, 130–134
merging files for mailing labels, 216
messages
  creating onscreen, 447–455
  when defining macros, 6–7
MID command, 470–471
mnemonic letter choices, using, 116
mouse, executing macros with, 13
moved text, retrieving, 193–194
moving a sentence, 191–194

moving macros to different directories, 11
multicolumn mailing labels, printing, 217

## N

**name** macro (signature), 4
Name Search feature
  in macro editor, 31-32
  using to select fonts, 324-325, 338
  when selecting keyboards, 96
named macros, 5, 8, 20
  *vs* Alt key macros, 15, 16
names, alphabetizing, 152-156
naming a macro, 5, 20
NEST command, 65-72, 78, 80, 471
nesting macros, 62, 65-72
**newpara** macro (types standard paragraph), 63
**news** macro (sets newspaper column definition), 251
newspaper columns, 251-253, 271
**next** macro (view next screen), 147
NEXT command, 472
nonproportional fonts and Line Draw, 289, 304
normal type, returning to, 354
**note** macro (uses Small type for footnotes), 416
notes, macro for taking, 142
NTOK command, 468
**number** macro (automatic outlining/formatting), 368
numbering entries in an outline, 367-376
numbering graphics boxes, 292
numbering headings with an outline style, 376
numbering lines, 379-381
numbering paragraphs, 367-369

## O

^O merge code, 130-132, 134
**off** macro (turns columns off), 252
**oldtab** macro (restores tab settings), 207
**on** macro (turns columns on and off), 252
ON CANCEL command, 472, 447
ON ERROR command, 447, 465, 473
ON NOT FOUND command, 72, 74, 80, 320, 447, 473
**oq** macro (creates open quote), 200
organization chart, creating an, 285-288
organizing macros, 10-11
original keyboard, returning to, 89, 113
ORIGINAL KEY command, 474
**out** macro (sets up outline style), 370
**outl** macro (creates outline for graphics), 277
outline numbering, automatic, 367-369
outline style (version 5.1)
  changing, 364-367
  default, 364
  using an, 370
Outline mode, 75-76
Outline style, 222-223
outlines
  aligning text in, 225
  and automatic paragraph numbering, 369
  creating for presentation graphics, 274-282
outlining, turning on, 367-370
overhead transparencies, proportions of, 272

## P

page breaks
  deleting, in mailing labels, 216
  previewing, 342-343
page
  defined, 192
  moving to a specific, 149-150

page number
  inserting in footer, 242
  inserting, 40
  viewing, 329
page numbering, 240-242, 254-256
  in business letter, 234
  suppressing, 247-249
  style, 256
page size and mailing labels, 215
**pages** macro (prints selected pages), 349
pages
  printing selected, 348-351
  viewing, 331
paired format codes, searching for, 53-56
paper size, defining in version 5.1, 272
PARA DOWN/UP commands, 474
paragraphs
  capitalizing first word in, 162
  defined, 192
  deleting to beginning or end of, 175-178
  indenting, 177
  moving to beginning of, 150
  moving to end of, 151
  sorting, 393-396, 422-427
  typing with a macro, 63
paragraph numbering, 223-227, 365-366, 367-369, 376-379
paragraph style, 223
paragraph symbol, 110
parallel columns, 253-254
**parout** macro (switches to paragraph numbering style), 365
path names, using, 11, 63, 349-351
pause, inserting a, 31-33, 39-42, 48, 333. *See also* PAUSE command
PAUSE command, 32, 45-46, 467, 474-475

PAUSE KEY command, 467, 475
**pg#** macro (page *n* of *n*), 240
**pgbreak** macro (previews page breaks), 342
**pgn** macro (turns on page numbering), 255
PgDn, PgUp, in macro editor, 31
phone lists, alphabetizing, 393
presentation graphics, 264, 272-285
**prev** macro (view preceding screen), 147
previewing a document, 329-331
previewing page breaks, 342-343
primary file for mailing labels, 214-217
print attributes in displays, 449-450
print quality, 19, 335, 355-356
**print2** macro (prints two copies), 332
**printcom** macro (print document comments), 358
printer, stopping, 326-328. *See also* canceling printing
printer, testing your, 104, 409
printing
  canceling, 325-326, 328-329
  changing number of copies, 331-333
  document comments, 357-360
  macros for, 324-361
printing pages in reverse, 340-341
printing selected pages, 348-351
prompts
  adding, 234, 247, 280-281
  using reverse video in, 447
  in designing macros, 41
  *See also* PROMPT command
PROMPT command, 130-132, 134, 320, 455, 461-462, 467, 475
proportional fonts and Line Draw, 108, 405
PrtSc key, for marking files, 11

**pstyle** macro (changes paragraph numbering style), 222

## Q

**qual** macro (sets print quality to medium), 335
QUIT command, 129, 134, 476
quotation style, setting up, 221-222
quotations, creating displayed, 302-303
**quote** macro (formats a displayed quote), 222
quotes, using, 200-201

## R

rectangles, onscreen *vs* printed, 288
redefining keys. *See* keyboards
redlining, using, 409-411
references, in term papers. *See* bibliography
rehighlighting a block, 16
relative tabs, 206
renaming macros, 11, 20, 48, 78, 268
repeating a macro, 18-19, 21, 28-29, 48, 159
repeating a search, 28
replacing abbreviations with phrases, 173
replacing and searching, 52-56, 58-59, 80
**repsm** macro (replaces small codes for Ventura), 266
resetting margins, 386-388
RESTART command, 477
restarting the printer, 328, 333-335
restoring deleted text, 16, 181
restoring tab settings, 207-209
retrieving moved text, 193-194
RETURN CANCEL command, 459, 477
RETURN command, 459

RETURN ERROR command, 459, 478
RETURN NOT FOUND command, 459, 478
Reveal Codes, listed, 494-502
Reveal Codes key (Alt-F3), 17
reverse printing, 340-341
reverse video
  for prompts, 447, 455
  using in slide show, 284
**rmftr** macro (removes extra footer codes), 69
**rmmar** macro (removes extra margin change codes), 66
rows in tables, 434-437
**rprint** macro (prints pages in reverse), 341
ruler line, displaying, 143-144
running a macro, 4, 8, 20

## S

sales tax, calculating in tables, 437, 440
saving a document, 9-10
screen, rewriting the, 455
screen, splitting the, 141
Screen Down key, 143
screens, viewing next and previous, 147-148
scripts, using columns in, 253
scrolling windows, 142-143
search, extended, 195
Search feature, 52
  and spacing, 194
  *See also* searching
searching
  and conditional macros, 72
  using in macros, 26-30, 52-59, 80
  using the mouse with, 53
section symbol, 110
sentence
  defined, 192
  moving a, 191-194

sentences
  breaking a document into, 73-76
  spaces between, 191, 259-260
  transposing, 190
Setup menu
  changing default print quality
    with, 335
  for indicating macro directory,
    10-12, 20
  using to check keyboard in
    effect, 89
  using to select keyboards, 112
**shadefig** macro (creates 3-d
    bordered shaded box), 294
shading
  in graphics boxes, 269, 290-303
  in tables, 435
SHELL MACRO command, 478
Shift key, mapping macros to, 84
SHORTCUT keyboard, 86, 88
**show** macro (automatic slide show),
    283
sidebars, 302-303
single spacing, switching to,
    249-250
sizes, changing text, 171
slide show, creating a, 282-285
slides, creating, 272
**sm** macro (moves sentence), 192
**small** macro (converts Large type to
    Small), 171
small caps, changing headings to,
    309-311
small type
  changing to large, 55
  using in footnotes, 415-417
"smart" quotes, 200-201
snaking columns, 251-253, 271
soft keyboards, defined, 84
sort keys, using, 426
sorting alphabetically, 152-153
sorting paragraphs, 393-396,
    422-427

**sortpar** macro (sorts by paragraph),
    423
**space** macro (changes line spacing),
    249
Spacebar, executing macros with, 13
**spaces** macro (standardizes spaces
    between sentences), 260
spaces, as represented in macro
    editor, 28
spacing between sentences, 191,
    259-260
special characters
  assigning to keys, 94-95, 103
  searching for, 58
  testing your printer for, 104
specialized keyboards, creating,
    104-112. *See also* keyboards
speed factor, in macros, 36-37
SPEED command, 36-37, 305,
    478-479
Speller, starting the, 151-152
splitting the screen, 141
starting WordPerfect and opening a
    document, 239
startup macro, for print quality in
    version 5.0, 335
STATE command, 455, 467,
    479-481
STATUS PROMPT command,
    455, 475, 481
Step mode, 481
STEP ON/OFF commands, 481
stopping a printer, 326-328. *See also*
    canceling printing
strikeout, using, 409-411
stripping out items from a
    document, 386
style
  of paragraph numbering, 223-227
  outline, using (version 5.1),
    364-367, 370
style sheets, using, 317-320

styles
  naming, 317
  turning on and off, 317–320
Styles feature *vs* macros, 306
subroutines
  and nested macro, 65, 73–75
  defined, 52
  using, 123
  *See also* GO command, LABEL command
subscripts, 338–340, 406
subtotals, calculating, 442
superscripts, 338–340, 406
**suppress** macro (suppresses headers, footers, page numbers), 248
suppressing headers and footers, 247–249
switching to different keyboards, 84
symbol keyboard, 109–110
symbols
  character set numbers for, 508–511
  creating with macros, 408
SYSTEM command, 489

## T

**tab** macro (sets tab at cursor position), 207
tab, setting at cursor position, 206–207
tab settings, restoring, 207–209
Tab Align command, 228, 256–259
Tab key, in macro editor, 29
**table** macro (sets up table format), 434
table boxes, defaults for, 291
tables of contents
  creating, 427–432
  marking headings for, 59–62, 376
Table feature (version 5.1), 432–444
tables
  creating, 432–444
  cursor movement in, 435

tabs
  and ruler line, 143–144
  clearing, 205
  in version 5.0 *vs* version 5.1, 206
target, marking a, 241
temporary macros, 13–14, 21
text boxes
  default settings for, 269, 290
  using, 302
  using in organization charts, 286–287
text
  converting document comments to, 357–360
  copying, 197–199
  cutting and pasting, 193
  deleting, shortcuts for, 44
  editing with macros, 18
  formatting with macros, 16–17
  macros, 13–14
text quality, changing the, 335
TEXT command, 234, 447, 450, 455, 461, 489–490
**textbars** macro (creates nonshaded text box), 302
**thickfig** macro (creates thick figure box border), 299
tildes, using in Macro Command Language, 447
**time** macro (inserts time), 209
time, inserting, 209
Tools menu, Macro command on, 4
totals, calculating, 440
**tr** macro (transposes characters), 188
trademark symbol, 110
transferring control from one macro to another. *See* chaining macros, nesting macros
transparency, creating a, 282
transposing characters, 188–189
transposing sentences, 190–191
transposing words, 186–187

trsent macro (transposes sentences), 190
type style *vs* typeface, 336
typeface
  changing the, 336
  *vs* type style, 336
  *See also* font
types of macros, 5-6
typesetter's quotes, 200-201

# U

umlaut, 105
undeleting, 16, 181
underlining, 164-166, 168-171
  searching for, 27
  changing to italics, 168
unique identifiers, 33, 59, 307, 309, 314, 417-418
uppercase, changing to, 156-164
user input with CASE command, 122
user-defined boxes, defaults for, 291

# V

value, of variable, 14
values
  expressions of, 457
  in variables, 446-447
VARIABLE command, 490
variables, 14
  assigning, 231, 247, 456-457
  using, 122, 446-447
Ventura Publisher, 264-268
View Document feature, 329-331, 342-343
viewing graphics boxes, 291

# W

WAIT command, 129, 134, 356, 475-476, 490
WHILE command, 491
win1 macro (returns screen to one window), 145
win2 macro (splits the screen), 140
winding columns, 251-253, 271
window, returning to full-screen, 145
windows
  cutting and pasting between, 183-185
  scrolling, 142-143
word, deleting, 178-179
word list, creating, 34
Word Search, using, 128
WordPerfect 4.2 units, 406
  for mathematical typing, 109
WordPerfect character sets, 508-511
WordPerfect Library, Calendar in, 212
WordPerfect
  previous versions of, 504-506
  starting and opening a document, 239
  starting and restoring default format settings, 239
  starting with a macro, 19-20, 21
words
  capitalizing, 156-164
  transposing, 186-187
WordStar
  and opening blank lines, 181
  deleting a line of text in, 85
.WPK extension, for soft keyboards, 85, 97
.WPM, as macro extension, 5, 7
WP.MRS, 85
wrdlist macro (creates word list), 34

# WordPerfect 5.1 Macro Handbook

## Macros Available on Disk

If you'd like to use the macros in this book but don't want to type them in yourself, you can send for a 5¼" or 3½" DOS-format disk containing all the macros in the book. To obtain this disk, complete the order form and return it along with a check or money order for $20.00. California residents add applicable sales tax.

---

**Kay Nelson**
**5751 Pescadero Road**
**Pescadero, CA  94060**


Name  _____

Address  _____

City/State/ZIP  _____


_____  5¼" disk          _____  3½" disk


Enclosed is my check or money order.
(Make check payable to Kay Nelson.)
*WordPerfect 5.1 Macro Handbook*

---

SYBEX *is not affiliated with Kay Nelson and assumes no responsibility for any defect in the disk or macros.*

# SYBEX Computer Books are different.

## Here is why . . .

At SYBEX, each book is designed with you in mind. Every manuscript is carefully selected and supervised by our editors, who are themselves computer experts. We publish the best authors, whose technical expertise is matched by an ability to write clearly and to communicate effectively. Programs are thoroughly tested for accuracy by our technical staff. Our computerized production department goes to great lengths to make sure that each book is well-designed.

In the pursuit of timeliness, SYBEX has achieved many publishing firsts. SYBEX was among the first to integrate personal computers used by authors and staff into the publishing process. SYBEX was the first to publish books on the CP/M operating system, microprocessor interfacing techniques, word processing, and many more topics.

Expertise in computers and dedication to the highest quality product have made SYBEX a world leader in computer book publishing. Translated into fourteen languages, SYBEX books have helped millions of people around the world to get the most from their computers. We hope we have helped you, too.

### For a complete catalog of our publications:

SYBEX, Inc. 2021 Challenger Drive, #100, Alameda, CA 94501
Tel: (415) 523-8233/(800) 227-2346   Telex: 336311
Fax: (415) 523-2373

## TO JOIN THE SYBEX MAILING LIST OR ORDER BOOKS PLEASE COMPLETE THIS FORM

NAME _____ COMPANY _____

STREET _____ CITY _____

STATE _____ ZIP _____

☐ PLEASE MAIL ME MORE INFORMATION ABOUT **SYBEX** TITLES

---

**ORDER FORM** (There is no obligation to order)

PLEASE SEND ME THE FOLLOWING:

| TITLE | QTY | PRICE |
|---|---|---|
| _____ | ____ | ____ |
| _____ | ____ | ____ |
| _____ | ____ | ____ |
| _____ | ____ | ____ |

TOTAL BOOK ORDER _____ $_____

SHIPPING AND HANDLING PLEASE ADD $2.00 PER BOOK VIA UPS _____

FOR OVERSEAS SURFACE ADD $5.25 PER BOOK PLUS $4.40 REGISTRATION FEE _____

FOR OVERSEAS AIRMAIL ADD $18.25 PER BOOK PLUS $4.40 REGISTRATION FEE _____

CALIFORNIA RESIDENTS PLEASE ADD APPLICABLE SALES TAX _____

TOTAL AMOUNT PAYABLE _____

☐ CHECK ENCLOSED  ☐ VISA
☐ MASTERCARD  ☐ AMERICAN EXPRESS

ACCOUNT NUMBER _____

EXPIR. DATE _____ DAYTIME PHONE _____

CUSTOMER SIGNATURE _____

---

**CHECK AREA OF COMPUTER INTEREST:**

☐ BUSINESS SOFTWARE

☐ TECHNICAL PROGRAMMING

☐ OTHER: _____

**THE FACTOR THAT WAS MOST IMPORTANT IN YOUR SELECTION:**

☐ THE SYBEX NAME

☐ QUALITY

☐ PRICE

☐ EXTRA FEATURES

☐ COMPREHENSIVENESS

☐ CLEAR WRITING

☐ OTHER _____

**OTHER COMPUTER TITLES YOU WOULD LIKE TO SEE IN PRINT:**

_____

_____

**OCCUPATION**

☐ PROGRAMMER                    ☐ TEACHER

☐ SENIOR EXECUTIVE              ☐ HOMEMAKER

☐ COMPUTER CONSULTANT           ☐ RETIRED

☐ SUPERVISOR                    ☐ STUDENT

☐ MIDDLE MANAGEMENT             ☐ OTHER: _____

☐ ENGINEER/TECHNICAL

☐ CLERICAL/SERVICE

☐ BUSINESS OWNER/SELF EMPLOYED

CHECK YOUR LEVEL OF COMPUTER USE

☐ NEW TO COMPUTERS
☐ INFREQUENT COMPUTER USER
☐ FREQUENT USER OF ONE SOFTWARE
   PACKAGE:
   NAME _____
☐ FREQUENT USER OF MANY SOFTWARE
   PACKAGES
☐ PROFESSIONAL PROGRAMMER

OTHER COMMENTS:
_____
_____
_____
_____
_____
_____
_____

PLEASE FOLD, SEAL, AND MAIL TO SYBEX

**SYBEX, INC.**
2021 CHALLENGER DR. #100
ALAMEDA, CALIFORNIA USA
94501

SEAL